Shailaja Paik centers her history of western Indian Da[...] charged political field of education, which was a testin[...] realization in the context of colonial and postcolonial modernity. Drawing on a rich archive of oral history and insisting on gender as a generative force in the shaping of all Dalit experience, she documents the ways that Dalit women made history through their struggle with the state and the community itself. This doubleness was both the condition of their radical history and the limits of its horizon. Readers will feel the contradiction of that double bind even as they come to appreciate the variety of obstacles Dalit women faced as they took up the daily challenges of 'getting on and [getting] out from under'.

Antoinette Burton, *University of Illinois*

Shailaja Paik's study of education among Dalit women in urban Maharashtra is a ground-breaking contribution to historical work on caste and gender in South Asia. Based upon extensive oral interviews as well as exhaustive archival research, Paik's book provides critical analysis of a broad range of important historical concerns, including the limitations of the colonial and post-colonial educational systems, the failure of pre-independence feminists in addressing concerns of low-caste women, the views of B.R. Ambedkar and other Dalit radicals on education and gender, and the ways education transformed and failed to transform the professional and familial lives of Dalit women.

Douglas E. Haynes, *Dartmouth College*

Shailaja Paik examines the double discrimination faced by Dalit women in India when they strive, against many odds, to make the most of whatever educational facilities there are available to them. They are discriminated against both as members of a stigmatised community, and also as women. While the caste-based prejudice comes from outside the community, the gender-based prejudice comes too frequently from within, as male Dalits routinely devalue and curb the potential of female members of their families. This history of such discrimination cannot be studied adequately through written records, as it is largely an unrecorded one – it depends very centrally on the collection of women's narratives through interviews. Dr. Paik has carried out this task with energy and great commitment, revealing a fine empathy with those with whom she engaged. The result is a path-breaking and important piece of research and writing.

David Hardiman, *University of Warwick*

Shailaja Paik's *Dalit Women's Education in Modern India* stands out for putting the everyday experience of ordinary Dalit women in western India at the center of her analysis of Dalit access to education in the twentieth century. Drawing on a rich archive of English and Marathi sources, including oral histories, Paik provides an account of Dalit women's navigation of the hierarchies of gender, caste, class, power, and privilege. The triumphs and tribulations of Dalit women who both seized and challenged the new educational opportunities makes for a compelling narrative attentive to the inequities within upper-caste as well as Dalit communities.

Mrinalini Sinha, *University of Michigan*

Shailaja Paik gives us a very clear look at education, what it means, how Dalits enter into it and how negotiable their attitude about education is. The long-standing Mahar/Mang comparison has been expanded in very interesting ways. Of her many topics two that are most unusual are in-depth studies of middle-class Dalits. Usually the middle class is dismissed as a minor percentage of Untouch-ables who have managed to climb into the middle class. Shailaja deals with it very seriously.... It is probably one of the very few reports we have. She has given us a multi-faceted study of discrimination in terms of the field of education. The reformers, from B.R. Ambedkar and Mahatma Phule down to the present, have all stressed education as the key to progress. Shailaja has much to offer to the field of education and women.

Eleanor Zelliot, *Carleton College*

Shailaja Paik's book deals with an understudied subject, Dalit women's educa-tion. It covers pre- and post-1947 developments by relying on rich sources – archival and oral. During the Raj (and sometimes after!) Dalit women suffered from dual discrimination since they were neither welcome in the public schools – though these institutions were supposed to be for all children – nor necessarily sent to them by their parents. But some of them, in Maharashtra, seized the opportunity of their migration to the city to follow Ambedkar's recommendation, 'Educate'. Paik's remarkable exercise in ethno-history meticulously highlights the many faces of segregation based on language and location, as evident from her 'tale of two cities' which shows that to live in a slum of Poona implied more than a mere topographical periphery. Last but not least, *Dalit Women's Educa-tion in Modern India* argues that education did not always give jobs to women – sometimes because they married too young, sometimes because nobody wanted to hire them: a strong plea for job reservations, one of the major achievements of India.

Christophe Jaffrelot, *King's College, London*

Dalit Women's Education in Modern India

Inspired by egalitarian doctrines, the Dalit communities in India have been fighting for basic human and civic rights since the middle of the nineteenth century. In this book, Shailaja Paik focuses on the struggle of Dalit women in one arena – the realm of formal education – and examines a range of interconnected social, cultural and political questions. What did education mean to women? How did changes in women's education affect their views of themselves and their domestic work, public employment, marriage, sexuality and childbearing and rearing? What does the dissonance between the rhetoric and practice of secular education tell us about the deeper historical entanglement with modernity as experienced by Dalit communities?

Dalit Women's Education in Modern India is a social and cultural history that challenges the triumphant narrative of modern secular education to analyse the constellation of social, economic, political and historical circumstances that both opened and closed opportunities to many Dalits. By focusing on marginalised Dalit women in modern Maharashtra, who have rarely been at the centre of systematic historical enquiry, Paik breathes life into their ideas, expectations, potentials, fears and frustrations. Addressing two major blind spots in the historiography of India and of the women's movement, she historicises Dalit women's experiences and constructs them as historical agents. The book combines archival research with historical fieldwork, and centres on themes including slum life, urban middle classes, social and sexual labour, and family, marriage and children to provide a penetrating portrait of the actions and lives of Dalit women.

Elegantly conceived and convincingly argued, *Dalit Women's Education in Modern India* will be invaluable to students of History, Caste Politics, Women and Gender Studies, Education Studies, Urban Studies and Asian Studies.

Shailaja Paik is Assistant Professor of History at the University of Cincinnati, USA.

Routledge research on gender in Asia series

Dalit Women's Education in Modern India

Double discrimination

Shailaja Paik

Routledge
Taylor & Francis Group

LONDON AND NEW YORK

First published 2014 by Routledge

2 Park Square, Milton Park, Abingdon, Oxfordshire OX14 4RN
711 Third Avenue, New York, NY 10017

Routledge is an imprint of the Taylor & Francis Group, an informa business

First issued in paperback 2017

British Library Cataloguing in Publication Data
A catalogue record for this book is available from the British Library

Library of Congress Cataloging in Publication Data
Paik, Shailaja.
Dalit women's education in modern India : double discrimination / Shailaja Paik.
    pages cm. – (Routledge research on gender in Asia series)
    Includes bibliographical references and index.
    1. Dalit women–Education–India–Maharashtra. 2. Discrimination in education–India–Maharashtra. 3. Sex discrimination against women–India–Maharashtra. 4. Educational equalization–India–Maharashtra. 5. Maharashtra (India)–Social conditions. I. Title.
    LC2328.M34P35 2014
    371.822095479–dc23   2013048742

ISBN: 978-0-415-49300-0 (hbk)
ISBN: 978-0-8153-8414-4 (pbk)

Typeset in Times New Roman
by Wearset Ltd, Boldon, Tyne and Wear

For my parents
Sarita Deoram Paik and Deoram Fakira Paik
who educated me.

Contents

Figures

Tables

Acknowledgements

This book is a product of the staunch support, inspiration, consistent and rigorous engagement, love and constant enrichment of significant people in my life. I have accumulated numerous debts over a decade and a half and although these debts cannot be repaid, it is my great privilege to thank them.

This book has been possible because of my engaged interlocutors: Dalit women who welcomed me into their intimately private and public lives in order to discuss their histories, hurdles and hopes. I feel very honoured to have shared the company of such energetic, erudite and inspiring people. All contributed generously their time, affection and insight with incredible faith and trust, and have taught me in turn about the deeper roots and meanings of the Ambedkar movement; about their ideas, lives and actions; and, most importantly, about relationships to be cherished. Women shared their tears, anxieties, tragedies, elations and triumphs with me. I am indebted to all of them.

David Hardiman has been an excellent intellectual mentor from the very outset of this project. Over the years, I have benefited from his constructive criticism and guidance. I am deeply grateful for his unfailing support, incisive comments and questions, and ready feedback. When I decided to excavate the book from the dissertation, I found an insightful and generous mentor in Douglas E. Haynes. His critical comments, encouragement, astute suggestions and vast knowledge of history and other subjects are reflected in this work. Doug discussed the small and big ideas, and read most of the chapters in their different versions, as well as very closely reading the final drafts of some chapters. He readily and energetically engaged with my endless queries and offered insightful comments. He, along with David, also helped strengthen the articulation of ideas in and beyond the book. Doug's passion for intellectual debates and clear and innovative historical writing infused this work. Between Doug and David, I am indeed well schooled. I am deeply grateful.

As the book was nearing completion, I lost a dear friend and mentor, Sharmila Rege. Sharmila introduced me to methodological debates and shared her intellectual treasure. I miss her deeply. Eleanor Zelliot shared some valuable sources and has been a constant support and inspiring mentor over the years. Gail Omvedt has been greatly supportive from a distance. Thanks to everybody for writing innumerable letters for different fellowships.

A timely fellowship with Yale's South Asian Studies Council accelerated the finalising, revision and writing of most of the chapters. Yale also provided me with an intellectually stimulating environment to present and test my revised ideas. I made friends, like Karuna Mantena, who read some chapters, commented on and discussed my work. Christophe Jaffrelot also read some chapters.

The research for the book was funded by grants from the Charles Phelps Taft Research Center and University of Cincinnati's Research Council. I am indebted to audiences and engagements at a number of conferences, symposia and institutions: the Annual Conference on South Asia at the University of Wisconsin, Madison; the Annual Conference of the Association of Asian Studies; the National Women's Studies Association; the Annual Conference of the American Historical Association; Yale University; Columbia University; Amherst College; Bowdoin College; TISS; Dartmouth College; University of Iowa; University of Michigan; George Mason University; and the University of Pennsylvania. Chithprabha Kudlu has been with this project since its inception and has with great enthusiasm shared my fieldwork stories. We discussed different topics of interest during long conversations over the phone. Thanks, Chith! Shefali Chandra was always there for timely discussions on some issues, and she and Anupama Rao have been supportive in different ways. Anjali Arondekar read an earlier version of Chapter 3 and offered critical comments. I thank friends and colleagues for making efforts to arrange workshops and talks on my research. I thank my colleagues at the University of Cincinnati for their encouragement and support, especially Willard Sunderland, Nikki Taylor and Laura Jenkins. Special thanks to Hilda L. Smith and David Stradling who, though unfamiliar with the context, read some chapters and discussed them with me. Hilda has shared her erudite scholarship and experience, and has patiently engaged with my every query. She has become a wonderful friend over the years. My greatest debts are also to friends, anonymous reviewers and my writing group, who have read all or parts of this project. I found a superb editor in Sarah Grey. Her skills, thoughtful suggestions and help with making the book accessible are truly invaluable. Many thanks, Sarah. At Routledge, thanks to the patience and support of the editorial and publication team.

I want to thank the librarians and staff at Mumbai Marathi Granthsangrahaalaya, Maharashtra State Archives, Mumbai University and the India Office Library, as well as the private collections of the late Vasant Moon.

Without the unstinting support, love and encouragement of my *aai* and my family – *akkaa*, Rani and Ashok Waghmare (Sir), Maitreyee and Advait, and Kirti and Amit – I couldn't have endured these long years. Aai has been a model of fortitude and has taught me to pursue my interests single-mindedly and passionately and always believed in my endeavours. Thank you, Gargi, for your love, wit and humour, your questions, your journey from reading the titles of the books on the shelves to talking about our lives, and seeing and sharing the process of this wonderful dissertation-to-book project. Thanks for the boundless joy and understanding! And of course I cannot name it all because it is beyond words, but thanks to you, Pravin, for everything in the past, present and future.

Introduction
Education for the oppressed

Without *vidya* [knowledge], intellect was lost; without intellect, virtue was lost; without virtue and morality, dynamism was lost; without dynamism, money was lost; without money Shudras were demoralised: all this misery and disasters were due to *avidya* [the lack of knowledge]!

Mahatma Jotirao Phule (1827–1890), Pioneer of Dalit and women's education

(Phule 1969, 189; Phule 2002, 117)

Ever since the revolutionary Jotirao Phule critically analysed the fundamental importance of knowledge seeking for women and Shudra-Ati-Shudras during the mid-nineteenth century, formal education has occupied a central place in

Figure I.1 Pune, Mumbai and Nagpur in Maharashtra, India (schematic map by author).

discussions of Dalit civic rights. From the last two decades of the nineteenth century onward, Dalit *streepurush* (women and men) in Bombay Presidency have actively engaged with philosophical notions and methods rooted in 'modernity' and viewed education as critical to achieving it. Revising and extending Phule's agenda of education and exposing the nexus of caste, gender and knowledge in the twentieth century, the radical leader B.R. Ambedkar (1891–1956) declared that '*shaalaa haa uttam naagarik tayaar karnyachaa kaarkhaanaa aahe* (schools are workshops for manufacturing the best citizens)' and motivated Dalits to 'educate, organise, and agitate' (Ambedkar 1927). The project of education also galvanised Dalit women to make their historical contribution to the Dalit movement and the programme of Dalit modernity. Phule, a Shudra Mali (gardener caste), and Ambedkar, an Ati-Shudra (Untouchable) Mahar, along with upper-caste, elite nationalists and educators, expended tremendous amounts of energy on the reform of women. Phule and Ambedkar were particularly innovative in deploying the modernist grammar of secular education, equality, human rights, dignity, and inclusive and egalitarian citizenship from within the institutional and discursive constraints of the state apparatus.

Dalits make up about 17 per cent of India's population. Historically, they have suffered from severe social, economic, political and cultural discrimination. Yet, since the mid-nineteenth century, inspired by egalitarian doctrines, Dalits have been fighting for their ordinary human and civic rights to access education, water tanks, temples, restaurants, *dharmashaalaas* (buildings to accommodate travellers) and streets. Many factors contributed to advancing Dalit education and empowerment: missionary schooling, colonial institutions, the limited introduction of liberalism into India, reform efforts by upper-caste leaders, experiences of civic space, migration to cities, public equality, struggles for political rights, and – most importantly – the efforts of Dalit radicals. Within this repertoire of factors, this book focuses on the struggle of Dalit women in one arena: the realm of formal education.

The primary concern of this book is to analyse the contradiction between the promises of education as envisioned by leaders such as Phule and Ambedkar and the form of education provided in practice by the modern Indian state. Studying this contradiction is important because both Phule and Ambedkar focused on the state and sought its intervention to resolve the Dalit question. They also critically analysed how high-caste males' *kaavebaaji* (cunning) subjugated both men of low castes and women of all castes by excluding them from their *maanavi hakka* (human rights), including the right to education. Dalit radicals in the early twentieth century interpreted their exclusion from common schools as a barrier both to individual freedom and advancement and to their collective ability to secure equal rights. Analysing these realities from the vantage point of Dalit women, I seek to understand the ideas, actions and changing values that have revolutionised their lives.

This book explores the nexus between caste, class, gender and state pedagogical practices among Dalit women in the cities of Pune, Mumbai and Nagpur to analyse the social, economic and historical circumstances that hindered as well as contributed to their education. A discussion of these processes and the changes they brought about is necessarily interdisciplinary in character. On the one hand, I focus on ordinary Dalit women's historical experience and trace a richly textured social and cultural history. On the other hand, I explore the kinds of politics that have developed in response to those experiences. What did education mean to women and why was it so important to them? In the context of education, and in a situation of continuing and existing discrimination, what were the distinct experiences of Dalit women? Did education contribute to Dalit women's social mobility and empowerment? How did changes in women's education affect their views of themselves, their domestic work, marriage, sexuality, and childbearing and rearing? How did women compare their lives with their mothers' and grandmothers'? Did education inhibit or promote Dalit women's involvement in wider politics? In sum, what does the dissonance between the rhetoric and practice of education tell us about the history of the modern as it unfolded in Dalit communities? In order to answer these questions, I pay attention to the social and emotional histories of individuals as well as their social circumstances, which shift and are subject to renegotiation and reconstitution. My story recounts a nuanced understanding of informal learning and formal education, and how both helped to shape Dalit women's lives: a journey of getting on and out from under.

Considering their personal and group preoccupations and needs in specific situations and intellectual contexts, Dalits in Maharashtra have interacted critically with the universal, modern discourse of scientific and social progress through local, vernacular Marathi concepts to suit their own purposes. This book thus centres on the dialectics of the Dalit modern: the possibilities and pitfalls shared by creative Dalit women and men in their historic engagement with the experience of modernity. I am concerned with Dalit women's *historical experience of space and time*, a *modern* experience, a paradoxical unity that has propelled them to tear down caste confinement and rigid roles to transform themselves and find their potential, while at the same time facing the threats of the maelstrom of perpetual struggle: contradictions, ambiguity and anguish. Moreover, the anti-caste politics of Dalit radicals and of some nationalists produced techniques through which Dalits engaged in *governmentalising* the self and community;[1] Dalits' access to the public was intimately tied to their ability to regulate, define, reorder and practise self-cleansing, self-disciplining, self-fashioning and self-development as well as political self-rule. Dalits actively expressed their ideas, emotions, fantasies and desires, and refused to be merely products of the agenda of self-transformation. I am thus deepening Michel Foucault's analysis of governmentalising techniques of transformation and extending them from the self to that of the community. While Foucault does not provide an explicit theory of the subordination of women or the colonised, his theoretical frames help me conceptualise substantive changes that took place in Dalits' social, political and sexual mores and, most importantly, their construction of their selves and community.

Dalit radicals' engagement with modern education in western India

By tracking the twisted relationship between the rhetoric of modern secular education and pedagogic efforts and the production of Dalit women's subjectivities, this book seeks to make sense of the decision to *deny* education to specific groups and of their larger place within society and the body politic. The history of Dalit women's education has been a process filled with contradictions and circuits of triumphs and reversals as Dalits engaged with colonial, nationalist and upper-caste power. There are thus many different stories here, with varying outcomes. For Dalit radicals, the focus on women and their representation was inextricably linked to social and political processes: women were agents who made choices and had critical perspectives about their own situations. Most significantly, women were to be included in power, public work and activism. To them, education, social and moral reform, and political power were intimately connected; organised women were in the forefront of these struggles.

This book concentrates on the hitherto neglected intellectual contribution of Dalit radicals in the realm of education, and its wider applications. In the specific context of the early twentieth century, Dalits deployed a two-pronged programme of education – internal and external – consolidating individualism, subjectivity, and the struggle for the equal rights and citizenship always-already granted to 'other' Indians. Neither the colonial British government nor the elite nationalists could adequately address Dalits' requirements. Only very recently have mainstream scholars begun to train their gazes on Ambedkar's contributions to Indian social, political and intellectual history. Moreover, Phule's and Ambedkar's contributions to education in general and women's education in particular have been a neglected subject of study.

Female and male Dalit radicals significantly transformed the nature of modern education by fashioning new idioms of power and symbols, rooted in the indigenous Marathi language. Their politics emerged from their day-to-day struggles for power and social justice. Thus, Dalit radicals did not fight merely to attend schools or seek employment; attaining education constituted an equal right (*samaan hakka*) to the public domain, which encompassed *maanavi hakka* (human rights), *nyaya* (justice) and *naagarikatva* (egalitarian citizenship).[2] They insisted that education was necessary to disrupt dominant discourses that denied them access to the public realm, and gave it a unique flavour by infusing it with *maanuski:* human and civic rights, equality and justice. At the same time they deployed the 'technology of the self'[3] (Foucault 1988, 18; Paik 2011), which constituted human dignity and involved the shaping of the inner resources of *svaabhimaan* (self-respect), *svaavalamban* (self-reliance), *pratishthaa* (honour), *vyaktivikaas* (individuated development), *ijjat* (honour), *dhaadas* (daring), and most importantly *sudhaaranaa* (improvement) on both a personal and community level. They argued that, for Dalits, *svaavalamban hech khare unnatiche pratik* (self-reliance signified true progress) (*Janata*, 4 August 1934). Dalit leaders and spokespersons embraced more popular forms of rhetoric grounded in the principles and political processes that gave meaning to ordinary Dalits' day-to-day lives.

Most significantly, unlike the upper-caste nationalists, instead of focusing on merely 'modernising' education and gender relations, Phule and Ambedkar sought to *democratise* them. They emphasised egalitarian relationships as opposed to privilege, and combined critiques of knowledge, caste and gender hierarchies in ways that opened up new spaces for women in general and Dalit women in particular. Radicals like Phule, Ambedkar, and, in South India, E.V. Ramsamy (Periyar), analysed how the public institution of education became entangled with hierarchies of caste, gender, class, community and sexuality, and subordinated and shaped the lives of Dalit women in particular ways. This book dwells on hitherto neglected Marathi sources to document Dalit radicals' efforts to reorganise the politically contoured home and public lives of Dalit women. Ambedkar differed from the Brahmans' *miraas* (hereditary office, but here privilege) and the Brahmani (brahmanical) agenda of *dnyanasanchay* (knowledge accumulation) rather than *prasaar* (dissemination) (Ambedkar 1920), which initially did not allow women to seek education and later insisted that women were still to follow men. The radicals challenged the limited reforms produced by nationalists and feminists of the time and introduced possibilities for Dalit subjectivity and held that, by questioning both upper-caste men and women and Dalit men, Dalit women would forge new agencies and refashion themselves and their futures.

Refashioning Dalit women

I concentrate on how the 'interlocking technologies'[4] of gender, caste, class, family, community, sexuality and education shaped and in turn were transformed by Dalit women's historical experience: the shaping of their ideas and self-development, the intimate processes of critical transformation, and the emergence of their subjectivity.[5]

For Dalits, the politics of caste, gender, education and moral reforms have complicated modes of political participation, the cornucopia of claims to 'rights' and 'freedoms', and their subject formation in a colonial context, which has always-already precluded the production of individual agency. Their struggle for equality, social justice and self-respect emerged out of their particular experiences of a stigmatised selfhood and of erasures by the colonial government and upper castes, and involved contradictory practices and development. The subjectivities of Dalit women emerged out of the local, vernacular, Marathi grammar and their personal struggle for self-development in specific historical contexts, and granted them a new sense of exhilaration and enlargement, new capacities and feelings, even as these have been concomitantly thwarted by profound insecurity, frustration and despair.[6]

I unravel how gender emerged as a *generative* process and became a fractured and unstable category. Dalit radicals' narratives penetrated Dalit women's mentalities; no longer mere rhetoric, these narratives transformed into fundamental truths that shaped women's affect, behaviour, and – ultimately – subjectivity as individuals and as members of the community. The force of Dalit radicals' rhetoric, discourses and education practices helped women to develop self-respect, self-confidence, self-humanisation and dignity. Through such purposive practices Dalit women structured the possibilities for further action. Rather than making women vulnerable, as in the case of the upper castes, Dalit radicals constructed a 'masculine Dalit womanhood' which incorporated 'masculine' attributes such as *svaavalamban* (self-reliance), *nirbhay* (fearlessness), *dhaadas* (courage), *karaaripanaa* (daring), *manodharya* (tenacity of the mind), *nischay* (resoluteness) and *dhadaadi* (daring) into the feminine. In stark contrast, from the eighteenth century onward, upper-caste Brahmani elites not only restricted women's education but also constructed a fickle-minded womanhood, dependent on males. Nationalists in the twentieth century sought to revise this agenda and to infuse the feminine into the masculine as an anti-colonial strategy, but they also concentrated on upper-caste and middle-class women alone.

Dalit radicals' powerful discourse shaped Dalit women, who participated ritualistically in collective action for education and empowerment. Yet, despite Dalit leaders' promises and efforts to expand (or democratise) educational opportunities, their connection of modern education with gender and moral reforms had unsettling implications for Dalit women, whose place in the body politic remained contested and uncertain. I reveal the disciplining of Dalit women's sexuality through upwardly mobile communities' caste strictures of monogamy and chastity as well as (second-generation) elite Dalits' construction of new and genteel 'femininity'. Thus, I also study the constraints on Dalit women's agency and the actual practice that thwarted Dalit leaders' promises and efforts to democratise or widen educational opportunity.

My study seeks to redress the scarcity of historical studies on Dalits. A few historians have studied Dalit resistance to both colonial and Brahmani hegemonic discourses and power and their struggle for modernity; however, we have yet to learn how education constituted a primary concern in Dalit leaders' – as well as women's and men's – appropriation of the modern in twentieth-century western India. Mainstream, feminist and Dalit historiography, as well as writings by Dalit activists, have overlooked ordinary Dalit women who have authored radical educational and social agendas in the Dalit movement. To date, historians have also generally relegated the field of education to the margins; there have been only a few studies of gender-segregated schooling during colonial times. Even these studies have neglected the ways in which caste discrimination affected women.

By focusing on municipal schools as an important conjunction for the multiple political, educational, social, cultural and intellectual battles of Dalits, I illustrate that the choices communities made about schooling help to illustrate larger questions about inclusion, exclusion and equality within Indian society. From the mid-nineteenth century, Dalits had to fight for the right merely to attend school. Their gradual appearance within western Indian classrooms in itself constituted a challenge to the hegemony of the high-castes. Prior to this, they were forced to sit outside the classroom. This process continued into the twentieth century. I address questions of *how* and *why* a theoretically 'liberatory' space – that of education – brought about modest emancipation but also became a site of humiliation and intimidation. I especially centre on Dalit girls studying in public or municipal corporation schools. At the centre of the book, therefore, are issues of citizenship and human rights, as well as the ways in which marginal groups were sometimes able to gain a more equal status and fight discrimination.

This book crosses the colonial and post-colonial divide to trace continuities and changes in Dalits' education access and process. Such an approach allows me to better comprehend the historically contingent, multiple and overlapping but conjunctive (social, educational, political cultural and gendered) processes which led to the construction of Dalit subjectivities. Instead of tracking a triumphalist narrative, this book examines the many hopes and hurdles, triumphs and tragedies, pressures and prejudices that Dalit women experienced over the years in their processes of education at different levels: primary, secondary, college and university. Focusing on shifting histories and entanglements of caste, class, gender and pedagogy and tracing the changes and continuities in the colonial and post-colonial periods, I seek to show how caste and patriarchy created for Dalit women a system of *double oppression* in particular historical conjunctures. This book reveals the physical and mental violence, the indignities and humiliations, to which Dalits in general and Dalit women in particular were and are subjected. As a subordinated people, Dalits share their struggles with other marginalised communities of the world. Central to this study are the discursive practices that led to the construction of Dalit womanhood and the specific experiences of Dalit women: what caste and patriarchy mean in their everyday lives; their vulnerability; their denigration; their insecurity; the erasure of their personhood and sense of self-worth – all seen in the context of their education. The book will also show how Dalits played a creative role by constructing a rhetorical platform to challenge existing education politics and to claim resources controlled by the government, as well as to disseminate educational (and civic) discourse deeper into Dalit society, thus bringing about the emergence of Dalit resistance.

This book thus addresses several important blind spots in the mainstream history of India as well as of the women's movement. It unravels the limitations of social reform movements and the mainstream feminist movement in engaging with the Dalit question. The dominant story of Indian nationalism has denied Dalits a space to debate or provide critiques of gender, caste and untouchability, and modernity. I also challenge dominant representations of Dalit women as 'lowly', 'poor' or 'unfortunate sisters' in the mainstream historiography of India, as well as of gender reforms, to examine how ordinary Dalit women's subjectivity was constructed through politics in the home and through their direct and indirect involvement in the Dalit public sphere that thrived in twentieth-century western India. Unlike the elite nationalists and colonial government, to whom Dalit women were objects of reforms, for Dalit radicals (especially Ambedkar), Dalit women's (and men's) selves had to be shaped out of a hierarchical and unequal society. Dalit women were to emerge as historical subjects out of the darkness of pre-modernity and pre-history into the light of the modern rule of law and egalitarian citizenship. This book documents the processes and efforts Dalit women made to attain modern education, as well as their everyday negotiations and lived experiences within and without the site of education.

Rather than 'going where women are' or 'recovering'[7] women through oral histories, I attempt to reconstruct Dalit womanhood and the radical *remaking* of their selves, collectively mediated by their personal experiences of schooling and the social and political struggles in which they actively participated. The book illustrates how Dalit subjects were formed within the limits of historically specific practices, what Foucault calls 'modes of subjectivation': the very processes and conditions that secure a subject's subordination are also the means by which she becomes a self-conscious identity and agent (Foucault 1980, 109–133; Foucault 1983, 208–226; Butler 1993 and 1997). This led to the construction of Dalit women's transgressive 'agency'.[8] Dalit women's capacities to recognise, reflect and reorganise for effective and purposive action, both as individuals and as part of a larger community, cannot be understood within the binary of enacting or subverting norms, or within the confines of liberalism. Rather, their networks of negotiations, abilities and skills to transform relationships of social injustice were constituted and enabled through their specific subordinated position. Dalit women's agency belonged to them as well as to the culturally specific and historically contingent arrangement of power in which they were located. This book thus centres on their shared socio-historical and emotionally contoured struggles for educational equality and on their visions of a democratic community. They provide fresh insights and nuanced cultural understanding of their particular predicaments – their collusions and collisions with the hegemony of the ruling classes.

This study's focus on education allows me to investigate not only the state and Dalit radicals' rhetoric and practices of modern education, but also the marginalised histories of ordinary Dalit women who were traditionally excluded from any sort of education. I unravel the intricate and complicated construction of Dalit women's subjectivities. I trace hitherto neglected familial, emotional and educational histories to explain how Dalit women constituted themselves as historical subjects, on however limited a basis, and consolidated their sense of personhood as they came into conflict on a day-to-day basis with Dalit men, upper-caste men and women, and the colonial and post-colonial states. I certainly do not wish to construct an individualised and individualistic 'heroine' or a voluntary autonomous subject, but I dwell on the confident and at the same time fragmentary and incoherent, discontinuous, knotty configurations of Dalit women's strategic redefinition of their subject position as they engaged with the collective in precarious and shifting political situations.[9]

I examine shifting histories of caste, class, gender, education, the anti-caste and anti-untouchability movement(s), and the political possibilities forged by Dalit social actors to offer a fuller understanding of Dalit women's social and cultural history and the realities of their educational experiences. Following the feminist scholar Joan Scott (1992, 37), I have focused on the 'discursive nature of experience' and how it is 'always-already an interpretation'. As such, I historicise Dalit women's experience by documenting how they were constituted as subjects in a particular political movement and at a historical moment. Dalit women's subjectivity was constructed discursively and their agency made possible by the ways in which they contested the historically contingent inner workings of power through the interlocking technologies of knowledge, caste, class, gender and sexuality.

Dalit women were constituted as 'subjects' through discourses and power of upper-caste exclusion and differentiation that sought to conceal or even repress them. During this process, upper-caste women took the lead in demanding rights for women and constructed 'liberal feminism', which reflected their concerns. They set the norms, which produced further contestations. This book speaks of the ruptures, tensions and failures in Indian feminism and lays out the conditions of the possibilities of Dalit subjectivity and agency. Dalit women faced overlapping difficulties, yet their collective and individual experiences also enabled numerous possibilities and choices.

The book also stresses homogeneity and heterogeneity in Dalit communities. Rather than a homogeneous group, the *Asprushya* (Untouchable) community represented many *jaatis* (caste, in this case sub-castes) which were fractured along lines of linguistic, cultural, regional and caste difference. The competition between Untouchable castes situated close together in social hierarchies often generated antipathy such that Mangs and Chambhars did not like to ally with Mahars for fear of being dominated by them. Hence, as less numerous and powerful groups, Mangs' and Chambhars' strategy was to keep their distance from the Mahars and to maintain their distinctive identity. Even during the famous temple entry movement of the 1920s, for example, the Mang leader Sakat allied with Gandhi and not with Ambedkar. When Ambedkar declared his intention to convert to Buddhism, many Mangs (including Ambedkar's Lieutenant Shivtarkar) deserted him.[10] Most importantly, in particular, historical and educational conjunctures – for example, that of the 1920s – diverse *jaatis* of Dalit women and men also came together to form fragile alliances. Thus they not only imagined a political community, constructed in the crucible of particular historical, social, intellectual, educational and political contexts – they actually lived in it.

Contested histories: caste, gender, education

This book brings into close conversation three hitherto separate strands of historiography and literature in the emerging field of Dalit studies, as well as women's studies and education studies. Moreover, my concept of 'interlocking technologies' allows me to deal with the entanglements of the disconnected historiographies in order to deal with a multiplicity of issues.

Modern Indian historiography's central dichotomy of colonialism and nationalism has actually contributed to the failure to acknowledge Dalits' role as historical subjects who were exceptional subjects of modernity.[11] Instead, I document Dalits' astute engagements with the social, economic and political processes, as well as institutions, of modernity, which they translated, contested, selectively embraced, and at times disavowed. These entanglements illustrate how Dalits strategically twisted and turned Western modernity for their own ends. They thus traversed the dichotomy between tradition and modernity, and engaged with their pasts and potent presents to refashion their futures.[12]

Although the British government permitted Dalits to study in municipal corporation schools, many who did so experienced humiliating and discriminatory treatment from both teachers and higher-caste pupils. The public right to education turned in practice into a right merely to a segregated education for Untouchable students. As a result, modern formal education *not only* became a significant site of conflict between imperial and upper-caste powers and Dalits; it emerged as a *field of forces* and a *political process* involving power, everyday negotiation, constant accommodation and much resistance. While the colonisers and their elite upper-caste agents were cautious about mass education, for Dalits education became a signifier, a language for speaking about rights and about their abduction by Brahmani forces in Maharashtra. They saw education as a particularly important means for their self-assertion and refashioning of personhood as well as their inclusion as citizens in the Indian body politic. Phule's and Ambedkar's militant struggles highlighted the hidden potential of education as a tool for social change, for Dalits' individual and collective transformation, and for gaining political power.

Yet the situation was particularly problematic for Dalit girls, because caste prejudice was compounded by prejudices against female education. Historically speaking, by 1931, Dalits had won by their own efforts 'the right to be taught'; yet, until 1981, about 54 per cent of the Dalits in Pune district were illiterate. But Dalits were on the move, encouraged by their leaders and activists to abandon oppressive village life and migrate to the cities, which they saw as more liberating. Nonetheless, as Dalits made some advances, some limitations and caste practices were also renewed in the modern cities of Pune and Mumbai. For example, during the 1940s, when the feminist Kumud Pawde rebelled against caste discrimination in her school by drinking water at a water-post meant for the upper castes, her teacher beat her (Pawde 2000). Despite this, she refused to be cowed and ultimately gained her Master's degree in Sanskrit, the classical, sacred language that only high-caste men had hitherto been permitted to study. Such experiences continued for Dalit girls into the latter part of the twentieth century. When she was a student in 1986, Bharati Kamble was teased and tormented at her school: 'The school workers taunted me for belonging to a "dirty" caste. Classmates hid my bag and pencils and harassed me.' Bharati, unable to fight this verbal abuse and psychological violence, dropped out of school (Kamble 2000).

Once we seek to uncover more subjective historical experiences, we encounter many silences. Although this is true for the history of the subaltern in general, the extensive official archive relating to the peasantry, tribal peoples and the working class has been read 'against the grain' in ways that have allowed for writing their histories in more thorough and sympathetic ways. This exercise has been carried out in particular in the twelve volumes published in the *Subaltern Studies* series. Until the fourth volume, however, women were ignored; although this lacuna was addressed strongly in later volumes, the whole series has continued to be remarkably silent about Dalits. In all, it has published only two articles on Dalits, neither of which is about Dalit women (Ilaiah 1996; Prashad 1999). Furthermore, Dalit thinkers – notably Phule and Ambedkar – have been overlooked and relegated to a 'subaltern' position even in the *Subaltern Studies* project.[13] More generally, post-colonial theory has yet to provide critical analyses of caste, gender and sexuality.

Most significantly, scholars, including Ambedkar, have critiqued (Brahmani) arguments which saw attempts to question the graded structure of 'Indian' society as essentially centrifugal to national integrity and neglected the minute power capillaries and the material reality of caste and gender oppressions and their concrete connections with patriarchy, thus highlighting the constructions of caste and untouchability across time and space (Deliege 1999; Leach 1969; Omvedt 1995; O'Hanlon 1985; Chakravarti 1998, 2003; P. Chatterjee 1989, 169–209; Juergensmeyer 1980). The anthropologist-historian Nicholas Dirks has provided a historical analysis of the colonial power's construction of caste in modern India through, for example, census enumeration. However, caste was not contrived anew by colonial modernity through its modern practices and technologies of governance; instead it was codified in pre-colonial times. What is significant, however, is that Dirks argues that by making caste traditional and political, the colonial state enabled a new politics of caste and civil society, in the process amplifying caste feelings and competition.

Scholars have also sought to engage with the Dalit question, in particular, to understand the ways in which Dalits dealt with the domination of the ruling classes and resisted both colonial and anti-colonial nationalist efforts in order to fight for their emancipation. In the process, this scholarship has led to the founding of Dalit studies. To me, Dalit studies as an intellectual inquiry is in fact a *conjuncture*: a potentially productive site of diverse perspectives which can initiate dialogue among different disciplines and scholarships and bring together disparate analytical categories and conceptual tools to understand social, economic, political, religious, cultural and environmental issues, as well as lives of the marginalised in different parts of the world.

My project makes a significant contribution to the emerging field of Dalit studies. This book situates itself within this historiographical approach and in the context of western India, of which scholars like Eleanor Zelliot, Gail Omvedt, Jayashree Gokhale, Philip Constable, Christophe Jaffrelot, Gopal Guru, and recently, Sharmila Rege and Anupama Rao are the leading figures. Yet this book departs from prevailing historical approaches to study Dalits in several different respects. Most historical works on Marathi Dalits focus on Ambedkar and on the history of Dalit activism (Zelliot 1992, 1994; Gokhale 1993; Omvedt 1994; Rao 2009). Rao significantly advances such studies by interlinking a history of the remaking of caste with an account of India's secular modernity. She also illustrates how even the process of adapting colonial modernity and secular education was paradoxical because it was thwarted by novel technologies of segregation. Benefiting from and building on these efforts, I delve into the everyday experiences of Dalit women to reveal education and formal schools as key institutions in the Dalit march towards modernity. My book also deepens Gyanendra Pandey's analyses by concentrating on the processes that led to Dalits' vernacularised engagement with the universal modern in the specific realm of education. I unravel how certain universalist ideas like rights, interests, individual independence and choice played out in a particular historical and regional context of Dalit education, social history, family life, and affective, emotional and inner resources that shaped Dalit women's consciousness. Moreover, I dig deeper into the early decades of the twentieth century and scour the past to analyse hitherto neglected Dalit agendas of creating the 'modern' citizen, and I also offer a nuanced reading of the ways in which the most marginalised group – Dalit women – navigated questions of gender, caste, class, power and privilege.

Surprisingly, only one historian, Zelliot, has documented Dalit initiatives in education; her research is yet to be published. *Dalit Women's Education in Modern India* certainly dwells on Dalit radicals' promises and practices for turning education into a fundamental battle with the colonial and post-colonial state and upper-caste nationalists. However, it shifts significantly away from previous movement-centric stories and leader-centric historiography to examine the practices of prejudice and discrimination, and the construction of ordinary Dalit women's subjectivities through their ideas about *shikshan* (education), *svaabhimaan* (self-respect), *sudhaaranaa* (self- and collective improvement), family, community and the wider society.

Most significantly, my book departs from earlier work by making the role of gender central to its historical analysis. However, in the context of north India, some historians like Ramnarayan Rawat have also occluded women and the working of gender relations in their revisionist reconstruction of Chambhars' history. The two most important exceptions to these generalisations are the noteworthy studies by the feminist historian Anupama Rao and the feminist sociologist Sharmila Rege. In her introduction to an edited volume, Rao theoretically addresses the nexus between caste and gender to point out the specific hurdles of Dalit women. Her book-length project *The Caste Question* (2009) recounts the story of Indian modernity from a male Dalit vantage point; however, most significantly, Rao also illustrates how issues of caste and gender complicated Dalits' political participation and modernisation. In one case study, she explores the intersection between law, violence and Dalit identity that produced Dalit women's sexual vulnerability, mainly in post-independence India (Rao 2009, 217–240; Rao 2003, Introduction).

My work builds on and departs from these scholars by drawing significantly on women's oral narratives that focus on both their political agency and their everyday life experiences. I gender modernity itself and seek to show that both women and men experienced and shaped modernity in different ways. Men may seem more vocal, articulate and 'political' compared to women, yet women actively engaged. I elaborate on men's work but also dwell on women's contributions to study the forces of history that shaped women's access to modernity. I make major advancements in the study of caste and gender in relation to Dalit women and their subjective complexities. I thus seek to advance theory and conceptual categories to deepen an understanding of the nexus of caste and gender by stressing the role of Dalit women as social actors and draw upon oral sources.

Moreover, I deepen the analysis of Ambedkar himself. In articulating deeper processes of women's historical engagement with modernity and upper-caste, elite nationalists and colonial power, I show in Chapter 4 how women actively engaged with radically modern technologies. Rege, in her introduction to *Writing Caste/Writing Gender: Narrating Dalit Women's Testimonios*, seeks to break new ground by arguing for 'Ambedkarite feminism'. In her introduction to Ambedkar's writings she recently focused on his 'feminist' analysis of caste and Brahmani patriarchy (Rege 2006, 2013). Like her, I focus on the significance of Ambedkar's contributions to resolve the 'woman question'; unlike her, however, I centre on Dalit women's ideas and practices, as they not only actuated but extended and critiqued Ambedkar's feminist praxis by challenging the politics of local leaders and men inside the household, however limited.

Most importantly, what gets occluded in extant scholarship is the fact that caste is at both ends and in the middle of the social structure – and that 'gender' also includes men. Many a time even notable scholars have often mistakenly and directly substituted caste with Dalit and gender with women. This also applies to publishing houses and the pressures of publishing, and hence the use of these categories in the titles of books. Moreover, existing scholarship does not attend to the ways in which Dalit women at once used the 'modern' Ambedkar's ideas and writings and also experienced transformations that went beyond his expectations. My study centres on how caste and gender constraints prevented Dalit women from achieving Ambedkar's expectations and the ways in which they faced new, reconstructed gender- and caste-based hierarchies over time and yet contributed to political activism and feminist practice. Although I predominantly focus on Dalit women, both men and women actively participated in the Dalit movement. Men and women were interdependent and constituted each other. Men supported women's political practices and at the same time discriminated against them as sexual and gendered subalterns.

In addition, I historicise and provide theoretical frames to further understand Dalit women's writings. In the wake of the Dalit literature of the 1960s, Dalit women and pioneering feminists like Baby Kamble, Shantabai Kamble, Urmila Pawar and Kumud Pawde, to name a few, wrote and published a significant amount of literature. They provide details not only of their plight, suppression, humiliation, dilemmas and exploitation, but also their challenge to communitarian notions of a singular Dalit community; their social, economic, religious and political deprivations; and their struggle and current status in society.[14] Dalit women have also analysed their 'double jeopardy' due to gender and caste oppression (Pawde 2005; Pawar 2005; Lanjewar 2005; Challapalli 1998; Basu 2002, 195). They argue that Dalit women are 'slaves of the slaves', 'Dalits [in relation] to Dalit men'; thus they are 'doubly Dalit' as they bear the burden of gender and caste oppression.[15] Nevertheless, with the exception of two notable women (discussed later in the book), none of the women I interacted with had written autobiographies.

This book also contributes to the literature on Dalits in urban history. It corrects the widespread belief among non-Dalits and Dalits alike that the power of caste is diluted in the cities. Indeed, in the Dalit imaginary there was a powerful conception of city life as caste-free, liberatory and democratic. One Dalit woman, Surekhatai Punekar, responded when I asked her about caste: 'There is *no* caste in the city. Why are you asking me about my caste? How does it matter? In fact, you are exacerbating caste distinctions by asking such questions' (Punekar 2002, emphasis added). Yet scholars like Kancha Ilaiah, Owen Lynch, Nandini Gooptu, Vijay Prashad, Nicholas Dirks, Anupama Rao and Gopal Guru have analysed the shattering of the modern 'caste-free city' dream.[16] There is a lack of historical studies on Dalits in the cities of western India. Urban geographers, sociologists and political scientists have once again excelled in comparison to historians; only one historian, Zelliot, has documented Dalit history in urban Pune. This gap in literature has led to incomplete understandings of the processes of education and social change that have shaped Dalits over time. This book is a small contribution towards grappling with Dalits' urban history.

Interlocking technologies of caste, class and gender

Historically speaking, like mainstream historiography, much of the mainstream feminist historiography has neglected the presence of 'caste communities' to focus on gender categories. Moreover, much scholarship on 'Women in Modern India' has also focused on upper-caste and, most significantly, Brahman women and their caste difficulties in terms of sati, enforcement of widowhood, widow remarriage and child marriage. In the process, however, these scholars have re-signified Brahman women's problems as those of Hindus and therefore Indians. By fixing Brahman women and Brahmani practices as 'Indian', some scholars have subsumed the powerful collusion of (upper) caste, class and patriarchy into 'Indian identity' itself.[17] Most significantly, such an intellectual strategy seems to be predicated on the scholars' reliance on the historical construction of 'liberal feminism' as de-classed, de-caste, or even de-sexed, and on its at times potent amalgamation with the upper-caste logic of a Hindu nation, which significantly occluded Dalit women as historical agents and rights-bearing citizens of the state.

Only over the past two decades have feminists critically analysed caste patriarchy and the power and privilege enjoyed by select castes and classes both historically and contemporaneously. A set of feminist scholars have drawn attention to the neglect of lower-caste and peasant women; some have also provided a corrective by addressing the theoretical and material aspects and the compounded nature of caste, class and gender (Sangari and Vaid 1989; Pardeshi 1998; Chakravarti 2003; Rao 2006, 2009; Rege 2006). Yet this scholarship rarely deals with ordinary women. Moreover, we still know little about the historical and complicated processes by which education has affected the hierarchies of caste, class, gender and sexuality. Social histories of education and colonial education policy have been written, but exclude the exigencies of gender and caste as they have affected Dalit women. Some feminist scholars have studied colonial education but have confined their studies to upper-caste, elite Hindu or Muslim women, thus neglecting Dalit women altogether (Forbes 1979; Minault 1981). Even the educational philosophies and practices of non-Brahman and Dalit leaders are overshadowed by those of upper-caste elite women and men. There is also little historical study of the post-colonial period.

Moreover, scholars have barely studied the potential connections between public institutions such as education and private realms like the family, gender, marriage and sexuality (Mukhopadhyay and Seymour 1994). Quite recently, the historian and feminist scholar Shefali Chandra provided a corrective by persuasively demonstrating the processes by which 'native codes of gender and sexuality shape[d] the history and symbolic power of English [education], and how, in turn ... English infuse[d] conjugality, desire, and caste' (Chandra 2012, 4). She 'explores how some [upper-caste, Brahman] Indians symbolically and materially reinterpreted English [or education, for my purposes] through the vocabulary of gender in order to produce sexual difference, sexual desire, and thus new regimes of caste exclusivity'. Chandra explicitly illuminates (upper-) caste privilege by focusing exclusively on upper-class Parsi and Brahman women's engagement with English education.

My book continues her conversation of education studies but significantly shifts the gaze to Dalit women's experiences of intimate practices of prejudice as they negotiated the colonial and post-independence state and upper-caste power. In the process, my monograph seeks to intertwine the 'domestic' with 'public' education in the context of Marathi Dalits. Historians have paid little attention to the critiques of gender, caste discrimination, family, marriage and modernity that Dalits produced. My book breaks new ground by attending to the deeper complexities of caste differentiation in everyday school practices and the production of micro-histories of affect, documenting how politically contoured personal and emotional experiences have allowed Dalit women to sharpen their sensitivities to injustices and silences over caste, class, untouchability, gender and sexuality. Dalit women's subjectivities emerged in particular historical conjunctures and their education nurtured new social and affective networks.

Dalits and education studies

More so than historians, political scientists, sociologists, anthropologists and demographers have mined the field of Dalit education. Some have also examined the deeply contentious territories of caste and education in independent India (S. Chitnis 1981; Velaskar 1998, 210–240; S.K. Chatterjee 2000; Jeffrey *et al.*

2005). Yet social scientists face limitations due to their primary concern with the contemporary period. Although some scholars have long recognised the matrix of overlapping structural difficulties in Dalit education, at the same time, others have denied the existence of caste discrimination in educational institutions (Khan 1993, 211–242; Kakade 1979). Perhaps these latter scholars failed to pick up on practices of caste differentiation in their studies, since few Dalits like to talk about such discriminatory practices.

Nonetheless, there is a significant lack of in-depth, qualitative investigation of Dalit women's education in colonial or post-colonial western India. Significant work by anthropologists like Patricia Jeffery, Craig Jeffrey and Veronique Benei has made a compelling case, cautioning that, despite India's more accessible and much improved education system, the Indian economy has failed to create large numbers of secure jobs for those it educates. This serious shortcoming has created a serious problem of unemployment among educated Dalit youth in North India (Jeffrey *et al.* 2005, 2008; Jeffrey 2010; Benei 2008). While this anthropological research is valuable, it lacks historical depth. The work of these scholars does little to explore the complicated historical processes involved in the construction of Dalit exclusion since the mid-nineteenth century, as well as the shaping of Dalit women's subjectivity over time. This book's unique study of untouchability in Marathi schoolhouses fills this lacuna.

My study departs from the above works by discussing the varying outcomes of Dalit women's formal education. Dalit women reported that 'they were indeed privileged to get whatever education they could' at local municipal schools. They argued that their education, however limited, also helped them to fight poverty, patriarchy, social injustice and inequality. Significantly, my historical work expands on Benei's anthropological study to argue that schools not only discipline and shape women in particular ways, but at the same time encourage them to an extent to develop their own understanding of social and political life.

The book does not offer a comprehensive review of education; I have purposefully made some choices. With its 'civilising' mission, the colonial government embarked upon opening up educational opportunities, yet it cautiously controlled the dissemination of knowledge within upper-caste and upper-class locations. The colonial state's limited liberalism and (pre-colonial and colonial) Brahmani discourses of education were thus mutually reinforcing. Many a time upper-caste elites thwarted British plans to 'modernise' education. My work departs from and deepens Veena Naregal's (2001) analyses of such 'laicisation' of education by tracking the processes, not in elite enclosures but in the everyday lives of ordinary lower-caste women. I focus on historical processes and events in the day-to-day living of Dalit students who accessed municipal schools in Mumbai, Nagpur and Pune.

This book also dwells on the internal divisions among Dalits and the complicated lives of some elite Dalits who were torn between borrowing and disavowing upper-caste practices in terms of dress, food habits, education and language. Many scholars have argued that education is generally beneficial for all and that there is a positive relationship between education and socio-economic status.[18] The feminist sociologist Padma Velaskar has examined the hidden role of education in the Dalit struggle for liberation and how it has acted as a mediator in 'contested reproduction' as well as in 'contested change' of the structures of caste inequality and untouchability (Velaskar 1998). In a study of Dalit college students carried out in the 1970s, M.B. Chitnis found that while 85 per cent of the students' parents and guardians were illiterate, three-quarters showed a strong interest in the educational progress of their wards (M.B. Chitnis 1973; B. Joshi 1986, 47–49; S. Chitnis 1981). This finding struck a blow at those who blamed Dalits for their own illiteracy and ignorance. Parents might be illiterate and unable to afford books for their children, but they still had very positive attitudes towards education.[19] Nevertheless, although educational uptake among Dalits has certainly improved greatly in recent years, there were still gaping holes, such as rising dropout rates (S. Chitnis 1981). Understandably, there was dissent among competing Dalit communities, with some more motivated than others to access and complete their educations (Kurane 1999; Abbasayulu 1978, 130–131; Sachidananda 1976; Singh 1969, 47, 57; the latter three are quoted in S.K. Chatterjee 2000). It is also well known that only a relatively small upper stratum of Dalits makes full use of the opportunities that are opened up through education (Dushkin 1979, 1999; Beteille 1992). A related issue is that increasing education has also led to competition among Dalits for a larger percentage of the pie of reservations. The sociologist G.G. Wankhede (2001) argued that in Maharashtra, the Mahars took the largest share of reservations and were thus disliked by other Dalit groups such as the Matangs and Chambhars. Lelah Dushkin reports that some Mahars were thriving and accruing immense benefits due to reservations. This, however, gave rise to an upper-class elite among them.[20] Several studies have highlighted the ways in which education and the economic betterment that results from it created internal divisions among Dalits (Sachidananda 1976, 277; Malik 1979, 50–55; Wagh 1986, 1994). However, I deepen these investigations by dwelling on the 'inner' gendered and class conflicts that education actually produced.

Double discrimination: the present project

This book is organised chronologically and thematically around its primary concern: to recover the contradictions between the rhetoric and the practice of modern secular education. To this end, the book tracks the dynamic dialectic and reconstructs the interlocking and shifting history of caste, class, knowledge and gender in relation to pedagogic rhetoric and efforts on the one hand, and the shaping of Dalit women's new subjectivities on the other.

The novel experiments of colonial modernity unleashed by the British government opened as well as closed opportunities for Dalits, thus constructing a unique *educational conjuncture* in early twentieth-century Maharashtrian politics. With their toil and taxes, Dalits contributed to establishing and maintaining the systematic apparatus of education, yet were virtually excluded from its benefits. Chapter 1 explains the historical and educational conjuncture centred on Dalits' complicated struggle for the right to education and modern citizenship in early twentieth-century Mumbai. I illustrate how education became a political process involving struggles over power and politics between the coloniser and the colonised. It also reveals how the presence of the colonial British government shaped and shifted this terrain of struggle among the colonised – touchables and Untouchables – situated in asymmetrical social and political positions. Working through the educational conjuncture, I offer an examination of smaller and broader debates about the potential and pitfalls as Dalits sought to become 'modern', fully human 'citizens' or full members of a community, as well as about their individual and collective social, familial and emotional battles in specific historical circumstances. Focusing on government municipal schools, the book examines how education is an important arena of struggle – one form of social activity within a broader network of experience, history and collective struggle.

The official story of British initiatives and policies of education figure very little in this book. Actually, the colonial state, like its agents, was torn by contradictions about its perceptions of the figure of the Untouchable, as well as on the Dalit question. Although the state diligently recorded education statistics, it had limited or no understanding of Dalit social life, the constitution of the Dalit programme of education, or Dalit womanhood.

The discourse of the colonial state was reinforced by internal colonialism among the colonised; both failed to include Dalits in their educational efforts. Events that took place in Mumbai's municipal schools amply reveal the contradictory relationships between institutional and policy developments 'at the top' and the 'lived experience' of ordinary Dalits. The upper-caste orthodoxy supported caste distinctions in schools, opposed executing the government's resolution, and wanted the decision to extend education as a right to all to be erased. In a similar vein, in the municipal corporation meeting, some hard-core Congresswallas were also against *ekloti* (one drinking-water pot for all castes): they did not want the touchables to be polluted and hence enforced the law of segregated drinking-water pots. Certainly, the decisions Indian society made about educating its children reveal to a great extent how it imagined their future civic contributions. Chapter 2 dwells on Phule's and Ambedkar's rhetoric of formal education, intellectual history of education, and culling of the education programme when it challenged the state as well as elite nationalists, including Gandhi. Dalit radicals' modern rhetoric identified the innermost task of *shikshan* (education) to build their human dignity by reviving the *svaabhimaan aani svaavalamban* (self-respect and self-reliance) and *naagarikatva* (citizenship) always-already denied to them, unlike the upper castes. I show how the rhetoric of education and intellectual and social history shaped and was transformed by Dalit social actors.

Chapters 3 and 4 historicise the struggles for Dalit women's access to education and reveal the convergences and contradictions between Dalits' and upper castes' agendas of education, *streeshikshan* (women's education) and the reform of women. Chapter 3 critiques the upper-caste, modern middle-class agenda of education as connected with *streedharma* (the model of conduct for women) and the gender logic of the Hindu nation, which strategically excluded Dalit women altogether. Although 'liberal feminists' as well as laywomen were closer to Dalit women and men in terms of educational exclusion, they still failed to include the latter in their broader missions. I explore the reasons for such repression and exclusion. Chapter 4 is devoted to the emergent modern historical subjects – Dalit women – who struggled for the right to education, which was interconnected with gender and moral reforms and discipline within the Dalit community. Although constrained by the very processes that enacted the modern reforms of education and women's rights, Dalit women carved out their agency, however limited, and continued to make enormous gains. Dalit masculine womanhood (which will be discussed in Chapter 4) emerged from Dalit women's growing sensitivity to social injustice, educational exclusion, civilising and cultural anxieties, and political consciousness as they appropriated modernity, 'respectability' and 'honour'. This process involved education, access to the public domain, politics, democracy, and a certain rationality in multiple and interconnected processes.

Dalit women constructed their agency through everyday struggles with Dalit men, upper-caste women and men, and the colonial and post-colonial states. Their day-to-day battles constitute their history. These processes involved Dalit radicals' gradual reorganisation of the Dalit public sphere and energetic efforts to include Dalit women as bearers of modernity and to restore their rights as women, however limited. Chapter 5 tells the story of first-generation Dalit women's initial experiences of school in rural areas and city slums. It challenges the promise of modern urban spaces which sought to erase caste and class power and privilege. Second- and third-generation modern middle-class Dalit women's educational journeys are explored in Chapter 6. Chapter 7 provides accounts of educated Dalit women's struggles for and in employment. The final chapter, Chapter 8, investigates middle-class marriage and childrearing practices among educated women to uncover deeper contradictions around gender and class within the Dalit community.

Reflections on methodology

Methodologically, *Dalit Women's Education in Modern India* straddles the borderlands where history and anthropology intersect. I trace ordinary Dalit women's social and cultural history by contextualising their lived experiences of formal education in government municipal schools in twentieth-century western India. The book employs multiple sources, extensive archival documentation and oral narratives to elucidate and make nuanced claims about the complicated relationships between caste, class, gender, family, sexuality, citizenship and educational opportunity.

The story unfolds in three cities – Pune, Mumbai and Nagpur – which supported educational initiatives and had an active history of social reform movements. I have also retained the ways in which Marathi-speaking communities have addressed the cities, as Pune and Mumbai. Thus, I use the colonial names Poona and Bombay only when contemporary sources have referred to the cities as such. Moreover, my use of 'Puneri' alludes to the quint-essential Brahmani ethos of Pune, while 'Punekar' refers to those coming from Pune. I began this project with a typical survey of the literature on Dalit women's education, which exposed abundant quantitative studies on enrolment, levels of education, resources spent and literacy levels, as well as some 'sad' but 'true' stories about the increasing number of Dalit students dropping out of schools or unable to access higher education. Amid a host of such studies by social scientists, what was lacking was an adequate appreciation of the logic of the inner workings of the historical processes that enabled Dalit exclusion and failure in formal institutions of education in the first place. Moreover, qualitative and detailed information on Dalit women's access to and process of education was continuously neglected. Hence, I set out to document Dalit women's lived experiences of education in order to understand their multiple and overlapping struggles to follow the promise of education.

Dalit Women's Education in Modern India is divided into two parts which draw upon different materials and methods. While the first part is devoted to Marathi and English archival data, the second concentrates on oral narratives to reconstruct Dalit women's experiences of education. This two-part structure unravels the dissonance between the rhetoric and practice of secular education. Part I is devoted to explicating the educational conjuncture in Maharashtra, as well as to Dalit radicals' rhetoric of modern education, moral and gender reforms to uplift Dalit community and serve the Indian nation. Part II elicits the complex ways in which Dalit radicals' and the state's rhetoric of education were thwarted in practice and reveals Dalit women's complicated lives at the conjunction of caste, class, gender, sexuality and education amid a host of social, sexual, cultural, affective and political formations. By shifting my focus and method to documenting the lived and everyday experiences of ordinary Dalit women in Part II, I seek to challenge the common narrative of the straightforward value of modern education. Each chapter focuses on a distinct theme. To paint the fullest possible picture of education, my investigation looks beyond the schoolhouse and analyses a range of other institutions, such as the family and the workplace. In this manner, my project offers a fuller understanding of Dalit women's education and history.

By using the feminist framework of 'intersectionality' or, as I prefer to call it, 'interlocking technologies', the book seeks to intertwine the domestic with the public domain. By weaving together Dalit struggles to access the public institution of education with Dalit women's personal battles in terms of gender, family and sexuality, I explore the tensions between the public and private domains to construct the intimate lives of Dalit women in twentieth-century urban spaces. By examining what actually happened within families – between men and women, parents and children – as they grappled with issues being debated in public, I focus on providing a fuller understanding of the growth of Dalit women's education in particular circumstances. Dalit men were dominated and dominating. They thus mapped the colonial–native, Brahman–Dalit and man–woman relationships upon their marital bonds.

Most importantly, I combine theories and practices of macro- and micro-history to analyse particular events in the lives of Dalit women in order to study the social structure, local economies and political relationships that illuminate relations of power. In this manner, I examine the minute details of Dalit women's first-hand accounts, contextualise them in socio-historical terms, and place their ideas, actions and lives in a wider historical perspective. Moreover, I theorise Dalits' everyday experiences by tying them to systemic phenomena: the anatomy of caste, class and gender hierarchies. By combining ethnographic evidence from historical fieldwork with hitherto-underused public and private archival sources, my monograph illuminates the reshaping and remaking of the Dalit self and community. This deeper investigation of caste from the inside, along with my lived experience, allows me a leverage to explore *our* worlds. I examine the actual reality of the educational experience of Dalit women and connect it to their history and struggles for identity and consciousness.

Archive

The question of the archive has been both a central and contested one in the process of reconstructing an often 'invisible', 'broken', 'ambiguous', 'eccentric subject' that never constituted a 'fully human community' or even 'womanhood'. To weave together a complex narrative of Dalit women's experiences of education, I researched a diverse array of archival sources: newspapers, autobiographies, published and unpublished public documents, government reports, education magazines, private manuscript collections and quantitative data (education statistics) at different archives. As it is, there is a deep problem of structural and theoretical exclusion of women's voices and subjectivities in the production of public records. Moreover, detailed official compendiums centred on colonial projects and goal-oriented education policies, rather than on their uneven implementation or unintended social and political effects. The 'official' records, both colonial and post-colonial, often objectified Dalit women, lacked in-depth information on them, and rarely commented on the Dalit educational programme or process. They did little to illuminate the ways in which Dalit women engaged with the government's policy, politics or local social practice and familial relations, and in the process of engagement remade themselves. Hence I have relied more on newspapers, pamphlets, writings produced by Dalits, the private archives of some Dalit individuals and oral histories of Dalit women.

In order to capture subtle markers of untouchability in urban educational spaces, an interdisciplinary and integrative methodology of various sources, both written and oral, is required. Dalit women's history cannot be studied through written records alone, as it is largely unrecorded. Women in general have had a vexed relationship with the kinds of documents and histories that archives typically contain; Dalit women's histories barely figure in these store-rooms. Where they have found a small space, they have often been depicted in an objective, arithmetic and algorithmic vocabulary: numbers, percentages, graphs, pictures of their poverty and destitution. Thus traditional archives have not only excluded but also distorted Dalit women's history. I use hitherto underused Marathi sources that capture the emotional and political contours of Dalit women's inner resources and experiences, as well as the changes they underwent. My unique contribution is the evidence I have gathered from extensive 'historical fieldwork' in Pune, Mumbai and Nagpur. Unlike elite Hindu and Muslim women, many Dalit women with whom I interacted did not write autobiographies, produce writings out of leisure or publish systematically. Instead, I worked with an alternative archive: the oral tradition, 'to challenge exclusionary, local, national, and colonial histories'.[21] Neither oral nor written sources are wholly reliable because both are fragmented. I have relied on a combination of both, because combining them offers a fuller account of the Dalit past. Different types of sources, some even fragmentary, create a discursive field in which they communicate, question, talk back to, interrupt, or even ignore one another. Dalit women were absent or completely erased from official and mainstream voices. For example, the fragments of Dalit women's ideas of education were absent or even avoided in the official story of education.

Oral history

Through oral histories, the book documents social, familial and emotional histories of Dalit women. It disentangles the affective and emotional power entangled in their experience of education. Advancing the efforts of oral historians, this book illustrates that oral sources illuminate the expressive cultures that have shaped Dalits' pursuit of their rights, emotional desires and affective networks to appreciate the extraordinary emotional pressures and challenges faced by women of different generations in their efforts to pursue their fantasies and desires.

Oral sources are a necessary condition for a history of the non-hegemonic (Dalit) classes; they are less necessary for the history of the ruling classes, who have had control over writing and leave behind much more abundant written records.[22] Hence this work takes oral history seriously in order to engage with Dalit women's own understanding of their history and to write a richer and more multi-layered account of their lives.[23]

By drawing on the significance of Dalits' oral history, I hope to 'draw attention to the lacuna in the theoretical analysis of historical sources and to remedy it by examining the value of oral traditions as a historical source'.[24] I contacted women from all backgrounds – rural and urban, educated and uneducated, employed and unemployed – to provide detailed accounts that related to the objects of this study, always paying attention to the uniqueness of each case rather than merely looking for abstractions (Atkinson 1998; Portelli 1990, 35).

Collecting such life stories provides a way of putting on record the experiences of relatively powerless Dalit women whose ways of knowing and seeing the world are rarely acknowledged, let alone celebrated, in the expressions of a Brahmani hegemonic culture. Telling and listening to these stories also creates vital links among participants and can be a powerful and practical instrument of conscientisation.[25] The personal narratives of Dalit women offer a place from which to reflect upon our past experience and to scrutinise our stories, which carry agency, meaning and information about the social and psychological positions we inhabit. It is also significant to explore what becomes of these stories. The current popularity of autobiography and narrativity in feminist research is a measure of the significance now attached to experience, reflection and psychoanalytic understanding as a counterbalance to the kinds of public and external evidence available from historical and structural analysis and political economy. The feminist historian Carolyn Steedman (1986, 143) exemplifies the theoretical genre perfectly while insisting that 'once a story is told, it ceases to be a story; it becomes a piece of history, an interpretative device'.

Dalit women's experiences are also contested and, like traditional sources of history, open to interpretation. I have sought to draw upon Dalit women's oral histories and memories in order to document and historicise their lived experiences, which were situated at a crucial intersection of colonialism and nationalism, public and private domains, and the personal and political. Since the year 2000, I have interviewed Dalit women from three generations, from different levels of education and age groups, and from slums and middle-class backgrounds to illuminate the reshaping and remaking of the Dalit self and community. Through narratives of Dalit women as usable sources of history, the book seeks to enlarge the scope of history itself.

I recount this story through the voices of two sets of Dalit women: the first generation, who entered schools for the first time and moved from rural areas into the city neighbourhoods, and the second and third generations, who moved from city slums to middle-class apartments and advanced towards modernity and 'middle-class' identity. My interlocutors were not shy in their willingness to be critical of leaders' and state policies, household and social tension, and past, present and future. Indeed, they narrated their stories enthusiastically because, for the first time, they found a chance to talk to and be recorded and photographed by someone interested in their lives, views and long-neglected stories.

Rather than providing a 'pure' and 'authentic' account of the past, this book attends to its own porousness and messiness and asks what we might learn from the oral narratives of Dalit women. Although in a different context (Africa), the historian Luise White reminds us that 'the inaccuracies in [such] stories make them exceptionally reliable historical sources as well: they often offer historians a way to see the world the way story tellers did, as a world of vulnerability and unreasoned relationships' (White 2000, 5). This book pays attention to the evasion, opacity, affect, anxiety, desire, agency, passionate and psychological truth claims through which Dalit women have talked back to Dalit men in the family, Dalit activists, state projects, and destabilised feminist 'recovery' projects of 'making the woman visible', 'sisterhood', and the long trenchant debates among feminists over prioritising individuality/family/community.

It has been a challenging task to weave through the life stories of our 'unheard', 'unsung', 'forgotten' Dalit women intricately through my own subjectivation.[26] Such a study requires not only reflecting on certain fundamental issues of Dalit self and society, but also carefully handling Dalit women's diverse thoughts and experiences, both localised and scattered. I have had some very intriguing and engaging experiences while conducting ethnographic interviews with 'my' Dalit women interlocutors which would almost certainly have been closed off from researchers who were not from my background. Most of the time they used the collectives *aaplyat* (in our community), *aapan* (we) and *aaplaa samaaj* (our community), thus talking to me as a Dalit woman. Women felt proud that *aapali mulgi* (our Dalit daughter) was researching *our* lives. Instead of calling them by their formal names, I often used the Marathi particle 'Tai' to address them with affection and respect. Our collective memories and shared experiences of the Dalit movement certainly helped me easily to enter into their private and public lives and to engage with them fully. My historical fieldwork has required me to take the question of experience into account seriously, deconstructing and reconstructing history in order to develop critical knowledge and a critique of knowledge itself.[27] I thus bring doubly marginalised Dalit women's lives to the centre of historical practice in order to document their history, in which they were claiming a historical voice produced from the crucible of their individual and collective political struggles for education and equality both at home and in public.

Notes

1 My debt to Foucault is evident here. See Foucault (1997, 281–282).
2 Editorials and articles in newspapers like *Bahishkrut Bharat, Mooknayak* (Leader of the Voiceless) and *Janata* (People) provide ample evidence of vernacular idioms in Dalit social and political thought and agendas. See, for example, *Mooknayak* (28 February 1920) for vernacularised expressions of Dalits' desire to become 'modern' citizens.
3 To Foucault, governmentality on an individual level involved the 'technologies of the self' and allowed individuals to effect

> by their own means, or with the help of others, a certain number of operations on their own bodies and souls, thoughts, conduct, and way of being, so as to transform themselves in order to attain a certain state of happiness, purity, wisdom, perfection.
>
> (Foucault 1988, 18)

4 My debt to feminist scholars of 'intersectionality' is obvious here. I combine their conceptualisation with Michel Foucault's articulation of 'technologies' as the disciplinary forms of power that were a product of the European Enlightenment. See Foucault (1993, 1988, 18), as well as D. Scott (1999).
5 I have conducted oral interviews with Dalit women in Pune, Mumbai and Nagpur. The number of interviews conducted in Pune and Mumbai was higher than in Nagpur. The women belonged to six castes: Mahar, Mang, Chambhar, Khatik, Dhor and Valmiki. For the purposes of this book I have concentrated on women for the first three castes. Dalits are classified into many *jatis* (castes) and are not a homogeneous group; however, I do not enter into the competitive politics among these groups. I do, however, draw upon caste differences among Dalits as and when enforced by Dalit women and men.

6 I have benefited here from Marshall Berman's study of the experience of modernity. See Berman (1982).

7 Leading feminist historians like Antoinette Burton and Mrinalini Sinha have well rehearsed the 'recovery' of the (upper-caste, middle-class) female subject in South Asian history.

8 Instead of limiting agency to those acts and practices that disrupt hegemonic power relations, I have benefited from Foucault's analysis as well as Saba Mahmood's (in a different context), which departs from the reductive binaries of resistance and subordination to dwell on the 'different modalities through which agency operates: performativity, transgression, suffering, survival, and the articulation of the body within different conceptions of the subject' (Mahmood 2005, 188).

9 The trajectories of their lives unravel every 'subject-effect', thus constituting an act of resistance. For the concept of 'subject-effect' see Spivak (1988, 3–32).

10 See Paik (2011, esp. pp. 234–235).

11 I am referring to Dipesh Chakrabarty's programmatic reading of the political idea of modernity by using the trope of the 'peasant' to 'stand for all that is not bourgeois (in a European sense of the word) in Indian capitalism and modernity' (Chakrabarty 2000, 11). Chakrabarty, like his Subaltern Studies colleagues, has forcefully denounced Eurocentrism and argued for a demand for subaltern histories.

12 Manuela Ciotti (2010, 35) coins the phenomenon of 'retro-modernity' to demonstrate the processes through which aspiring middle-class Chambhars embraced a form of passé modernity while remaining at the margins of what it means to be modern in contemporary India. 'The explanatory salience of retro-modernity lies in highlighting the tension between *a past modern and a contemporary one* in which the Chamars are caught in.'

13 Although Partha Chatterjee has a chapter entitled 'The Nation and Its Outcasts' in P. Chatterjee (1993), nothing is said about this Dalit tradition, or about Phule or Ambedkar. Only recently, Gyanendra Pandey's (2013) book *A History of Prejudice: Race, Caste, and Difference in India and the United States* was published; see my critical review (forthcoming) in *Social History* for further detailed analysis.

14 Muktabai Salve, Baby Kamble, Shantabai Kamble, Mukta Sarvagod, Meenakshi Moon, Saroj Kamble, Asha Thorat, Hira Bansode, Jyoti Lanjewar, Sugandha Shende, Surekha Bhagat, Aruna Lokhande, Susheela Mool, Meena Gajbhiye and Vimal Thorat. Sugava (Pune) and Asmitadarsha (Aurangabad) are two Dalit publishing houses that have provided a potent platform for many Dalit writers.

15 Lanjewar (1995, 2005). Caste politics has always been dominated by male leaders, with the issue of gender being either subsumed within its general rhetoric or simply set aside as trivial or frivolous. Only recently have some feminist renderings investigated the multiple and changing manifestations of caste in Indian society in order to understand the particular forms in which gender inequality and sex subordination are produced. Especially see how they have explored gender troubles faced by Dalits: Pawar and Moon (1989), Rege (2006), Rao (2003) and Chakravarti (2003).

16 Ilaiah (2002, 43). Ilaiah draws upon Phule's *shetji-bhatji*, or Brahman-Bania alliance, which oppressed Dalits. See also Lynch (1969), Gooptu (1993), Prashad (2000) and Dirks (2001).

17 My argument is fortified by Shefali Chandra (2012).

18 An M.Phil. dissertation by Swati Mutalik (1992) also underlined the positive effects of education on social mobility, social change and social participation. Anjali Kurane is of the opinion that education determines aspirations, productivity, and vertical and horizontal mobility. See Kurane (1999) and S.K. Chatterjee (2000).

19 Another study indicates that, though far less educated, of poor economic means, and needing immediate financial help from adult family members, nearly nine-tenths of the students received encouragement from their fathers, mothers and brothers. Thus, it may be said that the members of the older generation, irrespective of their own

educational level, understood the value of education, and therefore encouraged younger members of the family to take up education. See M.B. Chitnis (1973, 45–46), S.K. Chatterjee (2000) and Kananaikil (1998).

20 Dushkin (1999, 212, 218) argues that protective discrimination as a whole has become a mechanism for social control – an instrument of distributionist politics. See also Dushkin (1979, 661–667).

21 My debt to feminist scholarship is evident here. See Burton (2003, 23). Although in a different context, that of China, I have benefited from Gail Hershatter's work (2011).

22 This issue is raised by Portelli (1990, 1997) and Massey (1994, 4–6).

23 For examples of such work, see Hardiman (1987, 1995, 92, and 1996), P. Thompson (1978, 88–90), Omvedt (1980), Bhave (1988), Lalitha *et al.* (1989), Atkinson (1998), J. Thompson (2000), and most recently Hershatter (2011).

24 I draw upon works of oral historians like Vansina, Portelli and others. See Vansina (1961).

25 This refers to the concept of 'critical consciousness' discussed earlier. For Phule, Marx, Gramsci, Ambedkar, Freire, and so on, this means the awakening of the slave to the idea of his slavery and thus leading to a rebellion. I also draw upon Jane Thompson's insightful work on working-class women's education in England. See J. Thompson (2000), Allman (1999).

26 I draw once again upon Foucault's paradoxical character of 'subjectivation of the prisoner' (*assujetissement*) (Foucault 1977, 203).

27 I draw upon some feminists' commendable work on debates of identity and experience. See Mohanty (1994, 147–163), Moya (1997, 145). See also Ilaiah (2002, xi–xii). Drawing upon feminist methods, Ilaiah underlines that narratives of personal experiences are the best contexts in which to compare and contrast social forms.

References

Abbasayulu, Y.B. 1978. *Scheduled Caste Elite: A Study of SC Elite in Andhra Pradesh, Hyderabad*. Ph.D. dissertation, Department of Sociology, Osmania University, Hyderabad, India.

Allman, Paula. 1999. *Revolutionary Social Transformation: Democratic Hopes, Political Possibilities and Critical Education*. Westport, CT: Bergin and Garvey.

Ambedkar, B.R. 1920. *Mooknayak* (Leader of the Voiceless), 31 January.

———. 1927. *Bahishkrut Bharat* (India of the Excluded), 3 June.

Atkinson, Richard. 1998. *The Life Story Interview*. Thousand Oaks, CA: Sage.

Basu, Tapan. 2002. *Translating Caste*. New Delhi: Katha.

Benei, Veronique. 2008. *Schooling Passions: Nation, History and Language in Contemporary Western India*. Stanford, CA: Stanford University Press.

Berman, Marshall. 1982. *All That Is Solid Melts into Air: The Experience of Modernity*. New York: Simon and Schuster.

Beteille, Andre. 1992. *The Backward Castes in Contemporary India*. New Delhi: Oxford University Press.

Bhave, Sumitra. 1988 *Pan on Fire*, trans. Gauri Deshpande. New Delhi: Indian Social Institute.

Burton, Antoinette. 2003. *Dwelling in the Archive: Women Writing House, Home, and History in Late Colonial India*. Oxford: Oxford University Press.

Butler, Judith. 1993. *Bodies that Matter: On the Discursive Limits of 'Sex'*. New York: Routledge.

———. 1997. *The Psychic Power of Life: Theories in Subjection*. Stanford, CA: Stanford University Press.

Chakrabarty, Dipesh. 2000. *Provincializing Europe: Postcolonial Thought and Historical Difference*. Princeton, NJ: Princeton University Press.

Chakravarti, Uma. 1998. *Rewriting History: The Life and Times of Pandita Ramabai*. New Delhi: Kali for Women.

———. 2003. *Gendering Caste: Through a Feminist Lens*. Calcutta: Stree.

Challapalli, Swaroopa Rani. 1998. Dalit men's writing in Telugu. *Economic and Political Weekly*, 25 April: 22.

Chandra, Shefali. 2012. *The Sexual Life of English: Languages of Caste and Desire in Colonial India*. Durham, NC: Duke University Press.

Chatterjee, Partha. 1989. Caste and subaltern consciousness. In *Subaltern Studies VI: Writings on South Asian History and Society*, ed. Ranajit Guha. New Delhi: Oxford University Press.

———. 1993. *The Nation and Its Fragments: Colonial and Postcolonial Histories*. Princeton, NJ: Princeton University Press.

Chatterjee, S.K. 2000. *Education Development of Scheduled Castes: Looking Ahead*. New Delhi: Gyan.

Chitnis, M.B. 1973. An educational, social and economic survey of Milind College students. In *Milind College Annual*, Vol. 10. Aurangabad: People's Education Society.

Chitnis, Suma. 1981. *A Long Way to Go: Report on a Survey of Scheduled Caste High School and College Students in Fifteen States of India*. New Delhi: Allied Publishers.

Ciotti, Manuela. 2010. *Retro-Modern India: Forging the Low-Caste Self*. New Delhi: Routledge.

Cohn, B.S. 1987. *The Chamars of Senapur in Uttar Pradesh: An Anthropologist among Historians and Other Essays*. New York: Oxford University Press.

Deliege, Robert. 1999. *The Untouchable of India*, trans. Nora Scott. Oxford and New York: Berg.

Dirks, Nicholas. 2001. *Castes of Mind*. Princeton, NJ: Princeton University Press.

Dubois, Abbe. 1906. *Hindu Manners, Customs and Ceremonies*, translated, annotated and revised by Henry K. Beauchamp. Oxford: Clarendon Press.

Dumont, Louis. 1970. *Homo Hierarchicus: The Caste System and its Implications*. Chicago, IL: University of Chicago Press.

Duskhin, Lelah. 1979. Backward class benefits and social class in India, 1920–1970. *Economic and Political Weekly*, 14(14): 661–667.

———. 1999. Scheduled caste politics. In *The Untouchables in Contemporary India*, edited by Michael Mahar. Tempe: University of Arizona Press.

Forbes, Geraldine. 1979. Women's movements in India: Traditional symbols and new roles. In *Social Movements in India*, Vol. 2, ed. M.S.A. Rao. New Delhi: Manohar.

———. 1996. *Women in Modern India*. Cambridge: Cambridge University Press.

Foucault, Michel. 1977. *Discipline and Punish: The Birth of the Prison*, trans. Alan Sheridan. New York: Vintage Books.

———. 1980. Truth and power. In *Power/Knowledge: Selected Interviews and Other Writings 1972–77*, ed. and trans. C. Gordon. New York: Pantheon.

———. 1983. The subject and power. In *Michel Foucault: Beyond Structuralism and Hermeneutics*, ed. H. Dreyfus and P. Rabinow. Chicago, IL: University of Chicago Press.

———. 1988. Technologies of the self. In *Technologies of the Self: A Seminar with Michel Foucault*, ed. Luther H. Martin, Huck Gutman and Patrick H. Hutton. Amherst: University of Massachusetts Press.

———. 1993. About the beginnings of the hermeneutics of the self. Transcript of two lectures in Dartmouth on 17 and 24 November 1980, ed. Mark Blasius. *Political Theory*, 21(2): 203–204.

——. 1997. The ethics of the concern of the self as a practice of freedom. In Michel Foucault, *Ethics, Subjectivity and Truth*, ed. Paul Rabinow, trans. Robert Hurley *et al.* New York: New Press.

Gandhi, M.K. 1916. Speech on caste system. Ahmedabad, 5 June. In *Collected Works of Mahatma Gandhi*, Vol. 15 (June).

Ghurye, G.S. 1969. *Caste and Race in India.* Bombay: Popular Prakashan.

Gokhale, Jayashree. 1993. *From Concessions to Confrontation: The Politics of an Indian Untouchable Community.* Bombay: Popular Prakashan.

Gooptu, Nandini. 1993. Caste and labour: Untouchable social movements in urban Uttar Pradesh in the early twentieth century. In *Dalit Movements and the Meaning of Labour in India*, ed. Peter Robb. New Delhi: Oxford University Press.

Hardiman, David. 1987. *The Coming of the Devi: Adivasi Assertion in Western India.* New York: Oxford University Press.

——. 1995. Community, patriarchy, honour: Raghu Bhangare's revolt. *Journal of Peasant Studies*, 23(1): 88–130.

——. 1996. *Feeding the Baniya: Peasants and Usurers in Western India.* New York: Oxford University Press.

Hershatter, Gail. 2011. *Gender of Memory: Rural Women and China's Collective Past.* Berkeley: University of California Press.

Hutton, J.H. 1963. *Caste in India: Its Nature, Function and Origins.* Oxford: Oxford University Press.

Ilaiah, Kancha. 1996. Productive labour, consciousness and history: The Dalitbahujan alternative. In *Subaltern Studies IX*, ed. Shahid Amin and Dipesh Chakrabarty. New Delhi: Oxford University Press.

——. 2002. The emergence of neo-Kshatriyas and the reorganization of power relations. In *Why Am I Not a Hindu: A Sudra Critique of Hindutva Philosophy, Culture and Political Economy.* Revised edn. Calcutta: Samya.

Janata. 4 August 1934.

Jeffrey, Craig. 2010. *Timepass: Youth, Class and the Politics of Waiting.* Stanford, CA: Stanford University Press.

Jeffrey, Craig, Roger Jeffery and Patricia Jeffery. 2005. Broken trajectories: Dalit young men and formal education. In *Educational Regimes in Contemporary India*, ed. Radhika Chopra and Patricia Jeffery. New Delhi: Sage.

——. 2008. *Degrees without Freedom? Education, Masculinities and Unemployment in North India.* Stanford, CA: Stanford University Press.

Joshi, Barbara, ed. 1986. *Untouchable! Voices of the Dalit Liberation Movement.* London: Zed Books.

Juergensmeyer, Mark. 1980. What if the Untouchables don't believe in untouchability? *Bulletin of Concerned Asian Studies*, 12(1).

Kakade, S.R. 1979. *A Study of the Integration of the SC in Indian Society: A Case Study in Marathwada.* Ph.D. thesis. Pune: University of Pune.

Kamble, Bharati. 2000. Interview with the author, August.

Kananaikil, Jose. 1998. Marginalisation of the Scheduled Castes. In *Scheduled Castes and the Struggle against Inequality*, ed. Jose Kananaikil. New Delhi: Indian Social Institute.

Karve, Irawati. 1961. *Hindu Society: An Interpretation.* Pune: Deshmukh Prakashan.

Ketkar, S.V. 1979. *The History of Caste in India.* Ithaca, NY: Asia Book Corp. of America.

Khan, Shahrukh. 1993. South Asia. In *Women's Education in Developing Countries: Barriers, Benefits and Policies*, ed. Elizabeth M. King and M. Anne Hill. London, and Baltimore, MD: World Bank.

Kurane, Anjali. 1999. *Ethnic Identity and Social Mobility*. Jaipur: Rawat Publications.

Lalitha, K., Vasantha Kannabiran and Rama Melkote. 1989. *We Were Making History*. New Delhi: Kali for Women.

Lanjewar, Jyoti. 1995. Dalit literature and Dalit women. In *Dalit Women in India: Issues and Perspectives*, ed. P.G. Jogdand. New Delhi: Gyan.

———. 2005. Interview with the author, 10 October. Ambazhari, Nagpur.

Leach, Edmund, ed. 1969. *Aspects of Caste in South India, Ceylon and North West Pakistan*. Cambridge: Cambridge University Press.

Lynch, Owen. 1969. *The Politics of Untouchability: Social Mobility and Social Change in a City of India*. New York: Columbia University Press.

Mahmood, Saba. 2005. *Politics of Piety: The Islamic Revival and the Feminist Subject.* Princeton, NJ: Princeton University Press.

Malik, Suneila. 1979. *Social Integration of the Scheduled Caste*. New Delhi: Abhinav Publications.

Massey, James, ed. 1994. *Indigenous People: Dalits*. New Delhi: ISPCK.

Minault, Gail, ed. 1981. *The Extended Family: Women and Political Participation in India and Pakistan*. New Delhi: Chanakya.

Moffatt, Michael. 1979. *An Untouchable Community in South India*. Princeton, NJ: Princeton University Press.

Mohanty, C.T. 1994. On race and voice: Challenges for liberal education in the 1990s. In *Beyond Borders: Pedagogy and the Politics of Cultural Studies*, ed. Henry Giroux and Peter McLaren. New York: Routledge.

Mooknayak 28 February 1920

Moraga, Cherrie and Gloria Anzaldua, eds. 1983. *This Bridge Called My Back: Writings by Radical Women of Color*. New York: Kitchen Table.

Moya, Paula. 1997. Postmodernism, 'realism', and the politics of identity: Cherrie Moraga and Chicana feminism. In *Feminist Genealogies, Colonial Legacies, Democratic Futures*, ed. J.M. Alexander and C.T. Mohanty. New York: Routledge. Originally published in *This Bridge Called My Back: Writings by Radical Women of Color*, ed. C. Moraga and G. Anzaldua. New York: Kitchen Table, 1983.

Mukhopadhyay, Carol and Susan Seymour. 1994. *Women, Education and Family Structure in India*. Boulder, CO: Westview Press.

Mutalik, Swati. 1992. M.Phil. dissertation. *Education and Employment of Women in Pune City*. Pune: Indian Institute of Education.

Naregal, Veena. 2001. *Language, Politics, Elites, and the Public Sphere*. New Delhi: Permanent Black.

O'Hanlon, Rosalind. 1985. *Caste, Conflict and Ideology: Mahatma Jotirao Phule and Low-Caste Protest in Nineteenth-Century Western India*. Cambridge: Cambridge University Press.

Omvedt, Gail. 1980. *We Will Smash the Prison*. London: Zed Books.

———. 1994. *Dalits and the Democratic Revolution: Dr. Ambedkar and the Dalit Movement in Colonial India*. New Delhi: Sage.

———. 1995. *Dalit Visions: The Anti-Caste Movement and the Construction of an Indian Identity*. New Delhi: Orient Longman.

Paik, Shailaja. 2011. Mahar-Dalit-Buddhist: The history and politics of naming in Maharashtra. *Contributions to Indian Sociology*, 45(2): 217–241, esp. 234–235.

——. 2014. Review of Gyanendra Pandey's *A History of Prejudice: Race, Caste, and Difference in India and the United States. Social History*, 39(2): 141–143.

Pandey, Gyanendra. 2013. *A History of Prejudice: Race, Caste, and Difference in India and the United States*. New York: Cambridge University Press.

Pardeshi, Pratima. 1998. The Hindu Code bill for the liberation of women. In *Gender and Caste*, ed. A. Rao. New Delhi: Kali for Women.

Parekh, Bhiku. 1989. *Colonialism, Tradition and Reform: An Analysis of Gandhi's Political Discourse*. New Delhi: Sage.

Patwardhan, Sunanda. 1973. *A Change among India's Harijans: Maharashtra – A Case Study*. New Delhi: Orient Longman.

Pawar, Urmila. 2005. Interview with the author, 5–7 September. Borivili, Mumbai.

Pawar, Urmila and Meenakshi Moon. 1989. *Amhihi Itihas Ghadavala: Ambedkari Chalvalit Streeyancha Sahabhag*. Pune: Sugava.

Pawde, Kumud. 2000. Interview with the author, June.

——. 2005. Interview with the author, 16 October. Dhantoli, Nagpur.

Phule, Jotirao. 1969. Introduction to 'Shetkaryacha Asud' (Cultivator's Whipcord). In *Mahatma Phule, Samagra Vangmay*, ed. Dhananjay Keer and S.G. Malshe. Mumbai.

——. 2002. *Selected Writings of Mahatma Phule*, ed. G.P. Deshpande. New Delhi.

Portelli, Alessandro. 1990. *The Death of Luigi Trastulli and Other Stories: Form and Meaning in Oral History*. Albany: State University of New York Press.

——. 1997. *The Battle of Valle Giulia: Oral History and the Art of Dialogue*. Madison: University of Wisconsin Press.

Prashad, Vijay. 1999. Untouchable freedom: A critique of the bourgeois-landlord Indian state. In *Subaltern Studies X*, ed. Gautam Bhadra, Gyan Prakash and Susie Tharu. New Delhi: Oxford University Press.

——. 2000. *Untouchable Freedom*. New York: Oxford University Press.

Punekar, Surekha. 2002. Interview with the author. Kasba Peth, Pune.

Rao, Anupama, ed. 2003. *Gender and Caste*. New Delhi: Kali for Women.

Rao, Anupama. 2009. *The Caste Question: Dalits and the Politics of Modern India*. Berkeley: University of California Press.

Rege, Sharmila. 2006. *Writing Caste/Writing Gender: Narrating Dalit Women's Testimonios*. New Delhi: Zubaan.

——. 2013. *Against the Madness of Manu: B.R. Ambedkar's Writings on Brahmanical Patriarchy*. New Delhi: Navayana.

Sachidananda. 1976. *The Harijan Elite*. London: Thompson Press.

Sangari, Kumkum and Sudesh Vaid. 1989. *Recasting Women: Essays in Colonial History*. New Delhi: Kali for Women.

Scott, David. 1999. *Refashioning Futures: Criticism after Postcoloniality*. Princeton, NJ: Princeton University Press.

Scott, Joan W. 1992. Experience. In *Feminists Theorize the Political*, ed. Judith Butler and Joan W. Scott. New York: Routledge.

Singh, Anant Santokh. 1969. *The Changing Concept of Caste in India*. New Delhi: Vikas Publications.

Spivak, Gayatri Chakravorty. 1988. Subaltern studies: Deconstructing historiography. In *Selected Subaltern Studies*, ed. Ranajit Guha and Gayatri Spivak. New York: Oxford University Press.

Srinivas, M.N. 1962. *Caste in Modern India and Other Essays*. Bombay: Asia Publishing House.

——. 1996. *Caste in Its Twentieth-Century Avatar*. New Delhi: Penguin.

Steedman, Carolyn. 1986. *Landscape for a Good Woman: A Story of Two Lives*. London: Virago.

Thompson, Jane. 2000. *Women, Class and Education*. London: Routledge.

Thompson, Paul. 1978. *The Voice of the Past: Oral History*. Oxford: Oxford University Press.

Vansina, Jan. 1961. *Oral Tradition: A Study in Historical Methodology*. Chicago, IL: Aldine.

Velaskar, Padma. 1998. Ideology, education and the political struggle for liberation: Change and challenge among the Dalits of Maharashtra. In *Education, Development and Underdevelopment*, ed. Sureshchandra Shukla and Rekha Kaul. New Delhi: Sage.

Wagh, Vilas, ed. 1986. Dalit Madhyam Varga (Dalit Middle-Class). *Sugava*, special Deepavali issue, November–December.

——. 1994. Dalitanna Brahmani Saunskrutiche Akarshan (Dalit's attraction for Brahmani culture). In *Sugava Ambedkari Prerana Visheshank*. Pune: Sugava.

Wankhede, G.G. 2001. Educational inequalities among Scheduled Castes in Maharashtra. *Economic and Political Weekly*, 36(18): 1553–1558.

Weber, Max. 1958. *The Religion of India: The Sociology of Hinduism and Buddhism*. Chicago, IL: Free Press.

White, Luise. 2000. *Speaking with Vampires: Rumor and History in Colonial Africa*. Berkeley: University of California Press.

Zelliot, Eleanor. 1992. *From Untouchables to Dalit*. Delhi: Manohar.

——. 1994. *Dr. Babasaheb Ambedkar and the Untouchable Movement*. New Delhi: Bluemoon Books.

Part I
Education

1 The right to education

In the early decades of the twentieth century the ostensible public right to education turned, in practice, into a right merely to a segregated education for
Untouchable students in the Bombay Presidency. The rhetoric of civil liberties,
mass education and individual freedom adorned modern British colonial policies, but in practice, social exclusion (of non-Brahmans and Dalits) and
inequality were embedded in public education from its inception. Moreover,
upper-caste Marathi nationalists participated in and supported the colonial discourse because state policy was intrinsically interlinked with dominant Brahmani pedagogical practices. Hence, both the modern state and upper-caste elites
hesitated to resolve the Dalit educational question. Both were ambivalent about
the Dalit question in general and converged, to a large extent, in their discourse
of excluding Dalits from the right to education and of constructing differences
between castes. Dalits had a tremendous hunger for education and continued to
attain as much schooling as possible, despite the difficulties this entailed,
because they believed passionately in its modern promise, its significance for
their existential freedom, and its power as a vehicle to social, economic and
political freedom: a way out and up from under. Theirs was a militant optimism.

In this chapter, I uncover the overlapping educational battles at a specific
historical conjuncture in the context of decolonisation. Schools became more
than a site of struggles between the touchables and Untouchables, who fought
their social, cultural and political battles in the colony as well as between the
colonised and colonisers. Rather, it was a political process. These 'uncanny'
double forces constructed a typical *educational conjuncture* in the 1920s. This
was the outcome of disparate interactions between colonial perceptions of Indian
society; policies devised to combat educational 'backwardness' and their cautious implementation; Indian elites' participation in the colonial discourse; and
Dalits' response and resistance to the state and upper castes. Within this political
and educational context of constantly shifting relations among Dalits, upper-
castes, nationalists and the state, Dalits shaped their movement and in turn were
transformed by it. Unlike upper-caste elites who kept Dalits at a distance from
civic politics, Dalit radicals developed a wide repertoire of constitutional tactics
to challenge British education politics and claim resources and rewards, and successfully diffused Dalit demands for the 'right to education' and 'freedoms' into

Dalit society. They wrested the modernising force of education from the Raj and Brahmans and shaped their own resistance.

Historians have neglected this story. To explain the educational conjuncture of early twentieth-century Maharashtra, Dalits' educational aspirations, and their systematic denial by Indian society fully, a number of questions must be raised. If the children of the poor (Brahmans and other high castes) were admitted freely into government institutions, why were Dalits prevented from doing the same? How did private initiatives by both Dalit and non-Dalit social reformers, as well as missionaries, interact with British colonial state policy and practice in early twentieth-century Bombay Province? How and why did education become an important vehicle of Dalits' modernisation, especially from the late nineteenth century? How did segregated education affect Dalits? To address these questions, I will examine how education and schools in the context of early twentieth-century Maharashtra became a central terrain for struggle over power and politics out of the lived experience of individuals and groups, touchables and Untouchables, situated in asymmetrical social and political positions.

Certainly, the British had a commitment to opening education up to more social groups. This was an important part of their claim to be 'civilising' India – yet their record was inevitably an uneven one. Similarly, although some high-caste reformers made efforts towards mass education, on the whole they failed to include Dalits and address their thirst for education. Theoretically speaking, the colonial state did subscribe to the 'equal right' to education, yet deeper investigations uncover how bureaucratic normalising technologies and the educational discourse of the modern state prevented Dalits from exercising this right. Victorian values were thus not confined to the metropole, but spilled out onto the colony; British and Brahman forces continuously colluded and conspired with each other out of strategic anxiety. Foreclosing on the promise of education led to Dalits' exclusion from the body politic.

Inside the colony there were interconnections and important discordances between high and low castes that affected the discourse of education and social change. While some liberal upper castes did support Dalit education, in general Brahman supremacy prohibited this. Thus, both the state and upper castes worked in conjunction to macromanage the pedagogical structure and micromanage Dalit individuals, revising the educational discourse for new political ends. Significantly, the presence of the colonial state also allows us an interpretive space to grasp the tensions between the upper and lower castes. Colonial power altered the terrain of struggles.

Although discrimination against Untouchables was formally prohibited, this ban was seldom executed. Students faced numerous obstacles while exercising their ordinary human rights, such as accessing common water-posts and *lotis* (pots) to drink water. Yet they were far from being 'docile' or 'indifferent', as the colonial state and upper-castes would have us believe, and they resisted on a number of occasions. The repetition of such disruptive events created fissures in the normal school routine and interrupted the upper-caste conception of education, as well as challenged the British policy of educating the masses. These disruptions also called into question the dominant modes of historical under-standing of education; they provide us with counter-histories from a Dalit perspective.

This chapter investigates *how* and *why* education represented such a critical part of the broader struggle for Dalit civic rights from the early twentieth century. Formal educational legislation based on principles of equity offered a new direction for Dalits' efforts to escape their 'savage slot': during the water-shed year of 1920, they demanded not charity but *compulsory and free* educa-tion. In order to unravel these complicated processes, the first two sections of the chapter focus on the period leading up to the 1920s to demonstrate that, although the colonial government and some high-caste liberals made genuine efforts for mass education, many were also ambivalent about Dalit education.

The third section concentrates on the advent of dyarchy, an ingenious con-stitutional device which split the functions of government in two, especially after the 1920s. The government set the pace of reform, which was to be slow and measured, and announced its objective of gradually developing self-governing institutions. With this arrangement, however, the British controlled the central administration; 'reserved' functions such as law and order, finance, agriculture, and education were transferred to Indian ministers who were responsible to local legislatures. Upper-caste Indian education ministers failed to provide mass education because they were increasingly threatened by the potential of the rising lower castes. By contrast, some non-Brahman and many Dalit activists and spokespersons were actively involved in articulating the need for Dalit education as well as compulsory mass education. The early decades of the twen-tieth century, then, were a field of forces within which Dalits emerged as modern citizen-subjects.

Educational policies and practices of the ambivalent colonial state

The colonial government, Christian missionaries, non-Brahman and Dalit leaders, and high-caste liberals began making efforts toward mass education at the end of the nineteenth century. Their efforts were inconsistent, torn by contra-dictions. While some sympathised with Dalits' quest for education and political rights and believed they would make 'loyal' subjects, others were cautious about Dalits gaining access to political privileges before they had reached a 'high' stage of consciousness. During both pre-British and early British rule, no attempt was made to educate the Dalits because, as with Brahmani policy, education was confined to the higher castes.

Although the British considered education a 'civilising' tool, they were silent for a long time on the question of promoting education among the native popula-tion. Nonetheless, with the Act of 1813, education became the responsibility of the colonial state and Brahmans lost their traditional monopoly over schooling. The British government did eventually take up the responsibility of 'civilising' the 'barbaric' Indians. Macaulay's 'Minute on Education' (1835) sums up

England's superiority and its task of transforming brown Indians by using law, free trade and, most importantly, education.

The government did widen educational opportunities, yet there were some limitations. Actually, the colonial state, like its agents, was torn by contradictions about its perceptions of the figure of the Untouchable, as well as on the Dalit question. On the one hand, the colonial state and its agents described Untouchables as 'weak', 'lazy', 'primitive' and 'backward', yet at the same time appreciated their 'intelligence'. For example, historically speaking, the Mahars were hereditary village servants and were significant among the *baaraa balutedars*.[1] The *Khandesh Gazetteer* in 1880 defined the traditional Mahar as a 'lazy', 'unthrifty' but 'intelligent' village servant, noting that 'they have gained a monopoly of the unskilled railway market' (Campbell *et al.* 1880, 116, 119, quoted in Zelliot 1994, 35). Another colonial authority spoke of the Mahars' skills, predicting that they would *excel* in any field and would be a growing force (Craddock 1899, 28, quoted in Zelliot 1994, 35).

Thus the British had divided opinions on the Untouchables. Although significant in British eyes for their menial skills, they held lesser and lower attention as compared to the upper castes. As a result, the British favoured different communities in particular historical conjunctures. When they did intervene to promote education among the lower sections of society, they were cautious and conservative about interfering with the social order or initiating any educational or social reform among Dalits. The colonial state embarked on such efforts only later – and that too discretely, sometimes miserly, and with less enthusiasm, in contrast with the efforts of social reformers, Christian missionaries, and Untouchables themselves. The state recorded educational statistics; however, their efforts were quite weak and they had limited or no understanding of Dalit social life, the constitution of the Dalit programme of education or Dalit womanhood. As feminists have noted, the colonial state was also biased towards upper-caste and upper-class women. This work thus concentrates on Dalit social actors in a regional context to document discourses, initiatives and actual practice in the Dalit push towards education and, consequently, social and political awakening.

While some British officers (like Major Candy, the principal of Poona Sanskrit College) and missionaries made efforts to educate non-Brahmans and Dalits, on the whole the government was ambivalent and somewhat less eager to offer them an education. When in 1821 the government started a Hindu college at Pune known as Poona Sanskrit College, it was open *only* to Brahman students. A few years later the college was opened to all Hindus, but again the scholarships were restricted *only* to Brahmans (Keer 1964, 51).

The first governor of Bombay, Montstuart Elphinstone, was president of the Bombay Education Society and was often hailed as a liberal administrator. He observed in 1824 that the lower castes made good students, but went on to warn against encouraging them because 'if our system of education first took root among them, it would never spread further' (quoted in Ambedkar 1928, 415). He described himself as very cautious and an especially 'firm advocate of ... gradual evolution of human societies' (Deshpande 2007, 73–74).

In 1854, Charles Woods set out the government's active measures towards mass education and expressed a readiness to increase expenditure for these purposes. Yet, at the same time, Ellenborough, president of the Board of Control, warned that

> education and civilisation [flow] from the higher to the inferior classes, and so communicated may impart new vigour to the community, but they will never ascend from the lower classes to those above them; they can only if imparted solely to the lower classes, lead to a general convulsion, of which foreigners would be the first victims.
>
> (Ambedkar 1928, 10)

Thus the Court of Directors wanted social change to start at the top and filter downward: 'if [they] were to diffuse education ... they would give it to the higher classes first' (Ambedkar 1928, 10).

Christian missionaries started schools for Dalits in Ahmednagar in 1855; the next year the question of admission of a Dalit boy into a government school in Dharwar was first raised. Working on their techniques of 'fair play', in a Despatch of 28 April 1858, the Court of Directors passed an order that 'the educational institutions of Government [were] intended to be open to all classes' (Ambedkar 1928, 10) – yet, simultaneously and deliberately, they also made education a preserve for the high castes. Although the Dalits, along with other communities, were granted the right to enter government schools in 1858, in actual practice the state made no effort to enforce this theoretical right for some years.

In a similar vein, after two and a half decades, the Hunter Education Commission Report of 1882 affirmed that all government-aided schools and educational institutions should be open to all castes and communities. It favoured admitting lower-caste children to government schools as a *matter of right*. Although the colonial state agreed that the question of Dalit rights was a practical and pressing one, at the same time it was 'fully alive to the fact that no principle, however sound, can be forced upon an unwilling society in defiance of their social and religious sentiments' (Indian Education Commission 1883, 516–517). In principle, all schools wholly maintained out of public funds were to be regarded as 'open' to all taxpayers, including Untouchables; yet the Commission emphasised that even in the case of government schools the principle must be applied with considerable caution:

> If the low-caste community seek an entrance into the cess-school, their rights must be firmly maintained, especially in the secondary institutions where there is no alternative of a special school for them to attend.
>
> (Indian Education Commission 1883, 516–517; Constable 2000, 383–422)

The Commission appeared to sympathise with Dalits and acknowledged the upper-castes' opposition to their education. The report added:

the opposition was not generally due to religious sentiments alone, but in a large measure to the unclean habits and the unpolished manners and conversation of low-caste boys. They are also occasionally due to the desire of the upper-castes to keep the low castes in a state of subjection and servility.

(Indian Education Commission 1883, 514)

Yet, in order to control the internal crises, the Commission tried to balance the opinions of various groups. Significantly, the Commission tried to appease the upper castes even as the British continued to subdue and conquer them, advising teachers and inspectors that 'it is not desirable for masters or Inspectors, to endeavour to force on a social change and ... undesirable to urge [the low-castes] to claim a right about which they are themselves *indifferent*' (Indian Education Commission 1883, 517, emphasis added). Some rural communities in Bombay also raised objections to the instruction of low castes on the ground that education would advance them in life and induce them to seek emancipation from their present servile condition. In these circumstances, the government agreed that Untouchables required 'special help', yet it considered that 'such help can often be best afforded without giving offence to other castes by the establishment of special schools' (Indian Education Commission 1883, 517). Ironically, the Commission restricted education even while opening up access. The colonial state affirmed the right of 'education for all', yet it constrained Dalits because it did not want to antagonise the upper castes.

H.P. Jacob, Educational Inspector, North-East Division, issued a directive that Mahar and Mang students be admitted to all government schools in the northern division of Bombay Presidency, but colonial administrators opposed him. T.S. Hamilton, District Assistant Collector in Ahmednagar, argued in July 1880 that Untouchable students were not to be allowed into schools because it would be offensive to caste Hindus, who would withdraw their children, resulting in the closure of the school (quoted in Constable 2000, 386). Some administrators, Elphinstone among them, admired Dalits both for their inquisitiveness and aptitude. By contrast, P.C.H. Snow, Assistant Collector of Pune, and E. Giles, Educational Minister, Northern Division, had a low opinion of Untouchables. Giles wrote:

to place untouchable students in a school was effectively to empty that school of caste-Hindu students ... and [nobody] can alter this situation by mere order. These Dheds, Bhangis ... are most *indifferent* to education and even when the children come to school, they rarely remain there any time, their attendance is usually mostly irregular. They see *no* benefit in education.

(Quoted in Constable 2000, 394, emphasis added)

Many colonial officers were influenced by bourgeois Victorian ideas and valued educational theories which upheld 'good learning' and 'godliness' among the Brahman *jatis*.

Similarly, a Bombay High Court judge underscored for the Education Commission in 1882 'the impropriety and impolicy of forcing high-caste Hindus and others against their feelings to sit with Dheds and others like them in the same place' (*Bombay Chronicle*, 3 December 1882, quoted in Constable 2000, 387). Even K.M. Chatfield, Director of Public Instruction, saw education as a prerogative of the higher *jatis*. These officials chose to clearly favour the caste Hindus and encouraged their attacks not only on missionary educational programmes but also on Dalit educational rights (Ambedkar 1928, 9), thus demonstrating a preference for the caste Hindus over educational aspirations of Dalit students.

Table 1.1 reveals the fruits of the state's favouritism of Brahmans (Ambedkar 1928, 9). Although mass education was a government policy, in practice the masses were excluded from it. In order to find a way out of this impasse, the government resorted to two practices: opening separate government schools for low-caste boys and offering special encouragement to missionary bodies to undertake low-caste education. Even so, these too were limited.

Although the colonial state provided free schools, inequality and social discrimination were rooted in public education from the beginning. During the 1890s, Ambedkar received his early education in Dapoli and later Satara at a camp school, though in a segregated setting. At the English-medium school at Satara he sat apart from the rest of the class, even outside the classroom, on a piece of gunny mat which he had to carry to the school daily. He often had to go without water because Untouchables had no right to drink from the common water-post (Ambedkar 1992). Similarly, five decades later (in the 1940s), Kumud Pawde, a Dalit feminist, was not allowed to touch the utensils to drink water at school:

> We had to drink water at the corporation tap which was very far. Then I wondered as to why should I do it, and I started to rebel, but the maid there abused me badly and took me to the teacher. The teacher *bai* [woman] beat me up with a *danda* [stick].
>
> (Pawde 2005)

Pawde's and Ambedkar's experiences reveal the deep conjunction between Dalits' access to education and their struggle for civic rights, even ordinary

Table 1.1 Caste make-up of students in Bombay, 1881–82 (by percentage of total student body)

Castes	Primary education	Middle school	High school	Collegiate education
Christians	0.49	12.06	2.26	3
Brahmans	20.17	30.70	40.29	50
Other Hindus	64.69	37.50	34.89	22.3
Low-caste Hindus	0.87	0.14	0	0
Aboriginal Tribes	0.87	0.05	0	0

Source: Ambedkar (1928, 9).

human rights, such as access to water, in the early decades of the twentieth century. The everyday experiences of Dalit students made them more visible in the schools. These events also ruptured the triumphant colonial narrative of educational advancement and further revealed that Dalits were not 'docile' or 'indifferent'.

The ambivalent colonial government thus followed contradictory open and closed policies at the same time. It hesitated to resolve the thorny Dalit question because it believed that forcing a social change upon Indians would lead to chaos. The British government clearly feared revolt in the colony and hence restricted knowledge at the moment of its dissemination. The potentials of emancipation and novel closures of colonial modernity thus produced a distinctive educational conjuncture. The bureaucratic normalising technologies of the modern state demanded order and normalisation. In the process of controlling chaos, it eliminated those (Dalits) who threatened it – what Foucault has called a 'defence of society against itself'. Etienne Balibar refers to this operation as the defence of a society's 'interior frontiers' (Balibar 1994; Stoler 2002, 378).

Nevertheless, the government was successful in creating the illusion of equal access to education and equal human rights. Some colonial officials failed to recognise discrimination on the grounds of untouchability and, for convenience, emphasised the merits of educating upper-caste Hindus and placed faith in them to channel education to the lower castes, turning a blind eye to their exclusion of Dalit students. They colluded with upper castes about the Dalits' 'innate difference' and attempted to discourage them from seeking education. Overall, the colonial state's efforts to educate Dalits were weak.

Ambivalent high-caste liberals and efforts towards Dalit education

Similar to some colonial officials, high-caste, elite nationalists in general saw mass education as crucial to Dalit modernity, but were ambivalent about the Dalit question. Hence they failed to adequately emphasise the discrimination Dalits faced in the educational system. Oblivious to their own hesitations, the reformers, on the other hand, insisted that the government give up its ambiguous stand. One member of the Hunter Commission, K.T. Telang, argued that the government 'must bestow brains on those who have only hands.... Without mass education the country will never be able to enjoy to the full the fruits which it has a right to expect from higher education' (Indian Education Commission 1883, 618). Similarly, some liberal Pune Brahman reformers like M.G. Ranade, G.K. Gokhale, R.G. Bhandarkar and Lokahitawadi strongly condemned untouchability, yet did not create educational opportunities or institutions for the Dalits.

For example, Gokhale's Servants of India Society (SIS) aimed to spread education among the Dalits and to promote cordial relationships among different communities. In fact, Gokhale asked members of the Society to take seven vows, including a promise to 'treat all Indians as brothers and to work for the advancement of all without distinction of caste or creed' (Servants of India Society 1905–16, 3). One Devdhar also made arrangements for Dalit girls to be admitted to the Poona Seva Sadan; three began attending in 1923 (Servants of India Society 1917–23, 31). This was a revolutionary feat considering the socio-historical context of traditional Puneri society. He also secured financial aid and provided boarding facilities for boys.

In 1924 some active members of the SIS, such as Limaye, also organised an anti-untouchability campaign in Pune in order to 'encourage the Depressed Classes to claim and assert their natural rights of civic equality along with other classes' (Servants of India Society 1923–26, 24). Similarly, in Bombay the Society struggled to secure sweepers the right to travel in tramcars.

Other reformers were apprehensive about Dalit uplift. When Mohandas K. Gandhi visited Gokhale's Society in Pune in 1915, he was apprised of the group's programme with regard to Dalits. He solemnly cautioned, 'I am afraid you will make Harijans rise in rebellion against society'. But Hari Narayan Apte, a member of the Society, replied: 'Yes, let there be a rebellion. This is just what I want' (quoted in Desai 1953, 52–54). Similarly, Bhandarkar supported Dalit education and underscored that 'Brahmans did not oppose the education of untouchable children but were only concerned with their too close vicinity' (Bhattacharya *et al.* 2003, 125). Based on the Brahmani purity-pollution ideology, other objections raised to the admission of Dalits into schools were their unclean habits, unpolished manners and conversations [among] low-caste boys (Indian Education Commission 1883, 514; Bhagat 1935, 144). In a paper laid before the Hunter Commission, one writer raised the risk of contagious diseases and remarks:

> to parents to whom the well-being of the children is of equal importance with their education, the practical working of the principle of equality is a perpetual source of dis-comfort as regards both the physical and the moral welfare of their children.
>
> (Indian Education Commission 1883, 514)

Reinforcing this writer's reasoning, the state agreed these were 'real and reasonable difficulties', but also noted 'that the aboriginal races, whose habits are equally unclean, are never objected to on that ground'. There was a 'deep-seated prejudice to the admission of low-caste boys into public schools and it was due to religious feeling, fear of physical and moral contagion' (Indian Education Commission 1883, 515).

Aware of the prevailing prejudice, Sir N.G. Chandavarkar, a renowned social reformer, lawyer and judge, sounded a warning that 'the Indian society must remember that unless it awakens it is bound to die' (Kaikini 1911, 76). He argued that there could be no reform or hope for the higher castes so long as the so-called lower castes were despised. Chandavarkar also advocated Dalits' admission to schools, access to public facilities and civic rights. In November

1917, as chairman at a meeting of the Depressed Classes (DC), he played a crucial role in passing a number of significant resolutions. These included the DCs' right to elect their own representatives, their right to educational facilities, and that the Indian National Congress must make efforts to remove all disabilities imposed by religion and custom on them. In a speech at Byculla, Mumbai, Chandavarkar affirmed that DCs should be electorally represented [in the Legislative Council] in proportion to their population and through elections in their constituencies alone (*Mooknayak*, 28 February 1920), and reinforced their political demands. However, along with Depressed Class Mission leaders like G.A. Gawai who were Congress sympathisers, he also argued that Dalit members should also join the elected members of the Legislative Assembly. Ambedkar denounced Chandavarkar's (and later on Gandhi's) position on the grounds that if DCs were to follow this directive they would be condemned to live in a subordinate position.

Nonetheless, Chandavarkar believed that by 'uplifting the Untouchables, the Hindus liberated themselves' (*Bahishkrut Bharat*, 29 March 1929). Hence, he arranged a number of conferences to discuss the removal of untouchability. During one such conference in 1912 in Pune, inter-dining was also arranged.[2] Perhaps these leaders wanted to 'co-operate with'[3] the Dalits and made efforts for them, sometimes concerted and sometimes scattered, but they clearly had limitations. Since its inception until 1950, the SIS had made no budgetary provisions for Dalit uplift (Sawant 1989, 123). It succeeded neither in elevating Dalits nor in eradicating untouchability. Even leaders of the significant Prarthana Samaaj denounced the caste system and idolatry, and emphasised social transformation in principle, yet they wanted to use moderate persuasion instead of active social change.

Most significantly, unlike these liberal Punekars, a large percentage of orthodox Brahmans believed that their traditional power, monopoly over education and administrative employment were threatened. In addition, in the colonial public sphere, caste feelings were transformed and in fact intensified as new opportunities opened up. Brahmans responded by opposing education for non-Brahmans, Untouchables and women. As a result, the Brahman pundits of Poona Sanskrit College refused to teach Sanskrit to the non-Brahman students. When Major Candy, principal of the College, took upon himself the task of teaching Sonars, Prabhus and others while Brahman teachers taught Brahman students, a majority of Sanskrit teachers threatened to resign rather than teach the sacred language to non-Brahmans (*Bombay Guardian*, 8 October 1852, *Dnyanodaya*, 2 August 1853, quoted in Keer 1964, 48–49).

Both Mumbai and Pune witnessed organised political activity. The educated class dominated the Pune Sarvajanik Sabha, but failed in the barely active associations of Mumbai. Unlike Mumbai, in Pune's monolithic structure, the Chitpavan Brahmans alone dominated not only due to education, wealth and political power but on numerical strength as well. They comprised about 20 per cent of the population and formed one of Pune's largest single groups, animating street politics and mass demonstrations, and organising young men. Brahman dominance also meant the superiority of the Puneri orthodox; moderate social reformers did not enjoy real power after 1895. Puneri reformers were organised and effective. They were united over public and political matters, but disagreed on social and religious reforms such as idol worship and caste (Masselos 1964, 479). By contrast, Bombay (per Masselos) was not systematically organised. Its political activity was always a result of an uneasy compromise between its two social classes: Shets/Shetias (Banias) and educated Brahmans (ibid., 556).

At times some Bombay pundits were more liberal than their orthodox Puneri counterparts. They taught Sanskrit and even repeated the Vedas in the homes of Prabhus and Sonars, as well as those of Europeans. Nevertheless, pundits such as Gangadhar Dikshit-Phadke, Narayan Shastri Abhyankar and Gopal Shastri Gokhale were outcast by their communities because they taught Sanskrit (at Poona College) to youth of all castes: Sonars, Shimpis, Prabhus, Parsis and Shudras. By contrast, Dhakji Dadaji Prabhu, a member of the Bombay Native Education Society (established in 1827) and a leader of the orthodox section of the Society, determinedly opposed Shudras' (Maratha, Koli, Bhandari) entry to schools. An order excluding Shudras was passed and these students of the Bombay Native Education Society were forced to leave the school.

In such a field of forces, the social revolutionary Jotirao Phule's theoretical and institutional critique of knowledge, gender and caste was an important development. By critically examining the failures of the government as well as of upper-caste reformers and the rise of new castes, Phule articulated his radical project for more inclusive education (Phule 1991b, 118). Low-caste reformers, including Phule, appreciated the government's limited efforts, as well as those of missionaries, but also indicted the colonial state for its imperial and racist policies of openly favouring the Brahmans.

In a speech to the Hunter Education Commission on 19 October 1882, Phule questioned the government's efforts for low castes and pleaded for compulsory primary education. He also requested that the Education Commission take measures to expand female primary education on a more liberal scale (Phule 1882). Like Ambedkar many decades later, he wanted the government to focus on the education of the *ryot* (*rayat*, peasants), who, he pointed out, contributed towards the state exchequer in proportion to their large numbers. Both of them wanted *kaayade*, laws to make education *saktiche aani mophat* (compulsory and free).

Both Phule and Ambedkar advocated higher education for Dalits. Phule argued: 'higher education [should] be arranged so as to be within easy reach of all, and the books of the subjects for Matriculation should be published in the Government Gazette' (Phule 1991b, 125). Augmenting his efforts, Ambedkar declared that there was no hope without higher education for the Dalits. This position was opposed by some Brahmans, like M.M. Kunte, sometime acting principal of Elphinstone College in Bombay. Kunte told the Hunter Commission he agreed that

> the question of the admission of children of Mahars and Dhers into Government schools is not raised by the Mahars and Dhers themselves. It is not

real, and has no practical bearing. It is a groundless agitation caused by sentimental English officials and unpractical native reformers.

(Keer 1964, 56; Bhagat 1935, 143)

Likewise, V.N. Mandlik, an eminent jurist and a member of the Bombay Legislative Council (1874–84), argued for 'gradual transformation from within'. He added that the legislature must be 'supremely cautious and avoid all interference with the social and religious fabric of the Hindus' (Mandlik 1865). Mandlik also emphasised that the Untouchables were not ready for education. Even Gandhi in the early twentieth century (as Chapter 2 will explore) emphasised the futility of writing, algebra and geometry, and higher education for millions, including himself (Gandhi 1986, 252–253).

The feminist historian Shefali Chandra points out that 'prominent Marathi nationalists deliberately opposed any possibility of social change for members of other communities and famously agitated against the reservation of free scholarships in the Deccan and Fergusson Colleges for Muslims and "backward" Hindu castes' (Chandra 2012, 15). This earlier opposition to mass education was forcefully articulated by the renowned Brahman revivalist B.G. Tilak. This radical Hindu nationalist suddenly adopted a conservative stance as a modest moderate with respect to Dalits and untouchability. By underscoring that Shudras should stick to their crafts and leave politics to Brahmans, Tilak emphasised separate learning and openly revealed his Brahmanism. He opposed the extension of education to Kunbi (peasant) children:

No reading, writing, and rudiments of history, geography, and mathematics [to Kunbis] as they have no earthly use in practical life. You take away a farmer's boy from the plough, the blacksmith's boy from the bellows ... with the object of giving him liberal education ... and the boy learns to condemn the profession of his father, not to speak of the loss.... Having done this the boy looks up to the government for employment; you remove from him a sphere where he would have been contented, happy and useful to those who depend upon him and teach him to be discontented with his lot and with the government.

(Tilak 1881, quoted in Rao 2010, 140)

Unlike Phule and Gokhale, Tilak opposed compulsory mass education and criticised the government's efforts to introduce education into the villages because it encouraged peasants to revolt. For him, 'education to Kunbi children [was] a sheer waste of money' (Rao 2010, 140). He also emphasised that 'the curriculum taught to other [upper-caste] children was unsuitable for Kunbi children and the latter [should] be taught only those subjects which would be necessary for their living' (ibid., 139).

Tilak's friend Vishnushastri Chiplunkar 'simultaneously quashed the anti-caste critique of Phule when the latter drew attention to the rise of Brahmanic control over language and power' (Chandra 2010, 15). When some reformers contended that municipal schools supported by public funds should be open to all – that only taxpayers had the right to decide how their money should be spent – Tilak questioned their efforts. He suggested that if the reformers insisted on mass education then 'the lower castes should be provided the kind of [special] education benefitting their rank and station in life' (Tilak 1881, quoted in Rao 2010, 140). He believed that disseminating education among them was a grave error.

Thus Brahmans firmly controlled education and administrative jobs.[4] In the year 1884, out of 109 students in the Deccan College of Poona, 107 were Brahmans, even though they constituted only 4 per cent of the region's population. The same year, in Bombay, Brahmans comprised more than 50 per cent of the students. They wanted to reinforce their power and protect their Brahmani supremacy. They would not tolerate any cracks in its walls, and opposed the Bahujans' entry even into primary schools.

By making systematic efforts to restrict low-caste members from accessing facilities they had enjoyed, many Brahmans reinforced social and educational inequalities and consolidated their caste and class positions. They drew boundaries around the low castes and made continuous efforts to prevent and prohibit Shudras and Dalits from seeking education. These efforts and structures of caste feeling were amplified by the colonial state's technologies. By making arguments about cultural competencies and affective sensibilities, and commenting negatively on Dalit intelligence and understanding, upper-caste Hindus and the colonial state helped the historical construction of caste.

Along with city dwellers, many rural communities in some parts of the Central Provinces and Bombay 'objected to the instruction of low-castes on the ground that education would advance [them] in life and induce them to seek emancipation from their present servile condition' (Ambedkar 1928, 18). Villagers actually boycotted schools when Dalit children were admitted. Upper castes threatened the property and personal safety of Dalit families and intimidated students. A Madras witness mentioned that Nayars and Tiyas used to waylay Dalit boys on their way to school and snatch their books. Similarly, when a low-caste pupil was admitted to school in Kaira district, five or six large schools were closed down for years. The huts and crops of low castes were burnt down in one village, and a heavy punitive measure was imposed upon the village for two years.

Paradoxically, the theoretical right to education for all also came with the practice of segregated education, which intensified stigma and humiliation for Dalit students even as they entered the schools and other anonymous spaces in the city, such as public halls, tramcars and restaurants. Dalits entered new public spaces like schools even as their access remained mediated through paradoxical structures of segregation. When they entered schools they also felt that their self-respect and human dignity were violated. Their experiences thus contribute to a critique of the anonymity and imagined way of living in a city.

The contests between the upper and lower castes in the educational arena were not confined to school admissions, but also included the advancement and opportunities that formal education brought about – for example, in the higher administrative services, army, police and postal services. Such economic opportunities, like social life, were stratified in terms of caste. For instance, Dalits could not be clerks, although Indian Christian, Anglo-Indian and caste-Hindu non-matriculates were regularly employed in that capacity. Likewise, Dalit railway workers remained gang men and were rarely employed as porters, because porters often worked as domestic servants; in railway workshops they were not admitted as mechanics.

Even when they were able to attend school, Dalit students were subjected to many challenges. They experienced humiliating and discriminatory treatment from both teachers and pupils of higher castes. In the government schools Dalit students were socially excluded. Many Dalits who were allowed to enter schools and fulfil the colonial mission of equal educational access were often forced to maintain a distinct distance from their classmates and classrooms. In one district, the Dalits provided a list of fifty-seven primary schools in which their children had to sit on verandahs or outside. In Nasik district,

> a Depressed Caste boy was made to sit on a platform (as used by cultivators when watching their crops) exposed to the sun and rain outside the school which was held in an upper room, whilst the teacher occasionally leaned out of the window to give instruction to him. On rainy days he had to go home.
>
> (Starte Committee 1930, 14)

Significantly, many schools were held in temples, which did not normally admit Dalit children. In some cases they were admitted but were made to sit outside or separately from the other children (Table 1.2).

In Sinnar, all Untouchable students sat outside school. Thus they faced severe disabilities when accessing formal education. They were not allowed to sit, had to sit separately, or at the door of the classroom, or even outside the school seeking distant education, so many did not attend school. Sulochana Kadam recounted her experience at the Deccan Education Society's College in Pune in the 1930s:

> I was the only Dalit girl in the college and I felt proud and intimidated at the same time. I had to sit separately during the *jevanaachi pangat* [communal meals]. I felt very insulted, but that was the practice. I had to accept it; otherwise I would not have been able to continue at the college.
>
> (Kadam 2001)

Sulochanatai was thus humiliated every day; but she did not resist for fear of dropping out of the system. She later successfully completed her Bachelor's degree and became a first-class officer with the state.

Statistically speaking, even in the year 1881 there were only seventeen (or 0.14 per cent) low-caste students in the middle schools of Bombay Presidency and none in the high schools or colleges (Ambedkar 1928, 416). By contrast,

Table 1.2 Problems of Untouchable students in relation to education in primary schools in Nasik district

Village	Type of school building	Seating for Untouchable students
Malegao 1 area		
Umarane	Rented	Outside the building
Chinch Gavhan	Rented	Outside the building
Yevale 2 area		
Mukhed	Rented	At a distance in class
Paaradgao	Local school board	At a distance in class
Sirasgao	Government *chaavdi* (village meeting place)	At a distance in class
Adgaosol	Rented	At a distance in class
Balapur	*Dharmashaalaa* provided by villagers	At a distance in class
Deshmane	Maruti temple	Not allowed to sit
Kaatarni	Government *chaavdi*	At a distance in class
Kasur	Government and villagers' *chaavdi*	At a distance in class
Nimgao	*Chaavdi*	Outside porch
Pimpalgaojalal	Village *chaavdi*	Inside porch
Pimpri	Gosaavi *matha* (hermitage)	Far off to one side
Rajapur	Ram temple	Far off to one side
Somthane	Donated by villagers	Far off to one side
Erandgao	Part of *matha*, provided by villagers	Separate but inside
Nashik 3 area		
Aadgao	Private building	At a distance
Devargao	Temple	A porch beside the temple
Samangao	Private building	A porch in front of the temple
Dugao	Private building	Porch
Niphad 4 area		
Ahirgao	Half of a temple	Not allowed to sit
Datyane	Temple	Not allowed in temple
Lonwadi	*Chaavdi*	At a distance
Nandurdi	Temple	Not allowed to sit
Pachore	Temple	No facility for Untouchable students
Palkhed	*Chaavdi*	Not allowed to sit
Shirasgao	Maruti temple	Porch
Raulas	Villagers' building	Designated areas
Shirvade	Private building	Not allowed to sit
Vanasgao	Maruti temple	No facility for Untouchable students
Vavi thushi	Villagers' building	Porch
Katargao	Maruti temple	Porch
Kherwadi	Private temple	Outside the school
Jalgao	Private temple	Outside the school

Source: *Bahishkrut Bharat* (31 May 1929).

middle schools included 30.70 per cent Brahmans. High school populations were 40.29 per cent Brahman and about 40 per cent other castes and cultivators. The Brahmans were losing ground to the non-Brahmans. By 1889, out of 507,752 students, only 95,919 were Brahmans, while 299,716 were other Hindus and 10,630 were low castes (*Mahrataa*, 16 March 1890, quoted in Rao 2010, 152). The *Mahrataa* perhaps inflated the numbers for low castes in order to instigate a potent rhetoric of 'Brahmans in danger'. Yet, certainly, the Brahmans were threatened by low-caste entry to education and made every effort to scuttle it.

By 1885, clashes were sharper between non-Brahmans and Brahmans. When the government of Bombay decided that half of the full scholarships would be reserved for the BC, the Brahmans opposed the policy fiercely. The Pune Sarvajanik Sabha protested against this resolution, which they argued amounted to state discrimination against the Brahmans. By contrast, the Din Bandhu (Brothers of the Vulnerable) felt that it was only fair that non-Brahmans should have access to an education.[5]

Nevertheless, when the Court of Directors passed an order opening up government schools to all castes, 'the opposition of the higher castes to the admission of [Dalit] boys to a public school was often so strong that, even with the best will in the world, the Department could do very little in the matter' (quoted in Nurullah and Naik 1951, 422). Many caste Hindus shared the government's lack of concern for the low castes. 'They feared pollution from Dalits and discouraged one another from attending mixed public schools because this would force them to associate with Dalits' (Ambedkar 1928, 11). Dalits were left 'in the cold because the touchable classes would not let them sit at the fire of knowledge which the Government had lit up in the interest of all its subjects' (ibid., 12).

Considering the multiple and overlapping challenges of Dalits, some Dalit and non-Dalit reformers as well as the colonial state offered separate schools as one kind of solution. In the last quarter of the nineteenth century the Gaikwad of Baroda opened eighteen special schools for Dalits in his own state (Nurullah and Naik 1951, 589). In 1882, there were sixteen special schools for Dalits in Bombay Province with 564 pupils. Only 2,862 low-caste pupils (0.87 per cent) were attending primary schools and none were in high schools or colleges (Ambedkar 1928, 9). The numbers increased somewhat towards the end of the century as an overwhelming majority of Dalits and some non-Brahmans fought for Dalit education (Nurullah and Naik 1951, 423).

In contrast to Madras, the number of separate schools in Maharashtra was never large. Both the Hartog Commission of 1923 and the Starte Committee of 1930 strongly recommended mixed schools, arguing that separate schools were inefficient and that the system of segregation emphasised rather than reduced differences between Dalits and other Hindus. It also intensified Dalit exclusion. This became especially difficult if a clever student wanted to enter the normal school or the high school. This proposal was also debated on financial grounds: 'special' or separate schools would mean additional expense, and in 'in rural parts the Backward Classes [could] seldom be found to be living in one locality in large numbers' (Ambedkar 1928, 16). The higher castes were not willing to pay additional taxes for this purpose. These realities severely hampered Dalit education.

Phule (and later Ambedkar) made compelling appeals to the government for justice, and argued for the colonial state's control of and expenditure on education because they believed that 'education of the masses was a significant duty of the government' (*Bahishkrut Bharat*, 15 July 1927). From the mid-nineteenth century, Phule questioned the government's favouritism towards the high castes and lack of concern for lower castes, as well as its utopian idea that education would filter downward from the higher to the lower classes. Phule argued that primary education was utterly neglected in the Bombay Presidency and should be made compulsory until the age of twelve. He also emphasised that education should be controlled by the Director of Public Instruction rather than by the local school boards, which 'consisted of ignorant and uneducated men, such as Patils, Inamdars, Sardars, and others, who [were] not capable of exercising any intelligent control over the funds' (quoted in Keer 1964, 173).

By contrast, nationalists like Tilak contended that by supporting and spreading education to the Dalits, the government was in fact interfering with Indians' religious beliefs. He also attacked the missionaries for their efforts towards Dalit uplift and demanded that

> the local municipalities should have the complete power to recruit teachers. The local bodies are the best agencies for the work. They know the wants of their own locality and they alone can adjust the course of instruction, the number of schools, the subjects to be taught and ultimately the grants to be given to local educational enterprise.
>
> (Tilak 1881)

Deploying a Machiavellian move, Tilak allowed the landed elite, who paid higher taxes, to use their electoral power to restrict Dalits' entry into schools. Some of his friends, like S.H. Chiplunkar and M.B. Namjoshi, dominated the proceedings and controlled the Pune Municipality. Namjoshi also suggested that local board members – the elite – should control teacher recruitment as well as deciding the number of schools, their level (primary, secondary), fees and scholarships. Tilakites established their own procedures for identifying public opinion in ways that excluded the underclasses of Pune and decided the fate of education. These nationalists, who controlled ten out of eleven municipalities in the Marathi-speaking areas of Bombay Presidency, opposed Gokhale's plan for mass education (*Mahrataa*, 25 January 1890, 18 January 1891, quoted in Rao 2010, 153). Many Brahmans supported Tilak because he was struggling to preserve their traditional power through state policies.

Moreover, upper-caste propaganda regarding DCs' aversion to education continued well into the twentieth century. Many Sanatanists were against Untouchables' entry into temples and schools. Chunilal V. Mehta, president of the Municipal Corporation of Bombay, wrote to the Secretary of State:

There are fifteen municipal schools but the percentage of DC population attending these is very small. The school committee intends to open more schools for these classes. But there are difficulties: These communities evince *no* desire for education rather they are averse to it. They are scattered and it is difficult to find central places suitable to a considerable number. Landlords are not willing to let rooms for the schools of classes regarded as untouchable. Another is the want of trained Untouchable teachers.... As regards moral condition of these people socially stigmatized and despised the corporation do not propose to deal with severe social and religious questions involved in the consideration of the subject.

(Mehta 1916, emphasis added)

Thus Mehta suggested the severe problems involved in DC education in Bombay.

Nevertheless, from the end of the nineteenth century, Dalits made a united demand that their children be admitted to government school classrooms like caste Hindus (e.g. Valangkar 1894). Phule, Valangkar and others stressed the wide inequalities the government's emphasis on high-caste education created and fought for education as a crucial part of their battle for equality. However, they also created independent educational institutions. Without totally depending on government and missionaries' efforts, some Dalits and non-Dalits in Bombay, Nagpur, Pune and Ahmednagar established separate schools and hostels. Janoji Khandare, G.A. Gawai and Janu Kachrya, among others, started boarding-houses in the Vidarbha region (Kshirsagar 1994, 245). Some twenty-eight adults also attended a night school in Akola for about a year (Kshirsagar 1994, 121). Shivram Janaba Kamble (1875–1940) from Pune, known also for founding a Marathi newspaper and leading the *murali* abolition campaign and the Parvati *satyagraha*, was active in the *aana* (pice) fund night school run by literate Mahars. He also started the Chokhamela Vidyavardhak Mandal, a night school for adults, in 1900, as well as a Backward Class Hostel for boys in 1921 and one for girls in 1956 (Zelliot n.d. 4; Kshirsagar 1994, 237–241). Kisan Phaguji Bansode (1879–1946) founded a press and printed various newspapers, brochures and books related to the reform of untouchability. He founded the Sri Satchidananda Vachan Griha library in Mopla, the town of his birth, and received thirty trunks of books from upper-caste Hindus interested in his efforts. Significantly, Tilak is also rumoured to have solicited books for the library. Bansode founded the Chokhamela Girls' School in 1907 and also opened a number of hostels with the help of Jaibai Chaudhari (Zelliot n.d., 5). Chaudhari (1890–1964), a remarkable woman who worked as a coolie, carrying things from Nagpur to Kamptee, a distance of ten miles, went on to establish her own Chokhamela Kanyashaala in (Nayabasti) New Colony, Nagpur, in 1924 (Meshram 1945). She went from house to house to collect contributions. By 1945, about 125 girls were studying in Jaibai's school, out of which three-quarters were from Depressed Classes.

Besides Mahars, some Chambhars and Matangs also contributed to education efforts. Lahujibuwa Salve (1811–81) encouraged Dalit children to attend school and also opened a *talimkhana* (gymnasium and wrestling centre) in Pune, where it is said that not only Phule but Tilak and the revolutionary Vasudeo Balwant Phadke were trained in martial arts (Zelliot n.d., 11; Kshirsagar 1994, 322–323). P.N. Rajbhoj, who was injured in the Parvati Satyagraha in Pune in 1928, founded the Mahatma Phule Hostel and the Kamla Nehru Hostel, both in Pune. R.G. Khandale, founder of the All India Matang Seva Sangh in 1932, also opened a hostel in Daund in 1959.

The Chokhamela hostel, established in 1925 by Bansode and Nanasaheb Gavai, among others, provided free boarding, free education and food, which were difficult for Untouchable students to obtain. R.R. Paranjpye, the first minister of education, opened a Depressed Classes hostel in Poona in 1922. It was the first institution established by the government in Bombay Presidency. There were fifty DC students in the hostel and not only their lodging and board but also their fees were paid. In 1923, a year after the establishment of the hostel in Poona, the Primary Education Act of 1923 provided for 100 scholarships for BCs in upper primary schools (Zelliot n.d., 120, 1994, 121). As a result of these efforts, by 1931 the number of Dalit literates had risen to 2.9 per cent (about 1.7 million in the Bombay Presidency) – a sharp increase from 1911, when only 0.48 per cent of the Dalit population (which totalled 2,145,208) was literate (Census of India 1931; Sawant 1989). However, by 1920 the number of Dalits attending schools had decreased – and the cause was entirely economic.

Dalits' battle for compulsory and free education from 1920 onwards

Dalit radicals fought their double jeopardy of double decolonisation – internal and external – against the Brahman hierarchy and the colonial state. Benefiting from and building on earlier efforts, Ambedkar forcefully articulated Dalit demands, especially after the 1920s. During this period wider social awareness, migration to cities, economic improvement and occupational mobility allowed Dalits to challenge their caste exploitation both in structural and ideological terms. Modern Dalits made continuous efforts to challenge the caste structure rather than merely attempting to rise within it or even imitate the upper castes, for example, by donning the sacred thread.

Debates around education grew thornier and clashes between the upper and lower castes intensified during the early decades of the twentieth century, when the colonial state and reformers dealt with the Dalit question. This was especially true during the 1920s. Widening political participation allowed several caste associations and other organisations to press the colonial government and Indian political parties to recognise their demands. The Congress, Muslim League, Depressed Classes, and other religious and caste communities were engaging in constitutional politics and the communal arithmetic that accompanied it, and in many cases seeking separate representation. In Pune, the older Brahman political leadership, extremist and liberal alike, seemed to falter. The

Brahman liberals left the mainstream nationalist movement and remained alienated from social and political upheavals.

On the other hand, Gandhi strategically developed Congress as a 'mass'
organisation. Deploying some theatrical tactics in his unsaintly capacity, Gandhi
very deftly captured Congress in 1920 and established the removal of untouchability as part of its creed. He went on to further enshrine this principle in the
party's Constructive Programme (Zelliot 1988, 182–188). At the same time, his
attitude towards the Dalits remained patronising, conservative and cautious. To
Gandhi, caste was an 'ineffaceable blot', but he preferred to create a consensus
between Hindus and Dalits rather than openly antagonising Hindu orthodoxy. He
made efforts to 'uplift' Dalits and make them worthy members of Hindu civilisation through education and sanitation.

By contrast, Gandhi's contemporary Ambedkar was a firm believer in the state
and constitutional politics and could not be easily dissuaded from his faith in communal representation and separate electorates. He challenged Gandhian gradual
reform and presented the case for a separate electorate for Dalits (along similar
lines to that granted to Muslims in 1909) to the Southborough Committee in 1919.
The year 1920 was most significant for Dalits because Ambedkar forcefully articulated the earlier demands of Dalit radicals, and education emerged as a significant
element in the repertoire of civic rights as well as egalitarian citizenship. That year,

Figure 1.1 Ambedkar and his associates in early twentieth-century Bombay Presidency
(courtesy of Vasant Moon Collection).

the Dalit educational agenda transformed from a plea to a demand: '*mulanna aani mulinna mophat aani saktichech praathamik shikshan shakya titkya lavkar* [free and compulsory primary education for all girls and boys as soon as possible]' (*Mooknayak*, 5 June 1920). The Dalits' struggle for secular, compulsory education went hand in hand with their migration from villages and the economic changes unleashed by colonial modernity (growing urbanism and factories). Ambedkar was thus not creating a new movement but building on long-standing grievances and a local, if slightly less effective, agitational tradition. Ambedkar's bilingualism was also highly significant: his recourse to the language of public politics, as well as to the public discourse and principles by which Dalits gave meaning to their own lives, provided him with greater assertiveness as well as an effective means of gaining the support of the Dalit population.

More than 10,000 women and men attended the Akhil Bhartiya Bahishkrut Parishad (All India Conference of the Excluded), held in Nagpur from 30 May to 1 June 1920. The conference passed significant resolutions on education, the consumption of alcohol and carrion, political representation according to population, and election of representatives to legislative councils, district boards and municipalities. Most importantly in terms of education, Dalits made the following demands:

1   To make primary education *saktichech* [compulsory][6] and free for boys and girls *shakya titkya lavkar* [as soon as possible].
2   Appointment of a non-Brahman Education Minister in the Council.
3   More Dalit male entrants in training colleges.
4   To do away with the age limit for Dalits to enter schools and to increase it by three years in government jobs.
5   A matric-fail Dalit representative should be held eligible to get a job.
6   No fees for Dalits in secondary and higher education.

(*Mooknayak*, 5 June 1920)

While passing the resolutions, S.N. Shivtarkar, Ambedkar's Chambhar lieutenant of fifteen years, said: 'Brahmans owned the key of education and hence [Dalits] need[ed] compulsory education for progress. Primary education should be *free and compulsory for boys and girls*' (*Mooknayak*, 5 June 1920, emphasis added). Shivtarkar pointed out that compulsory education had been legislated in Bombay Province in 1917; yet, after three years, only two or three municipalities had made recommendations to the government. Even in Pune, referred to as *vidyeche maaherghar* (home for knowledge), Puneri Brahmans rejected municipal compulsory education laws because they had already benefited from education and wanted to enjoy their claim over it, protect their supremacy, and prevent lower castes from seeking education and potentially rising against them. Compulsory education was instituted in the city of Pune only in 1943, thirty years after it was proposed (Zelliot 2000, 221).

Most significantly, although Dalits represented more an amalgam of *jatis* than a coherent social community, the political vocabulary in which their collusion or mutuality was expressed was produced in a crucible conjunction of particular historical, social, intellectual, educational and political factors. Strong alliances were formed as well as fractured at particular historical conjunctures, rendering the *Bahishkrut samaaj* (excluded community) perpetually tenuous. Like Ambedkar, Shivtarkar also emphasised the need for education and political power alike; he departed from Ambedkar, however, on the issue of religious conversion to Buddhism.[7] Chambhars and Mangs also questioned Ambedkar's representation of the Dalit community as a whole.

Yet heterogeneous Dalit communities with conflicting interests came together to form fragile alliances in the particular educational conjuncture of the 1920s. Dalit radicals' political programmes provided diverse Dalit communities with the means to comprehend their social and political subordination and at the same time suggest practical remedies to transform their situation, as revealed below by the *paani-loti* question.

The *paani-loti* (water-pot) controversy and the breaking of the *ekloti* (one-pot) order

During the 1920s, pressure from both Dalits themselves and Christian missionaries prompted the colonial state to renew its campaign for 'education for all'. The Director of Instruction ordered on 23 February 1923 that 'no disabilities were [to be] imposed on Depressed Class children in any school conducted by public authority in its own or hired building' (Starte Committee 1930, 13). If publicly funded schools did not allow Untouchable students, their funding would be cut off. The Forasroad Municipal School in Bombay responded that 'there is no distinction on basis of caste here'. However, according to a discussion among the Bombay government's Municipal School Committee on 18 October 1927, the practice of *lotibandi*, or stopping *Asprushya* (Untouchables) drinking in the *lotis* (small drinking pots) meant for *sprushya* (touchables), was widely prevalent (*Times of India*, 4 November 1927; *Bombay Chronicle*, 20 October 1927).[8] If the *sprushya* used brass *lotis*, it was tin *lotis* for *Asprushya*. The School Committee feared that any change would be resented by caste Hindus, and rightly so – Hindus closed the Bombay Stock Exchange 'as a protest' against common drinking pots in schools (*Bombay Chronicle*, 18 October 1928). Despite the order, nineteen schools in the Bombay region openly flouted the government's determination and refused to enrol Dalit students.

Nevertheless, after waiting for six long years, Dalit students from Forasroad School challenged the contradiction between their theoretical rights as legislated by the colonial state and the everyday discrimination they faced. They believed their patience was being tested and decided to implement the government's resolution at once. On 27 July 1929 some Dalit students drank water in *lotis* meant for the *sprushya* (touchables) in order to provoke Shri Khatkul, the headmaster, into implementing the 1923 legislation. He ignored them; nothing happened. After two days, on 29 July, the school peon refused to admit the Dalit students who had drunk from the touchables' *lotis*. This provoked another ten or twenty students, who proceeded to do the same. This led to a *gadbad* (disturbance) in the school. At once, the headmaster called the *Asprushya* students and questioned them:

HEADMASTER: What will you achieve if you drink water like this?

DALITS: Until today we have been insulted and this act will undo that.

HEADMASTER: If you start drinking water like this, the touchables will leave school. What about that?

DALITS: If touchable students want to follow caste discrimination they should not attend municipal schools at all. They should go to other schools. But, if they do so, *we will follow them there too.*

HEADMASTER: Why are you doing this unnecessarily? I will provide you and them with *chaangali svatantra* [good and separate] water-drinking facilities.

DALITS: Well, what is wrong with this one? You are actually strengthening social distinctions.

One upper-caste teacher, outraged by this exchange, menacingly challenged *Asprushya* students: 'Do whatever you want!' (*Bahishkrut Bharat*, 16 August 1929). Their patience tested, activists asked all *Asprushya* students to leave the school at once.

About 300 students, from kindergarten to grade seven, stood outside the school and shouted slogans: '*Shivaji Maharaj ki jai* (Hail King Shivaji, the protector of the masses)', *Sarasvati Mata ki jai* (Hail the goddess of knowledge)' and '*Ambedkar Maharaj ki jai* (Hail King Ambedkar)' for about half an hour. At this critical juncture some Dalit leaders arrived at the scene and opened negotiations with the authorities. The students demanded equal access to drinking water and that those teachers who followed caste distinctions or insulted Dalit students on the grounds of caste *tyanchaa bandobast karaavaa* should be brought in line. After some deliberation, the headmaster agreed. Far from being 'docile' or 'blind', Dalits spoke loudly and articulately. They were often disciplined, had clear objectives, knew how to negotiate with authority, and above all brought their strength swiftly to bear. In many ways their rejection of 'separate but equal' water facilities parallels the anti-segregation movement of African Americans against the Jim Crow system in the United States.

In the year 1930, the Starte Education Commission of 1930 applauded the government's efforts and rejoiced to find 'an important advance in the position of the Depressed Classes in Primary Schools in recent years and particularly after 1922.... Especially for 1927 [they found] that there [was] a rise of 57 per cent' (Starte Committee 1930, 13). The Commission also asserted that the advance was largely due to 'the policy of Government requiring the admission of the children of the Depressed Classes in the common schools conducted by public authority without distinction of caste or creed' (Starte Committee 1930, 13). Yet, in the very next sentence, the Commission pointed out that 'this policy of admission to Common Schools [had] unfortunately not been applied in all places': there was some discord between the colonial state's official story of triumph and the advancement of Dalit education in Maharashtra. The government kept detailed statistics on education, but deeper analysis suggests that numbers hide as much as they reveal.

The Maratha social reformer V.R. Shinde emphasised most Maharashtrian teachers' lack of empathy for students and revealed differences between Mumbai and Bengal:

> Madras and Bengal provinces fared very well in terms of women's and Shudra education in contrast with the Mumbai province. [Because] unlike Mahars, Mangs, or Marathas of Maharashtra, Namashudras of Bengal started their own schools and ran them well too. This was most importantly due to the self-dependence and courage of Namashudras to start and maintain schools, support from the Brahmosamaj, and development of good teacher-student relationships. Teachers [in Maharashtra] in fact scared Dalit pupils on their very first day of school and encouraged them to drop out of it.[9]
>
> Teachers discouraged Dalit students; some Dalits parents, well aware that their everyday living depended on upper-caste whims, withdrew their children from schools.
>
> (*Bahishkrut Bharat*, 15 March 1929)

Nevertheless, M.G. Bhagat's sociological study of Bombay in the early 1930s suggests that Dalits

> had become alive to the advent of education and in some places they were taking full advantage of the special schools established for them. The whole community was very poor, but some were willing to pay fees and thus they were trying to put forward their rights to getting admission to schools.
>
> (Bhagat 1935, 143)

Many Dalits began sending their children to primary schools. In 1917 there were 30,212 Dalit children attending school; by 1922 this number had increased to 37,892, and to 59,693 in 1927 (Starte Commission 1930, 13). We need to note, however, that this was out of a population of 1.6 million in 1917 and 1.46 million in 1928. According to M.G. Bhagat, the increase in Dalit literacy noted above may be attributed to an increase in the number of Dalit primary teachers, most significantly during the first two decades of the twentieth century. Yet Bhagat does not provide us with any reliable statistics on teachers. Dalits struggled to attain the minimum requirements for teacher training – and if Dalit teachers were to be hired in common schools, their appointment presented some problems. For example, following the incident at Forasroad Municipal School mentioned above, Ganpat Mahadeo Sawant, the headmaster of Agripada School, openly challenging Dalits as well as the desegregation order, stated:

> since the *sprushya* teachers teach *Asprushya* students, in whatever way the *sprushya* teachers behave, even if they insult them to a large extent, *Asprushya var maan karta kaama naye* [Untouchables should not raise their

necks/heads to retaliate]. In our Konkan we do not allow your shadow to fall on us, how do you then think that we will allow you to drink water with us, *ekatra* [jointly]?

(Bahishkrut Bharat, 27 September 1929)

When a Dalit teacher, T.B. Kharat, was appointed to Sawant's school on 1 August 1929, Sawant warned him: '*Lakshaat thevaa* [keep in mind] – if you try to meddle with the *sovaleshaahi* [purity-pollution hegemonic structure] in my school, *khabardaar* [beware]!' Sawant was a brutal bully to two or three other Dalit teachers as well. He walked into their classrooms and humiliated them in front of the students, calling them *Mhaardey* and *Chambhaardey* [derogatory terms for Mahars and Chambhars] (*Bahishkrut Bharat*, 27 September 1929). The school also supported discrimination by distributing classes according to caste: *sprushya* students had *sprushya* teachers and *Asprushya* students had *Asprushya* teachers, as in earlier times. In this manner, the school successfully trampled upon the School Committee's orders of *ekloti* and equality in education. Even the touchable and Untouchable teachers drank water separately. During the daily break, while tea was served to all touchable teachers, *Asprushya* had to visit a Muslim hotel for refreshments.

Asprushya teachers and students faced segregation and were given separate *lotis* (pots) for drinking water (*Bombay Chronicle*, 20 October 1927). When a subcommittee of the Schools Committee recommended that all children should be given the same *lotis*, some members objected, fearing resentment from the caste Hindus. While Professor V.G. Rao told the *Bombay Chronicle* that this was a revolutionary change, D.G. Dalvi, a social reformer, mentioned a legal fear that some parents might file a suit against the Committee 'for enforcing an obligation which was by no means a legal one' (*Bombay Chronicle*, 20 October 1927). However, students were not obligated to use the *lotis* provided by the schools: scrupulous high-caste parents could give children their own *lotis*. But for Dalits the insult remained and the question was unresolved.

In Pune, on two occasions, non-Brahmans who proposed to open public water taps and cisterns to all citizens irrespective of caste or creed met with 'tooth-and-nail' opposition from Brahmans who claimed to be nationalists and Tilakites. Moreover, according to the *Times of India*,

> the language used by so-called Nationalist champions of sacerdotal privilege was grossly and even indecently insulting to the non-Brahmans and the indiscreet arrogance of some Brahmans, particularly the reckless champion of *sanaatan* Brahman superiority, the newspaper *Bhaalaa* [or *The Spear*, founded by the outspoken Brahman advocate Bhausaheb Bhopatkar, also known as Bhaalaakaar] added fuel to the fire.

(Times of India, 4 September 1925)

Bhopatkar was of the view that 'it will take twenty-one generations to completely eradicate villages of the curse of untouchability' (*Nirbhid*, 8 December 1935).

Another such event suggests once again how the Hindus attempted to resolve the Dalit question and the problem of *ekloti*. On 17 September 1929, when a Dalit student at Agripada School tried to drink water meant for the touchables, Headmaster Sawant spotted him and said: 'Hey you, don't you understand? Where are you going? Have you abandoned your *dharma*?' Kharat, an *Asprushya* teacher standing close by, questioned Sawant: 'Master, which *dharma* are you talking about? Don't you remember the government's circular order? How long do we keep silent?' (*Bahishkrut Bharat*, 27 September 1929). Subsequently, the headmaster asked the office boy to mix the waters: both touchables and Dalits drank the water together. This seemed like a happy ending to the *paani-loti* controversy.

The matter was more complicated, however. The very next day (18 September 1929), even before school began, two to four *shipai* (policemen) visited the school. Some touchable students, instead of attending school, went on strike; several Untouchable students felt threatened by these actions and returned home. Some Untouchable parents did not send their children to school because they felt intimidated by the touchables' strike. The touchable students had a conference with the headmaster, who convinced them to come back to school and call off the strike, but Kharat was transferred to another school (*Bahishkrut Bharat*, 27 September 1929).

Upper-caste Hindus argued that, as long as Untouchables had access to education and water, what was the harm in keeping these separate for each caste? They proposed their own agenda to resolve the caste and education question while maintaining 'difference'. For example, Panandikar, a Brahman, listed his views on what Untouchables should do to eradicate untouchability:

1   Untouchables should gradually give up their thoughts that they are *antyaja* [the last ones].
2   They should first do away with caste differences among themselves.
3   Without arousing *virodhbhaav* [antagonism], whatever rights they get they should feel obligated and not make a big *gaajaavaajaa* [hullabaloo] about it.
4   They should develop the habits of using clean clothes and keeping clean.
5   They should make use of good education and for this they should have separate schools.

(*Bahishkrut Bharat*, 1 July 1927)

This view held that Untouchables should carry out reforms silently and gradually to avoid renewed antagonism among different castes. Many Untouchables worried that if these Brahmans gained control over municipalities and local boards of education they would have to give up all hope (Ambedkar 1927). They decried Panandikar's reforms as hollow and contradictory. On the one hand, unlike Gandhi, who wanted the upper castes to change their hearts, he passed the burden of caste on to the Untouchables and asked them to leave behind their Untouchable *bhaavna* (emotions and thoughts). On the other hand, he directed them *not* to ask for equal education. Like Gandhi and Ambedkar, though, he emphasised discipline and cleanliness, with an eye towards normalising Dalits and keeping them in line. Perhaps such upper-caste reformers 'were reformers only in name' (*Bahishkrut Bharat*, 1 July 1927).

The Sanatanist Hindu orthodoxy was up in arms over *ekloti* politicies in municipal schools and threatened to institute legal action against the Corporation. Sir Manmohandas, during a public meeting at Madhav Baag, said:

This custom [of separate pots for drinking water] has the sanction of the Hindu religion according to 'Varnashrama Dharma' and a discontinuance of that practice would hurt the religious feelings of Hindus. The Corporation, by passing a resolution that no caste distinction should be made in regard to drinking water pots, has outraged the religious sentiments of the Hindus. It is the cardinal principle of every civic body to respect the religious injunctions of any particular religion.

(*Bombay Chronicle*, 18 October 1928)

Supporters of his 'selfish and dishonest' tendency (in the *Bombay Chronicle*'s words) passed resolutions to protect the Hindu religion, condemned those who voted for the proposition, and congratulated those who voted against it.

Other Hindus, however, condemned such orthodoxy. V.N. Chandavarkar described the Madhav Baag meeting as a 'big humbug and farce'. He argued that 'the people of his [Brahmin] class were really "*asprushya*" and those who were suppressed, oppressed, and depressed were really the "*sprushya*"' (*Bombay Chronicle*, 20 October 1928). He also expressed surprise that Mohanlal Desai, who had voted for discrimination against Untouchables in schools, was still a member of the Nationalist Party, which, like Congress, had pledged to eradicate untouchability. Some local Hindu Mahasabha party members continued to break the solemn pledges they had made to voters as well as the resolutions of the Congress Party, whose creed and policy they had adopted (*Bombay Chronicle*, 23 October 1928).

Despite Phule's continuous pleas, from the end of the nineteenth century, to allow states control over education, with the advent of dyarchy in the 1920s primary education was transferred from the colonial state and provincial governments to local bodies. As a result, state education policy was shaped by Indian ministers: unconcerned upper-caste elites, including many uneducated landlords, were in fact put in charge of modernising Indian education. They failed miserably.

The transfer took place in 1923, a landmark year in Bombay Presidency's educational history. The government claimed that handing over some 'important' departments to Indian ministers would prepare the colonised for self-government – and in the process absolved itself of its duty to educate the masses. Ambedkar declared that the 1920 reforms sent 'the Backward Classes in the Bombay Presidency from purgatory to hell' (Ambedkar 1928, 17). While upper-caste elites enjoyed their triumph and limited independence, the changes heralded the beginning of another tragedy for the Dalits. State policies served to fragment the colonised, bringing caste and communal differences into the educational arena in more pronounced ways. Focusing on this politics, Ambedkar argued, for example, that the Compulsory Primary Education Act (Bombay Act No. IV of 1923) was nothing but a fraud:

> Instead of making education compulsory the act underlined its voluntary nature and fixed no time limit to fulfil the obligation. [Also] unlike earlier where the Provincial Government controlled and managed Primary Education, the Compulsory Primary Education Act was to be managed by District School Boards which had their own executive officers.
>
> (Ambedkar 1928, 17)

Those officers were upper-caste bureaucrats already hostile to Dalit education. Hence Ambedkar declared that 'Local Boards and Municipalities were full of ignorant, Brahmani people who believed in *Varnashramdharma* and controlled these institutions' (Ambedkar 1927). He continued:

> These people are no experts on education and are incapable of serving on educational bodies. They have little idea about the aims and processes of education. In addition, they compete with each other due to differences in their castes and political affiliations.... Even teachers want to protect themselves and their profits and hence are involved in making every effort to seek favours from these members. In turn, the members need votes from the teachers and depend on them. Due to all these *bhaangadis* [internal politics] schools lack the kind of discipline they should actually have. If this is the state of Mumbai Municipality, we cannot simply think about other smaller municipalities and local boards.... Many a time among the Dalits and Muslims there is only one representative. He is absolutely helpless in the company of *vatandars* [landlords] in the local board.
>
> (Ambedkar 1929)

Ambedkar demanded that the provincial government should control education and, as a member of the Bombay Legislative Council, continued to work on democratising the local school board in the 1920s and 1930s. He contended:

> The government is mainly responsible for compulsory primary education and for extending it to the masses. It seems by pushing on the burden of education to local boards and municipalities the government wants to be free of its duties. However, the Local Boards and Municipalities members ... are not interested in the project of compulsory education.... Because [unlike in the Untouchable case], the spread of education in their castes and communities does not require any compulsion. *Tey kashaalaa kurhaad ghaalun ghetil tyanchya saamaajik varchasvaavar* [So why would they want to destroy their own social supremacy by providing education to backward castes]? Hence, the compulsory education law has made no

progress.... *First is mass education. Whatever happens, we should not post-pone the question of education.*

(Ambedkar 1929, emphasis added)

Ambedkar thus emphasised that the provincial government should shoulder the responsibility of education, suggesting that the government should collect tuition fees from those who could afford them and initiate new taxes (Ambedkar 1929). The upper castes opposed this move, since they did not want to pay more taxes.

Certainly not all the state's executives were unconcerned about Dalits; yet, even if some administrative officer was sympathetic, '[he] was bound to carry out the just and lawful order of the school board' (Ambedkar 1929, 71). These officers may have been more sensitive to local orthodox opposition:

> In one case ... the Administrative Officer had ordered the Depressed Classes to be made to sit inside the school, but as a result of local opposition the School Board passed a resolution, the result being that 25 Depressed Class boys were made to sit inside altogether in a separate building in the same compound.
>
> (Starte Committee 1930, 14)

Such practices continued in spite of the government's order to admit DC children to schools. Although the law implied that the children would be treated equally, this was not the case. In another instance in 1923 in Vinchur in the Nasik district, two Mahar boys were admitted to the sixth grade and allowed to sit alongside caste Hindus. The caste-Hindu parents opposed the move and withdrew their children from school, decreasing the student population from 240 to 65 (Sawant 1989, 54). Under these circumstances the Education Inspector had two alternatives: to close the school or to yield to the orthodoxy. The problem was resolved when the school authorities rented a separate building in which low-caste children could study.

Two Dalit activists – Rambhaji R. Bagare and Shankar D. Dhende – reported on the workings of the Pune School Board in February 1928, when it passed a resolution to open a free boarding-school for grades five to seven. When the decision reached the District Board, some officials refused to agree unless the government provided the funding. The government denied this request and the proposal ultimately failed. The District Board then issued its own, mocking agenda which declared that 'Untouchable supervisors should be appointed to check Untouchables' schools, and the government should fund this initiative'. Of course, the government refused this proposal too. Bagare and Dhende reported that 'both the above projects were of benefit to Untouchables. However, it would have been helpful if the upper-castes and the government had not exemplified their hollow/outward sympathies and just acted wisely to bring about some progressive and positive changes' (*Bahishkrut Bharat*, 1 February 1929).

The unfathomable gulf between the theory of education espoused in the law and its actual practice were a matter of grave concern for Dalit radicals in the

Bombay Presidency. For example, in 1921 to 1922 in India, there were about 20,522 Brahmans and 29,008 non-Brahmans in secondary schools and about 2,141 Brahmans and 1,558 non-Brahmans in English arts colleges for boys (*Bahishkrut Bharat*, 1 February 1929; Sawant 1989; Director of Public Instruction 1916–17). As Tables 1.3 and 1.4 reveal, in Bombay Presidency in 1923, Brahmans were a minority, only the fourth-largest demographic group in the population, yet they dominated all levels of education (Ambedkar 1927).

Although Dalits were the second-largest population group, they came last in primary, secondary and college education (Ambedkar 1927, 1982a, 421, 1982b, 42–43). By contrast, just 3 per cent of Brahmans held 80 per cent of jobs in the new administrative, educational, judicial and revenue institutions of the Raj. The statistics reveal the range of disparity in different communities' educational advancement. The disparity in educational progress between the Brahmans and non-Brahmans – which was particularly pronounced in Maharashtra – was partly responsible for the rise of the anti-Brahman movement. By the 1920s many non-Brahmans were developing a taste for Western ideas, knowledge and language, with their associated prestige and liberating potential. But the state of Dalits' education was deplorable. Compared to them, Muslims had made enormous strides and were closer to the Brahmans and allied castes in terms of education and employment.

Free compulsory education was introduced in the Pune wards of Nanapeth, Bhavanipeth, Ganjpeth, Gultekdi and Ghorpadepeth on 2 December 1929. It was applied to other parts of the city on 1 April 1943 (Sovani *et al.* 1956, 31), three

Table 1.3 Caste make-up of students in Bombay, 1923

Castes	Primary education, (students per 1,000 total population)	Secondary education (students per 100,000 total population)	Collegiate education (students per 200,000 total population)
Brahman	119	3,000	1,000
Muslim	92	500	52
Maratha	38	140	14
Untouchables	18	14	0

Source: Ambedkar (1928, 421).

Table 1.4 Prominence of castes in schools by level of education in Bombay, 1923

Castes of population in the Presidency	Order in respect of population	Primary education	Secondary education	Collegiate education
Advanced Hindus	4th	1st	1st	1st
Intermediate Hindus	1st	3rd	3rd	3rd
Backward Hindus	2nd	4th	4th	4th
Muslims	3rd	2nd	2nd	2nd

Source: Ambedkar (1928, 420).

decades after Gokhale introduced his bill in 1910, and went into effect city wide only after independence, in 1950. The scheme was not completely success-ful – more than half of the female population remained illiterate – and progress was fairly slow even in areas where compulsory schooling had been in place since 1929.

In sum, the transfer of power to school boards was brutal for Dalits. To contest its effect, Ambedkar's group, Bahishkrut Hitkarini Sabha, insisted that Dalits should enter public service and stand for election to self-governing bodies, from the Education Council to the local school boards. They also demanded that the transfer of primary education to school boards be stopped at once. Further-more, in order to ensure Dalits' ability to exercise the right to education they fought a *double battle* – both external and internal. Externally, they demanded special provisions like hostels, scholarships for higher education and reserva-tions. Internally, Ambedkar pushed Dalits to work on their most intimate sphere: self-consciousness and personhood (Ambedkar 1928, 19).

High castes generally prevented Dalits from entering public schools, access-ing public services, taking water from public watering places, and using roads and conveyances maintained out of public funds. This was not simply a social problem; untouchability was of the highest political importance, going directly to the fundamental question of Dalits' civic rights. In addition, the Starte Com-mission, as well as some high-caste liberals, did acknowledge these problems. Along with these agents, it was mainly the Dalit radicals who made widespread efforts to challenge in ideological and practical terms their exclusion from gov-ernment schools. Ambedkar, like Phule, argued that education was crucial for the *vanchit* (the oppressed and tricked ones) and for the progress of the nation.

As a member of the Bombay Legislative Council in the 1920s and 1930s, Ambedkar brilliantly examined the educational policies of the government as well as critiquing upper-caste education reforms. He diagnosed

> that the law of compulsory education was to be effectively implemented and executed, that too in *eksutripanaa* [a uniform manner, with propriety and equity]. Or else it is difficult to reap its results. Those classes who cannot afford to pay fees should have free education.... This is an innovative measure to bring together economics and sociology for the benefit of larger mankind. Upper-caste monopoly of education is dangerous. If you want education to be free and autonomous in the real sense it has to be made [compulsory and] available to all.
>
> (Ambedkar 1929)

Ambedkar thus sought to democratise educational practices. He also opposed the election of corrupt individuals on local school boards and their methods of education. Ambedkar further argued that 'education [was] a very different matter compared to the building of roads and cleaning of gutters' (Ambedkar 1929) and hence required more reflection and deliberation. He emphasised that school affairs needed to be handled in a disciplined manner, with propriety and equity.

Despite these arguments, however, ministers of the Indian National Congress who came to power in 1937 followed contradictory practices with regard to Dalits. In a 1940 speech (at the Mumbai Region Humanitarian Untouchables' Youth Conference) Shivram Balaji Moré attacked Congress' claim to be involved in 'special' work for Untouchables:

> The government had started a Backward Class Board for our *samaaj* (community). After the Congress came to power the Board made public the progress in the Backward Classes' education. The statistics reveal that before the Congress came to power in 1936–37 there were 61,667 Dalit students in common schools and 16,050 in separate schools. But, after the Congress came to power there were 60,928 in common and 13,649 in separate schools, in 1937–38. Thus, the children entering primary schools actually reduced after the Congress came to power.
>
> (*Janata*, 30 March 1940)

Moré also pointed out that the government proposed to change its earlier policy of admitting students to government schools, so that students would be admitted to semi-public high schools, and girls' high schools would replace the earlier government schools. This was a certainly a *visangat* (contradictory) and *dutappi vartan* (two-sided, ambiguous) strategy. Moré continued:

> Now that the government has closed the high schools our students have dropped out of schools and many have given up their education. The government has reasoned that it is closing down high schools because of the rising expenses. But instead of boys' high schools they want that of girls. In these high schools, *aaplya mulinche pramaan shunyaavar aahe* [the proportion of our girls is zero]. When our boys are facing a difficult time to educate themselves where will we find our girls to seek higher education? If we believe the government that it is making efforts for women's education, then we also need to understand that the percentage of literacy is certainly more among upper-caste women than in lower-caste men. In their women one can find thousands of degree holders and there are very few such men in our community. In these circumstances why should we not say that the Congress government is actually trying to [*maranyachi*] *kill* the progress and awakening among the Untouchables?
>
> (*Janata*, 30 March 1940, emphasis in original)

Thus Dalit activists and spokespersons questioned the dominant policies and practices that militated against their efforts for education and uplift. Upper-caste men appeared to reason that by replacing government high schools with girls' schools, they would set women against Dalits, creating a rivalry between the two marginalised groups.

Conclusion

Education emerged as not merely a 'site' but indeed as a field of forces and a political process between the colonial state and the colonised, and among Indians themselves. The colonial state did affirm a universal right to education in theory and accepted Dalits' entry to schools, but in practice it also cautiously foreclosed their opportunities. By favouring and importing the middle-class values of the Victorian metropole into the colony, the state transcended the metropole–colony binary, instilling its ideologies and inculcating its moral values into the upper-caste elites. The rhetoric and purposes of the colonial state were also embedded in and influenced by a political discourse shared by wider Indian society. This approach favoured elitist 'trickle-down' education strategies. The ambivalence of both the colonial government and high castes with regard to low-caste education led to further consolidation of a high-caste Hindu hegemonic structure for Marathi society.

As a result, educational policy was often contradictory and miserly. Educational discourse was intimately tied to upper-caste ideologies and practices, including Brahmani practices of discouraging Dalits from accessing education. Their rhetoric understood the modern paradigms of equality and social justice; yet, at the same time, they still wanted to maintain a distinct distance and difference and thus deepened caste distinctions. Marathi Brahman nationalists consolidated their caste and class power by restricting 'other' Indians from accessing facilities they enjoyed. In this manner, both the colonial state and upper castes further strengthened Brahman hegemony over education, administration and society, replicating and at times elevating colonial constructions of the 'docility' and 'roughness' of Dalits. Consequently, Indian education ministers, who were for the most part high-caste liberals, failed to provide mass education. The educational arena became a struggle between touchables and Untouchables, perpetuating the Dalit body as an object of pain and suffering in modern Indian schools.

Modern colonial power – along with its agents, the upper-caste elite – significantly altered the terrain on which Dalits accommodated and resisted. The British initiated new urban employment opportunities and disrupted traditional duties, enabling Dalits to work towards a unified social, pedagogical and political movement. Instead of remaining 'indifferent' or 'passive', Dalit radicals made continuous efforts to break through the formidable walls of Brahman supremacy and sought whatever education was available.

Dalits, on the other hand, believed in the modern promise of education as a way out and up from under everyday violations of their human dignity both inside and outside the classroom – a struggle for individual and collective freedom and political power. Diverse Dalit social groups, often with conflicting interests, came together in a political coalition to struggle for equal civic rights. In the specific educational conjuncture of 1920s Maharashtra, Dalits perceived their common interest in terms of 'Depressed Classes' – and not only imagined a community, but actually lived in it. In practice, however, Dalits were also fractured at other political moments, for example, over the issue of temple entry and religious conversion in the 1930s. Patterns of alliance and antagonisms continued to shift among contending Dalit castes situated close together in the social hierarchy.

This chapter has examined the intermeshed social, political and educational struggles of the Dalits; Chapter 2 weaves together its intellectual foundations. The profound resentments generated by Dalits' subordinate status, with its attendant humiliations and impediments, fuelled much of the intellectual radicalism of the early twentieth century as oppressed Dalits appropriated the modern discourse of human rights, struggled against their exclusion, opened schools and hostels, and began to politicise. All these efforts led to the refashioning of the Dalit self.

Notes

1 They were considered to be authorities in all boundary matters. They escorted the government treasurer, acted as guides and messengers to public officers, called upon landholders to pay the land assessment at the village office and village gate, and swept the village roads. Most of them enjoyed a small government payment, partly in cash and partly in land. Mahars were also largely employed by Europeans as domestic servants, particularly as butlers. They were highly employed as unskilled labourers and also worked as husbandmen, contractors and railway gang labourers. Many played kettle-drums at ceremonies.
2 I have drawn upon Shrirang Sawant's work for Chandavarkar's efforts. See Sawant (1989, 117–119).
3 According to Zelliot, these leaders represented a caste-Hindu attitude which led to cooperation with the Untouchables rather than service to them. They also made efforts through their writings (see, e.g. Bhandarkar (1913) and Gokhale (1903)).
4 Of the 384 employees of the executive and judicial branches of the Uncovenated Service in Bombay Presidency, 328 were Hindus, of which 211 were Brahmans, twenty-six Kshatriyas, thirty-seven Prabhus, thirty-eight Vaishyas, one Shudra, and fifteen Others. See Seal (1968, 118).
5 *Din Bandhu* was the public newspaper of the non-Brahmans. See *Din Bandhu*, 11 October 1885, quoted in Masselos (1964, 727).
6 By using the Marathi word *saktichech*, Dalits added weight to their emphasis on compulsory education.
7 Chambhars and Mangs later accused Ambedkar of being a 'Mahar' leader; the advancement of Mahars was a cause of animosity between different Dalit castes.
8 Despite the resolution that municipal schools in the city of Bombay should not discriminate by caste, Dalits were given separate pots. See Ambedkar (1982a, 457).
9 V.R. Shinde visited Bengal on two occasions: once in 1908 and again in 1923. He was very surprised about the progress of Namashudras at different levels of education as well as other sectors and made some significant observations (*Bahishkrut Bharat*, 15 March 1929, 29 March 1929).

References

Ambedkar, B.R. 1927. Aap ghari bata, baap gharihi bata (Disprivilege and injustice in one's private home as well as in the home of the paternal figure [the British colonial government]). *Bahishkrut Bharat*, 15 July.

——. 1928. State of education of the Depressed Classes in the Bombay Presidency. Speech to the Indian Statutory Commission on behalf of the Bahishkrita Hitakarini Sabha (Depressed Classes Institute of Bombay). In Ambedkar, *Writings and Speeches*, Vol. 2, ed. Vasant Moon. Bombay: Department of Education, Government of Maharashtra, 1982.

——. 1929. Mumbai ilakhyatil prathamik shikshanachi pragati (Progress of primary education in Mumbai Region). *Bahishkrut Bharat*, 31 May.

——. 1982a. *Writings and Speeches*, Vol. 2, ed. Vasant Moon. Bombay: Department of Education, Government of Maharashtra.

——. 1982b. *Dr. Babasaheb Ambedkar: Writings and Speeches*, Vol. 4, ed. Vasant Moon. Bombay: Department of Education, Government of Maharashtra.

——. 1992. *Dr. Babasaheb Ambedkar: Writings and Speeches*, Vol. 12, Part V, ed. Vasant Moon. Bombay: Department of Education, Government of Maharashtra.

Bahishkrut Bharat. 1 July 1927.

——. 1 February 1929.

——. 1 March 1929.

——. 15 March 1929.

——. 29 March 1929.

——. 31 May 1929. *Bahishkrut Bharat Puravani* magazine, pp. 9–10.

——. 16 August 1929.

——. 27 September 1929.

Balibar, Etienne. 1994. Racism as universalism. In *Masses, Classes, Ideas*. New York: Routledge.

Bhagat, M.G. 1935. *Untouchables in Maharashtra: A Study of the Social and Economic Conditions of the Untouchables in Maharashtra*. MA thesis, University of Bombay, India.

Bhandarkar, R.G. 1913. The Depressed Classes. *India Review*, 14: 482–485.

Bhattacharya, Sabyasachi, Joseph Bara and Chinna Rao Yagati. 2003. *Educating the Nation*. New Delhi: Kanishka.

Bombay Chronicle. 20 October 1927.

——. 18 October 1928.

——. 20 October 1928.

——. 23 October 1928.

Campbell, James, William Ramsay and James Pollen, eds. 1880. *Gazetteer of the Bombay Presidency*, Vol. XII. Bombay: Government Press.

Census of India. 1931. Vol. VIII, Part II. New Delhi: Government of India, Ministry of Home Affairs, pp. 435–437.

Chandra, Shefali. 2012. *The Sexual Life of English: Languages of Caste and Desire in Colonial India.* Durham, NC: Duke University Press.

Constable, Philip. 2000. Sitting on the school verandah: The ideology and practice of 'Untouchable' educational protest in late nineteenth-century western India. *Indian Economic and Social History Review*, 37(4): 383–422.

Craddock, R.H. 1899. *Report of the Land Revenue Settlement of the Nagpur District in the Central Provinces*. Nagpur: Government Press.

Desai, Mahadeo. 1953. *The Diary of Mahadeo Desai*. Ahmedabad: Navjivan.

Deshpande, Prachi. 2007. *Creative Pasts: Historical Memory and Identity in Western India, 1700–1960*. New York: Columbia University Press.

Gandhi, M.K. 1986. *The Moral and Political Writings of Gandhi: Vol. 1, Civilization, Politics, and Religion*, ed. Raghavan Iyer. Oxford: Clarendon Press.

Gokhale, Gopal Krishna. 1903. *Treatment of Indians by the Boers and Treatment of the Low Castes in India by Their Own Countrymen.* London: Christian Literary Society.

Indian Education Commission. 1883. *Hunter Commission Report.* Calcutta: Superintendent of Government Printing India.

Janata. 30 March 1940.

Kadam, Jyoti. 2001. Interview with the author, Yerawada, Pune, 21 October.

Kaikini, L.V., ed. 1911. *The Speeches and Writings of Sir Narayan G. Chandavarkar.* Bombay: MGPM.

Keer, Dhananjay. 1964. *Mahatma Jotirao Phooley.* Mumbai: Popular Prakashan.

Kshirsagar, R.K. 1994. *The Dalit Movement and its Leaders, 1857–1956.* New Delhi: M.D. Publications.

Macaulay, Thomas. 1835. Minute on Indian education, London, available at www.columbia.edu/itc/mealac/pritchett/00generallinks/macaulay/txt_minute_education_1835.html.

Mandlik, V.N. 1865. Native opinion, 19 March. In Richard P. Tucker, *Ranade and the Roots of Indian Nationalism.* Chicago, IL: University of Chicago Press, 1972.

Masselos, James. 1964. Liberal consciousness, leadership, and political organisation in Bombay and Poona, 1867–1895. Ph.D. dissertation, University of Mumbai, India.

Mehta, Chunilal V. 1916. Difficulties of Untouchable students. Letter to Secretary, General Department File. Maharashtra: Maharashtra State Archives, 30 November.

Meshram. 1945. (President, SCF Nagpur.) Mrs. Jaibai Chaudhari. *People's Herald*, 30 June.

Mooknayak. 28 February 1920.

——. 5 June 1920.

Nirbhid. 8 December 1935.

Nurullah, S. and J.P. Naik. 1951. *A History of Education in India during the British Period.* Bombay: Macmillan.

Pawde, Kumud. 2005. Interview with the author, 16 October, Dhantoli, Nagpur.

Phule, Jotirao. 1882. Memorial address to the Hunter Education Commission. Ganja Peth, Poona, 19 October. In *Collected Works of Mahatma Jotirao Phule*, Vol. II, trans. P.G. Patil. Bombay: Education Department, Government of Maharashtra, 1991.

——. 1991a. *Collected Works of Mahatma Jotirao Phule*, Vol. I, trans. P.G. Patil. Bombay: Education Department, Government of Maharashtra.

——. 1991b. *Collected Works of Mahatma Jotirao Phule*, Vol. II, trans. P.G. Patil. Bombay: Education Department, Government of Maharashtra.

Rao, Parimala V. 2010. *Foundations of Tilak's Nationalism: Discrimination, Education, and Hindutva.* New Delhi: Orient Blackswan.

Sawant, Shrirang. 1989. *Socio-Economic and Political Movements of the Depressed Classes in Western Maharashtra, 1890–1950.* Ph.D. dissertation, University of Mumbai, India.

Seal, Anil. 1968. *The Emergence of Indian Nationalism: Competition and Collaboration in the Later Nineteenth Century.* Cambridge: Cambridge University Press.

Servants of India Society. 1905–16. *A Brief Account of the Work of the Servants of India Society*, 12 June 1905 to 31 December 1916.

——. 1917–23. *A Brief Account of the Work of the Servants of India Society*, 1 January 1917 to 30 June 1923.

——. 1923–26. *A Brief Account of the Work of the Servants of India Society*, June 1923 to May 1926.

Sovani, N.V., D.P. Apte and R.G. Pendse. 1956. *Poona: A Re-survey, the Changing Pattern of Employment and Earnings.* Pune: Gokhale Institute.

Starte Committee. 1930. Primary education of the Depressed Classes. *Starte Committee Report.* Bombay: Government Printing Press.

Stoler, Ann Laura. 2002. Racial histories and their regimes of truth. In *Race Critical Theories: Text and Context*, ed. Philomena Essed and David Theo Goldberg. Malden, MA: Blackwell.

Tilak, B.G. 1881. Our system of education: A defect and a cure. *Mahrataa,* 15 May.

Times of India. 4 September 1925.

——. 4 November 1927.

Tucker, Richard P. 1972. *Ranade and the Roots of Indian Nationalism.* Chicago, IL: University of Chicago Press.

Valangkar, Gopal Baba. 1894. Letter to the editor. *Din Bandhu,* 15 April.

Zelliot, Eleanor. 1988. Congress and the Untouchables, 1917–1950. In *Congress and Indian Nationalism: The Pre-Independence Phase*, ed. Richard Sisson and Stanley Wolpert. Berkeley: University of California Press.

——. 1994. *Dr. Babasaheb Ambedkar and the Untouchable Movement.* New Delhi: Bluemoon Books.

——. 2000. The history of Dalits in Pune. *Journal of the Asiatic Society of Bombay*, 74.

——. n.d. Dalit initiatives in education. Unpublished paper.

2 'Educate, organise and agitate'

Non-Brahman and Dalit technologies of education

Many Dalits battled for the right to education, but it was Phule and later Ambedkar who forcefully articulated earlier demands, engineered educational technologies and sought state intervention. Ambedkar contended that justice between groups could not be achieved by educational means alone, advocating instead a multi-stranded strategy – social, political, economic and religious. In 1927, challenging some upper-caste, middle-class reformers, he argued that 'only by being educated [*sushikshit houn*] one cannot end untouchability' (*Bahishkrut Bharat*, 29 July 1927). Such an approach was missing in upper-caste, elite conceptions of social change, which considered untouchability to be an isolated phenomenon that 'education [alone] will eradicate' (*Bahishkrut Bharat*, 29 July 1927). For example, Gandhi suggested education and some cosmetic changes for Dalits, such as improving living conditions, rather than contesting the structures that constructed their social and educational exclusion in the first place. Although he posed a fundamental challenge to caste hierarchy and made efforts towards education, by adopting a reformist, moralistic and patronising attitude towards Dalits, Gandhi was also constrained from offering practical solutions to economic and social problems. He also rarely acknowledged Dalit radicals' agenda of educational reform.

By contrast, drawing upon the Enlightenment tradition, Ambedkar (and Phule) appropriated elements of a modern discourse of equal rights for Dalits and women and also looked upon them as *agents*. Unlike Gandhi, Ambedkar attacked caste technologies and argued that the question of Dalit education was part of a larger set of processes. It was embedded in power relations and was inextricably connected with social relations, the local economy, religious ideas, ideological battles and political movements. I investigate complicated caste articulations among different but entangled domains, rhetoric and discourses in a particular historical and educational conjuncture. In this chapter, I illustrate that by employing such 'rhizomatic'[1] methods, Ambedkar and Phule articulated an 'affective pedagogy' centred on possibilities, dignity and agency. Relatively few studies on these strategies for pedagogical and social action have been conducted to date.

Although Phule and Ambedkar saw Dalits as victims and also blamed them for their oppressed situation, yet they wanted them to take control. This chapter delineates the ideological, practical and contextual mechanisms through which Phule and Ambedkar sought to imagine Dalits as political *subjects* and create new Dalit *citizens*. For both men, the key dilemma at the heart of Dalit schooling and political life was how to make real the democratic promise of self-realisation within a caste apparatus that precluded self-determination for Dalits. The chapter explores their confrontations and negotiations with upper castes to understand how they constructed their demand for education in opposition to the constraints and controls of upper-caste and Gandhian nationalists. There was a rupture between Dalit language of rights and upper-caste sentiments for abolishing untouchability. In the repertoire of civic rights, education emerged as a significant force in the social revolt movements and political and ideological struggles at the end of the nineteenth century. Revolutionary anti-caste movements questioned upper-caste reformist approaches as well as the colonial state's cautious measures, and in this context education was infused with a new meaning and a radical social and political purpose. From a Dalit perspective, both colonial and nationalist policies and practices, discursive and non-discursive, emphasised a hegemonic agenda by conceptualising their lives in particular ways in order to not only fit but also *reinforce* the stereotype (explored in the previous chapter) of 'passive', 'docile' or 'indifferent' Dalits. They argued that 'sentiments' would have to be sacrificed, because public education could not be the private purview of a handful.

Thus, this chapter examines the competing models leaders articulated, debated and implemented with Dalits. It is devoted to explaining contested Dalit subjectivities produced out of the contradictions and convergences between non-Brahman/Dalit educational technologies[2] and Gandhian reformist agendas of education for Dalits. Challenging the colonial state's and Gandhi's insistence on gradual reforms, Dalit radicals insisted on autonomy and independence, denounced any sort of domination, and sought to exercise power equal to that of upper castes. While Chapter 1 examined the interwoven social, political and educational struggles of the Dalit movement for freedom, this chapter dwells on its intellectual underpinnings. As such, it deepens our understanding of the particular (and heretofore neglected) educational conjuncture in early twentieth-century Maharashtra: the historical and socio-political context of Dalits' right to education and the ideologies in which it was embedded.

Like the historian Philip Constable, I challenge earlier scholarship which gave primacy to Western agency – governmental and missionary – as the principal force behind Dalit educational change (Nurullah and Naik 1951; Forrester 1979; Oddie 1979; Kawashima 1998; Bayly 1989), and emphasise the role of Dalit radicals and their efforts for education. I go further to uncover the much-neglected wealth of Dalit educational ideas and activism, which provided one of the radical impulses for social, political and educational change. Scholars have mined Phule's and Ambedkar's contributions towards the social and political revolution in twentieth-century Maharashtra (O'Hanlon 1985; Zelliot 1992; Omvedt 1994; Gokhale 1993; Rao 2009; Jaffrelot 2004),[3] yet there is scant literature on Dalit leaders' educational ideologies and actions. Surprisingly, only one historian, Eleanor Zelliot, has focused on the much-neglected contributions of Marathi Dalit activists and spokespersons in the field of education,[4] and her article is yet to be published. Some sociologists have commented on Ambedkar's ideology of liberation and agenda of education,[5] but have made limited use of archival sources.

I centre on the theory of socio-educational reform advocated by non-Brahman and Dalit radicals: their philosophies, practices and initiatives in education as they sought to gain rights, as well as to refashion the Dalit self. This chapter weaves together the rationalising discourse of Phule's and Ambedkar's modern, radical educational technologies as they came into conflict with those of upper-caste, elite reformers. Their 'affective pedagogies',[6] which mapped possibilities and agency for Dalit students, were in fact 'technologies of the self'. Moreover, Dalit radicals in early twentieth-century Maharashtra interpreted Dalit exclusion from common schools as a barrier to both individual freedom and advancement, and to their collective ability to secure equal *maanavi hakka* (human rights) and *naagarikatva* (citizenship). Most significantly, Ambedkar declared that *shaalaa ha uttam naagarik tayaar karnyacha kaarkhaanaa aahe* (schools are workshops for manufacturing the best citizens) (Ambedkar 1927d). Benefiting from the social and political activism of earlier Dalits and some non-Dalits, he forcefully articulated the connection between their education and modern citizenship. This was essential for their deliverance from caste oppression.

Most significantly, the struggle of Dalits to live as full human beings embodied a combined critique of caste and gender hierarchies in a way that opened up new spaces for women. The education of girls and women was an integral part of Phule's and Ambedkar's discourse on education as a right. Both leaders appreciated the role of education in Dalit women's emancipation. Certainly, Ambedkar underlined its rationale for the women's movement because women were to be the collective 'civilising' agents of the Dalit world. Most significantly, challenging the upper-caste, middle-class agenda of 'feminised' education for women, Phule and Ambedkar aimed to use education as a tool to build critical consciousness. To them Dalit women were historical subjects, agentive forces who could uplift their community. The 'Dalit woman question' became a strategic part of the fight for human rights and could not therefore be separated from it, despite contradictions. (I deal with the details of Dalits' discourse on women's education and gender reforms in Chapter 3.)

To address these complex psycho-social, political and pedagogical technologies, the first section of the chapter historicises subaltern education in a transnational context to illuminate the international dialogue in which Phule and Ambedkar were involved. By critiquing the discourses and practices that led to their erasure, Dalit intellectuals developed transformative education reform theories and institutions. Their short- and long-term aims and struggles are dealt with in the second section. The final section outlines Dalits' internal and external strategies to discipline the self and to transform Dalit personhood. I conclude by juxtaposing Dalit and upper-caste/middle-class agendas of education, which shaped the particular history of Dalits' struggle for education in the twentieth century.

Phule's and Ambedkar's *trutiya ratna* (third eye) and its transnational connection

Although Phule and Ambedkar lived in different times, their revolutionary technologies of education (akin to those of John Dewey and Antonio Gramsci) both focused on using education as a tool for self-discipline and for the development of psycho-physical habits that were durably inscribed in the mind and body. These radicals had a common approach to fighting caste oppression and educational exclusion. Both strove to build Dalits' human dignity, confidence and resistance in order to accumulate *raajkiya sattaa* (political power). By incorporating social movement theory into pedagogy, they proposed an ethical theory of liberation in the historical setting of decolonisation. Although not usually considered educators in the same vein as educational philosophers like Tagore and Gandhi, Phule's and Ambedkar's influence on twentieth-century lower-class education was of immense importance.

Phule and Ambedkar derived their ideals from post-Enlightenment notions of modern rationality and humanism, and infused them with vernacular concepts and indigenous traditions offered by Kabir and Buddha. Non-Brahman and Dalit radicals were thus not untouched by (Western) modernity, as some scholars would like to believe; Dalits indeed conceptualised their ideology through an intricate construction of history and tradition. Moreover, their message penetrated cities as well as remote villages through the vernacular Marathi print culture, folk performances (*jalsaa*) and the power of the word: the practice of reading newspapers, pamphlets and poetry aloud. (Babytai Kamble, a feminist, witnessed such informal education and politicisation in the 1930s in her village of Phaltan, near Pune.) Dalit radicals thus selectively appropriated modernity, shaping and negotiating with it through symbolic actions and discursive practices, including indigenous idioms, the Marathi language, and day-to-day political struggles for power and social justice. Thus they strategically embraced and resisted both modernity and tradition to remake themselves as well as to articulate their collective identity, struggles and emancipation.

By tracing the social and intellectual history of radical anti-caste struggles as they enmeshed with educational technologies, I delve deeper into the socio-historical and political context of the Dalit movement and its intimate relationship with dignity and citizenship to deal with the pedagogical and political dilemmas of Dalit life. When Dalits were engaged in battles for civic rights and citizenship, the right to education emerged as pivotal, though tenuous in practice. Their arguments and choices were intimately connected with their social experiences and were informed by a high degree of political self-consciousness.

Phule's and Ambedkar's ideas of subaltern education have a transnational connection. They strongly resonate as well as interconnect with those of their contemporaries like Gramsci and Dewey as well as those after them, such as Frantz Fanon, Paulo Freire and Michel Foucault. What is gained from this international connection and dialogue is an understanding and appreciation of the significance of the narrative of liberation and education for Marathi Dalits. Most importantly, all of these theorists were concerned about the double colonisation (internal and external) of the subordinated and struggled to look upon education as a tool of emancipation. Benefiting from these conversations, I analyse the 'interlocking technologies' of social differences and prejudices, gender oppression, justice and equality to rethink Dalit women's education.

Informed, critical agency is important in combating all inequalities. Recently, critical pedagogues have cautioned that schooling has become increasingly corporatist, fostering a learning environment that stifles critical reflection and questioning, and encourages students to be consumers rather than critical thinkers, doers and active citizens in a democracy (see, e.g. Giroux and McLaren 1994). This argument is not new, but an old theme reconfigured in postmodern trappings. Phule's polemical play *Trutiya Ratna* (critical thinking or critical consciousness, literally 'Third Jewel') pressed his agenda of building a critical consciousness among those excluded from education for centuries. In order to achieve this goal he also opened the first schools for Dalits and women, in 1848 and 1852, respectively.

Phule believed that formal education would lead to the development of *trutiya ratna*, critical thinking or a 'critical consciousness' (Phule 1855), a concept that resonates throughout the twentieth century in the works of Ambedkar, Gramsci, Freire and Foucault. Metaphorically, the *trutiya ratna* symbolised the opening of the third eye and signified a mythically destructive ability to annihilate the prevailing power–knowledge nexus. In a similar vein, Ambedkar emphasised the need to cultivate the intellect, to disturb and unsettle pupils' minds. He was significantly influenced by John Dewey, his teacher in America; however, he had no such connection with his contemporary Gramsci, nor had Ambedkar read any of his work. Dewey's pragmatism and theory of enquiry aimed to produce independent thinkers rather than mere imitators or repositories of information (quoted in Queen 2000, 40).[7] Similarly, Gramsci greatly emphasised supporting and encouraging free, creative thinking among all citizens as 'vital to future society and government' (Gramsci 1971, 31–33).[8] Freire, the famous Brazilian educationist, borrowed the concepts of 'critical consciousness' and 'banking education' from Gramsci (Gramsci 1971, 30; Freire 1970). Phule's liberation of the Shudra-ati-Shudra was similar to – and in fact preceded – Freire's call for emancipating the Brazilian peasantry by almost a century.

Like Phule and Ambedkar, Gramsci advocated that pupils should criticise the curricula and the disciplinary structure of the old system and thus participate actively (Gramsci 1971, 37, 42). All of them understood the difficulties of the task, the 'extra effort' to be made in order to inculcate self-discipline and self-control. According to them this was significant in allowing the subaltern to compete successfully with more privileged classmates.[9] Gramsci also went on to analyse how education frequently endorsed structures of power, stating that the 'new type of school appears and is advocated as democratic, while in fact it is destined not merely to perpetuate social differences but to *crystallise* them' (Gramsci 1971, 40, emphasis added).

Gramsci, whose philosophy pivots on the significance of 'praxis', dealt extensively with the application and management of education in a future society

(Gramsci 1971, 29–30).[10] In this, he moved from an inspirational tone to a thoroughly practical exploration of what would constitute a more egalitarian and liberating system of schooling. Both Gramsci and Ambedkar clearly recognised that schooling constituted only one form of social activity within a broader network of experience, history and collective struggle (Gramsci 1971, 29). The school was thus one important site of struggle that could enable the subaltern to govern and not simply be governed.

Furthermore, Phule, Ambedkar and Gramsci affirm the interlinkage between political hegemony and pedagogic practices. Ambedkar argued that education was an essential prerequisite to occupying *maaranyachya jaagaa* (effective positions) in the government and to enjoy real *sattaa* (political power) (*Janata*, 15 December 1945). For Gramsci the 'pedagogical was inextricably grounded in a notion of hegemony, struggle, and political education articulated through a normative position and project aimed at overcoming the stark inequalities and forms of oppression suffered by subaltern groups' (Gramsci 1971, 103–104; Giroux 2002, 56). In a similar vein, Phule and Ambedkar analysed how 'Brahmans tricked Dalits and women by excluding them from all sorts of *maanavi hakka* (human rights)' (Phule 1991a, 448), including education. Hence, unlike Tilak and Gandhi, they concurred with Gramsci that 'education was a prerequisite for anybody in society, a right for all its members' (Gramsci 1971, 41–43), especially for women and low castes. Both Ambedkar and Gramsci also underlined the importance of 'common schools' for all classes in order to undercut rank and hierarchy.

Like Fanon, Phule and Ambedkar shared ideas on the 'double decolonisation' of the subaltern and charted out a 'narrative of liberation', the course of which is the movement from a historical moment of fighting Brahmani and British (or white/European imperialism in Africa, for Fanon) oppression towards universal freedom and dignity.[11] However, unlike Fanon, Phule and Ambedkar had faith in the state (via laws) that did not endorse spectacular anti-state violence.

Most significantly, I gender Fanon's articulations and underscore the emancipation of *streepurush*, women and men, who were excluded by high-caste males. In the Dalit pedagogical *telos* of freedom, the aim of the narrative is to influence individuals and modify them fundamentally; the *course* of the narrative is the movement away from a historically situated moment of Brahmani colonisation and towards an ethical subject.[12] In this process of double decolonisation, Dalits would learn to become women and men and assume full personhood. For Dalits, claiming personhood was a way of articulating their human dignity and expanding their rights.

Working with Fanon, I extend my focus on the disciplinary element in schooling, which owes much to Foucault's analysis of how the bourgeoisie have exercised their power through various institutions of governance such as the prison, army and hospital. Unlike Gramsci, Foucault did not focus on the school, though it is clear that this is a prime institution for such governance. Foucault, however, offered critiques of institutions that resonate with this study (Foucault 1977, 1980). According to him, the state and elites adopt their own disciplinary mechanisms that do not speak of a juridical rule but of normalisation (Foucault 1980, 106–108). Benefiting from him and Phillip Corrigan, I analyse how 'pedagogy works on the mind, and emotions, on the unconscious, and yes, on the soul, the spirit, *through the work done on, to, by, with, and from the body*' (Corrigan 1991, emphasis in original).[13]

Gramsci, who had a strong political agenda, was centrally concerned with the issue of delineating areas of resistance in order to facilitate the proletarian revolution. Building on his efforts, Foucault and Bourdieu foregrounded the overwhelming hegemony of the systemic structure but were pessimistic about the ability to resist something that was so internalised by those subjected to such power. In this they failed to grant agency to the subordinated. In his later work, however, Foucault did address this issue, arguing that resistance was possible within each sphere of power. The next section addresses how this global agenda of education worked in a local socio-political context.

Reconstruction: fighting caste and constructing educational paths to power

As we saw in the previous chapter, upper-caste reformism kept Dalits at a distinct distance. It denied them human dignity and education, and excluded them from the body politic. By contrast, the wealth of ideas and activism that emerged from Dalit civic, political and religious struggles was informed by the historical legacy and complexity of the Dalit experience in India.

Growing up as a Mali (gardener), a non-Brahman low caste, Phule faced social ostracism in everyday life. He also faced interruptions in his education, but was finally educated at the Scottish mission school. Like his upper-caste colleagues and friends, he thought the key to fundamental change in social attitudes lay in education. Unlike Phule, Ambedkar benefited from an educated family. His grandfather and father were associated with the military of the East India Company government, which made education compulsory for its soldiers. While children studied in the daytime, adults attended night schools. The Mahar platoon had its own school, and Ramji Ambedkar, Ambedkar's father, was headmaster at such a school for fourteen years (Ambedkar 1947b). All of the women and children in his family could read.

Ambedkar was haunted by the monster of untouchability however, and these experiences of being deformed and broken on several occasions, despite his intellectualism, had a deep impact on him. For example, when he expressed his wish to study Sanskrit, his teacher declared, 'I do not teach Sanskrit to Untouchable boys' (Ambedkar 1947a). He was forced to study Persian instead. The teacher also insulted Ambedkar's brother, which had a *vaiit parinaam* (bad effect) on the two boys' minds. Remembering these days, Ambedkar reported that he was 'restless to become a Sanskrit expert'. Sceptical and disillusioned, he questioned further: '[But] when will that *sudin* [good day] arrive?' (Ambedkar 1947a). Along with other Dalit radicals, he continued to fight for the 'good day' he imagined.

Ambedkar brought a nuanced understanding to his scholarly works and con-stitutional remedies. Unlike upper-caste agendas, Ambedkar's philosophy and actions were not isolated from his own background and social and political context. Phule's and Ambedkar's technologies were rooted in humanitarian and egalitarian ideas – in struggle and pride – rather than in the Brahman-mediated ritual orthodoxy, yet their educational visions were simultaneously contradictory and complementary.

Gandhi, an upper-caste member of the elite, attacked imperialism in all its forms and stood for decolonisation, but Phule and Ambedkar faced 'double colo-nisation' – both internal and external – by upper castes and British colonialism. Although colonial rule was to an extent liberating for Phule and Ambedkar, they also opposed the subjugation of India by the British. While externally they fought colonialism, as did Gandhi, internally they had to fight Brahmani domi-nation. Using the tool of education, they sought to fashion the new Dalit *streepu-rush* (woman and man) and make them full human beings.[14] They believed in the classically modern idea of the Dalit individual as a 'heroic' social actor carving out her own world and authoring her life – a veritably puritanical programme to be achieved through education.

Phule's and Ambedkar's spontaneous philosophy was critically derived from their shared experiences in social discrimination, which united them with their community in transforming the real world. Their revolutionary efforts to recon-stitute society on a new basis and to view the utopian condition immediately imminent stood in stark contrast to Gandhian conformity with the status quo of the prevailing institutional structures. This 'natural rhythm' was utopia for Gandhi, who belonged to a social group with a fairly continuous history. He thus responded psychologically to a Dalit crisis in a very different way from Ambed-kar, who had experienced the shocks of abrupt breaks.[15] The difference between these personalities is thus mainly due to the difference in their social and material backgrounds as well as their subjective experiences. It was also about the clash of competing economic interests, experiences and ideologies in dealing with social structures (especially untouchability). They agreed on many reforms and neither accepted the horrors of untouchability, yet there were differences: while Ambedkar resisted radically, Gandhi did not call for structural change and, like an organicist, emphasised conformity with the *varna* order. Yet later on in his life he separated caste from the *varna* system and challenged traditional ver-tical, hierarchical notions of *varna* to argue for a wider horizontal system in which all were equal. After the 1930s Gandhi revised his strategy and radically challenged caste practices and untouchability.

Gandhi was the father of the nation. By contrast, Phule's and Ambedkar's progressive movements, which represented empowerment and rights for Dalits, were marginal to the upper-caste, nationalist public sphere. Dominant groups that spoke for a 'common' public interest always made difference invisible. Clearly, there was a split between the authoritarian, paternalistic, 'majoritarian' agenda of nationalism and radical caste movements. Yet the 'minorities' had a clear understanding of their social, political and moral interests. Hence, they contested upper castes' religious and genealogical understandings of caste relations with their everyday lived experiences and challenged their own internal colonialism. Gandhian interests defined the necessity of education for a few, but risked casting Phule's and Ambedkar's demands for education as selfish interests or the greed of millions. Gandhi's efforts for Dalits' education and civic rights are well known. Instead of simply repeating them here, I will juxtapose them with Phule's and Ambedkar's to place them firmly in a specific social and historical context.

Democratising education: two aims, two phases

Phule, a radical humanist thinker, occupies a central and pioneering position in the struggle for the universal right to education. Through his Satyashodhak Samaaj (Society for the Seeking of Truth), established in 1872, Phule launched a vigorous polemic against the hegemony of the *shetji-bhatji*[16] alliance. As Ambedkar would later, he constructed a counter-history for the lower castes and identified their lack of education as the main culprit keeping them in mental slavery. Through Ambedkar's and Phule's writings and speeches, their affective pedagogy helped Dalit students understand the possibilities and constraints on their agency as it intersected with everyday life, social formation and political power. Such an approach involved complicated connections and overlapping processes, and empowered students to reconstruct their world and articulate their future in previously unimaginable ways. Phule and Ambedkar also submitted petitions to the government and sought remedies from within the state to educate the lower castes. Their strategies and efforts for social justice and for developing students' confidence to work for social change also extended beyond the classroom.

Some upper-caste elite (especially Brahman) reformers like Bhandarkar, Agarkar, and particularly Gokhale made strong statements about the need to educate the lower castes. Yet, when actual educational experiments were conducted, it was by non-Brahmans like Phule and V.R. Shinde, and Dalits like S.J. Kamble, K.P. Bansode and Ambedkar. Dalits reconstructed the boundaries of public domains (streets, wells, temples) and viewed education as particularly important to promote Dalit self-assertion as well as modern citizenship. Influenced by Dewey and benefiting from Phule, non-Brahman politics and his encouraging family background, Ambedkar seized the reins of the Dalit movement's leadership in Maharashtra in the mid-1920s.

During this time, Dalits' battle for education became a struggle for individual and collective freedom and political power. A dialectical understanding, where the individual is defined in relation to the community, was the cornerstone of Ambedkar's philosophy of Dalit liberation. While they shared a commitment to improving Dalits' educational status in Bombay Presidency, Phule and Ambedkar drew upon different political ideologies and practical strategies: indigenous ideals, Western thought and the language of political liberalism all guided their struggle for equality, human rights and justice.[17] Their ideologies and struggles for education, especially Ambedkar's, had two kinds of goals: short and long range. While short-range aims would make available basic literacy and citizenship training for Dalits' participation in a democratic Indian society, the long-range goals were to develop a class of *vishvaasu* (trustworthy) leaders who would guide the Dalits to freedom and equality (*Garud*, 12 October 1947).

Most significantly, these two kinds of aims fundamentally coincided with the two phases of Dalits' struggle for education which Ambedkar identified: first. to make it available; and second, to ensure that it was quality education on a par with that of other classes, designed to prepare Dalits for full citizenship. The first battle, what I consider a first-stage struggle, was to fight the social environment and win Dalits the right to be educated.

Brahman males monopolised education and criminalised lower castes who acquired education. They conspired to deny education to both Shudra-Ati-Shudras and women. Challenging this Brahmani orthodoxy, Phule started schools for low castes in the Budhwar, Rasta, Ganj Peths and Bhokarwadi neighbourhoods of Pune during the 1850s. He also formed a 'Society for Increasing Education amongst Mahars, Mangs, and Others' and opened a library for them. By educating the socially excluded – women and Untouchables – and bringing them into the process of learning and teaching, Jotirao and his wife Savitribai thus democratised education. In response, orthodox Brahmans threatened Phule and even attacked Savitribai. Nonetheless, the English weekly *Poona Observer and Deccan Weekly Reporter* observed Phule's initiatives as 'the heralding of a new age in the history of Hindu culture' (quoted in Phule 1991a, 608).

Along with Phule, Ambedkar was equally engaged in the first stage of the battle. However, Ambedkar revised Phule's agenda and extended it to the next stage. As a Dalit, he experienced first-hand discrimination and took an integral part in the second phase of the battle for education: to obtain education on a par with upper castes and to be given equal opportunities to use their qualifications to the best advantage.

Education and the manufacturing of modern Dalit citizens

What did education mean to Dalits? Education, for Ambedkar, had a social and political function: to provide a social continuity to Dalits' deformed lives[18] and to prepare them for their new role as 'modern' citizens in the democratic Indian body politic. Most significantly, 'schools are a *kaarkhaanaa* [workshop] to manufacture the *uttam naagarik* [best citizens]' (*Bahishkrut Bharat*, 3 June 1927). In his opinion, 'citizenship involved individual independence, individual safety, private property, equality, legal status to behave according to one's intelligence, freedom of language and expression, freedom to congregate, to fetch government jobs'; yet, due to social restrictions, Dalits were excluded from it (*Mooknayak*, 28 February 1920). By conceptualising *common schools as citizen-makers*, Ambedkar inadvertently provided ammunition for the devastating assertion that Dalits were neither citizens nor Indians, nor Hindus, for that matter. Thus politics was at the heart of the Dalit pedagogical question. Dalits had to fight double colonialism because in the imperial and (Gandhian) nationalist narratives they needed to be educated out of their ignorance, cleansed of their dirty past, because they failed to measure up to the 'secular' ideals of citizenship.

Significantly, Ambedkar emphasised that Dalits were to become *nirbhay* (fearless) citizens who had *svatantra vichaar aani vrutti* (independent thoughts and temperaments) (*Prabuddha Bharat*, 21 July 1956). In this manner, he interlinked Dalits' fight for education with their fight for equality, including equal rights to humanitarianism, human dignity, self-help, and most importantly citizenship. Thus Dalits did not fight merely to attend school or to obtain employment; their agenda went beyond that. Education was for dignity, empowerment, self-help, emancipation and community uplift. Ambedkar declared:

> what the Untouchables want is not education, but the right to be admitted in common schools. They do not want medical aid, but the right to be admitted to the general dispensary on equal terms. What they want is the right to draw water from a common well. They do not want their suffering to be relieved.

(Ambedkar 1989, 373)

He argued that education would be instrumental in fashioning and reinscribing Dalits as moral and modern citizens of India. Significantly, Dalits' different educational aspirations and needs grew from daily experience, thus representing their attempts to build a better future from an existing base. Dalits could not obliterate their suffering, but instead had to struggle continuously for their identities to be respected and their stigma removed. There is ambivalence here: by describing Dalithood, Ambedkar pointed out that Dalits were marginalised, outside the narratives of the Indian nation-state, and gestured towards their simultaneous emphasis/embrace and disavowal of subalternity. The label 'Dalit' later captured this paradox both literally and metaphorically, but Ambedkar did not use it extensively.

Bahishkrut and Harijan: contested self, contested subjectivity

Ambedkar identified Untouchables as the Bahishkrut (Excluded), riven by caste conflicts.[19] In a stark contrast, Gandhi hailed them as a homogeneous entity and called them Harijan (People of God). Thus the two leaders competed over the meaning, origins of and remedies for the removal of untouchability as well as over imagining Dalits as *subjects of history*.[20] According to Gandhi, Dalits were an inseparable part of Hindu society, but Ambedkar argued that they stood apart. The *varna* system, to Gandhi, was 'the gift of Hinduism to mankind', and the hierarchical caste system would meet the labour needs of society; to Ambedkar, though, caste was a division not of labour but of labourers. While the Dalits were a religious minority to Gandhi, to Ambedkar they were a social and political minority: educationally backward, economically poor and socially enslaved (Ambedkar 1928).

According to Ambedkar, the root of the disease of untouchability was the *manovrutti* (mind, thoughts and feelings) of people. He continued:

> I am an Untouchable and until my dining mess *bhat* [high-caste] cook knew about it, he served me tea and *bhaji* [pakoras] in a regular cup and saucer. But the day after a Gujarati newspaper published my photo and included information about my Untouchable background, the cook served me tea in a separate glass cup [meant for the Untouchables].
>
> (*Bahishkrut Bharat*, 29 July 1927)

Ambedkar was educated at prestigious universities in the US and the UK, but still suffered from the pangs of untouchability. He argued that 'while an ignorant Brahman could enjoy higher powers, an intelligent Untouchable was left aside because the former, though low by qualities, was highest by birth' (*Dnyanprakash*, 1 January 1930). Ambedkar contended:

> there was basically no difference between a poor, dirty, illiterate and a rich, clean, educated Untouchable. Hence there was no reason to believe touchables who wanted to pacify Untouchables by saying that once the latter were educated, they could be touched or treated equally [or even included].
>
> (*Janata*, 20 June 1936)

For these reasons, Ambedkar emphasised that education alone would not automatically eradicate untouchability, but by restructuring and transforming the entire anatomy of caste relations and attitudes one could certainly strike at the roots of social prejudices and inequalities. The individual and collective agency of the Dalits was essential for bringing about this social change.

Ambedkar argued that 'the Depressed Classes have their very persona confiscated. The socio-religious disabilities have dehumanised the Untouchables and their very interests are therefore the interests of humanity' (Ambedkar 1979b). By contrast, Gandhi wanted Dalits to gain self-respect without empowering them. Gandhi was a paradoxical figure. On the one hand, he argued that Dalits should have civic and human rights, including access to schools, temples and water tanks. On the other hand, he refused to attack the caste structure that essentially constructed their social exclusion. He adopted a similar approach to the woman question. Most importantly, by making it the duty of the upper castes to free the Harijans from the tyranny of custom, he ultimately denied Harijans the right to relieve themselves of their (Untouchable) burden. In this view Dalits would have to depend on the upper castes' gradual penance and subsequent change of heart and mind (Gandhi 1991, 487). Once again, upper castes were constructed as rational agents and subjects of history who would raise the Untouchables from ignorance to a state of advanced consciousness. Such nationalist techniques have ignored Dalits' role in making their own history. By contrast, Phule's and Ambedkar's militant, revolutionary agenda strengthened Dalits as agents who could think, make choices as individuals, and organise collectively without waiting for help from others. Ambedkar wanted them to be *himmatvaan* (courageous) like tigers and not sheep to be herded (*Janata*, 15 August 1953), as suggested in the Gandhian agenda.

Ambedkar was reluctant for a patient penitent and declared that the 'Untouchable question is not *Hindunchya gharchaa prashna* (a private one for individual Hindus); but, it is a national and to go further, it is an international problem' (*Janata*, 22 January 1936). He thus challenged Gandhi, who thought that the question of Untouchables, like that of women and the working class, should be resolved within the family. Underscoring Dalits' nationalism, he affirmed that just as 'Brahmans [like Tilak thought] that Swaraj [was] their birthright, so do the Mahars think' (*Times of India*, 1 January 1919). While Gandhi argued that he was fighting for the whole country, of which Untouchables were a part, Ambedkar believed that the Indian National Congress' fight would not bring real *svaraajya* (self-rule), but in fact would precipitate *aamchyavar raajya* (internal colonialism, a rule over Dalits) (*Times of India*, 28 February 1920), in which there were scarce chances of *suraajya* (good rule). Hence he affirmed to Dalits that 'without education [their] existence is not safe' (Ambedkar 1982a, 62, 1927a).

Ambedkar believed in Dalits' self-improvement and argued that 'human intellect is like marble. It will be moulded as you work on it.... Along with intellect a human being also needs *saunskar* [etiquette and morals].' Ambedkar argued that to achieve 'good *saunskar* was real education. A person needs a good educational foundation to prosper' (*Mooknayak*, 10 September 1920). The process of education would thus allow Dalit women and men to understand that they could both liberate themselves personally in the here and now and find a greater liberation in the future. Using education as a tool, Phule and Ambedkar sought to improve Dalits' socio-psychological environment to enable them to experience cultural joy.

By contrast, Gandhian idealism centred on cultural efflorescence. For Gandhi, 'real' education was a liberal education in harmony with nature. Phule's and Ambedkar's pedagogies of critical thinking were not absent in Gandhi's thought; however, he identified true education as knowing the *atman* (soul/self), God and Truth, and enjoying spiritual joy (Gandhi 1991, 296). His ashram was a basic school that trained people in different sciences of cooking and agriculture. By making education a *kamadhuk* (a mythical cow that will give whatever you wish for), Gandhi hoped to avoid fetishising it; but Phule and Ambedkar challenged him, emphasising education as absolutely vital for social and political reform.

By promulgating the slogan 'Educate, Organise, Agitate' in establishing his first organisation, the Bahishkrut Hitkarini Sabha (Society for the Welfare of the Excluded), in July 1924, Ambedkar underscored that education would be a primary factor in achieving Dalit emancipation. He thus made education the prerequisite for annihilating caste and for political awakening and power. The great leader himself became an ideal – a personification of what could be achieved by educated Dalits. Thus, in the Ambedkarite movement, education and social awakening were intertwined.

Contradicting Gandhi once again, Ambedkar reflected that once Dalits became 'well placed in the scale of social life they would become respectable and [this would change] the religious outlook of the orthodox towards them' (Ambedkar 1989, 382). But this was a difficult task, largely because Brahmans had a historical tradition of knowledge and learning. By the mid-nineteenth century they outnumbered all other groups in vernacular schools, government English schools and government employment in Bombay Presidency, as shown in the previous chapter.

Gandhi, by contrast, would not allow even an educated Dalit to seek higher education and employment. Although he changed his views dramatically on the right of Untouchables to acquire knowledge and learning, his view did not allow them to make use of their learning or choose their professions (Ambedkar 1991, 295). For Gandhi, caste had a ready-made means for spreading primary education. He said, 'each one of us has to earn our bread by following the ancestral calling [*svadharma*]' (Gandhi 1936). According to his belief in *varna vyavasthaa*, 'a Shudra would not make learning a way of living. Nor will a Kshatriya adopt service as a way or earning a living. The Untouchables must follow their hereditary professions' (Ambedkar 1991, 295, 276–277; Gandhi, quoted in Ambedkar 1979, 83).

Gandhi's Untouchable was a Harijan or even a Bhangi, an object of social reform. He was proud to call himself a scavenger in order to identify himself with them (*Young India*, 20 August 1925), because he spiritualised the act of cleaning the body and the toilet, as well as the street. Gandhi deployed the example of a scavenger to teach the highest Hindu to clean up his own refuse; in the process, however, he alienated the Dalits. Ambedkar bitterly criticised Gandhi's idealistic agenda of uplifting the Valmikis' (sweepers') broken pride by calling scavenging a 'noble' profession and transforming himself into an eternally skilled scavenger.

Fashioning modern Dalits

For Ambedkar, the modern Dalit self had to be carved out of an unequal, graded and often violent social structure. The Dalit self would thus have to emerge out of the darkness of pre-history and pre-modernity into the light of the modern, which consisted of equality, the rule of law, social justice and egalitarian citizenship. He continued:

> what Untouchables wanted was not *bhaakar* [bread], but *pratishthaa* [honour]. The want and poverty which have been their lot are nothing to them as compared to the insult and indignity which they have to bear as a result of the vicious social order. We are fighting for *ijjat* [honour and dignity].
> (Ambedkar 1991, 213)

Honour and human dignity were (and are) of immense significance to Dalits. Hence, Ambedkar argued that changing the social environment was important, and education was a tool to bring about this change. He epitomised the movement's visionary commitment to emancipatory education – to establishing their rights as *human beings and citizens of India*. Dalits were political citizen-subjects for Ambedkar.

Phule and Ambedkar diagnosed that democratising education among the lower castes would free their thought and allow them to analyse critically the religious–cultural–educational–social power hierarchy – that is, the Brahman Raj – and work towards dismantling it. Shudra-ati-Shudras could then actually transform power relations. Phule practised this ideology in 1855 when Muktabai Salve, a fourteen-year-old Dalit girl and his student, wrote a scathing critique of brahmanical hegemony. She studied with Phule for three years; her newly acquired literacy enabled her to describe in minute detail the sufferings of the Untouchables and to question the social hierarchy and power of the Brahmans. Indeed, children were not just 'imbibing' knowledge and information like sponges, contrary to the many pronouncements of pedagogy in primary schools. Rather, they were processing knowledge to develop understandings of their social and political milieu, however fragmentary these were.

In a similar vein, Ambedkar emphasised that enquiry and fearless reasoning would produce independent thinkers who would not await the transfer of knowledge from teachers to become mere databases of information.[21] Like Gramsci, Ambedkar asserted that the first stage in raising subaltern consciousness was schooling for all classes (Gramsci 1971, 30–31). In this agenda Dalit students would be agents and dissent against the pedagogical as well as against social structures to bring about their social and cultural emancipation. Phule and Ambedkar underscored methods of critical rationality, pragmatism and modern science.

The Gandhian modern shares with Ambedkar a concern for freedom of speech and enquiry, public health and civic awareness, yet it does not 'fulfill the condition of interiority that the discourse of rights both produces and guarantees for the citizen of the modern state' (Chakrabarty 2002, 62). Gandhi pathologised Shudra education while Ambedkar affirmed it. Gandhi argued that injunctions against Shudras studying Shastras or Vedas were justified; according to him a Shudra – a person without moral education, without sense and without knowledge – would completely misread the Shastras without prior preparation. He is correct that 'before anyone can understand such problems, he must have studied the elements of the subject, in order to prevent any distorted meaning' (Gandhi 1991, 79; 1925). Yet, in order to even misread the Shastras, we have to allow not only Shudras but also Dalits to access and read them. For them the right to reading *at all* came before the question of misreading any text. But the Brahmani social environment excluded Dalits from knowledge and punished their attempts to seek any sort of education.

In stark contrast, Phule and Ambedkar followed a more inclusive policy. They envisioned education as the practice of freedom or liberation for Dalits. Ambedkar argued:

due to the lack of education a [Dalit] remains *nirbuddha* [dull] and becomes another's slave. If one believes in the freedom of ideas, and that every person should have it, every person should develop the strength to protect their freedom and this cannot be done without education. This means every country should have freedom of the individual, only with this freedom the idea of protecting the nation can find its roots. And without education it can find no roots.

(Ambedkar 1927c)

Ambedkar emphasised that education was a weapon to protect Dalits' individual and collective freedom; he wanted students to be *shoor* (brave) and courageous, and to struggle consistently (*Janata*, 29 July 1950). His agenda closely parallels that of African-American movements in the early twentieth century as well as feminist pedagogies (Anderson and Kharem 2009; hooks 1989, 1994; Mohanty 1994).

The three leaders, Phule, Ambedkar and Gandhi, emphasised that informal education had at least as big an effect on people as did institutional formal education. Gandhi argued that a peasant's work may not change if he is bestowed with the knowledge of alphabets, since he does not need them in the field. Phule and Ambedkar both countered that any sort of education, especially reading and writing, will in fact enable the peasant to challenge his or her social discrimination and question the oppressor. Since education was intricately linked with the wider social and political context in which it was imparted, it certainly could be used for dissenting against hegemonic powers. Phule's and Ambedkar's affective and critical pedagogies, deeply embedded in the material and structural transformations in their lives, aimed to construct Dalit subjectivities. This was part of a wider struggle to change their material and social conditions.

Phule, Ambedkar and Gandhi struggled with the collisions and convergences between East and West to carve out a hybrid. Gandhi wrestled to preserve precious elements of an indigenous identity while investigating ways to accommodate the aggressive civilisation of the West. He attacked Western values of progress and civilisation, and was hence reluctant to offer this kind of education to the people (Gandhi 1991, 252). Ambedkar, however, was not an uncritical 'Westernist' or 'modernist'; indeed, he had a complicated relationship with modernity but at the same time could not use Indic tradition because of its hierarchical apparatus of caste and Brahman monopoly. He was attracted as well as repelled by tradition; he embraced Buddhism and underscored the roots of republicanism, rationalism and democracy in Indian intellectual tradition, thus building on the architecture of Western reason.

Gandhi rightly criticised the predominant system of education that was not for the millions but for a few as a false and rotten one (Gandhi 1991, 253). He further argued that literary education should be acquired through self-help. 'Those who possess it should take every opportunity to impart it to others and the latter should receive it from them', he concurred (Gandhi 1991, 297). The British government also shared Gandhi's doctrine of trusteeship and top-down approach. However, this Gandhian and British idealism failed to take into account upper castes' historical monopoly of education and Dalits' exclusion from it. How long were Dalits to stand at the doors of the citadels of knowledge and wait their turn?

Writing in the early 1870s, Phule attributed his rift with some Brahman reformers to their divergent ideas on the education of the lower castes. While these members thought that the lower castes should be provided with only the basic skills of writing and reading akin to their agenda for women's rudimentary education, Phule believed that 'they should be given thorough education, in order to get from it the power to distinguish between good and bad' (Keer and Malshe 1969, 141). In his address to the Education Commission on 19 October 1882, Phule outlined a more inclusive educational policy. He also pointed out the flaws in the colonial education policy which favoured high castes and commented on a number of themes, including the deplorable state of primary education in Bombay Presidency, the remodelling of the teaching machinery, course of instruction (for example, reading, writing, Modi and Balbodh, accounts, general history, general geography, grammar, lessons in elementary agriculture and on moral duties and sanitation), and the need of higher education for the masses. He also proposed 'special schools' for Mahar-Mangs, since they were shut out from all schools owing to caste prejudices. They were not allowed to sit alongside the higher-caste children (Phule 1882). The 'special schools' for Dalits that Phule envisioned were not a priority for the government or the upper castes. As noted in Chapter 1, for the upper castes this was a *double bind*: separate schools would protect their purity, but more schools also meant more taxes. Like Phule, Ambedkar was deeply troubled by the problems that compulsory education created. In his statement of 29 May 1928 concerning the state of education of the Depressed Classes in the Bombay Presidency (Ambedkar 1928), Ambedkar examined British educational policy's strategic neglect of Dalits, pointing out that the British propounded equality in theory, but inequality in practice. Although the ordinary schools entirely supported by the state were in theory open to all castes, in practice Dalits were denied admission to government schools – mass education was excluding the masses.

With their toil and taxes, Dalits funded education but were practically excluded from it. Like Phule, Ambedkar questioned the government's meagre expenditure on education, noting that 'while the amount spent on an individual's education was only 14 *annas*, the money recovered in the form of excise revenue was Rs.2.17' (Ambedkar 1982a, 39–40; 1927a). Phule and Ambedkar called upon the government to invest in free and compulsory education for lower castes – the strata of society with no inclination towards education. Ambedkar pointed out that education of the masses was a significant duty of the government (Ambedkar 1927c) and that the purpose of the Department of Education was to moralise and socialise the people (Ambedkar 1982a, 39; 1927c).

Ambedkar remained unconvinced by Gandhi's forceful argument that compulsory education would not be of use to everybody, for example, peasants. Ambedkar argued that it was not necessary to make education compulsory for upper castes, who had already benefited from education. Instead, compulsory education was necessary to strengthen a crippled community with few resources. He forcefully contended that:

> those who do not understand the importance of education and are *udaasin* [dispirited] about it need *saktiche kaayade* [compulsory education laws]. Compulsory primary education is the foundation of a nation's progress and not a question of the wishes of some people.
>
> (Ambedkar 1929)

Like Phule and other liberal reformers (for example, Gokhale and Sir Narayan-rao Chandavarkar), Ambedkar underscored the spread of primary education as the foundation for the advancement of the Indian nation and advocated for compulsory education laws to achieve this.

According to Gandhi, neither primary nor higher education, in practice, really enabled one to do one's *dharma* – to control one's mind, conscience and will. Gandhi's idealism and focus on spiritual power did not fit easily with Ambedkar's technologies of education and cultivation of intelligence and critical thinking for the Dalits. Intelligence, for Ambedkar, was necessary for *bhaakar* (bread), *shikshan* (education), *rajyasatta* (political power), and the human dignity and everyday existence of Dalits (*Janata*, 29 April 1933).

Further, Gandhi regarded the prominence of the English language as cultural imperialism. He rightly declared that 'to give millions the knowledge of English [was] to enslave them' (Gandhi 1991, 253). As it was, most Indians valued the knowledge of English over the vernacular and 'were enslaved by the English language' (ibid., 104); however, Gandhi bitterly criticised them and Macaulay's foundation of education. Gandhi was against the 'disease of civilisation' (254) and English education. But Gandhi was equally agonised, and rightly so, that '[elite] Indians had to discuss and spread Home Rule in a foreign tongue' (254). By contrast, Ambedkar was 'English education [as] like the milk of a tigress'. He argued:

> those who drink it will develop brilliance and new *sphurti* [stirring of the mind, enthusiasm]. Those who study English knowledge can study the history of European countries, and can also analyse the effects of uncontrolled domination and start thinking about independence.
>
> (*Mooknayak*, 28 February 1920)

For Ambedkar, however, the value of English-language education lay in the employment opportunities it would open up for labouring Dalit masses, the same way it had for the Brahmans. English would allow lower-caste representatives to deliberate on matters in legislatures, where all affairs were conducted in that language.

Many believed Gandhi's symbolic politics of donning a loincloth was firmly rooted in Indian culture and showed commitment to the poor. By contrast,

Ambedkar sought to fashion Dalits' self-confidence and dignity by adopting the unfamiliar style of an Englishman himself. Gandhi argued that Western civilisation was imbued with materialism and fought against what he saw as the self-destructive habits of the Indian middle classes, such as blindly mimicking English dress, diet and manners, and argued that they needed to limit their material needs. Gandhi's personal journey towards bodily decolonisation and appeal to reject delusory modernity failed, however, to grasp the Dalit dilemma. It is here that the equality of *difference* for Dalits is significant: by adopting English dress – the hat and three-piece suit of the coloniser, pertinent for recognition as a *saaheb* (high European officer)[22] – is to claim to be equal to the colonisers (internal and external) and to participate in the institutions of abstract equality such as citizenship, democracy and civil rights as well as for concrete gains: for example, gaining education and employment. Paradoxically, Dalits, including Ambedkar, suffered despite dressing like *saahebs*. Nonetheless, this *saaheb*-ness is fundamental to Dalits' everyday human dignity, self-construction and human rights because it supplements abstract equality and refuses to be defined by its terms. With this intelligent move it also renews European thought and dress by in turn gifting it 'what that thought by itself finds difficult, even perhaps impossible to think'.[23] The fashion of foreign cloth and dress, though expensive, starkly contrasts with Gandhian *khadi*, which was supposed to be 'cheap' (though in reality it was more expensive than mill-cloth), austere and simple, symbolic of indigeneity and purity. While Gandhi wanted to attack the middle-class values of upper-caste Indians, these imports were important to Dalits. They did not need to restrict their hunger by fasting as the middle classes did; their starving stomachs needed nutritious food.

Similar to many upper-caste reformers who upheld Indian spirituality and tradition, the Gandhian decolonising agenda aimed to drive out Western civilisation, and emphasised the cleansing of body and mind, of controlling one's mind akin to a *yogi purush* – basically an 'awakening of the natives'. Contradicting this ideological stance, Ambedkar, a modernist, believed in the grammar of rights. Instead of mortification, he called for the cultivation of the mind in order to resurrect the new modern Dalit personhood. Gandhi, like Nehru, effected a division between liberal education, which entailed knowing for its own sake, and practical training for mechanical occupations. Upper-caste, elite reformers' bourgeois ideas glossed over the monetary gains education would bring, since they already enjoyed them, and emphasised that 'education will take [one] closer to [one's] Maker' (Gandhi 1991, 312).

Would Dalits' social and material context allow them this life of leisure and luxury? Ambedkar, like Dewey, sought to eliminate educational distinctions such as the dualism between labour and leisure (as in liberal education), and constructed a combined course of intellectual and practical studies. He believed this would resolve the problems of education in a democratic society (Dewey 1916, 185). In order to ensure quicker employment opportunities, Ambedkar stressed the need for technical education – hands-on training – so that Dalits could seek different kinds of employment. Gandhi too celebrated traditional manual labour and, to an extent, he and Ambedkar seemed to agree on the importance of such 'education of the hand' (*Young India*, 12 March 1925). By arguing that 'expansion of the mind will come from hard experience, not necessarily in the college or the schoolroom' (*Young India*, 24 June 1926), Gandhi worked to improve the dignity of labour. But with this idea, again, he was making a case to upper castes and the middle classes for the dignity of physical labour.

Dalits had, on the other hand, had enough of experience of the hand and hard physical labour; what they wanted instead was the education of the mind. Contradicting Gandhi's idiosyncratic mixture of conservatism and change, Ambedkar challenged Dalits to free their minds and become scholars, experts, and eventually effective leaders. In order to undertake this arduous task, he wanted Dalits to cultivate self-discipline and regular habits of study. This was not the Gandhian self-discipline of mortifying oneself to get closer to the Maker, but one of cultivating the intellect. Ambedkar constantly entered into dialogue with Dalit students and cited examples from his everyday life to underscore the importance of hard work. Certainly he understood that not all Dalits would take to research; however, he believed it was necessary to develop a taste for enquiry in all people. To this end he established libraries, social centres, learning centres, study circles, laboratories, debating societies and magazines in which Dalits could engage with and publish on scholarly, social and political debates. He also suggested ideas for pooling college and university resources to minimise waste and facilitate research.[24]

Ambedkar and Gandhi agreed that cleanliness was necessary for Dalits to be easily accepted by the higher castes. Ambedkar constantly urged Dalits to wear clean clothes and abandon their caste markers, like heavy jewellery. In a similar yet stricter manner, the Gandhian paradigm of health and hygiene sought to first develop a culture of clean habits and 'correct' word pronunciations for Dalits, who had no home culture in education. Gandhi argued that there should be:

> a preliminary school for them in teaching good manners, speech, conduct. A Harijan child sits, dresses any way, his eyes, ears, teeth, nail, nose, hair are often full of dirt. For the first three months of school they should be taught cleanliness. On the first day bodies should be minutely examined and thoroughly cleaned. [Teachers] should use no books for the entire first year. One should talk to them about things they are familiar with – correcting pronunciation and grammar. Teach new words to them.
>
> (Gandhi 1970, 85)

Gandhi wanted the schools and teachers to impart discourses on the proper ideals of life, cleanliness and morality in such a way that Dalits could come into immediate contact with a better and cleaner way of life and effect a change in their social environment (Gandhi 1986, 178). A clean body was a prerequisite for service to the nation and citizenship. Once again, however, in the Gandhian model of education, disempowered Dalits would depend on their teachers and imitate the culture of upper castes. Dalits, like *adivasis*, were similar to younger brothers to upper-caste nationalists and had to be helped out of their Dalitness or primitiveness. This was a central theme in Gandhian and nationalist thought and social work; the Harijan Sevak Sangh was modelled along similar lines.

Thus, Gandhi aimed at bringing about a gradual change of heart in upper-caste Hindus while making Dalits dependent on Hindus. Ambedkar's combative agenda, on the other hand, was to fashion Dalits as critical agents to create a crisis for the Hindu. 'This crisis will compel [the Hindu] to think, and once he begins to think he will be more ready to change than he is otherwise likely to be', he asserted (*Bombay Chronicle*, 26 November 1932). Ambedkar thus challenged Gandhian diplomatic paternalism; he wanted Dalits to force the Hindus to alter their ways.

Phule, Ambedkar and Gandhi all underlined morality in education. Ambedkar's socio-political agenda for education included creating capacities for rational and critical thinking, developing leadership abilities, inculcating self-respect and a culture of self-help, and devising a *maanavi* (humanitarian) culture and ideology for Dalits. Socially, his goal was to trigger a process of fostering, cultivating and nurturing 'immature' Dalits and shaping their dispositions (Dewey 1916, 11). Politically, he aimed to build them as leaders of the community. By recreating Dalit beliefs, ideals, hopes, happiness and practices, in a process which paralleled the concept of reconstruction that Dewey introduced to the US working class, Ambedkar aimed to refashion them (ibid., 5). He believed this would provide Dalits with a continuity of social life. Education for him, then, was a process of 'continual reorganising, reconstructing, and transforming' (38) of Dalits' social environment and mental faculties. To accomplish this restructuring and transformation, Phule and Ambedkar suggested some internal and external technologies, to be discussed in the next section.

Shikshan, svaabhimaan, svaavalamban: building a robust Dalit community

In order to achieve their goals of obtaining education in the short term and fashioning Dalits as citizens and leaders in the long term, Dalits had to wage two significant battles: external and internal. By external (or visible) battle, I mean fighting Brahmans and the British government to obtain access to education and constantly agitating for constitutional remedies. By internal battle, I refer to psycho-social struggles: the invisible technologies that addressed the difficult task of developing a 'taste for education' among those excluded from knowledge. For example, many among the lower classes believed education was meant only for Brahmans. The popular belief was that education is nobody's concern except the Brahmans' (Ambedkar 1928); to dismantle it, a critical refashioning of the Dalit self was necessary.

The inner struggle

Although ideologically he argued that education would bring about freedom, Phule agreed that, in practice, special inducements in the form of scholarships and half-yearly or annual prizes could encourage the masses to willingly send children to school and create in them a taste for learning (Phule 1991b, 125). Many poor Dalits believed education would enfeeble their children, who would be withdrawn from physical labour and spend most of their time engaged in intellectual exercises. Phule and his colleagues in the Society for Increasing Education among Mahars, Mangs, and Others even blamed the idleness of Mahars and Mangs for their condition (*Dnyanodaya*, 15 July 1855, quoted in O'Hanlon 1985, 119).

Ambedkar argued with Gandhi that the solution to untouchability lay not in self-refinement but in the self-respect that Untouchables would build for themselves. Hence, dignity (i.e. to become *svaavalambi*, self-reliant, and inculcate svaabhimaan, self-respect) was most important to Dalits (*Bahishkrut Bharat*, 3 May 1929). Dalits had to fight poverty as well as for the right to even attend school. Ambedkar contested that:

> To effectively fight the Brahman Raj, Dalits need to first accumulate *saamarthya* [power or strength], both material and mental, because many of them seem to have lost their confidence, enthusiasm, dignity, and aspirations and have become meek and submissive and lack vigour. Hence, they have to build their strength and competence.
>
> (*Janata*, 20 June 1936)

Ambedkar also argued that the population had not realised the vital necessity of education within the population. The popular belief among Dalits was that Brahmans possessed the *veda-puranas* and therefore had an exclusive right to education. In order to challenge this false conviction, Ambedkar exerted them to cast aside their inferiority complex:

> Coming as I do from the lowest order of Hindu society, I know the value of education. The problem of raising the lower order is deemed to be economic. This is a great mistake. The problem of raising the lower order in India is not to feed them, to clothe them, and make them serve the higher order, as is the ancient ideal of this country. The problem of the lower order is to remove from them that *nuangand* [inferiority complex] which has stunted their growth and made them slaves to others, to create in them the *jaaniv* [understanding] of the significance of their lives for themselves and for the country, of which they have been cruelly robbed by the existing social order. Nothing can achieve this except the spread of higher education. *Aamchya sarva saamaajik dukhnyanvar uccha shikshan hech aushadh* [This is the solution to our social troubles].
>
> (*Janata*, 15 and 22 September 1951)[25]

Education was a means of overcoming an inferior status and state of mind, of wresting power from the powerful. Ambedkar uttered this eloquent expression of his vision for education towards the emancipation of Dalits during the foundation-laying ceremony of the Milind Mahavidyalaya (College) in Aurangabad in 1946. *Vidya* (knowledge), *pradnya* (understanding and insight), *karunaa* (compassion/empathy), *sheel* (virtues), *maitri* (friendship) and *samataa* (equality) were the six fundamental elements upon which students were to build their character (*Janata*, 17 December 1955).[26] They underscored Ambedkar's hopes for democratic education.

Ambedkar also deployed the techniques of formal and informal education through folk performers, newspapers, lectures, debates and speeches to the community. He constantly discussed his ideas with Dalits and invited them to participate as subjects – he wanted them to reflect, act on and carry out their revolution. For example, during his presidential address at the eleventh Untouchable Conference held in Pune in 1938, Ambedkar advised youth that '*khadtar tapascharya heech yashaachi gurukilli* (continuous and consistent hard work is the key to success)' (*Janata*, 17 September 1938). Almost half a century before Foucault's theoretical insights, Ambedkar and Gramsci (Gramsci 1971, 37, 41–43)[27] underscored that some 'special training' and 'discipline' were necessary for the disadvantaged.

Like Dewey, Ambedkar saw formal school as a site for not only training students, but also transmitting good resources, habits and self-discipline. He wanted Dalits to develop active habits that involve thought, invention and initiative in applying capacities to new aims (Dewey 1916, 40). He recounted his own rigorous working schedule as a student:

> Seeking knowledge is my *vyasan* [determined addiction]. We – my parents and siblings – lived in a ten-by-ten-foot room in Mumbai's development department chawls, and I studied with the help of a kerosene lamp. I finished my Ph.D., which normally takes eight years, in only three years' time because I studied for twenty-one hours a day. Even today, when I am forty years old, I work for eighteen hours sitting in my chair. But youth these days, if they sit in a chair for half an hour, they have to sniff snuff or smoke a cigarette or stretch. But all these actions do not provide any enthusiasm. I do not need all this in this old age either.
>
> (*Janata*, 17 September 1938)

Ambedkar thus underscored the durable inculcation of some psycho-physical habits. Further, he did not want Dalits to merely seek degrees and attain academic benchmarks, but also to critically develop their mental faculties through a formally disciplined regimen.

Ambedkar argued that Dalit students also needed to develop their self-confidence, because there was no *daivi shakti* (divine energy) in store for them (if they indeed believed there was). Rather, they were to believe in themselves and not in *daivi shakti* and build *aatma vishvaas* (self-confidence) so that they were not afraid to defeat others. He advised students not to feel ashamed that they were born to illiterate parents, but to affirm that *mee je kareen tey hoil* (what I will do will happen) and study hard to be the best. He continued:

You don't need just a BA. You have to compete with the forward castes and show your brilliance, in order to make *cheej* [a feat] of your education. These forward castes are in power, they have oppressed your ancestors and they will oppress you too. Hence, you should not only seek education, but *jhatun abhyas karaa* [study strenuously]. Continue your education and all our students have to be *saras* [excellent].

(*Janata*, 17 September 1938)

Ambedkar's stance here aligns with that of Gandhi, who saw advanced degrees as ornamental. Ambedkar did not want degrees without freedom: 'Dalit students must not only work harder, but also to outshine the upper-castes. Only if they exceeded the upper-castes *tyanchya barobariche ganale jau* [could they be on par with them]' (*Janata*, 17 September 1938). Thus, I slightly disagree with Zelliot that Ambedkar did not merely want Dalits to 'rise to the level of upper-castes' (Zelliot 1992, 62, 158); he wanted them to certainly compete with and, indeed, excel them.

Both Gandhi and Ambedkar agreed that building *sheel*, moral virtues, from the primary levels of education would provide a strong foundation for building a society and a nation. The most important education was the training of character. At the same time, for Ambedkar, scholarship played a more central role. Along with these internal battles, Dalits also had to fight many external battles to seek education.

External battles and constitutional remedies for Dalits' education

Dalit parents were doubly burdened if their children attended school. They not only lost their income from the children's labour, but had to bear the additional cost of their education. In his 1882 report on the progress made by Mahar and Mang children, Moro Vitthal, Member and Secretary of 'The Society for Promoting the Education of Mahars Mangs', pointed out that their short period of attendance during the rainy and the cold seasons was very precarious, since they did not have any means of protecting themselves against the inclement weather (Vitthal 1969, 636). In addition, Mahar and Mang children prepared their lessons at school during school hours because they had, for the most part, no friends willing or competent to encourage or compel them to learn their tasks at home (ibid., 637). Low-caste children were also not permitted to drink at public cisterns and wells, so Phule paid for drinking water as well as clothes and books for the students (Keer 1964, 29).

Teachers and transformation

This was a double jeopardy: the schools became a political, social and cultural process between touchables and Untouchables as well as between the colonised and colonisers. Phule, Ambedkar and Gandhi understood Dalits' predicament and all called for a thorough remodelling of the teaching apparatus. Phule analysed how the colonial state's policy and dominant Brahmani pedagogical practices were intrinsically interlinked. The teachers employed in the primary schools were almost all Brahmans; very few were trained in the Normal Training College. These untrained men were unfit for teaching professions because they exercised their Brahmani powers and mostly engaged the class at their will and pleasure. Most of the teachers who worked in these schools were unqualified (Phule 1991b, 143; Ambedkar 1927c).

All three leaders commented on teachers' ability to teach and agreed that much of their teaching was very dull. Gandhi too concurred that teachers were responsible for stimulating a student's reasoning faculty (*Young India*, 24 June 1926). Due to inefficient teachers, he argued, students learned chemistry without ever touching a metal (Gandhi 1986, 313). Phule, Ambedkar and Gandhi were against such teaching that dampened critical thinking; they wanted teachers to be trained to *teach*.

Phule and Ambedkar were also cognisant of upper-caste teachers' discrimination against Shudra-Dalit pupils in schools. Hence, in his preface to *Gulamgiri* (Slavery), written in 1873, Phule raised the slogan, 'Let there be schools for the Shudras in every village, but away with all Brahman school-masters' (Phule 1991b, 121). Phule proposed that teachers should be trained for primary schools and called for plurality in their appointment. Social discrimination had penetrated the classrooms, so he wanted teachers from the cultivating classes, who would be able to mix with students and understand their wants and wishes, unlike the aloof Brahman teachers (Phule 1882, 123).

Ambedkar also challenged the upper-caste agenda of traditional education. He underlined that the flow of education was *tumbalaa* (blocked) due to caste and the centralisation of education. He argued that the brahmanical education system should be decentralised and encouraged efforts to develop a more democratic and empowering approach that looked to teachers as leaders in transforming educational practice. He emphasised a teacher's responsibility:

> Teachers were in fact *saarathi* [guides and leaders] who were to mould individuals and society. School is not like a Hindu restaurant where a Brahman cook can manage everything. Even if everybody can enjoy food made by Brahmans, the education delivered by Brahmans may not work in contemporary times.
>
> (Ambedkar 1927b)

Since there was an intricate relationship between education and the social good, schools and teachers should aim to make children's minds *susaunskrut* (cultured) and guide them towards *samaaj hita* (social beneficence). Teachers were indeed 'cultural workers' and 'transformative intellectuals' who supported the oppressed and remained committed to advancing progressive projects through the educative process.[28] Ambedkar also wanted to break the traditional relationship between knowledge dissemination and Brahmans. By underscoring that teaching was immensely suitable for Dalits, like Phule, he emphasised plurality in the teaching occupation.

Remodelling the administration of formal education

The main agenda for Phule and Ambedkar was to empower Shudra-Ati-Shudras to capture positions of authority in all administrative departments, including education. Ambedkar argued for plurality in the representation of different castes on the Bombay University Senate. He also requested adequate Dalit representation on everything from local school boards to university councils and suggested remedies to cure the ailing Bombay University administration (Ambedkar 1982a, 305). In 1926 he provided a broader plan for the development of university education, including the founding of ten universities. During the debates regarding the Bombay University Act Amendment Bill I, presented on 27 July 1927, which proposed changes to the structure of the university, Ambedkar suggested that in order to succeed in promoting research and higher education, the university had to transform its primary constitution as an examining body (Ambedkar 1982a, 45, 50, 61). He argued that its fundamental function should be to bring the highest education to the doors of the needy and the poor, not merely to deal with problems of examinations and granting degrees (Ambedkar 1982a, 61).

Ambedkar was a great scholar, and he wanted to develop a similar taste for knowledge and learning not only in Dalit students but also in lecturers employed at both the college and university levels. He questioned the distinction between undergraduate and postgraduate teaching and suggested that faculty engaged in teaching particular subjects should be pooled so that students in different colleges could attend their classes as a special college. In this manner lecturers would be relieved and could pursue other special work and focused research, which would lead to robust postgraduate departments (Ambedkar 1982a, 47). Ambedkar opposed the separation of teaching and research, and wanted them to work in tandem: 'Where research is divorced from teaching, research must suffer' (Ambedkar 1982a, 298).

In his reaction to the 1927 Report on Education in Bombay Presidency, Ambedkar reiterated that education was the most *amogh* (productive) medicine for the social disabilities of Untouchables. Hence he supported concessions and special facilities for the *sarvavanchit* (most neglected) Untouchables, to grant them a new life and to make them knowledgeable and *vichaarpravrutta* (thoughtful):

> The Brahmans have excelled and the Muslims have progressed, but Untouchables are backward because they did not have any facilities. If two persons are strong, then giving *malidaa* [a cake of milk and sugar] to one and *bhusaa* [chaff or husk] to the other and starving him seems very unfair. But if one is sick and the other is healthy then giving husks to the healthy and good food to the sick is very appropriate.
>
> (Ambedkar 1927c)

Ambedkar thus argued that to bring the unequal onto the same platform, Dalits must be provided with special concessions and facilities as well as government support. Bringing Dalits up to par with upper castes would help eliminate the conflict between the two, ultimately ending caste struggle altogether.

Moreover, unlike Gandhi (1991, 252–53), Phule and Ambedkar advocated higher education for Dalits. For Phule, 'higher education [should] be arranged so as to be within easy reach of all, and the books of the subjects for matriculation should be published in the Government Gazette' (Phule 1991b, 125). Ambedkar argued that Dalits could not forgo their right and opportunity to seek higher education to the fullest extent (Ambedkar 1982a, 62).

Gandhi's Harijan Sevak Sangh supported the education of Dalits, granting scholarships to high school students and establishing hostels for them. However, a greater part of the Sangh's educational activities involved maintaining separate schools for primary-aged children in places where there were no common schools or where common schools were closed to them (Ambedkar 1989, 366). However, when G.M. Thaware (1902–52) approached him with the idea of a separate university for Dalits, Gandhi did not encourage it (Kshirsagar 1994, 351). This was perhaps because Gandhi wanted Dalits to assimilate into the wider community, as well as the fact that he did not value university education for everybody.

The question of separate or common schools

With regard to 'separate' or 'common' schools, the three leaders differed from each other. Both Phule and Gandhi insisted on separate schools for Dalits. Although Dalits gained some access to schools, their entry was thwarted by novel technologies of segregated education and corporal punishment inside the schoolhouse. To avoid caste discrimination at the hands of Brahman teachers, classmates and school inspectors, Phule advocated separate schools specifically for Mahar and Mang children (Phule 1991b, 92). The government established some such schools, but only in large towns. In the whole of Poona, for a population exceeding 5,000 children, there was only one school which was attended by fewer than thirty boys. Gandhi advocated separate schools for his own reasons: if Hindus were reluctant to accept Dalit students in the schoolhouse, he did not want to force them. He would wait until the Hindu cleansed his heart and understood the Dalits' oppression.

Ambedkar, on the other hand, like Gramsci, wanted common schools, which he believed would open up social intercourse with upper castes and undercut hierarchy (Ambedkar 1979b; Gramsci 1971, 31). Common schools would develop self-respect in Dalits. He argued that Hindus were divided among themselves and needed *social osmosis*. Only later on, in the 1940s, did he begin to emphasise that 'pride and dignity would be inculcated in a student in an institution which had been established by one of their own, and in which values were not dominated by those at the apex of the caste hierarchy' (Zelliot n.d., 14). Common schools, he argued, would assist in providing a 'free and equitable intercourse, sharing interests and fostering intellectual stimulation' (Dewey 1916, 62). Dalits were already hampered by the social isolation imposed upon them by the caste system:

Due to caste there is no common plane on which the privileged and the subject classes can meet. There is no endosmosis, no give and take of life's hopes and experiences. This separation has caused the educated to become slaves and created the psychological complex which follows from a slave mentality. But those affecting the privileged class, though less material and less perceptible, are equally real. The isolation and exclusiveness following upon the class structure creates in the privileged classes the anti-social spirit of a gang.

(Ambedkar 1991, 285)

Thus, for Ambedkar, education was a means to help Dalits balance their lives as well as to build a democratic India. He was interested in using education as a means to uplift Dalit individuals as well as the community and to gain political power to resist Brahmanism.

In addition to the Bahishkrut Hitkarini Sabha (Society for the Welfare of the Excluded), Ambedkar encouraged an important student organisation known as the Bahishkrut Vidyarthi Sammelan (Excluded Students' Organisation). It published a Marathi monthly, *Vidya Vilas* [Expanding Knowledge], to which students contributed articles (*Bombay Chronicle*, 29 April 1926). Ambedkar also established the Depressed Classes Institute in 1925 to give this programme a sound basis. His Independent Labour Party also focused on free and compulsory education, including adult and technical education, and aimed to reorganise higher education (*Times of India*, 15 August 1936). The work was consolidated

Figure 2.1 The laying of the foundation stone of the P.E. Society's College at Aurangabad. President Rajendra Prasad with Dr B.R. Ambedkar, Chairman of the P.E. Society (courtesy of Siddhaartha College Library).

in later decades by other educational societies, such as the People's Education Society (PES), founded in 1945. The PES established Siddhartha College in Mumbai to promote higher education among the poorer and weaker sections of society. The foundation of the PES gave a great impetus to the admission of girls to schools and colleges. The society had branches around Maharashtra, in Pune, Mahad, Nanded, Pandharpur and Bangalore, with good schools, colleges, diploma institutes, research centres, libraries and hostels to encourage the younger generation to pursue education.[29] Following Ambedkar, the PES emphasised attention to the physical fitness and intellectual growth of students. Today the PES boasts that it has carried higher education to the doors of the poor and downtrodden irrespective of caste (Talwatkar 2000).

Limitations of an educated generation

All of these efforts, over the course of a century, constituted and were constitutive of a new Dalit personhood. Yet Dalit radicals' rhetoric and efforts at education also had some limitations. On 20 July 1952, Ambedkar said bitterly that educated Dalit youth had failed him, and that he was scared of them, asking, 'Are the educated helping with the progress of the community?' (*Janata*, 26 July 1952). He complained that educated Dalits had become selfish after availing themselves of educational and employment opportunities, and had forgotten about the efforts of others that had made their education possible (*Janata*, 26 July 1952). He directed administrators to streamline the admission process and to make the educated responsible to their community. During his speech at the Bombay Presidency Depressed Classes Youth Conference, held on 12 February 1938, he declared:

> education is like a sword, and being a double-edged weapon it is dangerous to wield.... An educated person without *sheel* [moral character] and *saujanya* [humility] is more dangerous than a beast. If education was detrimental to the welfare of the poor, the educated person was a curse to society. Character is thus more important than education.
>
> (*Janata*, 26 February 1938)

Without character, then, education had no value (*Janata*, 13 June 1953). Ambedkar argued that education alone would not help to develop *yogyata* [aptitude]: 'Not every educated person is of use to society, because the educated also develop bad qualities' (*Dnyanprakash*, 1 January 1930). He continued:

> If the educated terrorise the ignorant peasants, such education should be abandoned. The educated seem to be scared to their *haadimaasi* [bones and flesh]. They do not even come forward to assert their rights. Hence they could not engage in efforts to open public wells, demonstrate on public highways and roads, and so on.... They should *kambar kasali paahije*

[make good efforts and continuously strive] to establish small social armies and centres and forcefully fight to establish their *nisargasiddha* [natural] rights.

(*Janata*, 26 February 1938)

Ambedkar seemed to be disillusioned by the inactivity of the educated and was concerned about the progress of the community. He wanted the caravan to continue its journey, but too few were prepared to make the degree of sacrifice he demanded from them. Here his failure was akin to Gandhi's; both men were cognisant of this unwillingness of the educated elites to make sacrifices. At the same time educated Dalits still did not find good employment and were discriminated against in the process. They were disappointed in this, and prevalent social prejudices dampened their spirits. Ambedkar also drew attention to the fact that despite the scholarships and boarding facilities, many Dalit students were failing in their studies. Hence, he wanted them to study harder and pass their grades (*Janata*, 15 December 1945). Certainly, his advice had the desired effect and many Dalits obtained education at different levels.

Conclusion

This chapter has juxtaposed Phule's and Ambedkar's political practices of vernacularising the universal modern, affective pedagogies and technologies of education as they challenged Gandhian reformist ideological viewpoints in the early and mid-twentieth century. In other words, it has dealt with competing models of Dalit emancipation and Dalits' social, material and ideological battles as they contended with idealist conceptions of education. In the process, I focused on the contested Dalit self and subjectivities as imagined by Phule, Ambedkar and Gandhi. While for Gandhi the Dalit self was vulnerable and dependent on the upper-caste Hindu, for Ambedkar, in stark contrast, the Dalit modern self was to emerge out of the queer nature of unequal society into a modernity that encompassed the rule of law, justice, egalitarian citizenship and democracy. In the process, formal education would play a fundamental role.

I articulated the overlapping two aims and two stages of Dalit education: short and long term, internal and external. The fight for education meant not only entering schools, but a socio-political movement for Dalits' liberation as well as their political power to fight internal and external colonialism. Thus politics was intricately connected with the Dalit education question. As such, the right to education involved overlapping and multiple aims: it was crucial for reinscribing Dalits as modern citizens and historical subjects, as well as agents, and to discipline and refashion the Dalit self. The remaking of the social and the reinvention of the Dalit self were dialectically synchronous, mutually informing and constitutive processes.

These complex and multiple processes, Phule and Ambedkar argued, would bring the modern, material, mental and moral benefits of employment as well as intellectual strength and capabilities to Dalits. Inscribing habits and discipline would help Dalits change their social environment and work towards a better future both individually and collectively. Ambedkar's puritanical programme and political practices called for Dalits to achieve education and economic improvement through hard work, prudence and keeping away from idle amusements. The battle for education was rooted in methods of modernity, and involved a broader social, psychological, economic and political struggle. As such, it was fundamental to achieving not only *bhaakar* (bread) but also *samaan hakka* (equal rights), *maanavi hakka* (human rights), *svaabhimaan* (self-respect), *vyaktivikaas* (individuated development or even self-improvement), *saamarthya* (competency), *svaavalamban* (self-reliance), *pratishthaa* (honour), *nyaya* (justice), *samataa* (equality) to strive diligently for *sudhaaranaa* (improvement) and to seek modern egalitarian citizenship (*naagarikatva*).[30] As a result, Dalits would deploy internal and external resources to achieve modern human dignity and finally *raajkiyasattaa* (political power).

Gandhi was an exemplary leader who brought the Untouchable question to the forefront. Yet his idealism and symbolic politics could not successfully deal with the complex processes of Dalit education. The constant dialectics between Dalit and non-Dalit leaders' continued engagement with the educational discourse shaped Dalits' political and social history in a particular way and was linked to their emotions and commitment. Moreover, the consistency of Dalits' ideas and efforts provided the dynamism of their historical development. Further, their educational discourse also brought gender and the reform of women into its ambit.

Yet, Dalit radicals' staunch optimism and liberation narrative did have some limitations. Their promises often failed to materialise in practice. Ambedkar's rhetoric of education, set in relation to Dalit social and political struggle, allows us to examine the imaginative possibilities he offered Dalits. Their educational programme constituted a politics that provided them with a means to grasp their situation and change it. Ambedkar began to tackle the question of power relations in the classroom by starting the PES, opening schools, hostels and libraries, and providing funds, floating scholarships and books; yet he did not actually envision schools as an arena where gender inequality could be broken. Nonetheless, the very act of entering the citadels of knowledge that had excluded them in the past was empowering to Dalits. Despite multiple difficulties, the complex processes of education and participation in public life helped many Dalit women to envision their selves and refashion their personhood. The next chapter analyses the deep connections between educational discourse and the reform of women.

Notes

1 See 'The Freaky Method of Experiment and Collage' in Deleuze and Guattari (1987), and Giroux and McLaren (1994, 18).
2 I am drawing on Michel Foucault's concept of 'technologies of the self'. See Foucault (1988, 18).
3 Rosalind O'Hanlon and Gail Omvedt have thoroughly investigated and recorded Phule's Satyashodhak movement, inspired by natural philosophy, and his efforts to

set up schools; however, we have yet to learn about Ambedkar's work and ideas of education. Jaffrelot's biography of Ambedkar provides an excellent insight into the leader's ideals and activism; however, it fails to capture the essence of the underlying philosophy and actions of Ambedkar in the realm of education.

4 I thank Eleanor Zelliot for sharing her unpublished paper 'Dalit Initiatives in Education' with me.

5 Padma Velaskar (1998) has analysed the role of education in the social changes among Buddhists in Maharashtra and summarised Ambedkar's ideology of education. An upper-level bureaucrat and UPSC member, K.S. Chalam, has diligently recorded Ambedkar's efforts in education (Chalam 2008). What is missing in this work, however, is a conceptual reading of his efforts and ideologies. Recently, Sharmila Rege has offered a corrective; see Rege (2010, 88–98).

6 I am borrowing this concept from Giroux and McLaren (1994, 18).

7 I also want to underscore that Dewey developed his ideas in Chicago and in conversations with women ideologues like Jane Addams. Thanks to Hilda Smith for this point.

8 Gramsci believed that children should first acquire and learn the basic tools of free intellectual thought, and to understand the cultural assumptions and systems necessary to express ideas in society. Learning spelling, reading, arithmetic, basic history, and some common morals and ethics would equip each child with the fundamentals of 'intellectual inquiry'.

9 According to Gramsci there is a dynamic tension between self-discipline and critical understanding. For Gramsci, education was 'a prerequisite for anyone in the society, is a right for all its members, and does not truly occur unless the pupil is led to his own, free discovery of knowledge and sometimes through coercion acquired the psycho-physical habits' (Gramsci 1971, 37, 41–43).

10 In describing how a school system should function, Gramsci details how the age of first attendance should be set and the various ages at which students should embark on the different phases of their education.

11 For an excellent reading of Fanon's decolonisation as learning, see Mostern (1994, 253–271).

12 I am attempting here a conversation between Phule, Ambedkar and Fanon. I am reading Phule and Ambedkar's pedagogical aims along with Fanon's revolutionary narrative of decolonising Africa to construct a Dalit narrative of pedagogical and theoretical practice. See his *Wretched of the Earth* (1963) and *Studies in a Dying Colonialism* (1965).

13 Gore (1998) engages with a similar argument.

14 I have benefited here from reading Fanon's views on decolonisation as the veritable creation of new men (1963, 36) and applying them to education and learning, but I am also gendering Fanon's articulations.

15 Here I have benefited from reading Dewey. Of course, Dewey does not deal with Dalits or Ambedkar, but he addresses how individuals coming from different backgrounds may respond differently to similar situations. See Dewey (1916, 232).

16 A Marwari-Brahman (Bania-Brahman) alliance who harassed the lower castes. See Phule (1969, 149).

17 For a brilliant study of this context of Phule's ideological framework and his distinctive radicalism in conversation with Protestant missionary polemic, European influence, Enlightenment ideas and religious radicals, see O'Hanlon (1985, esp. ch. 3). Phule was receiving new ideas from heterogeneous institutions; the family, schools, local communities, anti-British Brahman peers, debates and discussions, individual British administrators, and the new vernacular press were all significant agents of change.

18 Once again, Dewey did not deal with Dalits; however, his views on the social continuity of life are helpful in understanding the broken lives of Dalits. See Dewey (1916, 5).

19 Ambedkar was deeply cognisant of caste differences and rivalries among Dalits; he consistently exhorted them to think beyond their respective *jatis* and to work towards their common interests. He warned the Mahars and Mangs that a false sense of pride should not affect their relations (*Janata*, 13 June 1936). He also challenged those Mangs and Chambhars who called him a 'Mahar leader' and mentioned that his efforts for schools and social activism benefited every Dalit *jati*, not just Mahars. He also adopted a Mang boy.

20 I have benefited from Joan Scott's (1992, 34) meditation on 'experience'. According to her, 'subjectivities are produced in complex ways and ... subjects are constituted discursively'. This essay appears in many versions.

21 There is a resonance here with Dewey. See Dewey (1916, 39). See also the insightful article by Queen (2000).

22 Also note the *saaheb* suffix in Babasaaheb Ambedkar: the way the community refers to him proudly and affectionately.

23 I have benefited here from reading Ajay Skaria's distinctive way of questioning European thought. See Skaria (2009, 59).

24 See Ambedkar's efforts to remodel the structure of the Bombay University (Ambedkar 1982a, 45–50, 61, 298).

25 Ambedkar expressed his thoughts on the inauguration of the PES in Aurangabad. Also quoted in Talwatkar (2000).

26 Ambedkar underlined these principles during a speech at Milind College.

27 Foucaultian technologies require the development of habits and perceptual categories that can be inscribed in the body. See Foucault (1977, 1980).

28 See Gramsci (1971) who refers to teachers as 'cultural workers' actively involved in a cultural struggle of the oppressed. Also see Giroux (1988), Apple (1988), and others' work on the teacher as a transformative intellectual. See Carlson and Apple (1998, 26).

29 People's Education Society (2005, 13). This volume is evidence of the multi-faceted People's Education Society and its many activities.

30 Editorials and articles in newspapers like *Bahishkrut Bharat* (Outcast India), *Mooknayak* (Leader of the Voiceless) and *Janata* (People) amply reveal Dalits' idioms and agendas.

References

Ambedkar, B.R. 1927a. On grants for education, 12 March. *BLC Debates*, Vol. 19. In *Dr. Babasaheb Ambedkar: Writings and Speeches*, Vol. 4, ed. Vasant Moon. Bombay: Department of Education, Government of Maharashtra, 1982.

——. 1927b. Nyaya tari dya (At least give justice). *Bahishkrut Bharat*, 3 June.

——. 1927c. Aap ghari bata, baap gharihi bata (Disprivilege and injustice in one's private home as well as in the home of the paternal figure [the British colonial government]). *Bahishkrut Bharat*, 15 July.

——. 1927d. *Bahishkrut Bharat*, 29 July.

——. 1928. Evidence before the Indian Statutory Commission, 23 October. In Ambedkar, *Dr. Babasaheb Ambedkar: Writings and Speeches*, Vol. 2, ed. Vasant Moon. Bombay: Department of Education, Government of Maharashtra, 1982.

——. 1928. Motion submitted to the Legislative Council, Bombay, on behalf of the Bahiskrita Hitakarini Sabha (Depressed Classes Institute of Bombay) to the Indian Statutory Commission, Damodar Hall, Parel, Bombay, 29 May.

——. 1929. Mumbai ilakhyatil shikshanachi pragat. *Bahishkrut Bharat*, 31 May.

——. 1947a. *Navyug*, 13 April.

——. 1947b. *Navyug*, 14 April.

——. 1979a. *Dr. Babasaheb Ambedkar: Writings and Speeches*, Vol. 1, ed. Vasant Moon. Bombay: Department of Education, Government of Maharashtra.

——. 1979b. Evidence before the Southborough Commission. In Ambedkar, *Dr. Babasaheb Ambedkar: Writings and Speeches*, Vol. 1, ed. Vasant Moon. Bombay: Department of Education, Government of Maharashtra, 1979.

——. 1982a. *Dr. Babasaheb Ambedkar: Writings and Speeches*, Vol. 2, ed. Vasant Moon. Bombay: Department of Education, Government of Maharashtra.

——. 1982b. *Dr. Babasaheb Ambedkar: Writings and Speeches*, Vol. 4, ed. Vasant Moon. Bombay: Department of Education, Government of Maharashtra.

——. 1989. *Dr. Babasaheb Ambedkar: Writings and Speeches*, Vol. 5, ed. Vasant Moon. Bombay: Department of Education, Government of Maharashtra.

——. 1991. *Dr. Babasaheb Ambedkar: Writings and Speeches*, Vol. 9, ed. Vasant Moon. Bombay: Department of Education, Government of Maharashtra.

Anderson, Noel S. and Haroon Kharem, eds. 2009. *Education as Freedom: African American Educational Thought and Activism*. Latham, MD: Lexington Books.

Apple, Michael W. 1988. *Teachers and Texts*. New York: Routledge.

Bahishkrut Bharat. 3 February 1927.

——. 3 June 1927.

——. 3 May 1929.

——. 29 July 1927.

Bayly, S. 1989. *Saints, Goddesses and Kings: Muslims and Christians in South Indian Society, 1700–1900*. Cambridge: Cambridge University Press.

Bombay Chronicle. 29 April 1926.

——. 26 November 1922.

Butler, Judith and Joan W. Scott, eds. 1992. *Feminists Theorize the Political*. New York: Routledge.

Carlson, Dennis and Michael Apple, eds. 1998. *Power/Knowledge/Pedagogy: The Meaning of Democratic Education in Unsettling Times*. Boulder, CO: Westview Press.

Chakrabarty, Dipesh. 2002. *Habitations of Modernity: Essays in the Wake of Subaltern Studies*. Chicago, IL: University of Chicago Press.

Chalam, K.S. 2008. *Modernization and Education: Ambedkar's Vision*. Jaipur: Rawat.

Corrigan, P.R. 1991. The making of the boy: Meditations on what grammar school did with, to and for my body. In *Postmodernism, Feminism, and Cultural Politics: Redrawing Cultural Boundaries*, ed. Henry A. Giroux. Albany: State University of New York Press.

Deleuze, Gilles and Felix Guattari. 1987. *A Thousand Plateaus: Capitalism and Schizophrenia*, trans. B. Massumi. Minneapolis: University of Minnesota.

Dewey, John. 1916. *Democracy and Education: An Introduction to the Philosophy of John Dewey*. New York: Macmillan.

Dnyanprakash. 1 January 1930.

Fanon, Frantz. 1963. *The Wretched of the Earth*, trans. Constance Farrington. New York: Grove Press.

Forrester, D.B. 1979. *Caste and Christianity: Attitudes and Policies on Caste of Anglo-Saxon Protestant Missionaries in India*. London: Curzon Press.

Foucault, Michel. 1977. *Discipline and Punish: The Birth of the Prison*, trans. Alan Sheridan. New York: Vintage Books.

——. 1980. Truth and power. In *Power/Knowledge: Selected Interviews and Other Writings 1972–77*, ed. and trans. C. Gordon. New York: Pantheon.

——. 1988. Technologies of the self. In *Technologies of the Self: A Seminar with Michel Foucault*, ed. Luther H. Martin, Huck Gutman and Patrick H. Hutton. Amherst: University of Massachusetts Press.

Freire, Paulo. 1970. *Pedagogy of the Oppressed*. New York: Herder and Herder.

Gandhi, M.K. 1925. The meaning of the *Gita*. *Navjivan*, 11 October.

——. 1936. Dr. Ambedkar indictment: II. *Harijan*, 18 July. Available at www.gandhiserve.org/cwmg/VOLO69.

——. 1970. *My Views on Education*, ed. Anand Hingorani. Bombay: Bhartiya Vidya Bhavan.

——. 1986. *Gandhi on Education: The Moral and Political Writings of Gandhi, Volume 1: Civilisation, Politics, and Religion*, ed. Raghavan Iyer. Oxford: Clarendon Press.

——. 1991. *The Essential Writings of Gandhi*, ed. Raghavan Iyer. New Delhi: Oxford India.

Garud. 12 October 1947.

Giroux, Henry A. 1988. *Teachers as Intellectuals: Toward a Critical Pedagogy of Learning*. Granby, MA: Bergin and Garvey.

——. ed. 1991. *Postmodernism, Feminism, and Cultural Politics: Redrawing Cultural Boundaries*. Albany: State University of New York Press.

——. 2002. Rethinking cultural politics and radical pedagogy in the work of Antonio Gramsci. In *Gramsci and Education*, ed. C. Borg, J. Buttigieg and P. Mayo. Lanham, MD: Rowman & Littlefield.

Giroux, Henry A. and Peter McLaren, eds. 1994. *Between Borders: Pedagogy and the Politics of Cultural Studies*. New York: Routledge.

Gokhale, Jayashree. 1993. *From Concessions to Confrontation: The Politics of an Indian Untouchable Community*. Bombay: Popular Prakashan.

Gore, Jennifer. 1998. On the limits of empowerment through critical and feminist pedagogies. In *Power/Knowledge/Pedagogy: The Meaning of Democratic Education in Unsettling Times*, ed. Dennis Carlson and Michael Apple. Boulder, CO: Westview Press.

Gramsci, Antonio. 1971. *Selections from the Prison Notebooks of Antonio Gramsci*, ed. Q. Hoare and G. Nowell Smith; trans. G. Nowell Smith. London: Lawrence and Wishart.

hooks, bell. 1989. *Talking Back: Thinking Feminist, Thinking Black*. Boston, MA: South End Press.

——. 1994. *Teaching to Transgress*. New York: Routledge.

Jaffrelot, Christophe. 2004. *Dr. Ambedkar and Untouchability: Analysing and Fighting Caste*. New Delhi: Permanent Black.

Janata. 29 April 1933.

——. 22 January 1936.

——. 13 June 1936.

——. 20 June 1936.

——. 26 February 1938.

——. 17 September 1938. Khadtar Tapashcharya heech vidyarthyanna yashachi gurukilli: Ambedkar's advice to students.

——. 15 December 1945.

——. 29 July 1950.

——. 15 September 1951.

——. 22 September 1951.

——. 26 July 1952.

———. 13 June 1953.

———. 15 August 1953.

———. 17 December 1955.

Kawashima, K. 1998. *Missionaries and a Hindu State: Travancore 1858–1936*. Delhi: Oxford University Press.

Keer, Dhananjay. 1964. *Mahatma Jotirao Phooley*. Mumbai: Popular Prakashan.

Keer, Dhananjay and S.G. Malshe, eds. 1969. *Mahatma Phule Samagra Vangmay*. Mumbai: Maharashtra Rajya Sahitya ani Sanskrti Mandal.

Kshirsagar, R.K. 1994. *The Dalit Movement and Its Leaders, 1857–1956*. New Delhi: M.D. Publications.

Mohanty, C.T. 1994. On race and violence: Challenges for a liberal education in the 1990s. In *Between Borders: Pedagogy and the Politics of Cultural Studies*, ed. Henry A. Giroux and Peter McLaren. New York: Routledge.

Mooknayak. 28 February 1920.

———. 10 September 1920.

Mostern, K. 1994. Decolonisation as learning: Practice and pedagogy in Frantz Fanon's revolutionary narrative. In *Between Borders: Pedagogy and the Politics of Cultural Studies*, ed. Henry A. Giroux and Peter McLaren. New York: Routledge.

Nurullah, S. and J.P. Naik. 1951. *A History of Education in India*. Bombay: Macmillan.

O'Hanlon, R.. 1985. *Caste, Conflict and Ideology: Mahatma Jotirao Phule and Low-Caste Protest in Nineteenth-Century Western India*. Cambridge: Cambridge University Press.

Oddie, G.A. 1979. *Social Protests in India: British Protestant Missionaries and Social Reform, 1850–1900*. Delhi: Manohar.

Omvedt, G. 1994. *Dalits and the Democratic Revolution: Dr. Ambedkar and the Dalit Movement in Colonial India*. New Delhi: Sage.

People's Education Society. 2005. *The People's Education Society's Sixty Years of Glorious Existence Commemorative Volume, 1945–2005*. Maharashtra: People's Education Society.

Phule, J. 1855. Trutiya ratna. In *Samagra Vangmay*, ed. Y.D. Phadke. Mumbai: Maharashtra State Literary and Cultural Committee.

———. 1882. Memorial address to the Education Commission. In *Collected Works of Mahatma Phule*, Vol. II, ed. P.G. Patil. Bombay: Education Department, Government of Maharashtra.

———. 1969. Marwadi, Bhat yanche kasabavishayi. In *Mahatma Phule Samagra Vangmay*, ed. D. Keer and S.G. Malshe. Mumbai: Maharashtra Rajya Sahitya ani Sanskrti Mandal.

———. 1991a. *Samagra Vangmay*, ed. Y.D. Phadke. Mumbai: Maharashtra State Literary and Cultural Committee.

———. 1991b. *Collected Works of Mahatma Phule*, Vol. II, ed. P.G. Patil. Bombay: Education Department, Government of Maharashtra.

Prabuddha Bharat. 21 July 1956.

Queen, Christopher. 2000. Reflections in the light of Ambedkar's philosophy of education. *Siddharth College Magazine*: 40.

Rao, Anupama. 2009. *The Caste Question: Dalits and the Politics of Modern India*. Berkeley: University of California Press.

Rege, Sharmila. 2010. Education as *trutiya ratna*: Towards Phule-Ambedkarite feminist pedagogical practice. *Economic and Political Weekly*, 45(44): 88–98.

Scott, Joan W. 1992. 'Experience'. In *Feminists Theorize the Political*, ed. J.W.S. Scott and J. Butler. New York: Routledge.

Shukla, Sureshchandra and Rekha Kaul, eds. 1998. *Education, Development and Under-development*. New Delhi: Sage.

Skaria, Ajay. 2009. The project of provincialising Europe: Reading Dipesh Chakrabarty. *Economic and Political Weekly*, 54(14): 52–59.

Talwatkar, K.B. 2000. People's Education Society: A glorious heritage, 1945–1973. *Siddharth College of Arts and Sciences Silver Jubilee*: 77–83.

Times of India. 1 January 1919.

——. 28 February 1920.

——. 15 August 1936.

Velaskar, Padma. 1998. Ideology, education and the political struggle for liberation: Change and challenge among the Dalits of Maharashtra. In *Education, Development and Underdevelopment*, ed. S. Shukla and R. Kaul. New Delhi: Sage.

Wittul (Vitthal), Moro. 1969. Public examination of the Poonah Mahar and Mang Schools, 2 February 1858. Bombay: Gunput Crushnaji's Press, 1858. In *Mahatma Phule Samagra Vangmaya* (Collected Works of Mahatma Phule), ed. D. Keer and S.G. Malshe. Mumbai: Maharashtra State Board for Literature and Culture.

Young India. 12 March 1925.

——. 20 August 1925.

——. 24 June 1926.

Zelliot, Eleanor. 1992. *From Untouchables to Dalit*. Delhi: Manohar.

——. 1994. *Dr. Babasaheb Ambedkar and the Untouchable Movement*. New Delhi: Bluemoon Books.

——. n.d. Dalit initiatives in education. Unpublished paper.

3 Education, reform of women and exclusion of Dalit women

The Brahmani agendas of the colonial state and of elite Brahmans regarding education and reform of women, which defined women's social worth in familial terms, excluded the issues of Dalit *streepurush* (women and men). Although upper-caste, middle-class women shared social and educational exclusion with lower castes and shared gendered identity with Dalit women, they still failed to include the latter in *their* liberal-feminist movement. A few Brahman feminists from the late nineteenth century, like Pandita Ramabai, vehemently attacked caste structures and Brahmani patriarchy and forged a liberal feminism; yet even they significantly failed to converse and establish connections with their non-Brahman supporters, like Phule. The failure of the nationalist and feminist movements to include the concerns of lower-caste women led Dalit and non-Brahman radicals to severely critique upper-castes' instrumental agenda of education for women as well as their promises and efforts to expand educational opportunities.

During the Akhil Bhartiya Bahishkrut Parishad (All India Conference of the Excluded), held at Nagpur from 30 May to 1 June 1920, more than 10,000 Dalit *streepurush* resolved to fight for free and compulsory education. The Marathi language use of the term *streepurush* (women and men) is intriguing: unlike in the English, *stree* (woman) and *purush* (man) are joined together in a single word. Dalit radicals' deployment of the concept *streepurush* underscores their emphasis on gender differentiation, unlike the upper castes who sought gender-neutral unity for the cause of nationalism. Along with other *streepurush*, Dalit woman activist Tulsabai Bandasode attacked the upper-caste, middle-class agenda for excluding Dalits from the benefits of education (*Mooknayak*, 5 June 1920). She argued that education was in fact more important for Dalit girls than for upper-caste girls. She demanded boarding-houses for Dalit girl students in every district. Most significantly, she contended that, due to Dalit women's lack of education, upper-caste women kept them at a distinct distance. Bandasode thus signalled that Dalit women's inclusion in the modern, middle-class liberal-feminist agenda was contingent on the former's education. Her views were further reinforced by Rukmini Kotangale, who narrated her experiences of being ignored by upper-caste women and men as well as by the colonial British government.

Why was education so important to Dalit women? If women shared a common gendered identity and oppression, why did upper-caste women ostracise and isolate Dalit women? Of course, not all upper-caste women were isolated from Dalits; indeed, some actively supported their struggle for education and equality. But in general, if upper-caste women shared educational exclusion with low-castes, why did they then fail to build alliances with them? By explaining how the entanglements of the elite Brahman educational agenda and gendered moral and social reforms failed to include Dalit women, this chapter highlights the blind spots in the mainstream historiography of both India and the liberal-feminist movement.

From the mid-nineteenth century, and especially at the turn of the twentieth century, reformers contested the appropriate agendas of education, moral reform, social change and self-disciplining for *streepurush* of all castes, including Dalits. Indians who participated in the formation of colonial modernity undertook these practices of self-fashioning. The development of a modern state required the surveillance of social, sexual, moral and, most importantly, educational reform. Moreover, Dalits had to deal with a *double surveillance*: colonial and indigenous. Thus education reform was at the heart of not only the colonial 'civilising' mission, as we saw in Chapter 1, but also of Indian's modernising project because education would enable Dalits – women and men – to discipline and fashion themselves, and to prepare them for community and nation-building activities. This chapter focuses on the discursive practices that led to the formation of 'womanhood' in this context.

Much of the scholarship on the nationalist and women's movements has dealt with high-caste patriarchy and the position of elite women in family, marriage and kinship networks. This scholarship has engaged with caste issues through some anthropological and sociological studies on poverty and NGOisation, women and their stigmatised labour, and so on. The absence of an intertwined critique of caste and gender relations has indeed been a problem for feminists. Scholars have addressed the theoretical aspects and the compounded nature of caste and gender (Pardeshi 1998; Chakravarti 2003; A. Rao 2003, 2009; Rege 2006), yet they have rarely engaged with the reality of the historical experience of Dalit women in western India (cf. Rege 2006). We also know little about how education reinforced the oppressive nature of the two hierarchies. Only recently, the feminist historian Shefali Chandra (2012) has provided a convincing corrective by demonstrating how Brahman castes contained English education within their caste and class locations, thereby domesticating and even gendering the English language. This chapter deepens her analyses by shifting the gaze from Brahman enclaves to intimate caste practices in Dalit women's lives in order to examine the tangled and complex interplay of different education agendas, castes, genders, feminisms and masculinities.

Some upper-caste *streepurush* argued that education led to the disruption of family values or gender hierarchies and hence opposed women's education. Nevertheless, at the same time, many upper- and lower-caste reformers identified failure to educate women as the primary cause of the decline of Indian society. Education was more important for colonised women, who were seen as *doubly* 'ignorant' and 'backward' compared to men. *Streeshikshan* (education of

women) would serve two tasks: first, it would enable them to discipline themselves and become modern; and second, it would train them to teach, nurture and
prepare *their* children (read: sons) to become citizens of modern India. These
tasks were relevant to women of all castes. Yet Dalit women faced a *double
burden* because unlike non-Dalit women they also needed to develop their self-
respect and self-confidence. Most significantly, this *self-formation* especially
through formal education was crucial for Dalit women in the advancement of
their ethnic self-esteem, community development, nation-building and construction as modern citizens of the nation. As Ambedkar declared, schools are the
workshops to manufacture the best citizens (*Bahishkrut Bharat*, 3 June 1927). In
this complex field of forces, education emerged as a significant instrument to
discipline the body, nurture new standards of comportment and cultivate bourgeois respectability so that Dalits could become *modern citizens*.

Interestingly, there were interconnections as well as discordances among
high- and low-caste rhetoric, agendas for education and developments. In this
chapter and the next, I historicise Dalit women's struggle for access to education
in the early twentieth century. Specifically, in this chapter, I deal with the different ways in which Dalit women challenged elite Brahman agendas of education, the feminist movement and nationalist patriarchy. Chapter 4 continues this
investigation by focusing on the complexities of women's reform and education
within the Dalit community itself.

Unlike upper-caste elite women, Dalit women did not write or publish magazines of their own in the early decades of twentieth-century Bombay Presidency;
there is some fragmentary evidence in the form of quotes included in newspapers
or short essays written by women themselves. Certainly, in comparison to elite
Hindu and Muslim women, Dalit women were only beginning to enter schools;
they could not systematically write or publish their views, unlike their counterparts in other regions, for example, the Namashudras of Bengal. Even the colonial government was indifferent to Dalit women and maintained silence
regarding their issues. Anthropologists and census officers recorded many
anthropometrical details about Dalits: for example, their houses, dress and food
habits (or lack thereof), and village services. They created rich compendia of
educational statistics, but failed to provide any qualitative information on Dalit
women's education. The British opened schools for all, but remained ambivalent
about their interference in the social fabric of the country and did not fully
support Dalits. As a result, the colonial state failed to record these lowly lives
and their educational efforts, philosophies and agendas.[1] Scholars have extensively discussed the educational agendas as well as the caste and class consciousness of the colonial government, which favoured high-caste, high-class
women and their traditional norms over the lower classes. Moreover, except for
some autobiographies, there is a lack of sources on Dalit women's ideas about
education.

This chapter is organised thematically. The first section begins with an analysis of the ways upper castes forged an elitist, modern, but modest agenda of
education for the 'new woman'. The second section unravels how the elitist

agenda excluded the public, 'unruly', 'low' Dalit woman. Most importantly, the nationalist and liberal-feminist discourses on domesticity and education interpellated women as subjects of class, caste and nation, once again reconstructing class power, caste privilege and inequality. The third section addresses why feminists could not successfully present an ideology that would specifically address issues relevant to all Dalits. The conclusion brings together the tangled lives of women to reveal that, although liberal-feminist rhetoric alluded to all women as 'depressed', it failed to build bridges to actual Depressed Class women.

Streeshikshan: education or policing of women?

Streeshikshan is women's education and *streedharma* is a moral code of conduct for women. Note that there are no such equivalents for men because the subordinated women are 'different', not men. It is the subordinated who will be measured against the standard: women with men and Dalits with Brahmans. In late nineteenth-century Mumbai and Pune, as in other urban spaces of colonial India, women emerged as the most vexed objects – and later subjects – of social and moral reform. Indians lamented that their 'backwardness' – material and intellectual impoverishment – was due to their national 'weakness', 'passivity' and 'docility'. It was because they were 'effeminate', Hindu nationalists argued, that masculine colonial rule had turned Indian men womanish. Hindu nationalist discourse also emphasised how Hindu men's weakness led to their failure in protecting their religion and women. As a result, to counter and subvert the aggressive masculinity of colonial rule, nationalists strategically attempted to make the weak into the strong by appealing to women as powerful tools for regeneration of (Hindu) masculinity and modernity. In the process, private issues were vehemently discussed in public; there was no neat management of the two 'separate spheres'.

Divergent views on the role of women's education

Significantly, nationalists looked upon women as symbols and made them responsible for upholding the prestige of the household and thereby the nation. They believed social, educational and moral reforms were all necessary. Domesticity, intimately tied to notions of Indian womanhood, was at the heart of both the nationalist and imperialist projects. Both revivalists and reformers debated constructive suggestions for social reform, including the spread of women's education and its appropriate boundaries. Because women were (are) seen as the repository of tradition and were to hold the culture and caste line, the regulation of their behaviour was critical. Thus, women had a special burden.

The Brahman feminist Pandita Ramabai argued in her book *Stree Dharma Niti* (Morals for Women) (1882) that denying Indian women education was at the root of their anaemic health and the consequent degradation of childcare and children's health (quoted in Kosambi 2000, 139). She believed that women could elevate themselves as well as their children through education and self-development (ibid., 90). Her views are commonly discussed at length in the mainstream historiography of India and the women's movement. What is often ignored, however, is that in the same year and city (Pune), the non-Brahman leader Phule begged the Hunter Education Commission to be 'kind enough to sanction measures for the spread of compulsory primary female education on a more liberal scale' (Phule 1882). Like the Pandita, he vehemently attacked Brahmani orthodoxy, but unlike her he also revealed how it oppressed not just upper-caste women, but women of *all* castes and men of lower castes. It also, as a rule, excluded all women and lower-caste men from the benefits of education. Phule established the first homes to offer shelter, education and means of economic independence for Brahman widows well before the Pandita or the famous educator D.K. Karve (1858–1963). Yet historians have consistently paid little attention to his contributions to women's reforms and residential schools.[2]

On the one hand, Phule's plea for mass education gained support from some elite Pune Brahman liberals, like M.G. Ranade, Gopal Hari Deshmukh (Lokahitawadi), R.G. Bhandarkar, K.T. Telang, G.G. Agarkar (Babar 1968, 114) and G.K. Gokhale. On the other hand, however, there were some limitations to the liberal reforms which these reformers espoused. Although sympathetic to the non-Brahman cause, they believed in reforming society gradually; they would not radically attack the caste system because they had moderate notions of change. They retained their social base in their upper-caste locations and thus favoured a 'social' rhythm to bringing about change in parts of the existing structures. But, they also faced the threat of the real power of excommunication, so they were not ready to break with their caste-fellows by radically overhauling the social and economic structures.

Some revivalists and Hindu nationalists like B.G. Tilak vehemently combated both low-caste and female education (*Mooknayak*, 28 February 1920). Tilak was extremely critical of educated and independent women like Ramabai and Dr Rakhmabai. He argued that teaching women to read and write would ruin their precious traditional virtues and make them immoral and insubordinate. According to him, 'women should not be taxed with subjects' – like history, English, mathematics and science – 'that were beyond their power to understand' (quoted in P. Rao 2010, 105). When questioned if education should be made available to all children or if girls' education should follow that of boys, Tilak said, 'We'll see about that later' and postponed the matter, claiming that weak government finances rendered women's education a low priority. When he made this argument, the audience attacked him with eggs and tomatoes and drove him off the stage. To Tilak and some other politicians, politics in the public realm was men's work; they disliked women participating in public work or even standing and speaking in front of an audience.

Education, Brahman womanhood and the Hindu nation

Indian social reformers, Christian missionaries, philanthropic foreigners and the British government were the four main agents of women's education during this period. Men vibrantly discussed both the social position and agenda of women's education in the print culture. As educators, editors and critics, Brahmans controlled the dissemination of the new medium of modernity.[3] They dominated all walks of life and thus shaped new debates over society, culture and politics. An exploration of literature from mid-nineteenth-century Maharashtra (and other parts of India as well) suggests that the agenda for women's education was first formulated within the context of middle-class domesticity, of women's traditional family roles as *supatni* (good wives) and *sumaataa* (good mothers). Yet, embedded in this construction also lay the fear and danger of education's potential to turn women into 'bad' wives.

Reform of women, including their education, was thus intimately tied to women's sexuality. Nationalists and reformists were aware of the hopes as well as the hurdles or even dangers in educating women. Hence, although they embraced the modern discourse of women's education, they also cunningly circumscribed it. For instance, an 1837 essay penned by a Tailang Brahman in the newspaper *Durpan* declared: 'women without knowledge turn blind because they do not understand anything. They become detestable, which means the family is condemned' (quoted in Bhagwat 2004, 77). He thus suggested that moral education was necessary to curb women's sexuality, their untamed animalistic behaviour and their innate promiscuity (ibid., 75–82). For many upper-caste men education became a disciplinary tool to tame *streesvabhaava*, women's innate nature and their unbridled sexuality, and to transport them to an orderly world of culture in order to fulfil their *streedharma* of fidelity to their husbands and family (Bhagwat 2004, 79; Chakravarti 1998, 201).

In the process, reformers also experienced an embourgeoisement. As a result, they increasingly emphasised women's value in the household. The function of the school then was to prepare girls directly for domestic duties and the domestic economy: *gruhakaarya* (housework) and *gruhashikshan* (home education) or, even better, home science. Women's education was viewed as essential to their service and to the success of their sons and husbands, and ultimately of the (male supremacist) nation. In the year 1864, *Streebhushan* (*Women's Ornament*), a magazine from Mumbai, announced its motto in a poem:

> *Desh sthiti sundar vhavyaate* (A country's condition can become good)
> *Dnyani karaavya aadhi ho striyante* (If it first imparts knowledge to women)
> *Sudnya dise mukhya upaasanaa hi* (Those intelligent will see this as a significant task)
> *Yavaachuni anya upaaya naahi* (There is no other remedy without educating women).
>
> (quoted in S. Karve 2003, 73)

Thus, reformers underscored the intimate connection between women's education and the (Hindu) nation's progress. In other words, *dnyani svatantra stree hee rashtraachi shakti va vaibhav aani maanavjatiche saundarya hoya* (an educated and independent woman is the strength and glory of a nation and the beauty of humanity).[4] In this way educated mothers would regenerate Indian society through nurturing and socialising their children and advance the general condition of the country. Modern nationalists thus constructed a discourse of the motherland and of women as mothers of the nation. Men valorised women as nurturers of man and the (male) nation without considering them to actually constitute part of it. Women had to be prepared for this task through a thorough and wholesome system of special education (Banerjee 1992, 3; Chakravarti 1998, 200–207).

How then did reformers negotiate the contradictions of gendered spheres while also pulling women into national political activity? By widely and deeply debating the reform of *streeshikshan* and tightly tying it to childcare, rationalised home management and sexuality, nationalists at the turn of the twentieth century, like their imperial counterparts, identified domesticity as the core of society. As some scholars have suggested (and it seems correct at times), elite Hindu nationalists emphasised separate gendered spheres.[5] Their view was of course untenable because the home was not neatly circumscribed from the world. Indeed, it spilled out of its boundaries and penetrated the public domain because women were also made instruments of nation-building projects. There were, however, severe restrictions on women's mobility and the extent of their participation.

According to the perspectives of the reformers, educated women were instruments of nurture, class socialisers and regenerators of future (male) citizens of the nation. In this scheme, women were also to control their sexuality and please their husbands by turning into their helpmeets and companions. Partha Chatterjee is partly right that the Hindu nationalist discourse constructed the 'new woman' to be schooled in 'new' patriarchy, which was distinguished both from the West and from the patriarchy of indigenous tradition, as well as from subordinate classes of maidservants, washerwomen and prostitutes (Chatterjee 1989, 244–245). Yet we must reconsider the metropole and colony as well as the 'public' and 'private' in the same analytical frame and work on actual relations between elites in the metropolitan and colonial cities. As feminists have made clear, the colonial structures of power indeed interacted with and buttressed indigenous patriarchy and upheld hegemonic upper-caste, elite norms and practices (Chakravarti 1998; Sarkar 1993, 1869). Considering the interdependence of these spheres in the lives and minds of reformers, a 'special' education and a proper 'feminine' curriculum were needed for a *double task*: to advance women's socialising roles and to bring out the best traits of (Hindu) Indian womanhood.

For example, an Aryasamájist, Krishnashastri Godbole, argued in a lecture delivered on 14 March 1880 that the essence of women's education was how to rear children scientifically (quoted in Bhagwat 2004, 94). He continued: 'Every female takes care of her child and hence they develop well ... no other business should hinder a mother's upbringing of her child. It would not be wrong to say that women are responsible to make a person strong or weak, useful or useless' (ibid., 95–96). Brahman male reformers like Godbole thus formulated a model for upper-caste, middle-class women that placed them in opposition to both the Western woman and women of lower castes. This emerging male vision of the ideal Hindu woman, the 'new woman', was to appropriate the modern in limited ways, nurture her upper-caste cultural values and maintain her distance from lower-class/caste, 'vulgar' women who were 'different' and who performed menial tasks.

In the process, elite Brahman nationalists projected the chaste, virtuous, exclusive Brahman woman as the normative married woman and as the (a)sexual symbol of the Hindu (Indian) nation. This social construction of 'woman' further exacerbated caste differences and systematically stimulated the Brahmanisation of Indian culture. Significantly, Godbole's agenda has a global connection: the notion that a woman's primary role was to cook and clean at home, bear and rear children, and thus construct a chosen cultural capital of women as a global phe-nomenon.[6] In the context of Bombay Presidency, this elite Brahman strategy was a deliberate move to make 'femininity' appear transhistorical and always-already natural. Moreover, the home science curriculum in western India, like its national, British and US counterparts, underscored women's acquisition of 'mother craft' and practical skills like sewing, food preservation and cooking (Hancock 1999, 150).

Thus, in Europe, the United States, and even locally, women from both lower and middle castes shared Godbole's agenda and underlined the role of women as 'custodians' of the community and their main responsibility to procreate and educate correctly. This perspective was even shaped by some women from lower castes. In her essay 'The question of education in a lower caste' (1911), Hirabai Nagshekar of the *kalaavantin* (dancing-girl) community emphasised women's education. She deplored her community's stress on dance education alone for women and wanted 'another' kind of education for them. Hirabai also called upon the wealthy to support the education of both boys and girls (quoted in S. Karve 2003, 119–121). In a similar vein, in 1919 Vatsalabai Bole wrote a prize-winning essay that stressed women's duties towards parents, God, the community, and the nation. Bole envisioned that, as a potter moulds clay to make pots, an educated woman was responsible for fashioning her children (ibid., 195).

The rhetoric of girls' schooling in late nineteenth-century India intimately linked the aims of knowledge and learning, as well as their meaning, purposes and specific views on curricula, to ideas about proper gender roles and relations. Domesticity was at the heart of the nationalist project and constant surveillance of caste, culture and gender(ed.) discipline in schools; outside the school walls, domesticity emerged as a constitutive part of nationalists' anti-colonial visions of modernity. In this manner, schools became a site to train women for marriage and motherhood and actuated gender trouble. Many social reformers and lay women and men argued that since the family was the basic unit of social organ-isation in India, and because women played an indispensable role in maintaining its stability, enhancing the position of women was thus crucial to reforming society (Mazumdar 1976). They firmly believed that 'educating a girl meant educating a family'; the traditional roles of women were thus reinforced through the medium of school curricula. Most importantly, these opinions were repeatedly expressed and contested in Marathi newspapers well into the final decades of the twentieth century.

Reformers concentrated on the Indian family and the children born into it, and considered women's role central in *baal sangopan* (childrearing) and housekeeping. Even educated men preferred educated and 'intelligent' companions, which motivated parents to send their daughters to school. Parents were keen to secure their daughters an education that would embellish their feminine qualities and improve their value in the marriage market (Richey 1923, 129). Such reasons, along with preparing women for their future roles as *supatni* and *sumaataa*, led to a rapid increase in the founding of educational institutions for women. Between 1916 and 1921, in British India alone, the total number of educational institutions for Indian girls and women increased by 4,393 (126). In Bombay Presidency the number of primary schools increased from 326 in 1881 to 768 in 1901 and secondary schools from twenty-three in 1881 to sixty-seven in 1901. The number of girls attending primary schools increased from 19,917 in 1881 to 76,068 in 1901 and in secondary schools from 1,581 in 1881 to 4,984 in 1901 (Babar 1968, 126).

Gender differentiation in education

Although statistically the number of schools and female students was on the rise, historically speaking, the prejudice against the expansion of women's education was embedded in a basic conviction that there was something special about a woman's nature. There was a major concern with women's 'difference' that resulted in much public debate about curricula, syllabi, textbooks, and even the best location for girls' education. Hence, a major issue in women's education was the emphasis on a 'feminised' curriculum. While a minority of liberal reformers like Agarkar, Ranade and Gokhale placed girls on a par with boys and believed in a similar curriculum for both, the majority – as well as the colonial government – supported a gender-differentiated one. As a result, certain subjects, such as music, home science and hygiene, emerged as 'feminine' subjects, while chemistry, mathematics and physics became 'masculine' subjects. Male reformers as well as some women even questioned the usefulness of algebra and geometry for women.

Many men and some women believed that the rudiments of reading, writing, a little arithmetic for daily budgeting, hygiene, needlework, tailoring, embroidery and some English (i.e. subjects of a 'practical' kind) were more than adequate. These traditional assertions echoed Gandhian ideas of education, as dealt with in Chapter 2. Girls were encouraged to take up needlework instead of 'Euclid, mensuration, and science', and in lieu of native accounts they could read 'a little poetry' (Richey 1924, 306). Even renowned Maharashtrian educators like D.K. Karve and G.M. Chiplunkar shared the colonial government's curricular goals and belief that women were psychologically and biologically different from men and hence needed a separate – 'masculinised' and 'feminised' – curriculum. D.K. Karve 'categorically believed that Indian women must learn Indian languages and woman subjects. Such training would reinforce their femininity and increase their contribution to contemporary society.'[7] Moreover, he 'alluded entirely to the reproductive function of women as shaping female identity and gender difference' (Chandra 2012, 94). A more gender-specific curriculum was at the heart of Chiplunkar's *Scientific Basis of Women's Education* (1930).

Even the radical extremist Tilak turned a modest moderate when it came to female education and curriculum. He insisted that girls, including those in high schools, should be taught only 'vernacular, moral science, Sanskrit, sanitation, and needlework' (quoted in P. Rao 2010, 105):

> The object of female education is *not* to make the women equal to man. It must be remembered that women have to perform the wifely and maternal duties.... Their education should be so planned as to give to their minds a minimum amount of useful culture and information with minimum expenditure of energy.
>
> (Ibid., 132)

Tilak adopted a conservative position regarding women's reform. He argued:

> Men and women have different spheres of activity allotted to them in domestic economy ... instruction which is to fit them for the duties pertaining to their respective spheres must be given on essentially different lines.... Religious and moral instructions ... high principles of ancient Aryan religious morality or the *Pathamala* or knowing the names of the Peshwa by heart.
>
> (115)

Thus Tilak believed that 'the brain of a woman on an average weighed less by five ounces than that of a man' (115), and therefore the subjects taught to boys would be a burden on girls. This attack was so powerful that during the following twenty years no new schools for girls were established. Against seventy-one boys' high schools, there were only seven girls' high schools. One woman writer in Tilak's Marathi daily *Kesari* also suggested that secondary schools should be replaced by institutions for domestic science which she argued would prepare girls for their familial roles (quoted in Gogate 1988, 18). Thus Brahmani and colonial masculinist anxiety about higher education for women created and reinforced a stereotype of educated but lazy women.

However, some moderates and radicals departed from Tilak's conservative agenda. Agarkar, of the moderate contingent, contended with Tilak over the issue of gender differentiation and focused on complete equality in the curriculum for men and women. Like Dalit radicals, he argued that '*streepurush aanni ekach shikshan ghyave, va tehi ekatra ghyave* (women and men should seek the same education, and that too together)' (*Sudharak*, 31 October 1892). In a similar vein, the radical R.D. Karve (son of D.K. Karve), a staunch opponent of the segregation of the sexes, strongly attacked conservative views. He upheld women's higher education, self-reliance, economic independence and moral equality. Moreover, he also pointed out that special courses and separate institutions for women's education expressed a covert segregationist attitude that promoted the practice of untouchability in India (Gogate 1988, 23). He thus made a powerful argument by interconnecting upper-caste, conservative men's construction of difference for women with that of difference for Untouchables. This was a devastating intellectual claim because Brahman women (and men) consistently denied such a connection between them (Brahmans) and the Shudras. The excluded Untouchables never figured in their vocabulary.

Most significantly, Agarkar, Ranade, Jotirao and Savitribai Phule, and later Ambedkar found redemption in 'Mother English', as discussed in detail in Chapter 2. Savitribai even declared that 'through English education, casteism can be destroyed and Brahmani teaching can be hurled away' (quoted in Omvedt 2006). She challenged the 'nationalist celebration of the indigenous-maternal' (Chandra 2012, 21) and argued that the British rule had certainly liberated some from Brahmani Peshwa rule. She also welcomed '*Ingraji Mauli*' (our mother English) as the harbinger of culture. Scholars have yet to investigate Savitribai's efforts and achievements.

By contrast, upper-caste nationalists like Tilak opposed English education, especially for women. Tilak, who had himself benefited from learning the language, declared that 'English education had a de-womanising impact on women, and denied them a happy worldly life' (quoted in P. Rao 2010, 105). Hence he felt that girls should be offered an education that would be useful in domestic life and that teaching English was not education per se. Moreover, as Chandra has compellingly demonstrated, 'the civilising, conjugal power could be harnessed to the particular needs of upper-class society' and the Brahman caste (Chandra 2012, 69). Thus there was a deep contradiction among the thoughts and practices of some national leaders: on the one hand, they fought for equal voting rights for women, while on the other they demanded a considerable delay in girls' compulsory education. Although by the mid-1940s these battles had receded into the background, the debate on the appropriate course content for female education continued well into the late 1980s.

Furthermore, some male reformers reasoned that women did not have to search for employment like men and hence did not need BA and MA degrees (S. Karve 2003, 129). They argued that the modern woman should be educated but not working or financially independent; a woman's education should be geared towards helping her perform her duties as a wife and mother, as previously discussed. Ornamenting a woman with a degree was in fact threatening and moved the focus towards women's accomplishments. Nonetheless, many orthodox men and some women opposed these conservative viewpoints. Some women argued that there was an inextricable connection between education and higher educational degrees. Degrees, they affirmed, would allow them to do away with the *polpaat-laatane* (a circular wooden base to roll chapattis and rolling-pin). Many upper-caste women earned their livings using the *polpaat-laatane* to cook in others' homes. They argued that they would certainly be happier to gain a prestigious job than to have to walk from door to door in search of irregular employment every day. They added that degrees would also relieve them from roaming about selling *govaryanchi peti* (crates of cow-dung cakes) on holidays and festive occasions (S. Karve 2003, 129). However, this resistance, which was at times fragmented, could not produce effective results and these voices ultimately slipped between the cracks of the politics of education and limited female agency.

Thus, the ambivalent and constricted agenda of upper-caste males outlined the dangerous consequences of women's exclusion from education. Reformers sought to make efforts towards improving women's status and strengthening the Hindu community (as well as the nation), yet they failed to concern themselves with women's issues in their own right. They argued for the necessity of education and simultaneously set limits to it. In the process, they articulated a public culture of domesticity and at the same time entrenched separate gendered spheres, reinforced Brahman caste power and constructed caste differentiation. As Chandra (2012, 31) argues:

> The records from the Alexandra Native Girls English Institution, the schools of the Students' Literary and Scientific Society, and the Female Normal Schools reveal a particular kind of woman and a specific constellation of affective expressions of consolidated caste power, along with intellectual and commercial interests, within native society.

Many middle-class women nonetheless benefited: they contested and created their own spaces and negotiated in the public, political sphere by writing in magazines and the periodical press. Unfortunately, there were no such magazines for or by Dalit women.

Contested agendas of education and the construction of 'difference'

Similar to female education, non-Brahman and Untouchable education was a hotbed of controversy. Most importantly, due to the homogeneous Chitpavan hegemony in Pune, the Brahmani orthodoxy was firmly entrenched. A small number of Brahman reformers made attempts to attack the caste system radically and some Brahman liberals did work, to an extent, with non-Brahmans. The presence of British power also widened the arena of caste contestations. Although the British ostensibly believed in 'fair play by all classes', access to education and new professions was enabling and disabling at the same time; though technically open to all castes, education was often closed in practice to the lower castes, as discussed in Chapter 1.

Most importantly, despite reformers' ideological beliefs in mass education, the practice of initiating actual institutional changes was even more complicated.

When Gokhale worked to pass the bill on free and compulsory education in 1910, it failed miserably. Out of twenty-two members of the Poona Municipal Corporation on education, sixteen opposed education for girls. Commenting positively on this vote, Tilak declared that 'representatives of people symbolise the people and they have rejected girls' education' (*Mooknayak*, 28 February 1920). Conservatives like Tilak thus displayed their Brahmanism: they upheld the caste system, opposed non-Brahman education, and argued that education should not be made compulsory for those 'to whom education was unsuited and useless'. Instead of mass education, Tilak supported technical schools for the villagers because, he argued, they needed 'the most ordinary trades, like those of a carpenter, blacksmith, tailor, and mason' (quoted in P. Rao 2010, 139). Implicitly, Tilak saw these occupations as involving *inferior* people from whom Brahmans had to maintain a distinct and respectable distance and 'difference'. As a result, Tilak, Chiplunkar and M.B. Namjoshi, who dominated and controlled the Poona Municipality, ultimately opposed Gokhale's plan of mass education.

One of the major reasons for the failure of the 1910 bill was a lack of government funds and the subsequent financial burden for the maintenance of educational institutions. In addition, many elite reformers in the Bombay legislature argued that it would be immoral to send upper-caste girls to school on their own and expressed fears about their daughters' safety (S. Karve 2003, 129). Some also questioned, 'If all women are sent to school, who will do the cooking, and how is one to find maids for housework? Some reformers thus placed their own luxurios first', and emphasised that education was *not* necessary for women of *all* classes and castes because some castes and classes were 'fit' to do only certain kinds of jobs (ibid., 129, emphasis added).

Some upper-caste women were successfully gaining entry to schools, colleges, and even Bombay University; Dalits, however, were struggling to be included in these public spaces. If anything, free and compulsory education was more essential to Dalits because their exclusion denied them egalitarian citizenship. However, Puneri Brahmans had a different agenda altogether. A writer in *Kesari* suggested that the 'Pune Municipality should spend funds on making schools beautiful: they should have gardens and playgrounds for physical exercise' (*Mooknayak*, 28 February 1920). Now that they had excelled in the realm of education, Brahmans were thus more interested in improving the existing facilities at the schools their children attended than in spending on compulsory education for Backward Classes.

Since Tilak's Hindu nationalism was predominantly upper caste in its ethos, the Congress leader was not serious about ending abuses against Dalits: he managed to find a way to not sign the Anti-Untouchability bill in 1918 (*Mooknayak*, 28 February 1920). Severely critiquing the *vichaarshunyataa* (lack of thinking) and *dutappi vartan* (double standards) of Puneri Brahman men, Dalit *streepurush* argued that laws for compulsory primary education should be implemented. The 1920 Akhil Bhartiya Bahishkrut Parishad was attended by more than 10,000 non-Brahman and Dalit women and men. On the third day of the conference, the attendees passed thirteen resolutions, including one in favour of the immediate implementation of *muli mulaansaathi shikshan mophat aani sak-tichech* (free and compulsory education for girls and boys at the same time). Tul-sabai Bandasode, a Dalit woman activist, affirmed the resolution:

> Since our community women are not educated they keep their children at home, in order to attend to their work.... They also do not know how to take good care of their children and hence their children suffer immensely. Due to all this we face many difficulties.... Even upper-caste women push us *dur dur* [far far] away because we are not educated like them. Hence, along with male education, female education is very significant and there should be boarding houses for girls in every district.
>
> (*Mooknayak*, 5 June 1920)

Bandasode emphasised the importance of Dalit women's education for *themselves* as well as for their children. Most significantly, she affirmed that their lack of education was responsible for the tendency of upper-caste women to exclude them and keep them at a distinct distance. While the colonisers dominated the upper and lower castes and constructed difference, within the colony itself, upper-caste women and men's internal colonialism reproduced similar practices in their relationship with Dalits.

During this period, schools were mainly located in towns; not many Dalits had the resources to live there. Boarding- and eating houses were therefore essential for their educational success. Significantly, the Dalit demand for boarding-houses was *not* similar to the concept of residential schools for women, as introduced by Pandita Ramabai through her experiments at the Sharada Sadan (Home of Learning), opened in Mumbai on 11 March 1889, and replicated by D.K. Karve's Anath Balikashram (an ashram for orphan girls) and Hindu Widows' Home (near Hingne), started in Poona in 1896. The latter institutions were established to offer shelter, education and the means of self-reliance to upper-caste women who had been widowed, fled home, or were otherwise rejected by society. Many had been deserted by their husbands and families and were without support. Karve's Seva Sadan housed two Depressed Class women out of a total of sixty-eight (Gadgil 1952, 286).

Reinforcing Bandasode's views, Kumari Rukmini Kotangale said:

> Due to lack of education we are denied in all places, and when we complain to the municipality and the government about it, nobody pays attention to us and our opinions. Girls should be educated along with boys. And along with girls and boys of other classes, our girls and boys should have facilities for education.
>
> (*Mooknayak*, 5 June 1920)

Kotangale thus underscored that both upper castes and the colonial government excluded Dalits. Reinforcing male Dalit radicals' agenda, she demanded facilities for Dalit children on a par with those of upper castes. Like Phule and

Ambedkar, she also underlined the need for non-Brahman education inspectors, who could be more sympathetic to Dalits and the importance of education in gaining government jobs, which Brahmans dominated.

One Manoramabai, quoted in the newspaper *Mooknayak*, also demonstrated a strong awareness of the socio-political ramifications of education reform:

> If every person decides to *sudhaaranaa* [improvement and here self-improvement], the progress of the entire caste will be achieved in a timely manner. Without women's education the community cannot advance because they make up half its body. *Women's education is in fact more important than that of men.* A woman shoulders the responsibility of her household and children and hence an educated woman is more competent than an uneducated one. It is not necessary to reiterate in a new language the already advancing efforts of education and its *achaat shakti* [limitless power], especially its necessity for the community in the present circumstances. It is due to knowledge that in the world today steam engines, electric power, and other new inventions have become only common. If we look at some developed nations, we can admire how an individual possessing such a power [of *shikshan*] can bring about the advancement of [her] family, community, and nation.... Unless the *bahujan samaj* [masses] are educated on a wider scale our nation will not change on social, religious, or political lines. Only after comprehending this did Gokhale introduce the Bill for Compulsory Primary Education. Yet, due to the cunning of our *svaarthi* [selfish] extremist camp [i.e. Tilak and his supporters] it was defeated. Fortunately, in 1917 Patel made efforts to pass a law mandating compulsory primary education for boys and girls at the same time. But it was only on paper. Because, as everybody is aware, our extremists advocating *svarajya* [self-rule] trampled it and stalled the work.
>
> (*Mooknayak*, 28 February 1920, emphasis in original)

Manoramabai thus underscored the necessity of women's education and also attacked Brahmani conservatives like Tilak who vehemently demanded *svarajya* but discouraged mass education. She connected the progress and advancement of the masses with the social, religious and political development of the nation. Moreover, unlike Dalit women, upper-caste women reinforced Dalits' demand for free and compulsory education for girls after only a decade – for example, at the Women's Day celebration in Pune in the 1930s (Gogate 1988, 111).

Most significantly, Anusayabai Kamble connected Dalit women's education with the development of human dignity, *svaabhimaan* (self-respect) and *svaavalamban* (self-reliance):

> Education of girls will light the wick of *svaabhimaan*. If the excluded want to progress and rise to the level of the *pudharalele lok* [progressive upper castes], they should take care of women, the other wheel [of the family cart]. Along with themselves they should allow women to reap the *laabha* [profits]

of education.... Only then will the family cart run smoothly and reach its desired destination in a secure manner. Although the Brahmans and other so-called higher-caste and -class people at times seem to hinder women's education, in actual practice they never keep their women away from education.... This can be gauged from the increasing activities of the Bharat Mahila Vidyapeeth [Karve's Indian Women's University, established in 1916]. What they want is that their daughters should pursue and profit from whatever education they like. Why will they then want to spend the municipality funds on the non-Brahman and the excluded community's education? They are *svaarthi* [selfish]; they want to hinder and stagnate this *pavitra karya* [pure act of education] and instead spend on their health, hygiene, and luxury. Thus, in these times, we should not sit idle, but *eksaarakhi dhadpad karoon* [consistently struggle all the time] to execute the *pavitra kaayadaa* [pure law] of compulsory primary education, make our *bhaavi pidhi* [future generations] drink *shikshaamrut* [the elixir of education], and clear their path in the journey toward *unnatishikhar* [the peak of advancement]. *Bhaavipidhit svaabhimaan nirmaan karaavaa* [Develop self-respect in the future generations].

(*Mooknayak*, 11 September 1920)

Kamble thus underscored that the fundamental agenda of education was to inculcate self-respect, self-confidence and dignity for a degraded community; Dalit women had a central role to play in this process. She challenged Brahmans and other upper castes who acted selfishly and sought to pollute the pure act of education by limiting it to their caste and class. She articulated these modern universal ideals and ideas in the local Marathi vernacular, much as Ambedkar did when he forcefully declared that '*svaabhimaanshunya jeevan kanthane naamardapanache aahe*' (to live without self-respect is to live effeminately, in cowardice) (*Bahishkrut Bharat*, 3 May 1929). In making these arguments, Ambedkar clearly drew upon problematic conceptions of masculinity and femininity that were almost universal among Indian political figures, including some feminists, during this period. Ambedkar was keenly aware about how feminine 'nature' had been essentialised. As a result, he argued that self-respect was applicable to masculine nature and to both women and men. Hence both must become more 'masculine', more self-conscious, and construct self-confidence and make their own destiny in a determined manner.

Most significantly, rejecting the lofty upper-caste, middle-class ideals of *saundarya* (beauty), *vaibhav* (wealth and prosperity), *streedharma* (moral codes for women), and the 'softer' virtues of beauty, compassion and submission, Kamble began and ended her essay by emphasising the development of the inner resources of *svaabhimaan* and *svaavalamban* that had been denied to Dalits. The fundamental task of education for most ordinary Dalit women and men was to build self-respect and self-reliance, and *remake*, not merely refine, their whole selves as upper-caste women did. Shaping *svaabhimaan* was also geared towards *sudhaaranaa* (improvement), nurturing, and the advancement of individual, family and community in the present and the future. Dignity was important to lowly Dalit women and children in refashioning their futures because for Dalits, *svaabhimaan* and *pratishthaa* were not an always-already natural given, or even a solitary individual achievement. Living in an oppressive, hierarchical and unjust society that subjected them to degrading conditions and systematic humiliation, they had to struggle to develop self-respect and individuality, and cultivate and express an identity they would generate out of their stigmatised selfhood.

The need for and programme of education for Dalit women and Dalit womanhood emerged out of Dalits' local, political, civilisational and cultural anxieties as they sought to attain a *vernacularised* modernity reflected in a variety of Marathi key concepts: *maanuski, sudhaaranaa* (improvement and reform), progress, *khare maanavi hakka* (real human rights), *samataa* (equality), *svaabhimaan* (dignity) and *vyakti olakh* (personal identity). To achieve this end, Dalit radicals' and especially Ambedkar's movement emphasised creating two key institutions: the Bahishkrut Bharat Samaaj Shikshan Prasarak Mandali (Excluded Indian Education Dissemination Committee) and Svaabhimaan Saunrakshak Mandali (Self-Respect Protection Committee),[8] and mobilising material as well as symbolic resources. In this local historical educational conjuncture, Dalits understood and appropriated the discourse of human dignity, which inflected their march towards a certain modernity. In the process, Dalit radicals provided a motive force for Dalit women's subject formation. By contrast, these double forces – the intertwining of education with Hindu nationalist and gendered discourse – depicted women (and elite womanhood) as weak, helpless, submissive and in need of protection, and at the same time as powerful tools for regenerating the nation.

Despite the opposition of Brahmans, women's education expanded rapidly during the period from 1860 to 1920. Revivalists' campaigns to prevent women and non-Brahmans from entering schools failed miserably, but progress for Dalits was very slow. The number of girls in all institutions in Bombay Presidency increased by about 30 per cent – from 52,941 in 1886 to 1887 to 187,265 by 1921 to 1922 (Richey 1924, 155), yet this attendance was a mere fraction of the millions of Indian women who remained illiterate. There were 1,252 non-Brahman and eighty-four Mahar and Mang girls, as against 1,102 Brahman girls, in the municipal schools (P. Rao 2010, 158). Statistics often hide as much as they reveal: the comparatively rapid progress of the advanced classes can often lead one to overlook the very slow progress of the 'others'. Compared to 150 Brahman and almost twice their number, 299 non-Brahman women, only *two* Dalit women attended college (Richey 1924, 42–43). In 1923 in the Bombay Presidency, about thirty-four girls and 1,235 boys attended state-run schools. In April 1923, when the Bombay branch of the Bahishkrut Bharat Samaaj founded a free school, it attracted only fifteen girls out of a population of forty-one students (Pawar and Moon 2008, 76).

Yet the *Quinquennial Report* of 1927 reported that 'with a total population of 1,983,415 Backward Class females in Bombay Presidency in 1927, only 5,739 girls were studying in the lower primary and only 159 girls in the middle classes, one in the higher classes and none in the University classes' (Starte Committee 1930, 23). Hence the Starte Committee of 1930, along with many Dalits, emphasised that, as the Hartog Committee had suggested, preference should be given to girls' education by providing scholarships and hostels for Dalit girls. The Starte Committee made further suggestions for women's teacher training colleges. It continued:

> The purpose [of the college] was to accelerate the growth of DC women teachers to take charge of the education of the DC. Also, the hostels were to be Boarding Schools in which besides providing accommodation to girls opportunities were afforded to others for instruction in useful Arts and Crafts with a view to open them to new ways of earning a living.
>
> (Starte Committee 1930, 23–24)

The colonial state gradually did make efforts towards Dalit female education and employment. However, in Bombay Presidency in the 1930s, only Pune Brahman women fared well in education. These women also competed with men to obtain scholarships: for example, Iravati Karve won the Humboldt Scholarship to study anthropology at Berlin University; Kamlabai Deshpande completed her doctoral studies at Prague University; and Paranjpay received her doctorate in meteorology from London University (Gogate 1988, 36–37). The highest level of education a Dalit woman could attain in Pune, though, was high school. There were only fourteen Dalit female students out of Pune's total high school enrolment of 2,395 girls, and only four were in the middle school (Gadgil 1952, 286). Even in 1954, only three could attain an eleventh-grade education (Sovani *et al.* 1956, 39). Therefore, in order to dispel the 'darkness of ignorance' (Deshbratar 1934), Dalit men and women demanded women's education both in villages and cities. Unlike many upper-castes, male and female Dalit radicals upheld Dalit women's higher education and advertised their accomplishments widely.

Educated women challenge Brahman male hegemony

While Dalit women struggled to educate themselves, upper-caste, middle-class women's literary talent found expression in autobiographies, novels and journal articles.[9] Even some middle-class men fought oppression and prejudice to enable women to become teachers, doctors and professionals in other fields. While Dalits fought for social equality and equal opportunity, demanding material benefits such as jobs, upper-caste bourgeois ideas over-emphasised feminised education and traditional roles for women. Women's education did expand; however, many upper-caste elite women were restrained in terms of their freedom, knowledge about their society and critical thinking. Except for a few, like Kantabai Tarkhadkar (discussed below) or Pandita Ramabai, most upper-caste educated women reinforced bourgeois cultural notions that embellished 'feminine' virtues: beauty, mellowness and moderation. Others spoke of the need for educated women to 'develop' such womanly virtues as chastity, self-sacrifice, devotion to their husband and patience. New social forms of disciplining and inculcating 'femininity' were in order: thrift, cleanliness, home accounting and hygiene.

Some women challenged the gendered discourse of Brahman orthodoxy and patriarchy. The irrelevance of *shastras* (religious scriptures) was a theme that emerged in the writings of several women. Continuing Phule's Satyashodhak tradition, the political precursor of challenging Brahmani hegemony and patriarchy in Maharashtra, Tarabai Shinde, a Maratha woman, expressed a growing frustration with Hindu orthodoxy in an 1882 polemical text *Stree Purush Tulana* (A Comparison of Women and Men). Shinde attacked Brahmani patriarchy and called for introspection among non-Brahman Kunbis regarding patriarchy.[10] Tarabai questioned the marginalisation of women's education, male reformers' mimicry of British habits, and the privileging of a masculinist public sphere. She exposed the nature of social degradation and caustically criticised non-Brahmans' unquestioned imitation of the Brahmani practices of enforced widowhood and censoring women. Unfortunately, however, she was perhaps ambivalent about these practices; she did not comment on social distinction and untouchability in Marathi society.

A decade later, continuing Tarabai's polemical tradition, a rare Brahman woman, Kantabai Tarkhadkar, emphasised that women writers should not be scared and must expose the *ashikshit* (illiterate) and *kroor* (cruel) traditions in the community as well as those affecting women of all classes – the 'trickery of *bhatbavaus* [Brahman priests] who for selfish motives forced oppressive traditions on ignorant people' (quoted in S. Karve 2003, 99). She continues:

> Our *shastras* [religious scriptures] and priests feel that when a woman even looks at a man her honour is in danger; however, how can the same scriptures allow a shameless barber to touch this woman? Don't *shastras* feel anything about this? There are problems of our traditions, for instance child marriages that cause thousands of losses of *santati* [lineage], wealth, honour, and the entire country's *dhuldhaan* [destruction]. Another problem is the marriage levy, which has almost become a tax, and the pride that priests take in exacting money.
>
> (Ibid., 102)

Like Phule's student Muktabai and the non-Brahman feminist Shinde, Tarkhadkar provoked her female readers to question the activities of *bhats* who incessantly pronounced their sacred scriptures, 'philosophised', and continuously contributed to others' *peedaa* (harassment/affliction). Significantly, she also wrote an essay about the problems of poor Kunbis (agriculturalists) who worked day and night to repay their ancestral loans. It was not the money-lenders who fleeced them, she alleged, but the Brahmans. Ultimately, she ended her essay with a prayer – 'May God keep you away from the [Brahmans'] reign of lies' (104). Tarkhadkar thus cautioned innocent women about the cunning practices of Brahman *bhats*.

The constraints of women's community

On rare occasions, some Brahman women also participated in Dalit *mahilaa samaaj* or women's community. For example, on 14 January 1929 at the *haldikunku*[11] ceremony during the Sankraant festival, women from Bhangi (Sweeper) as well as Brahman communities participated. The Bahishkrut Bharat Bhagini Sabha (Excluded Indian Sisters' Conference) also exchanged *tilgul*[12] and *haldikunku* with upper-caste women as well as participated in *bhajans (Navaakaal*, 14 September 1938). During one such *sprushya-asprushya* (touchable-Untouchable) women's *tilgul* event held on 19 January 1933 at Seva Sadan in Pune under the presidency of Tarabai Dabholkar, girls participated in many activities like skits, colloquy in English and drills. These events were inspired by Gandhian practices. In her speech, Dabholkar said:

> This event is new at Seva Sadan and it feels good to see that many Harijans have attended it. We should help them, encourage, consider them as our Hindu religious community and build bonds with them, and work towards erasing the blot of untouchability.
>
> (*Navaakaal*, 23 January 1933)

Following Dabholkar, Mainabai Jadhav, a Harijan woman, said:

> It is very satisfying to see that we all *sprushya-asprushya* women have come together for this event. You had embraced your tradition of generations and pushed us Harijans far away until today. But, I am happy that you have invited us to this sweet festivity. I thank the society for that. I request you to grant us equal rights as you would to the non-religious. I am extremely satisfied to see the touchable women and congratulate them for mixing with the Harijan women.
>
> (*Navaakaal*, 23 January 1933)

In a similar vein, in Amravati a *haldikunku* ceremony was held under the presidency of Mrs De, who emphasised the removal of distinctions between *sprushya-asprushya*. One Laxmibai Naik reported that another Brahman, Chandrabai Patwardhan, had also reiterated convincingly that 'caste discriminations should be abolished; [Dalit] women should live in a clean and tidy way as well as seek education' (*Bahishkrut Bharat*, 1 February 1929). Thus cleanliness and education were essential if Dalit women were to be included in the modern Hindu nation. Janakibai Apte of Ahmednagar had established the Hind Sevika Sangh and conducted literacy classes for Dalits. She also adopted an Untouchable girl, whom she brought up along with her own daughters in the 1960s (*Sadhana*, 1 September 1962). Efforts to adopt and employ Harijan children in the homes of the privileged castes were written into the bylaws of the Harijan Sevak Sangh's Constitution (Verma 1971, ix).[13] These significant efforts were celebrated in the pages of *Harijan* magazine.[14]

Despite these significant efforts, in general, upper-caste women entered into an alliance with upper-caste men and increased their corresponding social distance from the low castes. For many years, upper-caste women were denied education; they shared this exclusion with Shudras and Dalits. Brahman women like Anandibai Joshi, Anandibai Karve and Kashibai Kanitkar have described in detail the hostility they encountered while attending school or public meetings, yet they attempted to step beyond the threshold in a clandestine manner (see Kanitkar 1912; A. Karve 1951; Vaidya 1991). While some newly educated reformers insisted on their wives' and sisters' education, many orthodox family members at home and in public mocked, shunned and harassed them in different ways. Kashibai Kanitkar's misery was such that she repeatedly contemplated suicide. Although women shared their exclusion from the benefits of education with the lower castes, they continued to despise them and did not converse with them. The unschooled and lowly Dalit woman was the 'other' upon whom Brahman women could stage and even amplify their superiority. Even Pandita Ramabai attacked caste structure and Brahman orthodoxy and patriarchy as did non-Brahmans and Dalits, arguing that British rule and Hindu men crushed women, yet her discourse of reform did borrow from the dominant understanding of Hindu nationalism to construct the normative woman as high caste and Hindu[15] (as evident from the title and subject of her 1887 book *The High-Caste Hindu Woman*) or even her efforts for the Arya Mahilaa Samaaj (Noble or Respectable Women's Assembly), which she established on 1 June 1882 in Pune. Thus *anarya* (non-Arya) Dalit women were excluded altogether.[16] She, along with other women, failed to converse and establish connections with Phule, who hailed her as a champion, because that would have been another blasphemy (following her exit from Hinduism and conversion to Christianity).

Challenging upper-caste bourgeois ideals, Dalits' intense battle for education was deeply connected to their struggle for self-respect, dignity and self-confidence. Dalit women like Kotangale in fact underscored Ambedkar's 'second phase' of the battle for education by demanding Dalit education on a par with that of other classes.[17] With their toil, blood and taxes Dalits contributed to establishing and maintaining an education system from which they were practically excluded. The upper castes quickly grasped that if the free and compulsory education bill was passed they would have to pay more taxes; they defeated the bill.

Upper-caste men saw women's education, paradoxically, as enabling women to better fulfil their traditional roles, rather than creating new or different ones. Both Hindu and Muslim elite men wanted visibly virtuous bourgeois women to seek education, in order to make their own lives more harmonious and compatible but also to perpetuate their social and cultural positions. This puritanical agenda certainly aimed to maintain and even enhance their status. It revealed the double standards of morality and sex discrimination, and contributed to men's superiority over women. However, Dalit radicals departed from this project of constructing 'difference' by creating new spaces for women's autonomy in the politically contoured private and public spheres.

In sharp contrast to the middle-class goals of education to perpetuate traditional roles, a gendered framework of education was absent from the educational agenda of revolutionaries like Phule and Ambedkar. Most significantly, contradicting Brahmani ideas of policing women's congenital fickleness through education, Phule and Ambedkar declared that the primary function of education was to inculcate critical thinking that would enable both women and men to analyse the reasons behind the Brahman dominance that oppressed them and to struggle continuously in order to dismantle it. While upper castes underlined fundamental views of womanliness, Phule and Ambedkar aimed to construct Dalits – and especially Dalit women – as agents with a critical perspective on their own situation who would agitate and collectively organise against Brahmanism. While ambivalent upper-caste moderates did not want a complete overhaul of the socio-economic situation, many non-Brahman and Dalit radicals like Phule and Ambedkar aimed to strike at the roots of all structures and forms of Brahmanism.

Unlike Phule, Ambedkar and other Dalit radicals, very rarely did upper-caste, elite women deliberate on broader issues of the *Asprushya* and *asprushyata* (Untouchables and untouchability), and social discrimination, as well as the gender discrimination within. A perusal of literature penned by upper-caste elite women suggests how middle-class Marathi society existed and evolved during the turn of the twentieth century. Women wrote on a variety of topics, including the weather, the geography of different countries, domestic issues, sewing, embroidery, weaving, *raangoli* (floor patterns), *baal sangopan* (childrearing), home remedies, and so on. Some women also argued for systematic education for women and discussed scientific methods of cooking and weaving, women's behaviour, and national and international issues. Several upper- and middle-caste women contested forced widowhood, dowry, the age of consent for marriage, and health and sexuality for women (S. Karve 2003). They criticised some traditional practices, but did not link them to their own caste location and its privileges, and thus actually reinforced a Brahmanically stratified society. Their vision of enlightened domesticity and middle-class disciplinary rectitude was similar to the bourgeois values of Victorian society. However, Indian women compounded this with Brahmani values and constructed their own model of ideal Hindu womanhood that erased Dalit women altogether. Such discursive practices were a part of the colonial context, in which women knew their limited options and the art of the possible, and found spaces through opposition as well as accommodation with reformers. At the same time, erasing discussions of caste from their modern, middle-class discourse, they often remained silent on questions relating to Dalit women.

The boundaries and exclusions of liberal feminism

The (familial) closeness of upper-caste women to upper-caste men and their corresponding social distance from low-caste women and men led the feminist movement to focus particularly on elite, Brahmani education agendas. In striking a patriarchal bargain with upper-caste men, women conformed to existent social and patriarchal structures.

The 'respectable' woman as citizen-subject

Most elite women remained confined to their upper-caste social locations and were thus divorced from non-Brahman and Dalit challenges to Brahmani ortho-doxy. This may be due to several reasons. First, as Chatterjee has reminded us, the 'new woman' constructed by Hindu nationalist discourse was the reverse of the 'common' Dalit woman, who was coarse, loud, sexually promiscuous and subjected to brutal oppression by men. By maintaining a distinct distance from the prostitute, maidservant and washerwoman, nationalist patriarchs wanted to reform what they saw as the backward condition of women and regenerate the nation. The specific discourse of colonial modernity marked off the respectable, spiritual and domestic core from the disreputable, profane and public. National-ism thus conferred a new social responsibility and bourgeois respectability upon upper-caste women. They were to maintain spiritual and material purity by not imitating masculine habits (drinking, smoking) and, most importantly, by keeping away from Dalit women, who stereotypically could be indulging in these evils. They were also silently and vocally complicit in the selective knowledge-dissemination programme. In the process, in general high-caste, elite women excluded Dalit women altogether; at times they also constructed them as 'other and developed contrasts in order to constitute themselves as part of the exceptionalism of the Brahman caste.

Second, as Mrinalini Sinha has persuasively argued, 'the liberal discourse produced by middle-class Indian feminists was profoundly invested in the claim of the women's movement to be undivided by caste, class, and communal issues' (Sinha 1999, 218), as they sought to establish the new idea of the normative citizen-subject. Yet, in the process, some liberal feminists reinforced the upper-caste logic of the Hindu nation and aligned with mainstream nationalism. So while anti-caste movements offered radical critiques of gender, class and caste differentiation and untouchability, and remained independent from the national-ist and middle-class women's movements, in return the latter eclipsed non-Brahmans and Dalits because its 'liberal-feminist agenda ... was tied to the circulation of the national citizen-subject as the normative subject of political discourse' (217). Sinha continues: 'the alleged neutrality of the figure of the citizen-subject ... was sustained by a liberal-feminist politics that constructed itself as above considerations of caste, class, and sectarian divisions' (218).

But this strategy was not without costs. Indian history's and women's histo-ry's compelling constructions of a dream of perfect order, that is, liberal-feminist politics, for example, was 'disturbed by the nightmare of its random, hetero-geneous and often unruly' (Voss and Werner 1999, ii) and fragmented subjects: Dalit women. The liberal–feminist discourse did not consider the problems of untouchability or of Dalit women as worthy of discussion or even their participa-tion in the wider movement. As with Gandhian and nationalist rhetoric, Dalit, lower-class and caste struggles were peripheral to the project of any liberalism or liberal feminism. Some liberal Indian feminists attacked the structure of high-caste, Brahmani patriarchy for its oppressive caste practices. However, many of them, including Pandita Ramabai, could not stand outside these entanglements or engage with non-Brahman leaders like Phule; hence there were limitations to their radicalism. One reason for their adoption of such a position could be because feminists were strategically interested in making their cause *respectable*. In the effort to convince men to accept certain challenges to patriarchy, it was important for feminists to make the case that they were respectable people with respectable causes. For the same reason, perhaps, feminists did not embrace radical notions of sexuality.[18] In the process, however, they brought about a successful consolidation of liberal feminism with upper-caste, particularly Brahman, notions of the Hindu nation. At best, this branch of feminism merely paid lip-service to those (Dalit) women who were daily beaten down, mentally, physically, psychologically and spiritually, and who, unlike them, had no access to education.

Dalit women, liberal feminism and modernity

There is a problem with the assertion of women as a class or caste in the colony as well as post-colony. Although with this intellectual move the politics of liberal feminists challenged the double standards of the nationalists' patriarchal agendas, their politics were further divorced from radical subaltern critiques and struggles. The liberal–feminist discourse also masked the violence at the heart of 'Indian' modernity, which reconstructed caste- and class-bound inequalities for women. By directing attention to the complicity of patriarchal nationalism and 'colonial' women (see also Sarkar 1993, 1869–1878), I attempt to provide evidence, even if fragmentary, of previously eclipsed accounts of Dalit women in order to re-materialise the complex terrains on which the politics of liberal feminism was carried out. Unlike elite feminists, Dalit women faced a *double patriarchy* comprised of high castes and Dalit men, a complex feature of their everyday life that was also reproduced, as we have seen, in the realm of education.

Caste identity rather than gender was the primary framework of political identity. While Dalit women battled to recover their individual and collective self-esteem and to uplift their community, they also faced social discrimination at the hands of their upper-caste 'fortunate sisters'. They were ostracised by some members of the All India Women's Conference (AIWC). For example, Anjanbai Deshbhratar, who attended the Nagpur Conference of the AIWC on 1 January 1938, remarked:

the Savarna sisters' behaviour toward their *Asprushya bhagini* [Untouchable sisters] was unfriendly and abrupt and demonstrates their despicable mental attitude. During meals they asked Jaibai and other Untouchable delegates to sit at a distance and thus insulted our community by regarding them as polluting.

(Pawar and Moon 1989, 134)

Referring to this humiliating experience for Dalit women, the Nagpur Untouchable Women's Conference passed a resolution condemning touchable women's behaviour and announced the establishment of a new association: Srimati Ramabai Ambedkar Sangh (after Ambedkar's wife's name). Dalit women's contestations invoked the plural term *feminisms* to signify a paradigmatic break and forged an inclusive Dalit consciousness. At the time, the general women's movement did not have the solidarity or political consciousness that the Dalit community had developed.

It was in this complicated conjunction of social, educational and political battles that Dalit women emerged as historical subjects. In these emotionally contoured political and personal struggles, Dalit women were constituted as subjects and agents through discourses, power and the efforts of upper-caste elites' exclusionary politics and caste differentiation, as well as repression of the truth of untouchability and the particular problems of Dalit 'womanhood'. The Dalit woman was produced by the processes of Dalit women's active critique of upper-caste (Brahman) exceptionalism, direct and indirect involvement in the politically charged programme of education and the founding of political organisations, and remaking of the self through expression of their desires, fantasies and transgressive capacities. The third All India Untouchable Women's Conference in 1945 critiqued the double standards of the AIWC's agenda of 'sisterhood' and argued for organising separately (Pawar and Moon 1989, 80) because the 'working of the AIWC and women's voluntary associations was often marred by petty bickering and attitude of class discrimination among its members'.[19] The attitudes of upper-caste female leaders discouraged poor and lowly Dalit women from participating in women's associations; they had no access to them because of caste and class differentiation. As a result, the clear departure of Dalit women from the perspective of the mainstream nationalist women's movement occurred during colonial times and within the national movement.

Such events and subjective experiences of Dalit women force us to ask difficult and different questions about the roots of modern Indian nationalism and Indian women's liberal feminism as de-class, de-caste and de-communal (and not de-sexed), as argued by Sinha.[20] The construction of a citizen-subject without even a glance at the existence of the lowest of the low, let alone including them in the imagined Indian nation, is problematic. It is predicated on the denial of politics that goes into the establishment of elite power and privilege. It not only erases Dalit women from history but also obscures upper-caste women's collaboration in the ideological and practical work of caste power. It clearly blanks out the conjuncture between unequal orders and systems in contradictions that can enrich our knowledge. Thus, once again, as with Gandhian rhetoric, there is no doubt about how upper-caste, elite women constructed themselves as the *agents* of history who were to represent *all* women, including Dalits.

In general, elite feminists – analogous to the upper-caste, elite reformers – distanced themselves from Dalit struggles during the twentieth century because they were ambivalent about Dalit and Dalit women's questions. Puneri Brahmans maintained their intellectual and social elitism and had no close relations with non-Brahmans or Dalits. One non-Brahman recalled that 'they were high intellectuals who did not mix with ordinary people' (Omvedt 1974, 205). Similar to Hindu nationalists, they did not include Dalits in the imagined Hindu community. By constructing Dalit women as helpless and degraded, elite feminists could express solidarity with them as women or as part of a 'depressed' whole. The AIWC claimed to represent all Indian women (just as Gandhi claimed to represent all Indians, including Dalits, or the nationalist movement claimed to represent India), yet this claim indicated their aspiration of the imagined community of women and could not stand in actuality. The activities of the AIWC did result in broadening social and political consciousness among women of the upper-middle class; it represented their reality. They argued for equality and used Indian womanhood as a rhetorical device, but at the same time, in practice, they denied ordinary rights to doubly oppressed Dalit women. In feminist discourses Dalit women did not appear as actors with their own agendas and initiatives but rather as low, downtrodden and unfortunate objects of reform.

Women: a depressed class?

In the early decades of the twentieth century, women's organisations underlined the rights of 'women as a minority' and argued for reservations for women in the legislature and councils. Earlier the AIWC had acknowledged the need for special provisions for the inclusion of Dalit women, but it later rejected all special concessions to them and other groups in favour of abstract 'equality'. In 1932, during the deadlock over the Communal Award, the AIWC passed a resolution that the practice of untouchability was a disgrace to the Hindu religion and by fasting unto death Gandhi had, in fact, brought immediate attention to it.

In 1933, by the time of the Lothian Committee, the AIWC refused to make any official distinctions among women. Amrit Kaur, the AIWC president, testified before the committee that 'we have eliminated the words "depressed classes"' (quoted in Sinha 2006, 244). She argued, and rightly so, that all women were depressed: economically, politically, or even mentally. Thus she referred to the category of 'Indian women' as persons exploited because of their gender. Yet such a claim of 'all' women as a single 'Depressed Class' obviously extirpated questions not only about the absence of Depressed Class women from the women's organisations, but also the problem of the specific suppression, separate interests and special considerations of these women.

Although some notable women, like Muthulakshmi Reddi and Subarayon, to an extent recognised the need for special representation of Depressed Class women, on the whole, women's organisations (like male reformers) in colonial India relegated caste, untouchability and caste-based gender oppression into the social realm and made it a special burden of Dalit women alone. By contrast, Dalit radical feminism turned caste into a potential political category. It is important to note that unlike liberal feminists and other reformers or nationalists, both Ambedkar and Gandhi wanted to pass the burden of caste on to upper-caste Hindus and not to Dalits. Yet, influenced by Gandhi's position regarding the representation of Depressed Classes, liberal feminists chose to follow Gandhi over Ambedkar and women delegates like Malini Sukhtankar recorded their personal dissent against special concessions even for women. Like Gandhi, however, Sukhtankar was willing to make an exception in the case of Depressed Classes as a temporary measure, and advocated that Depressed Classes' seats be filled under a system of joint electorates so that they were not separate from the general Hindu population.[21] Most mainstream women's organisations of the period thus addressed the issue of untouchability through programmes of 'Harijan campaigns' and did not support Ambedkar's demands for political representation. Women were struggling to incorporate Gandhian principles in everyday practice.

Moreover, some women, like Anandibai Prabhudesai, also demanded different education for different women's classes according to their specific needs (quoted in S. Karve 2003, 115) – at times sounding like Tilak in terms of education. Manakabai Laad also stressed that labouring in textile mills, selling vegetables and working as housemaids was the work of *khalchya pratichya*, a 'lower quality' of woman, and *not* of high-quality women. She also mentioned that Nikambi *bai* was also teaching tailoring to all upper-quality/class women (Laad 1892). It is intriguing to note Manakabai's use of the word *pratichya* (quality) instead of *varg* (class). She thus always-already equated lower classes with lower quality. In addition, her comfortable upper-class life allowed her the luxury of the education she liked. In a similar vein, in 1933, Arundhati Apte, while commenting on the competition in employment between women and men, discouraged women's attainment of such jobs in textile mills. She argued that the coming together of women and men in small workplaces engendered illiteracy, ignorance and proximity with lower castes, noting that such practices of gendered and caste subjects were, 'indeed, the cause of immorality in such mills' (Apte 1933). Thus, in both the colonial and Brahmani discourses, the heat of factories, like the heat of the tropics, fostered promiscuity that required vigilant surveillance.

Some elite Brahman women did comment on class or caste, but, like Tilak and Gandhi, also cautioned their upper-caste 'sisters' against intermingling with lower-caste/class/quality people. They alleged that physical association with low-quality, lower-class, non-caste women and men was contaminating; such people were to be kept at a respectable distance or even avoided. By deploying the discourse of class and referring to women as a homogeneous unit – *stree varga* (class), *stree samaj* (community) or *stree jaat* (caste) – most upper-caste women writers sought to mobilise gender identity for women as a whole, beyond the collective identities of communities. Yet in the process they sought to universalise Brahmani power, consolidate their caste exclusivity and class interests, and exclude Dalit women. Even the domestic pedagogy of home science was readily applicable to their middle- and upper-class and -caste homes and the 'betterment' of their poorer sisters.[22]

Dalit women's exclusion from modern feminisms

Arguments for Dalit women's emancipation through education were produced, made public and contested during the early decades of the twentieth century, as Dalit radicals struggled for civic rights and sought to refashion Dalit community. Except for a few upper-caste, elite women, many women studied within the strict enclosures of Hindu orthodoxy and *patisevaa* (husband-service) and were schooled to reinforce traditional patriarchal norms, for example, of female subordination and seclusion. Barring a few exceptions in both the colonial and postcolonial periods,[23] they were complicit in the Brahmani patriarchal codes of caste and gender regulations, and engaged in reproducing the material and ideological structures of their social group; for this they were rewarded as well as punished.

The upper-caste, middle-class political strategy of homogenising gender also led to the exclusion and invisibility of Dalit women. Sinha explains, 'the very act of imagining a collective identity for women on the basis of a shared gender oppression was a noteworthy achievement in colonial times' (2006, 10). I concur with her, but only to an extent, because I contend that the celebration of an inclusive and broad-based movement was problematic for many women. The insistence on a universal category of 'woman', based on a single axis of gender identification, occluded the simultaneous entangled processes involving caste and untouchability, community, class and sexuality for Dalit women. These homogenising efforts have been seriously problematic for understanding the situations faced by Dalit women, whose histories remain largely unscrutinised. Engaging with these contradictions will enrich our understanding of the women's movement. Dalit women's occlusion by upper-caste feminists also parallels the invisibility of women of colour in white feminists' renderings in the US and UK.

Feminists and their political struggle sought to forget their differences and ignore these causes of separation and suspicion with the mainstream feminist movement. In general, such historically contingent, upper-caste feminism has been unable to critically engage with and confront inequalities of caste.[24] In this way, power inequalities within the women's movement were masked. Talking in generalised terms about women shielded the questions of identity, agency, and how these categories were constructed in complex contexts. Similar to leftist liberals, members of the Indian women's movement rarely discussed caste; when they did, they focused on higher castes and excluded Dalit castes, assuming instead that caste identities could be transcended by a universal sisterhood among women as a class.

Some elite mainstream feminists also argued that Dalit women's first loyalty must be to their gender and urged them to see the ways in which they were exploited by their own community, and by their fathers, husbands and brothers. Conforming to their preoccupation with women's unity and empowerment some mainstream feminists critiqued Dalit patriarchy.[25] However, Dalit women and men had already criticised Dalit men's sexist and masculinist rhetoric and practice. Upper-caste, middle-class women and their avowedly non-sectarian organisations framed the women's question and education agenda normatively as upper caste, middle class and Hindu. These women entertained notions of 'backwardness' regarding their Dalit and Muslim sisters, and enjoyed the privilege and power of their 'normalcy'. Constructing alliances across these differences was certainly not impossible; however, most educated feminists did not attempt it. Although ideologically some delegates of the AIWC wanted women to think beyond their 'narrow' experiences, in practice, as Sinha rightly argues, 'neither the propaganda nor the membership of the organisation ever reached much beyond the lower middle classes in urban and *mofussil* (district-level) towns in India' (2006, 56).

In line with Gandhi's position, liberal feminists framed the problems of caste and religious minorities as 'private', social and religious; unlike him, however, they also constituted it as a special burden of lower castes alone. Women wanted to appropriate the universal 'modern'; this meant contradicting traditional remnants of caste and in the process pushing the special burden of caste onto Dalits. They saw untouchability as a retrograde tradition and a blot on Hinduism. It was difficult for elite women to critically evaluate their religion and caste privileges and the entanglements, as well as materiality, of caste and gender. Although many attacked upper-caste practices, only rarely did feminists like Tarkhadkar and Pandita Ramabai critique their particular communities. Even then there were some limitations. For many women, engaging in such an exercise amounted to 'airing dirty laundry in public'; women feared such exposure. Further, some upper-caste women (like Land) seemed to be almost nauseated by proximity to the lower castes – male or female – as well as with the idea of being treated as lower-class servants.

Upper-caste women and men thus often deployed the flexible idea of the 'feminine' not only to reinforce male authority, but also to privilege their (Brahman) caste and their difference from 'others'. Women hence represented one of the most symbolic and closely surveilled possessions of the elite. Often, as writers and academics whose hegemonic tendencies tended to colonise disempowered Dalit women, they acted, theorised and wrote as if they were best able to judge whether and when other women's voices should be heard.[26] Dalit women in the late colonial and post-colonial periods continuously asked: Were Dalits in general and Dalit women in particular only to be heard when their voices resonated with the dominant discourse? The danger here is that the mainstream appropriates the voice of the subaltern and then claims to speak in its interests and even for it, thus once again 'silencing the subaltern', to paraphrase Gayatri Chakravarty Spivak (1988).

In post-independence times, some elite feminists, like some Dalits, have romanticised Dalit patriarchy. They suggest that women of the lower castes, especially Dalit women, though economically deprived, lead more sexually liberated lives than upper-caste women because the social constraints of seclusion and widowhood were not demanded of them and because divorce was allowed in many lower-caste communities (Liddle and Joshi 1986, 91, 65–69). They contended that Dalit women could drink, smoke or beat up their husbands. Although upper-caste women were afflicted by some 'softer' forms of gender oppression, many educated upper-caste women were granted freedom to move and work in the public arena so long as they respected the rules of caste and class endogamy. On the other hand, Dalit women did not have such rights and were vulnerable to state and upper-caste domination in the public and Dalit patriarchy in the private. While it is difficult to rank these different oppressions, the reason for the disjunction between lower-caste women's freedom and upper-caste women's limitations stemmed from different patriarchal systems that afflicted different castes.

It is in and due to these repressive processes that Dalit women were closer to Dalit men, as we will see in the next chapter. Although some upper-caste women helped Dalit efforts, in general the feminist frames they adopted failed to see critically their complicity in the oppression of other groups of men and women, and to interrogate Dalit women's subordination as both 'Dalit' and as 'women'. Many, as I have revealed, failed to recognise the social humiliation of Dalit women that led to particular social injustice and inequality. Consequently, elite women attempted to universalise women's culture and subordination, which was problematic.

Thus there were deeper tensions within womanhood and feminism as constructed in a colonial context. My intention here is not to question the potential of the profound transformation that the liberal discourse of women's freedom actuated for women's and nationalist politics. Rather, I want to draw attention to the silencing and invisibility of Dalit women that was brought about by the particular politics of the historically contingent Indian feminist movement, which has essentially been an upper-caste and middle-class movement since colonial times.[27] Several recent mainstream feminist historians have pointed out that lower-class and Dalit women were largely ignored in earlier feminist writings (see e.g. Sangari and Vaid 1989). What was missing was a genuine dialogue between the different castes of women to forge a common programme. This colonial legacy has led to distrust and suspicion even in postcolonial times.

Conclusion

Elite, Brahman men were ambivalent about education for women. They thus allowed women limited agency to function in a well-marked domestic sphere and, through coercion and consent, made them complicit in upholding Brahmani raaj. They thus initiated caste and gender trouble. Although elite nationalists also revealed their ideas about limited female agency, urban, elite, upper-caste women in various forms expressed their 'feminist' interests. Women carved out spaces for autonomy and initiated a range of social reforms.

There were contradictions as well as connections between upper-caste and Dalit agendas of *streeshikshan*. Initially the upper castes believed that women or Dalits knowing how to write could be dangerous – this would allow them to have power over the written word and improve their capacity to disrupt Brahman men's lives or Brahmani hegemonies. Unlike them, however, Dalit radicals increasingly wanted women to read and write, to fashion themselves and their futures. For upper castes, the protection of girls' chastity and hence their families' and communities' honour was certainly more important than the development of their minds. To an extent (as we will see in the next chapter) Dalits shared this agenda; unlike them, however, Dalits did not make a fetish of it, because they increasingly valued the modern development of critical mental faculties. Upper-caste women and men talked unendingly about women's traditional roles and domesticity, and sought to use education to help do better what was planned for them: marriage, motherhood, home science and management. This was hardly the agenda of Dalit education: instead of being better managers of the home, Dalit women sought to improve their self-respect and dignity because they were levers to uplift their caste and strengthen the nation.

Contestations over caste, gender and education also led to new constructions of modern womanhood(s): Dalit womanhood was predicated on building *svaab-himaan*, *svaavalamban* and *sudhaaranaa*, unlike the Brahman creation of a modern but modest, mellow, dependent, bourgeois woman. I extend this argument in the next chapter, which dwells on the construction of Dalit women's subjectivity and feminism in colonial western India. Although some women, like Rakhmabai and Pandita Ramabai, challenged Brahman patriarchy, at the same time many women in general (including educated ones like Anandibai Joshi and Ramabai Ranade) consented to it and agreed with male reformers' ideals of companionate wives and patriarchal practices.

While many women put aside the caste (or even gender) struggle in favour of a broader (national) struggle, at the same time, under the mask of a progressive women's movement, many upper-caste women's writings were also agents of reinscribing a middle-class, upper-caste code of conduct because women had a real fear of being outcast. They offered little or no discussion of 'different' and difficult issues like untouchability and caste inequalities because (like Gandhi), perhaps, for them, Dalit women were still in the 'waiting room of history'. They defined the normative, ideal woman and paid little attention to Dalit women, making little effort to engage with them. Very few women used their subversive writings to challenge caste discrimination and patriarchal practices, thus ignoring the existence or development of Dalit struggles. Thus, the disciplinary educational project regenerated caste and class privilege and inequalities as well as the caste- and class-bound female public realm. Most importantly, unlike Muktabai, Savitribai and Jotirao Phule, and Ambedkar, elite women failed to take into account the historical legacy of upper-caste men's oppression of women and Dalit men.

The upper-caste rhetoric of reformism and feminism failed to accept the double-sided Dalit theory of education: Dalit advancement and women's advancement were not seen as thoroughly intertwined with one another. The disciplinary power of education shaped new ideas of chastity, virtue and marital devotion as well as consenting subjects, who reproduced upper-caste and gendered norms. From these historically contingent processes emerged Brahmans' exclusive control of knowledge and sexual normativity as well as upper-caste women's role in sanctioning Brahman exclusivity. Like the old Brahman factions, moderates and extremists alike, elite women failed to establish alliances with the Dalit movement and remained divorced from Dalit women. In this manner, although women gained immensely and were successful in agitating for many reforms, in the process the circumscribed liberal–feminist rhetoric, as well as practices, shaped education agendas and gendered norms, and in particular excluded Dalit women. Even upper-caste male reformers, barring a few notable exceptions, failed to address Dalit demands for mass education, which they perceived as a threat to their privileges and jobs.

Some upper-caste women and men wanted girls' education to follow boys', related women's education to their familial and feminine roles, and objected to women's higher education. Unlike them, however, Dalit radicals wanted women and men to enter schools *at the same time*. In addition, they did *not* advocate separate education: women and men were to receive the same education and in co-educational contexts. Moreover, women were to seek self-reliance and even economic independence. The Dalit agenda severely critiqued elitist agendas and in turn enriched them. There was a deep chasm between the quality of education, school settings and playground beautification sought by a newly assertive and growing middle class and the fundamental rights to education, livelihood, and dignity sought by most Dalits, who were driven to the wall.

As a result, Dalit women challenged their exclusion by elite women and articulated different aims: seeking *shikshan* (education) and developing *svaabhimaan* (self-respect) instead of *saundarya* (beauty). They also contended the colonial construction of the 'woman question' that stereotyped the problems of a minority of Brahman women as those of Indian womanhood in general and constructed their womanhood out of this repression and erasure. Consequently, they were to play a key role in the Dalit movement, as I will analyse later in this book. They actively participated in the Dalit struggle, both directly and indirectly, and from this engagement emerged a new political consciousness, which they creatively used to found their own autonomous space in order to uplift their *samaaj* (community). In a sharp contrast with elite agenda of schooling women in traditional patriarchy, proper deportment, correct ritual, domestic practice and *sanskruti* (culture), Dalit radical technology underscored self-respect, self-reliance, and intellectual and moral superiority, and instilled in women the agency to dismantle hegemonic control and consent. Women continued to gain more, not less.

Notes

1 In a punitive campaign, one British lieutenant treated Bhil women like their menfolk in a 'war of extermination'. Administrative authorities voiced no doubts regarding this treatment of women (Ballhatchet 1957, 223–224).

2 For example, see Forbes (1979). Only very recently have feminist historians offered a corrective. See Chandra (2012, 20–21). Chandra also comments on the contribution of Savitribai Phule, which is a much neglected aspect in the history of women in India.

3 As Gordon Johnson reminds us, at the turn of the twentieth century, more than 80 per cent of Marathi newspaper editors were Brahmans. See Johnson (1970, 105, 107).

4 *Gruhalakshmi* (Wealth of the Home) magazine had this slogan in 1927 (S. Karve 2003, 55).

5 Chatterjee (1993, 120–121). Many feminist historians have already provided correctives to Chatterjee's arguments.

6 British sociologist Ann Oakley's studies of housework as an occupation have focused on the division of labour within the household as a major cause of inequality between the sexes. See, for instance, her *Housewife* (1974a) and *The Sociology of Housework* (1974b). The aim even of Wellesley College, situated in the north-eastern United States, the heartland of progressive reforms, was to develop 'moral education' for women.

7 Chandra (2012, 85). Chandra provides a critical analysis of Karve's pedagogical ideals and practices (83–98). She argues that 'for all its pretensions of democratising education, [Karve's Indian Woman's University] actually legitimised the new caste- and class-based knowledge economy'. However, he was attacked and queried by the Bombay-based newspaper the *Indian Social Reformer* about the collapse between woman, marriage and reproduction that the university openly institutionalised.

8 Newspapers started by Ambedkar express these vernacular idioms and efforts of Dalit radicals. For one such example see *Bahishkhrut Bharat*, 15 March 1929.

9 Especially after the 1880s, women started writing and found their own space by writing stories, autobiographies and experiences, such as *Sumitra* (1855), *Stribhushan* (1864), *Anandlahari* (1861), *Gruhini* (1877), *Streeshikshan Chunuh iku* (1899), *Bhaiya nche Avadate Masik* (A Magazine of Women's Choice) and *Bhagini* (1941).

10 Shinde; see Bhagwat (1997) and O'Hanlon (1994) for an extended analysis of this piece.

11 The *haldikunku* ceremony involves women exchanging red vermilion and turmeric powder. It is tied to certain festivals like Sankraant, the New Year celebration, but it can be celebrated otherwise too.

12 Small, sugary sesame balls exchanged among men and women during Sankraant.

13 I am grateful to Joel Lee for this point and for providing the source.

14 For example, see *Harijan* 1, 23 (July 1933), which stated: 'One Harijan has been employed as a servant by a *savarna* gentleman in Gollapalem.'

15 My argument is endorsed by Grewal (1996, 185, 208).

16 Meera Kosambi, Pandita Ramabai's biographer, mentions some of Ramabai's efforts for lower-caste women. It seems that after her 'shift to Kedgaon she focused on lower-caste famine victims rather than upper-caste widows and because of this her activities were peripheral to mainstream society'. See Kosambi (2000, 12).

17 *Mooknayak*, 5 June 1920. See Chapter 2 for these two phases of the battle for education.

18 I am grateful to Douglas Haynes for this discussion.

19 *Stree* (Woman) October 1936 and December 1938, *Shramik Mahila* (Women Labourers) February 1949, June 1949, May 1949 and October 1949. Sudha Gogate's study of women's writings in Marathi media points out that some women's magazines, like *Shramik Mahila* and *Stree*, made these allegations. See Gogate (1988, 115, 117).

20 I am thinking of Gandhi here, who wanted a de-sexed woman to serve the nation. Sinha (1999) complicates it by tying it to class, caste and communal identities.

21 See these dissenting views on the mode of representation for Depressed Class women in Sinha (2006, 244–245).

22 K. Srilata (2003) and Sharmila Rege (2006) have argued that they failed to recognise their Brahmanism itself and thought in terms of feminism.
23 I am reminded of the Mandal reforms and upper-caste women's demand for cancellation of reservations for Backward Classes. They brought to light the effects of Mandal on their marital chances of finding suitable partners from their own castes – thus they were not ready for inter-caste marriages.
24 My argument is endorsed by Tharu and Niranjana (1999, 497). See also the works of Vandana Sonalkar, Sharmila Rege, Uma Chakravarti and Anupama Rao.
25 Madhu Kishwar in discussion with Jaya Jaitly in Jaitly 1998; see also Datar (1999, 2964). Vandana Sonalkar (1999, 24–25) criticises mainstream feminists.
26 bell hooks (2001, 36) also writes about these hegemonising/hegemonic tendencies of white feminists.
27 Significantly, this period witnessed the predominance of upper-caste and middle-class women's issues of Brahmani patriarchy such as sati, widow remarriage and prohibiting child marriage.

References

Apte, Arundhati. 1933. Purushanchya vyavaharkshetrat striyanchi spardha (Women's competition in the realm of men's work). *Mahila*, July.
Babar, Sarojini. 1968. *Strisiksanaci Vatchala*. Mumbai: Government of Maharashtra.
Bahishkrut Bharat. 3 June 1927.
———. 1 February 1929.
———. 15 March 1929.
———. 3 May 1929.
Ballhatchet, Kenneth. 1957. *Social Policy and Social Change in Western India, 1817–1830*. Oxford: Oxford University Press.
Banerjee, Himani. 1992. Mothers and teachers: Gender and class in educational proposals for and by women in colonial Bengal. *Journal of Historical Sociology*, 5(1): 3.
Bhagwat, Vidyut. 1997. *Maharashtrachya Samajik Itihasachya Dishene* (Towards a Social History of Maharashtra). Pune: Women's Studies Centre, University of Pune.
———. 2004. *Stri Prasnachi Vaatchaal* (The Journey of the Woman Question). Pune: Pratima Prakashan.
Chakravarti, Uma. 1998. *Rewriting History: The Life and Times of Pandita Ramabai*. New Delhi: Kali for Women.
———. 2003. *Gendering Caste: Through a Feminist Lens*. Calcutta: Stree.
Chandra, Shefali. 2012. *The Sexual Life of English: Languages of Caste and Desire in Colonial India*. Durham, NC: Duke University Press.
Chatterjee, Partha. 1989. The nationalist resolution of the women's question. In *Recasting Women: Essays in Colonial History*, ed. S. Sangari and S. Vaid. New Delhi: Kali for Women.
———. 1993. *The Nation and Its Fragments: Colonial and Postcolonial Histories*. Princeton, NJ: Princeton University Press.
Chiplunkar, G.M. 1930. *Scientific Basis of Women's Education*. Poona: S.B. Hudlikar.
Datar, Chhaya. 1999. Non-Brahman renderings of feminism in Maharashtra: Is it a more emancipatory force? *Economic and Political Weekly*, 34(41): 2964–2968.
Deshbratar, Krishnarao. 1934. Shikshanavishayi kahi vichar (Some thoughts on education). *Janata*, 5 May.
Forbes, Geraldine. 1979. Women's movements in India: Traditional symbols and new roles. In *Social Movements in India*, Vol. 2, ed. M.S.A. Rao. New Delhi: Manohar.

Gadgil, D.R. 1952. *Poona, A Socio-Economic Survey, 1945–1952*. Poona: Gokhale Institute of Economics and Political Science.

Gogate, Sudha. 1988. *Status of Woman Reflected in Marathi Media, 1930–1970*. Pune: Shubhada Saraswat Publications.

Grewal, Inderpal. 1996. *Home and Harem: Nation, Gender, Empire, and the Cultures of Travel*. Durham, NC: Duke University Press.

Hancock, Mary. 1999. Gendering the modern: Women and home science in British India. In *Gender, Sexuality and Colonial Modernities*, ed. Antoinette Burton. New York: Routledge.

Harijan, 1(23). July 1933.

hooks, bell. 2001. Black women: Shaping feminist theory. In *Feminism and 'Race'*, ed. Kumkum Bhavnani. Oxford: Oxford University Press.

Jaitly, Jaya. 1998. Samvad. *Times of India*, 15 August.

Johnson, Gordon. 1970. Chitpavan Brahmans and politics in Western India. In *Elites in South Asia*, ed. E.R. Leach and S.N. Mukherjee. Cambridge: Cambridge University Press.

Kanitkar, Kashibai. 1912. *Pa. Va. Sau Dr. Anandibai Joshee Yanche Charitra va Patre*. Bombay: Manoranjan Grantha-Prasarak Mandali.

Karve, Anandibai. 1951. *Majhe Puran*, 2nd edn, ed. Kaveri Karve. Bombay: Keshave Bhikaji Dhavale.

Karve, Svati. 2003. *Streevikasachya Paulkhuna* (Important Achievements in the Development of Women). Pune: Pratima.

Kosambi, Meera. 2000. Women, emancipation, and equality. In *Ideals, Images and Real Lives*, ed. Alice Thorner and Krishnaraj Maithreyi. Hyderabad: Orient Longman.

Laad, Manakbai. 1892. Striyankarita shivankamachi mahiti (Information for women on sewing). *Arya Bhagini*, April.

Liddle, Joanna and Rama Joshi. 1986. *Daughters of Independence: Gender, Caste and Class in India*. New Brunswick, NJ: Rutgers University Press.

Mazumdar, Vina. 1976. The social reform movement in India: From Ranade to Nehru. In *Indian Women: From Purdah to Modernity*, ed. B.R. Nanda. New Delhi: Vikas.

Mooknayak. 28 February 1920.

——. 5 June 1920.

——. 11 September 1920.

Navaakaal. 23 January 1933.

——. 14 September 1938.

O'Hanlon, Rosalind. 1994. *A Comparison between Women and Men: Tarabai Shinde and the Critique of Gender Relations in Colonial India*. New Delhi: Oxford University Press.

Oakley, Ann. 1974a. *Housewife*. London: A. Lane.

——. 1974b. *The Sociology of Housework*. London: Robertson.

Omvedt, Gail. 1974. Non-Brahmans and nationalists in Poona. *Economic and Political Weekly*, 9: 6–8.

——. 2006. Why Dalits want English. *Times of India*, 9 November.

Pardeshi, Pratima. 1998. The Hindu Code Bill for the liberation of women. In *Gender and Caste*, ed. A. Rao. New Delhi: Kali for Women, 2003.

Pawar, Urmila and Meenakshi Moon. 1989. *Amhihi Itihas Ghadavala: Ambedkari Chalvalit Streeyancha Sahabhag*. Pune: Sugava.

——. 2008. *We Also Made History*, trans. Wandana Sonalkar. New Delhi: Zubaan.

Phule, Jotirao. 1882. Memorial address to the Hunter Education Commission. Ganja Peth,

Poona, 19 October. In *Collected Works of Mahatma Jotirao Phule*, Vol. II, trans. P.G. Patil. Bombay: Education Department, Government, 1991.

———. 1991. *Collected Works of Mahatma Jotirao Phule*, Vol. II, trans. P.G. Patil. Bombay: Education Department, Government.

Rao, Anupama. ed. 2003. *Gender and Caste*. New Delhi: Kali for Women.

———. 2009. *The Caste Question: Dalits and the Politics of Modern India*. Berkeley: University of California Press.

Rao, Parimala V. 2010. *Foundations of Tilak's Nationalism: Discrimination, Education, and Hindutva*. New Delhi: Orient Blackswan.

Rege, Sharmila. 2006. *Writing Caste/Writing Gender: Narrating Dalit Women's Testimonios*. New Delhi: Zubaan.

Richey, J.A. 1923. Education of Indian girls and women. In *Progress of Education in India, 1917–1922, Eighth Quinquennial Review*, Vol. 1. Calcutta: Superintendent Government Printing.

———. 1924. Female education. In *Progress of Education in India 1917–1922, Eighth Quinquennial Review*, Vol. II. Calcutta: Superintendent Government Printing.

Sadhana. 1 September 1962.

Sangari, Kumkum and Sudesh Vaid. 1989. *Recasting Women: Essays in Colonial History*. New Delhi: Kali for Women.

Sarkar, Tanika. 1993. Rhetoric against age of consent: Resisting colonial reason and death of a child-wife. *Economic and Political Weekly*, 28: 36.

Shinde, Tarabai. 2004. *Streepurush Tulana* (A Comparison between Men and Women). Pune: Sumedh Prakashan.

Shramik Mahila (Women Labourers). February 1949.

———. May 1949.

———. June 1949.

———. October 1949.

Sinha, Mrinalini. 1999. The lineage of the 'Indian' modern: Rhetoric, agency, and the Sarda Act in late colonial India. In *Gender, Sexuality, and Colonial Modernity*, ed. Antoinette Burton. New York: Routledge.

———. 2006. *Specters of Mother India*. Durham, NC: Duke University Press.

Sonalkar, Vandana. 1999. An agenda for gender politics. *Economic and Political Weekly*, 34: 1–2.

Sovani, N.V., D.P. Apte and R.G. Pendse. 1956. *Poona: A Re-Survey, the Changing Pattern of Employment and Earnings*. Pune: Gokhale Institute.

Spivak, Gayatri Chakravarti. 1988. Can the subaltern speak? In *Marxism and the Interpretation of Culture*, ed. Cary Nelson and Lawrence Grossberg. Urbana: University of Illinois Press.

Srilata, K. 2003. *The Other Half of the Coconut: Women Writing Self-Respect History: An Anthology of Self-Respect Literature (1928–1936)*, ed. and trans. K. Srilata. New Delhi: Kali for Women.

Starte Committee. 1930. Primary education of the Depressed Classes. *Starte Committee Report*. Bombay: Government Printing Press.

Stree (Woman). October 1936.

———. December 1938.

Sudharak. 31 October 1892.

Tharu, Susie and Tejaswini Niranjana. 1999. Problems for a contemporary theory of gender. In *Gender and Politics in India*, ed. Nivedita Menon. New Delhi: Oxford University Press.

Vaidya, S. 1991. *Shreemati Kashibai Kanitkar: Atma Charitra ani Charitra, 1861–1948*. Bombay: Popular Prakashan.

Verma, Mukut Behari. 1971. *History of the Harijan Sevak Sangh, 1932–1968*. Delhi: Harijan Sevak Sangh.

Voss, Paul J. and Marta L. Werner. 1999. Towards a politics of the archive. *Studies in the Literary Imagination*, 32: 1.

4 Modern Dalit women as agents

Dalit women's modern and strategic subjectivity and agential capacities emerged out of the exigencies of the immense, discontinuous and shifting political situation, and from their complex *everyday negotiation* with Dalit men's ambivalences and civilisational and cultural anxieties as well as with elite feminism's discourse and power of exclusions, erasures and repressions. It is their *historical experience* of the modern: of life's possibilities and pitfalls, the socio-economic developments as well as the momentous subjective transformations that shaped their lives on the individual and group levels and concomitantly thwarted their creative potential. In a sharp contrast to the upper-caste elite agenda for education to embellish the 'softer' virtues of beauty, submission, compassion and kindness in women and to instruct them in self-refinement, Phule, Ambedkar and the larger Dalit community urged women to gain every possible educational qualification to develop self-esteem, self-confidence, determinacy and daring in order to channel their agency effectively towards cleansing the community as well as striking at the roots of caste and gender oppression.

Ambedkar did not conceive of a struggle for Dalit rights and uplift that did not involve women's education and emancipation. Tackling Dalit patriarchy was an integral part of this battle for women's self-development. Yet there were complications, because these male-centred efforts were also contradictory and ambiguous. Paradoxically, while Dalit radicals attempted to restore agency and dignity to Dalit women, they also restricted them to an extent by emphasising their central role in the family. Nevertheless, on the whole, these articulations and practices enabled Dalit women's individual and collective agency.

The previous chapter dealt with how Dalit women fought the contradictions between the rhetoric of elite, Brahmani agenda of education as well as liberal feminism and their practices and forged a new political consciousness. This chapter continues that conversation and deepens it further by dealing with the politicisation around gender reforms and education within the Dalit community itself. There were significant connections as well as contradictions between Dalits and upper castes. Dalits' cultural anxiety, combined with the agenda of modernity and education, embraced upper-caste, middle-class ideas and practices to an extent, yet also radically departed from them in many different ways. Instead of dwelling on merely modernising, Dalits actually sought to deeply democratise; that is, to emphasise egalitarian gender relations and undercut privilege.

How then did Dalit radicals resolve the actual 'Dalit woman's question'? How did they negotiate their contradictions between confining women to the private sphere and pulling them into the public sphere? How did Dalit women make sense of their communities' and their own identities and educational experiences, and understand their beliefs about civic inclusion through educational opportunities? How did they live at the intersection of vast systems of power, patriarchy, caste and colonialism? In these processes, what did Dalit women gain and lose?

I answer these questions by investigating the kinds of uncertainty, anxiety and authority that underwrote Dalits' experiments in achieving a certain modernity. Dalits negotiated with the liberal-rationalist version of modernity and transformed its meaning to serve their own purposes relevant to their specific circumstances. However, by emphasising equality between different castes and male and female genders they engaged in practices of democratisation and went beyond merely modernising and creating a 'liberal' space for middle-class women. As a result, Phule and Ambedkar appropriated forces of modern power and sought to arrange and rearrange social and political conditions (both discursive and non-discursive) so as to oblige Dalit women to re-form their subjectivities, make choices within constraints and transform themselves for *sudhaaranaa* (improvement). In the process, the micro-technologies of governmentality and power polished, disciplined and 'civilised' Dalit women while simultaneously restricting them.

By illustrating how Dalit political and cultural anxieties coalesced particularly around the bodies of Dalit women I reveal that Dalits' struggle for education, equality, freedom and power became intimately connected with the politics of radically *remaking* Dalit women as historical *subjects* and *transgressive agents* of social reform. This 'self-making' of Dalit women was *not* like the 'recovery' of women's subjectivities that some feminists have rehearsed well in the context of upper-caste, elite women.[1] Moreover, Dalit women were also *not* merely 'humble interpreters of a supernatural leader's vision', as the historian Pandey (2013, 179) has recently suggested.

I challenge the dominant renderings of mainstream historiography of both India and the women's movement, which cast Dalit women as the 'labouring poor' or 'unfortunate and lowly'. Scholarship is divided on interpreting Dalit women's lives: they are either looked upon as those 'broken', 'terribly thrashed' or who have 'smash(ed) the prisons'.[2] I prise open the gap between the two sets of scholarships and dichotomies to emphasise how Dalit women cannot be confined to such linear readings. Rather, I focus on the complexity of Dalit women's subjectivities as both victims and agents: their struggles against victimhood shaped their selves and agency. Unlike middle-class, upper-caste women, Dalit women have never figured as subjects or agents in historical accounts of either anti-colonial nationalist struggle or of gender reforms. Some historians and feminist scholars have worked on the theoretical and compounded nature of caste and gender (for example, Gail Omvedt, Uma Chakravarti, Pratima Pardeshi, Sharmila Rege, Anupama Rao and Vandana Sonalkar); however, they have yet to study how these entangled oppressions affected the lived and everyday experiences of Dalit female entrants in schools. Moreover, by dealing with the shaping of Dalit women's ideas of family and wider society, I examine the intricate processes of the construction of ordinary Dalit women's subjectivities.

I centre on Phule's and Ambedkar's creative roles in radically democratising gender norms. As a result, gender emerged as a *generative* process to imagine 'new' forms of public emancipation. The two leaders reconceptualised the shifting, porous and entangled nature of public and private realms, and pioneered struggles for women's education, rights and status within both the community and the wider society. I demonstrate how they articulated the interlocking technologies of education, caste, gender, community, moral reforms and sexuality in a particular historical and political conjuncture. While it is tempting to read the two radical men as feminists (Rege 2013), we need to also look at the ways in which they are indeed analysing gender deeply rather than confining it to a narrow feminist agenda. The feminism of colonial times, especially of the early twentieth century, was a constrained project that focused on granting women limited access to the public sphere, education and political participation. Like Phule and Ambedkar, many imperial and indigenous feminists and upper-caste men worked to dismantle hegemonic structures; however, unlike the former, the latter did not seek actual parity with men.[3] In the fraught process of challenging some inequities, some reformers actually produced them anew.

Moreover, Phule's and Ambedkar's work for women's education attracts far less scholarly interest than that of Brahman educators like D.K. Karve or Pandita Ramabai.[4] Scholars have also done little to study the potential connections between public institutions such as education and private realms like the family, gender, marriage and sexuality in the context of the Dalit community. This chapter analyses how gender and sexuality became critical elements in the politicisation of Dalits and were connected to women's education and access to and potential for participation in the public domain.

Formal schools not only trained Dalit men and later women, but refashioning women became the reason for making education central. Dalit women's construction as 'custodians' of the community also reinforced their creative social role as 'subjects' of social reform. The question of women's liberation was central to Dalit political and social programmes. By centring on women's education and self-making, Dalits departed from elite, Brahmani norms, which were initially against women's education. Even later, when education was extended to women, Brahmans restricted it and prescribed an instrumental agenda of education. Yet Dalits imitated some Brahmani patriarchal norms. However, these processes were fractured. Dalits' insistence on patriarchal values was complicated and shifting because they negotiated, and only selectively appropriated, bourgeois values. At the same time, by constructing Dalit women as *historical agents* with real and political, not just symbolic, value (such as in the Hindu nationalist gender discourse), Dalits radically departed from caste-Hindu norms.

Nonetheless, in the process, Dalit radicals seemed to tighten patriarchal restrictions on women; this held unsettling implications for Dalit women, whose place in the body politic remained contested and uncertain. Due to the numerous tensions and shifting combinations of acceptance and rejection of caste and gender hierarchies, Dalit women were (and are) burdened by male reformers' anxieties and contradictions around gender.

In this chapter, I analyse the historically contingent discursive practices that shaped Dalit women's political consciousness from the early decades of the twentieth century. The first section deals with Phule's articulation of the interlocking technologies of knowledge, caste and gender as they operated on *bahujan* (non-Brahman and Dalit) women's bodies. The second focuses on education, gender and moral reforms from 1880 to 1920 to unravel Dalit radicals' anxieties about female sexuality. In their battle for higher social status, Dalit reformers also sought the authority to control the sexuality of stigmatised women, as we see in the *murali* reform. In the third section, I dwell on Ambedkar's anxiety and authority in relation to gender norms. I articulate his *double task* of fighting *two* intimate battles – external and internal – at the same time. By the external battle, I refer to efforts to deepen democratisation by attacking Brahmani normativity and privilege; by the internal battle, I mean his deployment of 'technology of the self' to remake Dalit women and attack Dalit patriarchy by emphasising women's education and challenging gender inequalities. I also examine the major limitations of this radicalism, including its emphasis on women's central place in the family. These contradictions affect(ed) many Dalit women, who yet have continued to critique, express their desires, and transgress, in order to contribute to the movement and carve out spaces (even if only small) for themselves. Finally, the last section focuses on Dalit women's radical and effective activism and its constraints.

I want to reiterate that, unlike upper-caste elite women, Dalit women did not write for or publish magazines of their own during that period. Most of the time, I have had to understand their views and lives through the vision and ideas of male reformers who wrote regularly for printed Dalit newspapers and periodicals. Women had only begun to express themselves in writing and did not systematically publish their views.

Phule's *trutiya ratna*: contesting knowledge, caste and gender differences

Phule forcefully attacked the interconnectedness of knowledge, human rights, untouchability, caste and gender by starting schools for *both*: Untouchables in 1848 and widows' homes for Brahman women in 1854. In contrast with the upper-caste agenda of producing modest helpmeets, Phule sought to identify knowledge as the *trutiya ratna* (literally the 'third jewel'). In his first political play, titled *Trutiya Ratna* (1855), Phule deployed the jewel as a metaphor for the third eye, which would help knowledge-seeking women to examine oppressive social relations and the multiple operations of Brahmani hegemony (Phule 1855;

also mentioned in Phule 1963, 115–117). Thus the *ratna* would be an important weapon especially for non-Brahman and Dalit women and men to strike at the roots of caste, gender and educational oppression. It would also help *bahujan* women to fight against *double* patriarchy, both within their homes and outside. Towards this end, and to challenge the Brahman monopoly on education, Phule opened his first school for low-caste girls in 1848 in Pune, the orthodox seat of power.

Reinforcing Jotirao's efforts, his wife Savitribai Phule devoted her life to working for women's education and against caste practices. Along with her husband, Savitribai underscored the significance of challenging caste endogamy and also suggested an anti-caste, *bahujan* alliance of all women and Shudras and Ati-Shudras against Brahmanism. The Phules thus challenged Brahmani practices as they discriminated against lower castes and restricted the sexuality of upper-caste women. Advancing her teacher's efforts, Muktabai Salve, a fourteen-year-old Mang girl in Phule's classroom in 1855, wrote about the 'Grief of Mang-Mahars'. In her essay Muktabai exposed the deep social stratification in society and criticised Brahmani domination. She also questioned God's deployment of caste differentiation: 'You have given the Vedas to Brahmans and nothing to us?' (Salve 1855). She further examined the *kroor* (cruel) attitude of Brahmans towards Mang-Mahars, using 'Mang-Mahars' as a combined community.

Most significantly, Muktabai lamented lower castes' exclusion from specific forms of textual knowledge. In fact, she ended her essay by pleading to Mang-Mahars to study hard in order to open their *trutiya ratna*. *Trutiya ratna*, the tool of critical thinking, would help them to analyse their oppressed lives under Brahmani hegemony as well as patriarchy. Seeking education was akin to building critical consciousness in women to bring about social change. Like her teacher Phule and other Dalit women, Muktabai insisted that education would end Brahmans' ill treatment of Shudra-Ati-Shudras.

While comparing the reproductive labour of Dalit and Brahman women, Muktabai underscored the particularities of the experiences of Dalit women: 'Our women give birth to babies and they do not even have a roof over their heads. How they suffer rain and cold! Try to think about it from your own experiences' (Karve 2003, 171). In other words, Muktabai asked, 'Aren't Dalit women "women" who suffer the pains of womanhood?', thereby implicating the reader. Muktabai thus subverted the strategies of both nationalists and elite women who passed the burden of eradicating untouchability and caste oppression on to Dalit women alone. Rather, by making a moral and political appeal to upper castes, she, like Ambedkar and Gandhi, attempted to return the burden of caste to them. Her particularly powerful script teaches us to connect the personal details of experiences with structural oppressions in gender and caste politics in order to analyse the specific hurdles of Dalit women. Significantly, Muktabai revealed the contradiction between the ideological myths of genteel (Hindu) womanhood and the particular realities of Dalit women's everyday struggles. We can ill afford to ignore how she theorised her ordinary personal experiences of pain by tying them to systemic phenomena: the anatomy of caste, class, knowledge and gender hierarchies, local economy and power relationships.

In a similar vein, Phule critiqued upper-caste Brahmanism, articulating brilliantly the overlapping and graded ways in which Brahmani patriarchy exploited women of different castes (Phule 1991a, 111–114). Moreover, by analysing how interlocking technologies, or the matrix of caste and gender oppressions, interacted to shape the multiple oppressions of non-Brahman, labouring Kunbi and Dalit women, Phule's analysis introduced a feminist framework of 'intersectionality'.[5] He analysed that the fundamental differences between lower- and upper-caste women sprang from possession of material resources – the burden of work and the particular difficulties – of Dalit-Bahujan women, in contrast with the (Brahman) Bhat women who had servants to attend to their needs (Phule 1991a, 50, 111–114). However, to him, the Brahman woman was also oppressed by the Brahman man. Hence, although gender seemed the fundamental basis for women's oppression, its entanglement with caste created severe problems for lower-caste women.

Most significantly, in his *Sarvajanik Satyadharma Pustak* (*Book of the Universal Philosophy of Truth*), published in 1891, Phule addressed *sarva ekandar streepurush* (that is, all women and men together), and analysed the material aspects of women's oppression. He declared that women were indeed *sreshtha* (superior) to men (Phule 1963, 149). He questioned:

> Have you ever heard of a Brahman widower performing *sataa*? They can marry many times, [but] the same is not allowed to women. When a married woman dies, her old, worn-out, decrepit widower marries ignorant maidens and ruins their youth. However, men have produced strict strictures and practices not to allow girls to re-establish marital relations for the second time. If you [men] do not like women's practice of marrying two to three times, how will women accept such filthy behaviour from men? Because women and men are capable of enjoying all *maanavi adhikaar* [human rights], it is discriminatory to have different standards for women and for *dhurt* [cunning] and *dhaadasi* [bold] men. As a result, women's rights are usurped by men, and of course the reverse will not apply. This has happened due to some daring men's selfish fabrications of the religious books. The other castes [like *sonaars*, goldsmiths] also follow the Brahmans and subject women to the same miseries.
>
> (Phule 1963, 149–153, 154)

Thus, Phule emphasised the double standards of Brahman men and their religion as well as the reproduction of women's oppression among non-Brahmans. He argued that while men frolicked with prostitutes and mistresses, they enforced fidelity for women. He further explained that the causes of the secondary position of women and Untouchables were *not* their naturally inferior physical strength (as some upper castes believed) (Phule 1991c, 456), but because they were not as *dhaadasi* (bold) as the *lobhi aani dhurt Aryabhat* (greedy and cunning Brahman) men, as well as their lack of knowledge. According to Phule, it was due to the '*kavebaji* [cunning] of Aryabhat Brahman [men] who do not allow *Shudra-Ati-Shudras* to even look at or listen to their *granths*' (ibid., 447). Phule diagnosed the situation of women in similar terms, using the term *streejaat*, which combines the roots *stree* (woman) with *jaat* (caste):

> Since *streejaat* (woman-caste) is very *abalaa* [lacking strength and vulnerable], *lobhi* [avaricious] and *dhaadasi* [daring] men with great cunning have never consulted women, and in general all men have always dominated them. Since they did not want them to understand *maanavi hakka* [human rights], they denied them *vidya* [knowledge]. Due to this all women are oppressed.
>
> (Phule 1991c, 448)

In this manner, Phule affirmed that crafty Brahman men conspired to exclude women from education and human rights, and poured *julum* (tyranny) on them. Moreover, they reproduced a similar strategy and denied knowledge to Shudra-Ati-Shudras in order to maintain their dominance (Phule 1963, 156). History shows how they have established their claim to 'purity' by 'othering' women. Yet, as we saw in the last chapter, some Brahman women consented to and supported Brahman men. Hence, for Phule, if women and Untouchables wanted real *sattaa* (power) they would have to seek education and fight Brahmanism. His agenda was reinforced and revised in Ambedkar's programme of education in the twentieth century.

Phule was the first revolutionary to insist on using the term *streepurush* (women-men). He thus underscored women and men's equality and their claims to common human rights as well as emphasising gender differentiation instead of a gender-neutral unity, as underscored by upper-caste elites. In a sharp contrast to the upper-caste agenda of schooling women in traditional patriarchy, proper deportment, correct ritual, and domestic practice and *sanskruti* (culture), Phule's and Ambedkar's radical technologies underlined the construction of intellectual and moral superiority. They thus challenged the idea of the natural endowment of mental faculties on Brahmans. They also instilled in women the agency to dismantle hegemonic control and consent. Middle-class Hindu and Muslim men were ambivalent about higher education for women and allowed limited agency for them to function in a well-marked domestic sphere while upholding Brahmani hegemony. Unlike them, however, Dalit radicals supported Dalit women's pursuits in higher education and advertised their academic achievements widely.

Although some women, like Rakhmabai and Pandita Ramabai, challenged Brahmani patriarchy, many Brahman women, like Anandibai Joshi and Ramabai Ranade, also implicitly consented to it by agreeing with male reformers' ideals of companionate wives and the patriarchal practices laid down for them. Women were to be modern, but modest and mellow. Although Pandita Ramabai challenged both reformist and nationalist patriarchal agendas, which robustly

Figure 4.1 Kumari Shakuntala studied subjects like Sanskrit, Marathi, English and
Economics to gain her MA in 1964 from Pune University (courtesy of
Vasant Moon Collection).

reinforced each other, her object of reform remained the high-caste Hindu
woman. She was a pioneering feminist who attacked the alliance between local
patriarchal elites and their colonial counterparts, but at the same time she also
borrowed to an extent from the discourse of dominant Hindu nationalism.[6] Yet
Phule supported her and asserted her rights because she challenged Brahmani
orthodoxy by converting to Christianity in 1883.[7]

Phule envisioned an emancipatory *Bali rajya*, the kingdom of the non-
Brahman king Bali, which was grounded in equality, dignity and freedom and
included all humans, whatever their gender or caste (Phule 1991b, 8, 9, 152). He
also revised marriage rituals and underscored a *Satyashodhak* marriage ceremony that called upon men to be considerate of a woman's need for knowledge,
dignity, respect and freedom, and bound them with a *pratidnya* (oath and agreement) (Phule 1963, 229–232).[8] He challenged practices of child marriage and
enforced widowhood.[9] Thus Phule consistently attacked the dominance of men
and of Brahmani social structures, and emphasised male–female equality
because he was concerned with the position, rights, identity, desires and

emotions of women. The conversations and debates around the 'woman's question' grew sharper in the early decades of the twentieth century, when Dalits encountered modernity in multiple ways.

Morality, modernity and reform before 1920

Dalit activists challenged both external colonial rule and upper castes' internal colonialism. When the nationalists were increasingly working to incorporate the 'others' (lower castes, women, Muslims), upwardly mobile non-Brahman and Dalit radicals critiqued Brahman power and hegemony, which they argued had stunted their *vyaktivikaas* (individuated advancement). While both non-Brahman and Dalit radicals vied for educational and employment opportunities, they also emphasised their families' education, health and moral discipline. Dalit radicals interrogated false dichotomies like public versus private and masculinity versus femininity and transcended them by organising women and asserting their autonomy. The household was an economic and domestic realm, but it was also tied to the interests of the community. Hence, it was impossible to show where 'private' relations ended and 'public' relations began, since both were imbricated in the same total context. Dalit *streepurush* were helpmeets in private as they had been in public. In the process, the imagination of family with its affective and social and political relations, making the home a political space and reforming women and gender was critical to the discourse of Dalit emancipation. Thus, unlike upper castes, Dalit radicals centred their efforts on a *double task*: refashioning Dalit women and building their self-confidence as well as uplifting the community.

Non-Brahmans and Dalits were indeed *torn* between emulating Brahmani social and religious values and rejecting them to an extent. Similar to Hindu nationalists, they simultaneously exalted and subordinated women. They sought to challenge Brahmani caste ideology along with importing and reproducing certain novel and even harsher patriarchal practices into their own households. Yet Dalits' insistence on patriarchal values was not as automatic as it might seem. Dalits were *not* involved in simple mimicry of upper-caste values practices, as some scholars believe. In fact Dalits 'negotiated' strategically every day; they selectively appropriated certain Brahmani values, reshaping them constantly to produce spaces for themselves within the colonial Victorian and Brahmani order.[10] This complicated, contingent and intentional *everyday negotiation* involving the dialectic of appropriation and subversion operated at every moment in the social, cultural, educational and political realms. The Dalit community was constantly in a process of making micro transformations through everyday negotiations.

In general, and due to the emergence of the 'new woman' paradigm of patriarchal nationalism in particular, elite women and men had always-already ostracised Dalit women as 'unrespectable', 'unruly' and 'other'. To attack such social constructions and stereotyping, Dalit radicals insisted on middle-class bourgeois *respectability* and honour: correct, 'cultured', decent manners; proper, full attire;

propriety of behaviour; and sexuality standards that were stricter for women than for men. In an effort to decentre upper castes, Dalits embraced to an extent the gendered discourse of morality; women emerged as the principal means of asserting the rhetoric of moral superiority. Thus, echoing nationalists, the metaphoric deployment of womanhood and domesticity was tied to fashioning Dalit modernity, and women bore the burden, as icons or status markers of the community. Unlike the nationalists, however, women were agents to remake themselves and uplift the community. Although these tenuous processes were fractured, by emphasising the constitutive role of women and gender in its construction, Dalit radicals sought to politicise the community through a reform of education, family and female subjects. To gain bourgeois respectability they sought to control sexual relations and denounced the immoral lives of some *baatalelya* (stigmatised) women like *muralis* and prostitutes. By emphasising their prurient interests, they expressed an anxiety about women's sexuality. Dalit radicals also underlined that Dalit women's sexual violation continued due to communities' prevalent 'customs' of abandoning Dalit girls as *muralis* and *jogtinis* in the name of God.

As a result, in 1909, Shivram Janaba Kamble of Pune and other reformers petitioned the British government to intervene in the *murali* matter, to end the practice of dedicating Mahar-Mang girls to the god Khanderao (or Khandoba) as *muralis* (Government of Bombay 1909, 1913). *Muralis* married to God were obligated to provide sexual services to men of all castes. Dalit reformers thus expressed their cultural anxiety over unbounded female sexuality by starting a criminalisation campaign. Their disciplinary tone underscored monogamous marriage and sex within marriage as the norm. Anything outside the institution of marriage was 'deviant' behaviour and potentially criminal, to be punished by law. Many non-Brahmans had already criticised the morality of upper-caste women as a strategy of resistance. Dalit radicals also negotiated with upper-caste hegemony by attempting to claim through gender reform the power denied to them by caste hierarchy, and valorised marriage and monogamy.

By adopting the popular medium of *jalsaa*, *powaadaa* and *tamaashaa*, Dalit troupes toured remote villages and modern cities and engaged in singing and music to bring about social change. In the process, however, Dalit radicals also sought to restrict celebration of the *jalsaa* to men so as to counter practices that they now considered immoral and degrading. They believed that by acting in such roles, Dalit women degraded the status of the Dalit community as a whole. Driven by a desire to 'modernise' their practices, they decried performance that they now considered 'backward'. In their battle for higher social status, Dalit reformers and the colonial state also sought the authority to control the sexuality of stigmatised women and criminalise their lifestyle, as we see in the *murali* reform of 1909. They thus sought to discipline and control the women of the Dalit community and thus one expression of their sexuality. This gave rise to a tangled politics of caste, untouchability, gender and moral reform in the colonial context. The logic of legal, bureaucratic and caste communities' regulation of *murali* sexuality was rooted in restructuring the self and based on modern middle-class sexual ethics.

Challenging the public redress and heavy and indignant censure from the press as deployed by Dalits and the colonial government, *muralis* like Shivubai Lakshman Jadhav provided in turn an internal critique by challenging the double standards of Dalit men. Shivubai declared that '*aamchyaavar tikaa karun haa prashna sutanaar naahi* [this question cannot be resolved by criticising us]' (quoted in Pawar 1989[2000], 90; see also Rao 2009, 63–65). She in fact held fathers responsible for the continuation of such 'evil' practices and for *muralis'* lives of shame, something ignored by male reformers. Shivubai called for a campaign against Dalit fathers, arguing that their superstitious beliefs and ignorance pushed their daughters into such caste-based sexual labour.

However, Dalit *streepurush* continued to inspire eloquent exercises in shame and sexual morality by arguing for chaste and respectable Dalit womanhood to maintain the pride of the community. To them, *muralis* stigmatised the entire community. Hence, women like Anusayabai Kamble from Rasta Peth, Pune, for example, called upon the community 'to provide every small assistance to *muralis* and *bhutyas* for their remarriage and resettlement' (*Mooknayak*, 11 September 1920). Kamble saw marriage as the only 'respectable' option for *muralis*. Dalit women's self-disciplining and monitoring of the sexual subject would thus constitute a respectable and powerful Dalit identity, most significant for a degraded community. In the process, however, Dalits also reintroduced gender hierarchies because, unlike women, men could get away with wrongdoing. The construction of family-oriented and chaste Dalit womanhood may, however, be read as Dalit radicals' effort to reclaim the morality of the community.

Historians have observed how the British constructed Indian men as 'weak' and 'lacking in manliness', even 'like women'. Indian elites challenged the colonial standpoint by arguing about Indian masculinity. Yet, while appropriating masculinity and historical subjectivity for themselves, upper-caste males in pre-colonial and colonial times deployed their internal colonialism within the colony by excluding Dalits (peasants, women, tribals) from history. They often stereotyped Dalit men as 'weak', 'stupid' and 'lacking self-discipline, intelligence, and manly virility' (Gupta 2010).[11] They also systematically disparaged and demonised low-caste Dalit women's sexuality to justify the nationalist movement, colonialism, casteism and racism. Both colonial and elite discourses and practices drew upon Brahmani frameworks of patriarchal hegemony (and strict surveillance of upper-caste women's sexuality) to create a dichotomy between the (upper-caste) goddess and the (lower-caste) whore. They also constructed Dalit women as public property and legitimised upper-caste men's access to the sexual labour of Dalit women, thereby socially constructing female Dalit sexuality. Due to caste practices of distinction between *anuloma* (hypergamous) and *pratiloma* (hypogamous) marriages, Brahman and upper-caste men constructed dominant discourses which strengthened connections between upper castes and chastity. In the process, upper-caste men always-already had open access to lower-caste women, whereas upper-caste elite women were a sign of power, a guarded possession. As the feminist Gayle Rubin has argued, discourses of 'sexual morality

[have] more in common with ideologies of racism than with true ethics [because they] grant virtue to already dominant groups' (1993, 15).

In this manner, upper-caste men crafted differentiations of gender, caste and sexuality, and amplified their morality and caste power. They accused the brutalised Dalits of 'loose' sexuality and through their practices forced many Dalit women to provide sexual services to them as *muralis*. Thus there was/is a chasm between upper- and lower-caste morality and the concept of womanhood: purity as opposed to promiscuity and desire, normality as opposed to deviance, superiority as opposed to subservience, order as opposed to disorder. Dalits were aware of these discontinuities and the ensuing tensions. Neither were non-Brahmans silent; they publicly criticised the morality of Brahman women as a strategy of resistance. Continuing to assert their morally superior public face and to challenge these Brahmani codes, as well as to underscore normative conjugality, Dalit radicals strategically sought to withdraw some Dalit women from the sex market. For them, such 'unchaste' women represented the backwardness of Dalits; they attempted to assert their superiority over Brahmans on this issue and to challenge their powerlessness.

Dalits negotiated with an upper-caste agenda of controlling women's sexuality and entrenching patriarchy by foregrounding institutions like family, marriage and chastity; yet they radically departed from it by interrupting upper-caste men's open access to Dalit women's sexual labour. Some scholars have argued that the impact of 'sanskritisation' entailed fresh restrictions for Dalit women as markers of higher social status [12] Yet, as I have revealed above, this would be too simplistic an argument that obliterates Dalits' intentionality. Indeed, Dalit politics emerged out of negotiating the historically contingent and contrary experiences that required Dalit subjects not to imagine the succession of the past but to recognise unprecedented changes in their present and to build their future. In their struggle to appropriate modernity, at times they adopted strategies of sanskritisation without much success, but also refused to be its prisoners and confronted the uncontested assumption of the sexual availability of Dalit women. They subverted their disadvantages through movements for self-respect and political empowerment as well as engendering cultural transformation. They thus twisted and turned the master narrative of modernity by reformulating their positions and pasts *within* Indian society and politics.

Significantly, in these entangled processes, there were *no* binaries; Dalits were thus *dominated* and *dominating* at the same time. Dalits emphasised marriage and sexual monogamy. With this strategy of elevating Dalit women's chastity, however, they limited the earlier flexibility of Dalit women's domestic arrangements. Such strategies were significant to protect Dalit personhood and social progression, to protect their crumbling woman/manhood or even human rights, as well as to build the confidence and dignity of women and the community as a whole. Thus control of sexuality was related to practices of Dalits' social regulations and was important in regenerating and modernising their society. This was a means of asserting a morally superior face to the upper castes, but of course, this strategy came with costs.

In the 1920s and especially the 1930s, the 'woman question' penetrated the Dalit public sphere. Dalit women represented the most symbolic and guarded possession of some Dalit elites. They associated women's status and *ijjat* and *aabru* (honour, respectability) with that of the community. Their strategy was perhaps similar to Victorian/imperial feminists', to upper-caste ideologies and reform around the woman question in the late nineteenth and early twentieth centuries, and to the universal agenda of women's work for the community and the nation. In the last decades of the nineteenth century, imperial feminists authorised a redemptive role for women in both the private domain of the family and public work. In this debate they used the trope of women as the 'producers' of the nation; their moral superiority and responsibility was extended from domestic to national functions (Burton 1994, 33–44).

To an extent, Ambedkar also shared the emancipation ideology of feminist debates and upheld Dalit women's gender roles as caretakers, transmitters of culture, class socialisers and civilisers of Dalit community. Similar to the nationalist and imperialist projects, he celebrated Dalit women's values of purity or chastity, honour, integrity and duty. Yet his construct of 'Dalit woman' both fits into this framework and radically departs from it in its attack on patriarchy within Dalit and non-Dalit communities. Most significantly, he challenged Dalit women through his writings, speeches and public activities, created possibilities, and worked for their individual and collective agency in order to be independent, organise effectively, uplift themselves and emancipate the Dalit community. In the process, Dalit women found a way to create agency, womanhood and a full humanity denied to them by both upper-caste elite nationalists and liberal feminists; they enacted their choices within constraints, and gained more, rather than less.

Anxiety and authority: Ambedkar and the empowerment of Dalit women

Unlike the upper-caste nationalists, Ambedkar, like Phule, dwelled on democratising patriarchal power relations rather than merely modernising gender relations. He attacked feudal and colonial structures which reinforced certain patriarchal forms and at the same time he pulled women into the public sphere. As a result, his rhetoric and practices helped women attain an enhanced sense of their agential capacities and self-respect rather than being restricted to familial and caste-based identities. Thus, Ambedkar centred on a *double task* of two intimate battles: an external one of attacking upper-castes and using the tool of education to uplift the Dalit community and, simultaneously, an internal battle of reforming women and gender. This section dwells on the ways in which Ambedkar negotiated the contradictions between emphasising Dalit women's domestic roles and pulling them into the public sphere. His politico-ethical rationality almost functioned in the way modern power produced subjects and governed their conduct: by altering 'the social and political worlds of the colonised and [attempting] to transform and redefine the very conditions of the desiring subject' (Scott 1999, 52).

Figure 4.2 Ambedkar at a meeting of women (courtesy of Ambedkar Collection).

Ambedkar was deeply and critically engaged in Dalits' self-making. His con-cerns for Dalit women indicate that the trope of Dalit womanhood as well as feminism and gender itself, had constitutive power in shaping Dalit ideology, discourses and the community. Dalit radicals' technologies generated a radical gender ideology that challenged in significant ways the basis on which women were excluded from power. These ideologies continued to shape the Dalit women's subjectivities and movement both in colonial and post-colonial India.

Streeshikshan was at the core of women's social reform. Ambedkar stressed the significance of *vidya aani dnyan* (knowledge and understanding) for both girls and boys:

> Knowledge and learning are not for men alone; they are essential for women too. Our ancestors were aware of this. If they had not been aware, the people serving in the platoons would not have educated their girls as they did. They say: *khaan tashi maati* [as is the quarry so will be the stone]. So you must remember that if you want *sudhaaranaa* [improvement] for future genera-tions, educating girls is very important. You cannot afford to forget my speech or to fail to put it into practice.
>
> (*Bahishkrut Bharat*, 3 February 1928)

Ambedkar thus emphasised cultivating women's intellects and self-development for genuine freedom. *Sudhaaranaa* became a metaphor for reform, and Ambedkar argued that without education and improvement women would remain 'backward' and unable to provide intelligent training and discipline for their children. Most significantly, Ambedkar wanted Dalit women to provide education for and create a sense of self-respect and ambition in their children. He wanted them to 'awaken [children's] *mahatvaakanksha* [aims and ambitions] gradually. Emphasise in their minds that they will be *thor* [respectable]. Do away with their *heengand* [inferiority complex]' (Ambedkar 2002a, 426). In this manner, he sought to link the emancipation of Dalit women through education with the internal transformation of the culture and ethos of the family. These processes led to possibilities. Education was also a marker of respectable status.

Yet Dalit radicals to an extent, like Hindu nationalists, nurtured an instrumentalist view of education for women. Women, by virtue of their caretaking functions and role as transmitters of culture, were 'custodians' of the community, responsible for its uplift and improvement. As feminists have argued, the social, cultural and political institutions of motherhood and marriage have proven to be fertile grounds for the restriction of women. However, in the case of Dalits, and in the particular historical, social and cultural contexts, this was a significant battle to uplift a degraded community and improve its human dignity.

Similar to the middle-class ideology of the upper castes, Ambedkar wanted Dalit women to produce healthy, educated and well-trained children. Yet he differed from the upper-caste agenda of education, which initially did not allow women to seek education (and when they did, women were to follow men). Rather, Ambedkar constantly emphasised Dalit women's rights to live as human beings, to have their individual consciousness and to think critically. To Dalit radicals, Dalit *women and men should enter schools at the same time* (see, e.g. their agenda at the All India Outcast Conference, published in *Bahishkrut Bharat*, 3 June 1928). Most significantly, by articulating a multi-pronged strategy along with social, religious and political reforms, Ambedkar stressed the importance of education for annihilating caste and for the Dalit struggle towards equality, freedom and citizenship. He fought for Dalits' access to all levels of education and deployed informal education through newspapers, speeches and conferences to instruct the Dalit community and especially Dalit women to battle against their difficulties.

Reinforcing Ambedkar's ideas, a Dalit activist, S.V. Gaikwad from Mumbai, reiterated:

> Women and men should have the same rights. Women do not have the freedom to think or express their choices. They should be given education. Without education we are trapped, we do not have the strength to *pratikaar* [resist]. In all this, the more women lose their freedom of thought, it will be beneficial to men. Men have been trying to *maarnyachaa* [kill] women's power to think. Hence women need social and political rights, freedom, and prestige like men.
>
> (*Janata*, 8 June 1940)

Like Phule, Gaikwad identified men's cunning in excluding women from critical thinking. In a sharp contrast with upper-caste women and men, he emphasised that women's education was indeed important for their selfhood, for equality with men, and for enabling them to fight for their basic human rights as well as social and political freedom.

Moreover, Phule and Dalit radicals, including Ambedkar, unlike their upper-caste counterparts, did not waste time and were not interested in drafting a distinct feminine curriculum for women, because for them the fundamental battle for Dalits was first to enter schools. The Dalit agenda contradicted those of the emerging middle classes, which emphasised basing women's moral education in everyday life. While the upper castes conceived of women's nature as libidinous and perceived women's agency negatively, Phule and Ambedkar constructed the positive agency of Dalit women.

Most significantly, these educational and political programmes were not erected on rhetoric alone. Indeed, the leaders and lay Dalits shared mutual interests, though these were of course contingent upon particular and shifting historical, political and intellectual contexts. Thus, Dalit radicals, and especially Phule's and Ambedkar's ideas and practices, did not simply stimulate Dalit *streepurush* into action, as if they were waiting be acted upon, but in the process the latter could indeed grasp their situation with greater clarity and forcefully forge strategies to radically change their conditions. Dalit women actively engaged in their subject formation by interpreting radical political discourse not only to explicate their situation but also to construct a concrete method for changing it. Indeed, for Dalits, '*svaavalamban hech khare unnatiche pratik*' (self-reliance became the symbol of true progress and advancement) (*Janata*, 4 August 1934). Anusuya Shivtarkar emphasised:

> It is not impossible for *aaplya* [our] educated women to work for the social, religious, and educational advancement of our community. We should educate *our* children, teach them to be clean, and instil in them their role in uplifting the Dalits. We clearly need *shikshan* [education] and *svaabhimaan* [self-respect]. Our women should be ready to contribute to the movement along with male brothers. Our future is in our hands, so we should work under the leadership of Ambedkar, participate in the movement, and prove our credibility.
>
> (Shivtarkar 1934)

Thus, Anusuya articulated the fundamental role of educating Dalit women and the practice of the 'technology of the self' in transforming themselves. Like many Dalits, she used the collective '*aapalya*' to signify the close-knit community as well as to produce individual and collective subjectivity. Most importantly, in this particular historical conjuncture, Dalits rarely used the names of their caste communities (like Mahar or Mang) to address educational or political reforms. This collective mentality certainly favoured Dalit militancy, and a united struggle for the Bahishkrut Samaaj (Community of the Excluded), especially in the contingent political conditions, yet there were contradictions in other ideologies of protest: for example, religious conversion. For Anusuya, like

Ambedkar and unlike the middle classes, reinforcing domestic ideology through women's education went beyond familial and individual uplift. She emphasised that by using their *shikshan, svaabhimaan* and *svaavalamban*, Dalit women were to work towards individual as well as community uplift and empowerment. Unlike for upper-caste women, fostering self-respect and self-confidence along with education was most significant to Dalit women.

Dalit women thus reinforced Ambedkar's agenda. Ramabai Gaikwad, daughter of Dadasaheb Gaikwad (Ambedkar's lieutenant), remembered his (Babasaheb's) words: 'Why should we live like insects and vermin, why should we rot in this dirt? We must uplift ourselves. We also must send our children to school; they must cast their light on the world' (Pawar and Moon 1989, 258). She was very influenced by his words, and taught her children while organising a *mahilaa mandal* (women's association).

Thus, education was not isolated from social and moral reform or from the construction of respectability, honour and dignity for women. As in the case of imperialists and nationalists, educated women were expected to exercise a 'civilising' influence. Dalits also aspired to the middle-class model of 'pure' womanhood. But the battle for Dalit women was *doubly difficult* because they had to acquire the bourgeois respectability that was always-already given to elite women while also actively disciplining and fashioning themselves. The embourgeoisement of the modern Dalit woman was also predicated on the creation of a social split between her and the *baatalelya* (stigmatised), uncultured 'others', so that Dalit radicals continued to dwell on the woman–community nexus. Some twenty-five years later, after the *murali* question had disappeared, during the Mahar *Parishad* of June 1936, Ambedkar emphasised that Mahar women of Kamathipura, the red-light district of Bombay, were a stain on the community. He forcefully declared: '*bhagininno, samaajaalaa battaa lavanaarya dhandya paasun mukta vhaa* [sisters, emancipate yourself from the business that stigmatises the community]' (*Times of India*, 17 June 1936; *Janata*, 4 July 1936). He continued:

> Because of you the Mahar community in Mumbai city has to lower their heads in shame. Every Mahar is sad to see other communities violate the honour of their sisters. If you want to go along with your caste members, you should leave your *durgandhit ayushyakram* [foul living]. Only if you are ready to do this can you join us. Not otherwise. Every society values the character of women *streejaat samaajaacha aalankar aahe* [because women are its ornaments]. Every man makes efforts to find a companion from the best *kul* [lineage] because he understands that his children, his family, and the prestige of his lineage depends on women's *sheel* [moral virtues]. But your lifestyle is a *battaa* [blot] on the community and woman-caste. So you should abandon your dirty living and improve your own prestige and dignity as well as that of your caste.... If you want to be called Mahar, you have to leave this *galichha* [filthy] life at once.
>
> (*Janata*, 4 July 1936)

Ambedkar thus sought to regulate the sexuality of some Dalit women. Yet, we need to grasp the specific context in which he emphasised morality, shame and respectability for the already degraded Dalit women, who were the ornaments and carriers of the (Mahar) caste line. He restricted the unruly lives of Dalit prostitutes while bringing respectable Dalit women into the public sphere. Educated Dalit women were to aspire to modern status, normative conjugality and higher gendered respectability in the public sphere. He also declared that he was not responsible for providing them with a means of making a living, because he believed that they would take care of themselves – but he supported their right to marry if they wished. He was also very disturbed when a Muslim man questioned Mahar (men): 'Why do you think it is a problem if we take many Mahar women?' Ambedkar wondered, how could men in general have open access to (Dalit) Mahar women?

Ambedkar thus expressed his contradictory position on prostitutes: they were victims who had to be cleansed and yet a blot worthy of blame. His dilemma on the prostitute question was shared by the Indian National Congress when prostitutes, the 'fallen women', insisted on participating alongside their 'respectable' bourgeois sisters in Gandhian campaigns during the early decades of the twentieth century. The resolution to save women from falling into evil rested uneasily with the assumption that such women were themselves evil. Like Gandhi, Ambedkar insisted that prostitutes give up their unfortunate profession, but did not make it a fetish or even naturalise 'pure womanhood', because he also understood the ritualised and routine sexual oppression of Dalit women. He also did not want women to 'follow him'. Rather, he made a deeper emotional appeal to women's *astitva* (being) and their circumstances. His advice was connected to building *svaabhimaan*, so he consistently invited Dalit women to participate in the very public discourses which concerned them as well as the community. He refused to confine them to the social realm, instead recognising their independence and encouraging their involvement in the Dalit movement as subjects and historical agents of democratisation.

Similar to Phule, Ambedkar underscored that the special burden of Dalit women was due to the operation of the interlocking technologies of caste and gender. He brilliantly theorised the much-debated origins of the caste system in India. Refuting the claims of other scholars of caste, he underscored the significance of endogamy or the 'closed-door system' as the fundamental characteristic or 'essence' of caste: 'Endogamy [is the] key to the mystery of the caste system.... It is only through the maintenance of equality between the sexes that the necessary endogamy of the group can be kept intact' (Ambedkar 1916, 1–21). Most significantly, by initiating this intellectual enquiry, Ambedkar articulated a gendered analysis of the construction of castes in India. He pointed out the role of sexuality in safeguarding the intellectual monopoly of the Brahman caste.

Ambedkar argued that women seemed to be 'gateways to the caste system', because it was due to the Brahmani articulation of the endogamous nature of caste, mainly through the regulation and control of women's sexuality, that caste enclosures and purity of blood could be maintained. Women's sexual subordination was institutionalised by ancient male lawgivers as well as by the masculinist state. Most significantly, Ambedkar exposed the close ties between sexuality and caste: Brahmani patriarchy and gender codes closely guarded and highly valued the sexuality of upper-caste 'surplus' women; 'sati, enforced widowhood, and girl marriage were primarily invented to solve the problems of both the *surplus man* and *woman*' and prevented them from transgressing the boundaries of caste. 'Strict endogamy could not be preserved without these customs' (Ambedkar 1916, 1–21). On the other hand, such practices almost institutionalised upper castes' sexual access to lower-caste women, as noted above.[13]

Sexuality itself was thus socially constructed. Ambedkar uncovered the fundamental functions of endogamy. This understanding of endogamy as a structuring principle of both caste and gender had underpinned the eugenic anxieties of upper castes. Extending Phule's agenda, Ambedkar also interlinked the struggles of fighting caste with that of radically fashioning lower-caste women. He investigated ancient Hindu literature to put forth a passionate critique of the lower position of Shudras as well as that of the Hindu woman (Ambedkar 1987, n.d.). Moreover, it was not a mere coincidence that Ambedkar wrote two articles almost replacing Shudras with women in the titles: 'Shudras and the Counter-Revolution' and 'Woman and the Counter-Revolution'. In his *Rise and Fall of the Hindu Woman*, Ambedkar argued that Brahmanism

> denied women the right to acquire knowledge which [was] the birthright of every human being. It was an insult because after, denying her the opportunity to acquire knowledge, she was declared to be as unclean as untruth for want of knowledge; she was also denied the right to realise her spiritual potential.
>
> (Ambedkar n.d., 14)

Some eighty years after Phule, Ambedkar examined the continued degradation of Shudras and women by some influential Brahman men. He thus established connections between the role of sexuality and Brahman castes' intellectual monopoly, which was predicated on their selective knowledge dissemination. They had cunningly restricted non-Brahmans, Dalits and women from learning. Only gradually, 'with the permanence of the marriage arrangement',[14] could Brahman men command Brahman women's compliance with their connivance. By sharing some of the knowledge privilege with upper-caste women, Brahman men thus shaped consenting women subjects, who in turn emphasised Brahman exclusivity.

Ambedkar attacked the Hindu law codes, especially that of Manu, who he argued was responsible for the fall of women. Ambedkar forcefully contended that for 'Manu a woman was a thing of no value'. Manu 'does not prevent a man from giving up his wife. Indeed he not only allows him to abandon his wife but he also permits him to sell her…. He prevents the wife from becoming free' (Ambedkar n.d., 20). Manu did not allow women any domination over property. He also granted men the right to physically punish women. Ambedkar also revealed the crevices and cracks in Manu's law of divorce:

Many Hindus also thought that Manu saw marriage as a sacrament and therefore did not allow divorce. This of course is far from the truth. His law against divorce had a very different motive. It was not to tie a man to a woman but to tie the woman to a man and to leave the man free.

(Ibid., 20)

Ambedkar thus articulated a powerful critique of Brahmani patriarchy and the sanctity of Hindu marriage, which could not be violated by divorce. He extended Phule's agenda and confronted some powerful Brahman men who accumulated power and deprived women of their freedom. Moreover, Ambedkar valued women's individual choices and construed marriage as a 'social contract', an agreement between women and men that could be broken at will.

Similar to some reformers in others parts of India, Shahu Maharaj, the non-Brahman leader, and Dalit radicals, including Ambedkar, supported inter-caste or mixed marriages in order to fight the organic connection between caste and gender inequality; the closing of certain caste groups against others; and those upper-caste Hindus who wanted to protect the cohesiveness of the community against pollution. However, it was Ambedkar who forcefully declared: '*The real remedy for breaking caste is inter-marriage. Nothing else will serve as the solvent of caste*' (Ambedkar 2002b, 289, emphasis in original). But Ambedkar was not the only one to broach such ideas.[15] During the historic Mahad Satyagraha of 25 December 1927, conducted under Ambedkar's leadership, his close associate G.N. Sahasrabuddhe, a Chitpavan Brahman man, burned a copy of the *Manusmriti* (Manu's law codes), thus rejecting its implication for everyone: Brahmans, Shudras, Dalits, women and men (Zelliot 1994, 77). While some feminists have rejected the implications of the *Manusmriti* for women, for others the very 'linking of women and Shudras *together* is one more evidence of the low position of women' (Desai and Krishnaraj 1987, 33, emphasis added).[16] They appear to be more concerned with the linking of women with the Shudra than with the subordination of the Shudra. Whatever happens to the Shudra woman?

During his speech at the Mahad Satyagraha women's meeting that evening, Ambedkar specifically placed the burden of social responsibility and of ending untouchability on Dalit women:

The problems of annihilation of caste and everyday life have to be tackled by men and women together. If men alone undertake this work, I have no doubt that they will take a longer time to complete it. If women, however, take this up, I believe that *compared to men, women would do a better job and will soon succeed*. Therefore you *must attend* the *parishads* [conferences] and *help men in their work*. To tell the truth, the task of removing untouchability belongs not to men, but to you women.

(*Bahishkrut Bharat*, 3 February 1928, emphasis added)

Thus Ambedkar brought women into the political public sphere even as he expressed his cultural and patriarchal anxiety and authority. There were some contradictions in his attitudes towards women. He made the project of ending untouchability the responsibility of both women and men, and thus asserted gender equity and companionship, arguing that as the 'men have decided to work for community uplift; so should you' (*Bahishkrut Bharat*, 3 February 1928). On the other hand, by suggesting that women could do better than men, he seemed to question his emphasis on gender equality. He appeared to emasculate men by suggesting the superior moral and physical strength of the female gender. While this declaration of women's advantage on one level suggests a move similar to those of upper-caste nationalists, on another level it differs from them by over-turning the gender asymmetry in men's favour. Moreover, he fashioned Dalit women as 'civilisers' not only of the home but also of the public domain.[17] Yet by looking upon women as 'equal partners' in the fight for justice, he emphas-ised the Dalit community's internal reforms to build the community and open up spaces for Dalit women. Ironically, he also identified woman as the 'helpmeet' of man, perhaps also unaware of her own rights and equal status to man, and thus made her supplementary to man's primary political tasks, thereby reiterat-ing the traditional gender discourse. This suggests the complicated and differen-tial positioning of women within Dalit modernity. In the process, Ambedkar underlined some gendered duties.

Nevertheless, all in all, Ambedkar and Dalit women were involved in a crit-ical refashioning of Dalit women's emotional and corporeal selves. Ambedkar

Figure 4.3 Dalit women dressed in full saris marching resolutely ahead (courtesy of Vasant Moon Collection).

argued with Dalit women that 'you gave birth to us [men] and we are treated worse than animals' (*Bahishkrut Bharat*, 3 February 1928). He therefore challenged Dalit women to either stop producing children or fight the blot of untouchability borne of them. He continues:

> Other people can get respectable jobs in courts and offices, but the sons born of your wombs are held in immense contempt. When you know all this, how will you answer if someone raises questions about why you gave us birth? What is the difference between us and the children born of the Kayastha and other caste-Hindu women? Why are Dalits subjected to an inferior position, denied educational and job opportunities and simple human rights? You must think about this. You must realise that you possess as much virtue, character, and purity as a Brahman woman. Moreover, you have the *manodharya* [tenacity of mind], *karaaripanaa* [faithful and firm] and *dhamak* [power and daring], something that the Brahman woman lacks.... So you should now pledge that you will not live in a *kalankit* [stigmatised] condition henceforth. Men have decided to work for improvement of the community; so should you.
>
> (*Bahishkrut Bharat*, 3 February 1928)

Similar to Phule, Ambedkar brought out the contradiction between the status of women belonging to different castes, but unlike him he also commented on the children they bore. He provoked Dalit women to question upper-caste women's privilege and claims to purity, in contrast to their curse of impurity. Once again, he saw women as victims and also found them worthy of blame; yet, most significantly, he wanted them to take control of their lives.

Ambedkar thus made gender a 'generative' process to enable women to enjoy their human rights. He forcefully advised women to exercise their choice in both the domestic and public political domains; women in turn deepened the practice. In the process, gender thus emerged as an unstable and fractured category. On the one hand, Dalits reinforced masculinity and patriarchal power in the name of the community or ethnic self-respect, and women faced some restrictions on their autonomy, personal decision-making and mobility. On the other hand, and unlike the upper-caste strategy, by infusing 'masculine' attributes like *dhadaadi*, *karaaripanaa* and *nischay* into the feminine, they sought to constitute a *masculine Dalit womanhood*. In sharp contrast with Brahmani patriarchy's prescription of femininity and genteel behaviour for women, Ambedkar emphasised Dalit women's strengths in firmness as opposed to the Brahmani construction of a fickle female, their equality with Dalit men, and their masculine willpower and daring. In the process, he engendered the construction of a masculine Dalit womanhood, as against upper-caste genteel, gendered discourses. Unlike the patronising and moralistic Gandhian attitude towards women, which praised them for their strength and idealised them as models of purity, patience, devotion, dependence, self-sacrifice and other 'feminine' ideals,[18] Ambedkar resorted to the practical remedies of building inner resources of self-confidence, independence and courage. He guided women's attention to the specifics of their oppression by caste and underscored their subordination by the caste–gender compound: their simultaneous oppression as Dalits and as women. Hence, he emphasised that *the problem of untouchability eradication was every Dalit woman's responsibility*.

By constantly concentrating on Dalit women's inner resources, internal strength, 'progressive character' and superior moral attributes, Ambedkar aimed to build Dalit women's confidence and self-respect in order to re-empower them. Although this self-fashioning had the potential to encourage Dalit women to discover new public roles, it also redefined and reified their mothering roles and regulated their emotional and social existence. To an extent, Dalit women also became political and moral symbols. Unlike upper-caste women, however, they were constituted as *subjects and historical agents*: responsible, powerful, real-life activists. Ambedkar favoured Dalit women and focused on empowering them in the politically contoured home, organising them in the public space, and encouraged their contributions to the struggle for social and political change. Thus he redrew the boundaries of the social reform of untouchability as an inherently political concern for Dalit women.

Another significant task for Ambedkar was the radical rejection of some detestable identity markers of untouchability: clothing, jewellery, naming and housing, which had been strictly policed by upper castes since time immemorial. He urged: *Svaccha raahnyas shikaa va sarva durgunanpaasun mukta rahaa* [learn to be clean and stay away from all bad qualities]. This was a significant battle to uplift a degraded community socially and improve its human dignity. Records of colonial ethnographers in the Bombay Presidency reveal their selective amnesia while recording details about lower-caste women. For instance, in his ethnographic study of the Mahar community, the colonial officer R.E. Enthoven adopted an objective standpoint towards Dalit women, mentioning only material details like dress and ornaments (Enthoven 1922, 407). Such a distinctive construction of caste as a social category was significantly predicated on the recognition of difference between touchables and Untouchables. Ambedkar had grasped this connection, and he explained 'body politics' to women during the Mahad conference:

> You should abandon all *junya* [old] and *galiccha* [filthy] customs and *chaliriti* [literally 'rituals' but here 'ways of living'], that provide *olakhnyachi khun* [recognisable markers] of untouchability. Certainly, Untouchables do not have a stamp of their Untouchable status on their foreheads. But Untouchables can be immediately identified due to their *chaliriti*, [which] I think have been forced upon us. Hence, you should abandon all markers that will identify you as Untouchables. Your *lugade nesanyachi padthat* [style of draping saris] is one such *saksha* [marker]. You should destroy this evidence. You should make it a habit to drape saris like the high-caste women. Similarly, the many *galsarya* [necklaces] and silver and tin bangles up to your elbow are [also] a mark of identification. One necklace is enough. Clothes reflect a more elegant appearance compared to jewellery, so you

should spend money on good clothing. If you must wear jewellery, then get gold jewellery.... Also, pay attention to cleanliness. Change your sari-draping style before you go home.

(*Bahishkrut Bharat*, 3 February 1928)

Thus, dress more than jewellery emerged as a powerful way of presenting Dalit women's transformed personhood because it was the most obvious marker. At one level, similar to the European cultural critique of aspects of Indian culture as requiring a 'civilising mission', Ambedkar criticised the rife superstition and judged women's particular practices as 'backward'. However, at another level, he also contested caste and relations of power by which 'others' identified Untouchables and by which in turn Untouchables identified themselves. By giving up these specific styles, Dalit women asserted themselves against both Brahmani caste and gender codes as well as intra-caste patriarchies. Yet some also affirmed to Ambedkar that '*aamhaalaa naahi baaman vhayacha*' (we don't want to become Brahman) (*Janata*, 6 November 1954) and rejected his emphasis on the middle-class model of womanhood.

Dalit women thus bore different kinds of material and symbolic burdens. On one hand, their distinctive markers were signs of enslavement and had to be discarded to establish a sense of autonomy, *svaabhimaan*, and to produce new subjectivities and forms of respectability. On the other hand, and most significantly, by adopting the style of upper-caste women, Dalit women contested and challenged Brahmani practices and values, selectively appropriated them, sought their revenge and *made* them *Dalit*. By featuring themselves as paragons of *womanly virtue*, they politically performed the 'traditional', normative Brahman sari draping to claim an Indian subjectivity. Such highly politicised *body politics*, conflicts and practical strategies thus constituted a symbolic rebellion.[19] It was indeed a social transgression that helped Dalits to articulate their political intentions of disrupting their disrespectability, challenge their Dalitness, and significantly transform their everyday lives. In order to constitute themselves anew, they intentionally desired forms of full dress that were previously a privilege afforded to upper-caste women *alone*. Dalit women were not allowed to wear a full sari, so the politics of the sari were significant for remaking the self and the community.

To Ambedkar, the politics of attire was significant. He himself adopted the Western-style suit and tie. He emphasised wearing clean and neat clothing, even if it was torn. He asked Mumbai's Dalit railway workers, who were notoriously fond of their uniforms, not to wear them at all times. His discourse and programmes penetrated deeper and affected the ideologies of many Dalits. Immediately after his Mahad speech, helped by the radical upper-caste women Lakshmibai Tipnis and Indirabai Chitre from the Chandraseniya Kayastha Prabhu community, women readily draped their saris like upper-caste women, covering their legs down to their ankles.[20] To do so, everyone was given eight *annas* for *choli-baangadi* (blouse-bangles). Ambedkar's speech also affected the men: they gave up the wild-looking jewellery on their hands and ears. Even the sweeper in the Mahad municipality resigned from his job (*Bahishkrut Bharat*, 3 February 1928). After a decade and a half, in 1942, Ambedkar recorded a similar change in dress, manners and speech of about 20–25,000 Dalit women present during the All India Depressed Classes Conference in Nagpur (Ambedkar 1942, 28–29).

Some Dalit women remembered that Ambedkar insisted that women wear clean white saris for the Buddhist conversion ceremony on 14 October 1956. When some women could not find saris, they wrapped white *dhotar* around themselves. By draping themselves in clean white clothes and saris to commemorate important events in their lives, many Dalit Buddhist women have kept their promise with Ambedkar, both in late colonial and post-colonial India. During the Dhammadiksha Suvarna Jayanti Bauddha Mahila Sammelan (Golden Jubilee of the Conversion to Buddhism, Buddhist Women's Conference) held in Nagpur on 10 October 2005, many Buddhist women wore white saris or *salvaar-kameez*. Some women also draped themselves in starched saris and wore sleeveless blouses, thus symbolising their advancement to an elite status. They thus exhibited dispositions that were hitherto a purview of the upper castes, and threatened the latter's historic identity.

In the process, Dalit women shaped their selves, their political and emotional subjectivities, and values, and redefined their habitus. They reinforced Dalit male radicals' emphasis on changing clothing, in stark contrast with male Hindu reformers whose clothing concerns were especially directed at women. This gendered response speaks to how the latter 'wanted to attack women for their love of jewellery and fashion, seen as evidence of women's inherent frivolity, as conspicuous consumption and an irrational aesthetic, as a marker to their pleasures, passions, and desires' (Gupta 2002, 141). Hindu reformers and Gandhians who argued that women should practise thrift and give up their love of jewellery never included Dalit women, for whom a change of jewellery signified refashioning their selves.

Moreover, the public intruded on the private. Home also became a political space; women were as actively involved there as in public. Reinforcing women's authority inside the home and within family and kinship relations, Ambedkar instructed them to not tolerate or cooperate with their men if they acted against the community pledge to avoid eating carrion (*Bahishkrut Bharat*, 3 February 1928; Keer 1962, 70–71, 104–105; Pawar and Moon 1989, 90). They were also not to feed their husbands if they consumed alcohol. By also underscoring birth control, Ambedkar constantly affirmed women's autonomy over their bodies. Moreover, he also defended R.D. Karve, a birth-control advocate and sexologist, during a lawsuit against him. Thus, contrary to upper castes' strengthening of Brahmani patriarchy through consent and coercion, Dalit radicals like Ambedkar envisaged contesting and challenging Dalit patriarchy as part of the battle for Dalit women's rights. Working on the personal and collective agency of Dalit women through their education played a major role in this reconstruction.

By invoking the paradigm of dignity, good habits (no alcohol, no carrion), orderliness, decency and cleanliness, Ambedkar sought to inculcate in women and men new social forms of discipline. He emphasised that Dalit women would play a major role in representing the community in its march towards a certain modernity. He stressed that a woman was an individual who must enjoy individuated subjectivity, individual freedom and equality with men. In the process, he fashioned a new self and 'womanhood'. He not only aimed to establish a regulatory technique that constrained and at the same time induced every Dalit woman to work upon herself, control her body and make changes; he also encouraged her to appreciate these changes.

Dalit women were not merely symbols of the community's identity; they were themselves rights-bearing subjects of the state. In contrast to upper-caste, middle-class agendas of education and elite liberal feminism, Phule and Ambedkar's radical technologies underscored an inclusive framework of education and reconfigured Dalit women as *agents*. Dalit women were thus 'emergent historical' subjects: 'fully involved in producing new meanings and values, new practices and social relations – those belonging to the "modern woman" whom [they] alternatively feared and scorned'.[21] Dalit women and men were subjects and gendered selves created in a specific socio-historical context at the conjunction of political, cultural and educational, and intellectual battles. Due to the operations of multiple and interlocking technologies, Dalit women refused to be merely the 'site' on which Untouchables attempted to uplift and improve their *samaaj*.[22] In fact they were *historical agents* who understood the exigencies of the political and intellectual context, made choices, transgressed and sought access to the public realm by erupting into its discourse and disrupting their harmony, and whose active, political involvement in Dalit *sabhaas* (meetings), *satyagrahas*, *parishads* (conferences) and emancipatory agendas was of the utmost importance. Thus, the consciousness I am describing is not necessarily a freely choosing individual who is the normative male subject of Western bourgeois liberalism, but that which came into being in Dalit women's response and engagement with hegemonic discourses. Dalit women were part of immense, discontinuous knottings and discursive displacements that constituted a 'subject-effect' (Spivak 1988, 341). Dalit radicals' rhetoric and discourses (ideologies and practices) thus provided immense possibilities for them. Dalit women were also complex agents interpellated by multiple discourses; as a result, subject positions were created out of their lived caste and gender experiences. The complicated processes of mutual affiliation and differentiation between the colonial rulers, dominant upper castes and emerging Dalit radicals provided the larger discursive field from which emerged ordinary Dalit women's subjectivities and political consciousness.

In the educational conjuncture of the early twentieth century, upper-caste reformism and feminism failed to accept the double-sided Dalit theory of education. Dalit advancement and women's advancement were not seen as thoroughly intertwined with one another. Challenging Hindu nationalist discourse, elite feminist convictions, false essentialisms, and the dichotomies of home/world, spiritual/material, feminine/masculine and private/public, Dalit radicals, especially Ambedkar, encouraged Dalit women to organise. He favoured their involvement in politics and encouraged them to hold independent meetings and conferences, thus bringing them into the public sphere and resorting to constitutional reforms and state intervention. Most significantly, Dalit radicals' call to women to join the Dalit movement was connected to the remaking of self. Thereby the community contradicted upper-caste elites' claim to be saving the 'motherland' by linking idealised womanhood with nationalism. By contrast, many elite men and women feminists remained unmarked by caste because to them it was *gharchaa prashna* (a question to be solved inside the Hindu family or home). Contradicting them, however, Phule and Ambedar radically recovered caste from the realm of the personal and social, debated it, and made it political by bringing Dalit women into the public sphere. In the process, they attempted to release them from strict social status and rigid gender hierarchies, and encouraged a sense of tremendous possibility for women's self-development.

This new self-development brought about a profound sense of enlargement and new capacities and emotions; yet frustration and despair also concomitantly ensued. However, it is out of such social, political, emotional and intellectual agitations and turbulences that the expansion of experiential possibilities and self-enlargement, as well as new arrangements and derangements of Dalit women's strategic subjectivity, were born, which in turn fashioned the modern Dalit. Women's direct and indirect involvement helped to shape their views of themselves and of their broader mission. Such work was crucial to the formation of Dalit women's subjectivity as well as integral to the construction of Dalit culture and new forms of historical self-consciousness that were modern. Yet some Dalit men borrowed upper-caste, middle-class patriarchal practices, surveilled women's bodies and sexuality, and sought to reconstitute patriarchy.

Dalit women's radical and effective activism

The arrival of modernity and process of democratisation among Dalits was both enabling and constraining. Women actively participated in the public political sphere at different levels. Chandrikabai Ramteke, Jaibai Chaudhari and Sulochanabai Dongre were fearless leaders in the All India Dalit Mahilaa Congress. In 1945 Jaibai was also a major activist of the Scheduled Caste Federation. She attended men's meetings, put forth her views candidly and counselled women on many topics (Pawar and Moon 1989, 209). Laxmibai Naik established an Untouchable Women's Society in 1921 in Amravati. Dadasaheb Gaikwad's daughters Seetabai, Ramabai and Geetabai were in the forefront of the Nasik's Kalaram temple-entry *satyagraha* of 1930. Ratibai Puranik was responsible for organising the first Sisters of the Bahishkrut Bharat Conference and worked for the wider distribution of Dalit journals (ibid., 224). Geetabai Pawar, an educated activist of the Matang community, and a teacher, along with Madhalebai and Mainabai, started a *mahilaa mandal* in 1932 and spread Ambedkar's message in Bheempura, Kamathipura and the Range Hill area in Pune. She clearly remembered her first speech trials at Seva Sadan, when Vitthal Ramji Shinde urged her to speak: 'I did not quite know what I was saying, but I could hear the sound of clapping. Shinde patted me on the back' (228). She took part in inter-caste common meals and believed in Ambedkar's movement and leadership. Mukta Sarvagod organised women in Mumbai's B.D.D. chawls and established nineteen women's associations. Anjanibai Deshbhratar organised a conference of Untouchable girl students from Berar in the Nagpur Cotton Market from 21 to 25 May 1936. She was also instrumental in founding a hostel for Dalit girls. As a teacher she continued her participation in the liberation movement.

At this historical conjuncture of the 1930s, when the debate on separate electorates for Dalits was contested between Dalits, elite nationalists and the colonial government, another crucial question emerged on the issue of representation: who actually represented the Dalits? Contesting Gandhi's claim as the 'true leader of Dalits', Anjanibai and Radhabai Kamble attended a meeting held by the Untouchable Women's Reform Association at Imamwada on 26 April 1936 and resolved: 'Dr. Babasaheb Ambedkar is the *true* leader of the Untouchable community, and we Untouchable women will follow his footsteps and undertake reforms; this is our resolve' (Pawar and Moon 1989, 213, emphasis added). Women articulated their claims and made critical choices. Yet Ambedkar's claim to *truly* represent Dalits electorally was thwarted by Dalit sub-castes like Chambhars and Mangs, who contested his authority (as a Mahar) to represent the entire Dalit community. Thus the processes that sought to construct a united Dalit identity were also fractured along *jati* lines.

Indirabai Patil (1919–64) was general secretary of the All India Untouchable Women's Council when it held its annual conference on 20 July 1942. About 25,000 women attended. Dongre and Shantabai Dani were presidents of Women's Conferences of the All India Scheduled Castes Federation (AISCF) and enjoyed power, however limited. Dongre gave an inspiring speech in front of 25,000 women assembled from different parts of the country. She also attended the Women's Conference in Kanpur in 1944. Dani was also the chairperson of the Women's Council of the AISCF held in Kanpur in 1944 and was secretary of the SCF in Bombay Presidency.

Women thus gained political consciousness due to their direct and indirect involvement in campaigns, protests, demonstrations, *satyagrahas*, political debates, *mahilaa mandals* and social reform movement activities, for example, via the Bahishkrut Hitakarini Sabha. In 1946 the SCF candidate was Radhabai Kamble, who emerged as a workers' leader from Bardi. Although educated only until the fourth grade, she was adept at standing in front of thousands of people and delivering provocative and strong speeches. Once she also declared, 'We will win our rights whatever happens. If they don't give them to us we will grab them, take them by force, and snatch them away' (Moon 2000, 95). While working in the ginning mill in Nagpur, Radhabai would stop the men and women as they came out of the gate and hold meetings outside the mill. Everyone would stand still and listen to her fiery speeches. Women held processions when there was injustice or violence against Dalits and shouted slogans such as 'The blue flag of the Dalits is dear to us and we want to become a ruling community' (Pawar and Moon 1989, 273). By participating in public meetings, women improved their confidence. Such a collective struggle allowed them to identify and support the larger Dalit community actively, particularly when the issue of separate electorates erupted. Parbatabai Meshram agreed that they 'gained knowledge of the outside world, they became aware of injustice, oppression, and insult, and a sense of identity awakened in them. They preferred to work for the society instead of sitting around and gossiping' (ibid., 275).

Dalit women also participated in the activities of the Samataa Sainik Dal (Army of Soldiers for Equality, SSD), formed in 1927. Ambedkar instituted the SSD, a disciplined youth wing, as a volunteer corps that initially organised meetings, rallies and conferences, house-to-house publicity campaigns, engaged in physical and psychological training, and sought to protect Dalits from physical attacks and intimidation. But after 1942 it took up a broader programme of confronting and resisting injustice, inequality and atrocities. The Sainiks wore red shirts and khaki pants and followed military discipline. Some Dalit radicals rhetorically questioned women about their contribution to the struggle and also requested that they participate in the Samataa Mahilaa Sainik Dal (Army of Women Soldiers for Equality, the women's wing of the SSD):

> Both men and women should work toward the progress of the community. Like men have volunteered enthusiastically, so should women, in order to bring about *unnati* (advancement). Women should be more organised than men. Times are changing and cultured men understand that women can equally contribute to the struggle. You have strength of character, patience, perseverance, and toughness, and the movement needs your contribution. Women should remember that it is time to show their stellar qualities and fight for their rights themselves. Similar to the Samataa Dal, women should also have a *sainik dal*. Women in other countries are progressing and so should Dalit women. Abandon the 'Untouchable' feeling that you are *heen* [deficient/inferior] and by *dhadaadi* [undertaking daring feats] you should resolve to assist Babasaheb's efforts. We are struggling for human rights, we should be able to get them and we should have the *paatrataa* [ability] to preserve them too. It is our duty to build that ability. Since we are fighting for our rights we should work on advancing our *yogyataa* [fitness/aptitude] to possess them and for this an organisation is needed. Why can't women volunteer with *utsaah* [enthusiasm] and *svayamsphurti* [self-motivation]? I ask all Untouchable women: don't sleep. Wake up. Throw away your old ideas and imaginations. Organise and reinforce the movement. On Babasaheb's next birthday he should be gifted with a magnificent salute by the Samataa Mahila Sainik Dal. *Nischyane, chikaatine karyaas laagaa* [start working resolutely and consistently], *kartutva gaajavaa* [make big achievements], and you will find *yash* [victory].
>
> (Jangalgop 1940)

Thus femininity and masculinity were (and are) shifting and unstable categories. At one level, by feminising patience, perseverance and toughness, Jangalgop almost reinforced Gandhian gendered attributes. Yet, like Ambedkar, he also wanted women to work in a masculine fashion by using resoluteness, *dhadaadi*, *dhamak* and *nischay* to their fullest abilities. As a result, more than 500 women marched 'in martial array like disciplined soldiers' at the start of the Nasik Satyagraha of 1930 (*Times of India*, 3 March 1930).

Many women also actively supported the Hindu Code Bill. Women were the central core of the bill through which, by proposing reforming laws on property, marriage and divorce, Ambedkar sought to question the prevailing Hindu laws which were patriarchal, and denied women certain fundamental rights. Nalini Ladke, a teacher, was the chairperson of a Dalit women's conference held on 29 February 1949. Lakshmibai Naik, Arunadevi Pise and Hirabai Meshram made speeches at this meeting and also passed a resolution supporting the Hindu Code Bill. They challenged some Brahman men and women who opposed the bill (Pawar and Moon 1989, 266–267) and resolved that hostels be set up for Dalit women and that they be provided with free education (*Janata*, 26 March 1949). Women thus contested elections, participated in school committees, fought for landless labour, joined the Naamaantar movement to change the name of Marathwada University to Dr Babasaheb Ambedkar University, and continuously challenged the hegemonic ruling communities and the state.

In this manner, Ambedkar challenged patriarchy in the everyday lives of women, yet he and his followers were also limited in creating a new anti-patriarchal consciousness. While many women played leading roles, others faced certain restrictions. Chandrika Ramteke recounted that, taking into account her public work for the movement, her husband shamefully accused her of going out '*navare karayala tithe*' (to make many husbands there) (Hatekar 1999, 76). Women faced enormous resistance from the men if they undertook organisational tasks. Sindhutai Pagare, Sushila Jadhav and Bhagatai Kaasare reported:

> We merely participated in programmes outlined by men. We were never *karyakarinichaa sadasyatva* (members of executive committees) or decision-makers and remained subservient to men in Dalit organisations like the Bauddhajan Panchayat Samiti, the Republican Party, and the Dalit Panthers [in post-Ambedkar times].

> (Pawar 1999, 98)

Thus women complained that their roles were limited to preparing other women to participate in organisations, collecting dues, leading demonstrations, or *purushanna ovalanyapurtich* (honouring men) (Sonkamble 2002).[23] The last act was a type of offering in which women waved a platter with light wicks around leaders' heads (to remove all troubles and evil) and garlanded them. Some women did not gain significant positions in male-dominated political spaces. The prescription of the 'mother model' entered the public domain and the workplace and curtailed the mobility, as well as equal opportunity and equal treatment, of women. In a move similar to an extent to imperial feminists and upper-caste nationalists, Ambedkar (1936) emphasised that *streejaat samajacha alankar aahe* (the woman-caste was a jewel of the community) and used the power of Dalit women. He also maintained that 'educated women were to protect their *sheel* [virtues], understand their *kartavya* [responsibility], and work toward the community's advancement' (*Bahishkrut Bharat*, 4 November 1927). To an extent, like Hindu nationalists, he constituted them as symbols of the modernisation of the Dalit community as a whole, yet he clearly departed from this characterisation to deploy them as agents, as levers to uplift the community.

Dalit radicals made women the guarantors of the transformed home, with the responsibility to protect and build a confident, masculine Dalit womanhood. Ambedkar and other Dalit activists had grasped the crisis that was emphasised by social stereotypes and colonial perceptions. In order to challenge the stereotypes about themselves, women and men resorted to asserting their masculinities in different ways: political activities, making demands in public spaces, cultural performances, and so on. Unlike Tilak and Gandhi, who were uncomfortable with women assuming high-profile public roles and assigned them jobs they saw as more suited to their feminine nature, Dalit radicals wanted women in the forefront of their struggle.

Dalit radicals thus continuously challenged upper castes and worked to destabilise their firm faith in their existential superiority over Dalits. Through these actions they attempted to keep their distance from Dalitness, which was associated with marginality, vulnerability and subordination. Dalit radicals' rhetoric, actions and efforts were important for restoring *svaabhimaan* and *svaavalamban* – that is, dignity – to Dalit women and the community as it attempted to fashion a new, modern self in the present and the future. Dalit affective narratives turned rhetoric into powerful discourse that shaped Dalit women's affect, behaviour and subjectivity through their ritualistic participation in the collective action for education, citizenship and empowerment.

Describing the achievements of such a *Bhimvaaraa* (winds of change, inspired by the Ambedkar movement), Baby Kamble, a feminist who shares her aunt's passion for justice, records the impact of Ambedkar's speeches on the community, noting that after his speech at Jejuri:

> my father's aunt Bhikabai ascended the stage and stood in front of Baba to address the gathering. She said, 'What Bhimrao Ambedkar says is very true [*khara*]. We should educate our children. We will not eat carcasses. We shall reform the society. We shall take oaths with Ambedkar to fight. Let anything happen, but I am telling you all to follow him'.
>
> (Kamble 1990, 64–65, 113)

By participating in many *sabhaas* (conferences), Bhikabai had gained immense confidence. She supported Ambedkar, who reminded women of their pivotal role in the Dalit revolution and called upon them to usher in a new era. Ambedkar, like Periyar, did not limit participation to domestic matters, but extended it firmly into the sphere of politics and provided novel ways to link personal and political struggles. As Shantabai Dani aptly sums up:

We Untouchables took every word of Babasaheb's speeches as an inspiration. His words gave us identity, self-respect, independence, and the strength to fight against injustice. We can say that his words shaped our minds and our personalities.... I was living the life of an ordinary school teacher, an ordinary woman, but Baba's work made me a social activist. The change I underwent surprises me even now.

(Pawar and Moon 1989, 246)

Dani's emotions are reinforced by Babytai: 'Thanks to Babasaaheb, the Mahar retrieved their souls and changed their situation radically and for the better' (Kamble 1990, 121, 123). Although women like Dani and many others cite Ambedkar as their source of energy and inspiration, conceal themselves behind the male figures of their families or communities and minimise their own contributions, I need to reiterate, with many feminists, that this is a universal feature of women's writings and is not specific to Dalit women. What is, however, more important is that women's emotional subjectivity allows us to consider the intersections of *samaaj* (community) and family with 'history' and how Dalit radicals brought about a profound individual and collective change in the Dalit *samaaj*.

Most importantly, Dalit women exercised historical agency, piecing together whatever was available to actively engage in the political practices of constructing themselves and their communities. They were thus not merely 'humble interpreters of a supernatural leader's vision' (Pandey 2013, 179), as some historians (like Pandey) would like us to believe. Such approaches to studying the heretofore occluded history of women further diminish their creative roles and deny them even the small spaces available. Based on his reading of Babytai's translated autobiography, Pandey informs us that she was '*caught up in* the Ambedkarite movement from an early age' (ibid., 180, emphasis added). However, as this book will make clear, women were not 'caught up' or ensnared; they *chose* instead to engage critically with and contribute to the movement. Moreover, Babytai's original Marathi autobiography amply underscores how Dalits themselves articulated political concepts in their local, vernacular Marathi. She underscores that Ambedkar's movement led to the production of *sphurti* (enthusiasm and activity), courage and *khambirpanaa* (determinacy and positivity) in the Mahar community and details the processes through which '*ekaa ekaa vicharaalaa anek phaate phutu laagale*' (gradually one idea formed and sprouted forth many) (Kamble 1990, 108, 112, 113).

The tension between Babytai's reminiscences and scholarly interpretations of them prises open a critical space to investigate gender history. What counts as absolutely critical to some may not affect or be perceived similarly by others. This once again brings to light the limitations in mainstream (male) scholarship: Pandey is reading one Dalit woman's autobiography and placing the agentive forces outside the Dalit self, allowing Dalit males to assimilate her into the movement – without her approval! He portrays Dalit females as entirely dependent upon and derived from male deeds and desires. He does not question *why* women were 'caught up' and consented with men. Moreover, what Pandey neglects is that although Dalit women's subjectivity was at times fragmentary and incoherent, they also forcefully exercised choices and made certain decisions: for example, choosing the leadership of Ambedkar and Phule over Gandhi. Many women like Babytai had ideas, engaged with local politics (112–115), wrote about their sexual subordination, provided details of domestic violence and contested patriarchy, and were still firm about actively participating in the movement.

Significantly, Pandey falters again when he accuses 'Dalit memoirs, especially of women' and 'other writings of the same kind' of 'a persistent tendency to expel the political question from the domain of the family and locate it instead in the realm of the political party' or constitutional politics (Pandey 2013, 190). The problem with this argument is, first, that Pandey does not provide enough evidence to tell us who exactly the agents were. Are all autobiographies and women's accounts at fault for performing such erasures? Second, Pandey does not take into consideration the work of Dalit radicals, as I have revealed above, or recent feminist historiography, which, instead of 'shifting' the problem of the political to formal politics, has grounded it in the domain of the family, thus making the family a site of resistance and a political practice.

Historians thus need to ask adequate questions as well as provide some 'good' answers. For example, what was *Bhimvaaraa*? What did Ambedkar and *Bhimvaaraa* mean to Dalit women and men? Why was it so significant to them? How did women create the effect of a unified Dalit movement? Despite being 'brutally battered' and 'terribly thrashed', how did they articulate and write about the multiple struggles of the Dalit community in private and publicly? What was the movement's significance? How did women appropriate the agenda of the Dalit movement, the nationalist movement and their leaders for (un)intended purposes?

Most Dalits approached the concept of educational opportunity from a profound sense of shared responsibility. Few lost sight of how their achievements might affect Dalits still in villages, as well as women. To spread awareness among Dalit women, the Bahishkrut Bharat Bhagini Parishad was established and held conferences in different areas (*Bahishkrut Bharat*, 4 January 1936). During one such women's conference, held in Naigao, Mumbai, to support Ambedkar's *Dharmaantar* (conversion to Buddhism) on 31 December 1935, its president Devikabai Damodar Kamble said,

> Our leader Babasaheb Ambedkar has started *satyagrahas* in Mahad and Nasik to provide us equal status. But hard-hearted Hindu *sanatanists* opposed these efforts. Hence Dr. Ambedkar has decided to convert and we have gathered here to express our full support to him.
>
> (*Nirbhid*, 5 January 1936)

Seconding Kamble, the gathered Dalit women and men passed the resolution for *Dharmaantar*.

On 3 June 1953, in a public meeting under the auspices of the SC *mahilaa mandal* at Rawli Camp, Sion (Mumbai), Ambedkar addressed an audience of about 3,000 people. He advised women to carry on their programme of emancipation in spite of adverse criticism. The *mandal* contributed Rs.401 as its first instalment towards the SCF's Building Fund (Crime Investigation Department 1953).

Yet Dalit radicals' negotiations were contradictory, and the assertion and agenda of masculinity often encouraged patriarchal practices.[24] Control over women was also linked with more honour, dignity and respectability for them. Dalit radicals looked upon Dalit women as 'purifiers', responsible for the improvement of the community. Dalit women became saviours of Dalit men and the community. In making this political move, Dalit reformers could justify Dalit women's activity in the public sphere, which could lead (at least in some cases) to women's commitment and national activity. However, the roots of this outward-directed agenda were deeply embedded in women's place in the private sphere.

This was a double-bind: Dalit women's subjection was produced and restrained by the very structures of power through which they sought emancipation. Dalit women suffer(ed) from certain inherent contradictions in Dalit radicals' thinking, which raised as many questions about women and gender roles as it resolved. The management of female sexuality and the whole politics of honour and shame were a principal difficulty for most communities, including Dalits. Most of the time they were unattainable agendas. Another serious problem that reformers had to address was how to legitimate the need to educate women while simultaneously restricting them to the home as wives and mothers. Some emphasised conservative roles for Dalit women even as they incorporated their participation and thereby restricted their potential.

Dalit radicals did not consciously articulate gender equity as distinct from Dalit regeneration and the community's march towards modernity. Ideals of modernity centred on annihilating derogatory elements marking their caste and constructing a respectable replacement. The two aims of gender justice and community refashioning were part of the same project, so their gendered ideology and discourses did and did not change radically. Because of this they were to an extent unable to break free from gendered discourses, thus burdening women with private and public roles.

By emphasising the operations of interlocking technologies of education, caste, class, gender, sexuality, family and community, and persuading Dalit women to rethink their attitudes to womanhood, motherhood, public roles and employment, Ambedkar brought about a complete change in Dalit women's historical voice from the crucible of domestic and public politics. He wanted women to be independent-minded and daring; hence, he recognised their autonomous subjectivity, however conflicted and limited. Nevertheless, and most significantly, it is from the everyday ambiguity and negotiations of Dalit consciousness that actions, events and unintended results sprang forth actively. All the everyday contradictions and convergences of power and powerlessness, of vulnerabilities, of truth and illusions, of what women did and did not control, helped them to improve their knowledge of the means to transform their lives.

The post-1920 Ambedkar movement witnessed the increased prominence and self-assertion of Dalit women. They started attending schools and conferences, made public speeches (a truly revolutionary act for those who had been silenced and excluded), and became more confident. They recovered their self-respect, were actively involved in the movement, and agitated for their rights. They supported compulsory primary education, hostels and scholarships for Dalit girls and the appointment of Untouchable women teachers.[25] With these vital actions, struggles and organisations, women gained a consciousness that penetrated their everyday lives and elevated them to new, hitherto unachievable heights. However, these tasks involved many and different difficulties, as I will examine in the next chapter.

Conclusion

Education technologies interacted with social and economic structures, moral reform, and political power to work for Dalit emancipation. Hence, it is important to untangle these technologies' knotty relationships with different domains and with discursive and non-discursive practices in the Dalit march towards a certain modernity. Dalit women played a key role in this.

In the context of the Dalit movement, gender itself emerged as a very contested, unstable and fractured category. It became a *generative* process to imagine new kinds of emancipation and democratising techniques. Dalit radicals' critique of gender emerged from within the critique of caste and untouchability. Upper-caste men constructed hierarchies of gender, caste and sexuality in particular historical contexts. Phule and Ambedkar identified the cunning of upper-caste men and analysed the subordination of Dalit women, constructed Dalit women's subjectivities, and fashioned Dalit womanhood. The new Dalit woman was historically produced and her subjectivity shaped to enforce new forms of Dalit identity. She was an amalgamation of modernity and tradition for normativity, caste and sexuality as well as a rights-bearing subject of the state (unlike the upper-caste woman, who was always-already one). Dalit radicals, like Self-Respecters under Periyar in colonial South India, concentrated on female suffering and internal reform because the improved position of women was critical to them.

Moreover, Phule and Ambedkar were men who were deeply concerned about the feelings, emotions, desires, identity and dignity of women. Although they lived and struggled in different times, they shared a common approach to the nexus between knowledge, caste, sexual and gender discriminations. Yet there were differences: Phule, for example, was not concerned with any particular roles for women. Ambedkar, on the other hand, emphasised women's mothering roles and redrew the boundaries of the social reform of untouchability as an inherently political concern for Dalit women. There were contradictions in Ambedkar's approach to women. At one level, Ambedkar's disciplinary rectitude to an extent was similar to the bourgeois values of Victorian-Brahmani notions of womanhood. Yet, on the other and deeper level, with his agenda of democratisation, he brought women into the modern public sphere to discover their new roles within the family, community and nation. In addition, Phule seemed more radical than Ambedkar; however, the impact of the latter's ideology, practices and the overall movement was and is deeper.

There was both continuity and discontinuity between the upper-caste and Dalit agendas of education and gender reform. In contrast to upper-caste agendas of education, which policed women and their sexuality, non-Brahman and Dalit interlocking technologies critiqued the compounded nature of caste, class, gender and education, and sought to bring Dalit women into the public sphere instead of fully entrenching domestic ideologies. Most importantly, unlike some upper-caste and Gandhian nationalists, Ambedkar did not create a dichotomy between the social and political, nor did he confine Dalit women to the social. Instead, in the case of Dalit women, the social deeply penetrated both formal and informal political struggles, and women bravely annexed new arenas of life. Moreover, Dalit women and men grasped and appropriated Dalit radicals' discourse and efforts for education and self-making, and forged strategies to transform their conditions. From these mutual processes emerged their political consciousness. In addition, by connecting the construction of caste to practices of endogamy (such as sati, enforced widowhood and child marriage), Ambedkar has taught us to see how the security of the home or the domestic space depends on a just social order.

The production of the Dalit woman was a contested process predicated on caste, class, gender and sexuality differentiations. This chapter has documented the complicated processes of shifting masculinities and femininities by which Dalit radicals departed from upper-caste femininity to forge new constructions of a masculine Dalit womanhood, vernacularising and claiming universal ideas of human rights, education, individualism, daring, resoluteness and emancipation. Moreover, unlike upper-caste males who 'controlled femininity to bolster the resilience and agency of native-caste masculinity' (Chandra 2012, 81, 223), Dalits instead incorporated the masculine attributes into the feminine and carved out a heroic agency. This production process, however, was also thwarted by the power of old patriarchies and differentiation from 'other' stigmatised women.

Dalit women's strategic subjectivity was born out of the social, political, emotional and intellectual agitations and turbulences of this expansion of the self and its experiential possibilities, which in turn fashioned the modern Dalit. Dalit women's participation in the movement also shaped the movement for their rights and for an organisation separate from the all-India women's movement. Women gained on both social and psychological grounds; some said the Dalit programme had transformed their lives from empty gossip and boredom to vital engagement and commitment. Ambedkar's political project emphasised the agency of Dalit women in building self-respect and confidence in the community. They were not simply latecomers to history or modernity; they adopted and critically transformed bourgeois ideals for their own benefits. Certainly, the fulfilment of these promises proved difficult.

Notes

1 On such a retrieval and formulation of (upper-caste elite) women's subjectivity, see Burton (1994) and Sinha (2006).
2 Many scholars have focused on Dalit women's victimhood in terms of patriarchy, poverty and social injustice. See, e.g. Rao (2003) and, more recently, Pandey (2013). On the other hand, some scholars, such as Gail Omvedt in her *We Will Smash this Prison! Indian Women in Struggle*, and Maya Pandit, who translated Babytai Kamble's autobiography *The Prisons We Broke*, have focused on how women in peasant and Dalit communities have smashed the prisons.
3 I thank Shefali Chandra for these timely discussions.
4 Even a quick glance at the vast literature on 'Women in Modern India' will prove the scant attention paid to non-Brahman and Dalit initiatives in education compared with Brahman efforts mainly for upper-caste women.
5 I am referring here to the famous critical race theorists such as Kimberlé Crenshaw (2003) and Patricia Hill-Collins (1991), who have argued for 'intersectionality' as the primary analytical tool to analyse the multiple dimensions of marginalised subjects.
6 My argument is fortified by Inderpal Grewal (1996, 185, 208).
7 Phule continued to support Ramabai and to attack so-called modern reformers in his journal *Satsar* (Essence of Truth).
8 In colonial South India, Periyar started *svaabhimaan vivaha* (self-respect marriages) as a part of his Self-Respect Movement.
9 See his letters to the Parsi reformer B.M. Malabari, who submitted to Viceroy Ripon two notes on child marriage and enforced widowhood for action by the British government (Phule 2002, 191–197).
10 I am borrowing the concept of 'negotiation' from Douglas Haynes, who discusses interactive patterns of colonial political encounter and the creative role played by local elites (1991, 14). I extend it for my purposes.
11 Scholars have already studied masculinity in colonial India and illustrated how the British constructed Indian men as 'weak' and 'lacking in manliness'. See Nandy (2010, 1–63); Sinha (1995); Chowdhury (1998, 120–149); Parekh (1989, 172–206).
12 Various scholars have emphasised how women were used to counter their social marginalisation. See Lynch (1969), Cohn and Guha (1988, 255–298) and Bandyopadhyay (2004). For views on how women in turn asserted themselves, see Searle-Chatterjee and Sharma (1995), Jogdand (1995), Chakravarti (2003), Rao (2003) and Rege (2006).
13 Uma Chakravarti (1998, 3–31) has analysed how Peshwai upheld Brahmanya as Dharmarajya, to uphold the superior morality and purity of Brahmans; in fact, Brahman women carried the major responsibility of upholding Brahmanya.
14 Ambedkar examined the containment of knowledge alongside the exposition of the sexual division of labour: 'Brahmanism did succeed in making the Shudras and the women the servile classes. Shudras, the serfs to the three higher classes and the women the serfs to their husbands' (Ambedkar 2002b, 50).
15 Although in a different part of India, Charu Gupta has revealed that:

> C.Y. Chintamani, president of the Fifth UP Social Conference, pointed out that a bill was necessary for the removal of caste barriers. These voices were hopelessly outnumbered, revealing the unrepresentative character of the liberal reformers, and the bill could not be passed. Even branches of the Arya Samaj took public positions against the bill.
>
> (Gupta 2002, 139)

16 Shudras are the lowest stratum in the four-fold division of Hindu society. Unlike the Untouchables, Shudras are touchable.
17 The link between women and progress, on the one hand, and women and civilisation,

on the other, was made early and often by feminists. Henrietta Muller's declaration that 'the intelligence and status of the women of a country are a measure of its civilisation' was practically axiomatic in feminist writing. Women became thermometers of their civilisation (Burton 1994, 83–84).

18 The Brahman urban elite agenda certainly followed Manu's instructions. Although the Gandhian agenda of the twentieth century sought to manifest feminine qualities as superior to masculine ones, it was also not very different from the earlier construction of femininity; see, e.g. Patel (1988, 378).

19 On the history and politics of naming, see Paik (2011). Scholarship is divided on these caste practices: Srinivasan's concept of sanskritisation or Moffatt's study of imitation of higher castes by lower has been challenged by Zelliot (1994), Hardiman (1995) and Rao (2009), among many others.

20 It is important to note that during this time upper-caste males persuaded upper-caste women to wear six-yard instead of nine-yard saris because the latter revealed the legs of women and were less modern compared to the former.

21 I am borrowing from Antoinette Burton (2003, 98), who relies on Williams for her reading of Cornelia Sorabji as an 'emergent figure of Indian modernity'.

22 See Lata Mani's (1998) classic feminist reading of how the discourse of sati and Brahman women became 'sites' of the conflict between white colonial rulers and brown Indian men.

23 Chandrakanta Sonkamble is a female politician from Chinchwad, Pune.

24 For an insightful discussion of Dalit masculinity, see Gupta (2010).

25 Anusayabai Ingole presided over the Berar Untouchable Women's Conference in 1936, which passed important resolutions and marked the growing awareness of women in the social and political spheres (*Nirbhid*, 8 March 1936).

References

Ambedkar, B.R. 1916. Castes in India: Their mechanism, genesis and development. In *Dr. Babasaheb Ambedkar: Writings and Speeches*, Vol. 1, ed. Vasant Moon. Bombay: Department of Education, Government of Maharashtra, 1979.

——. 1936. *Janata*, 4 July.

——. 1942. *Report of the All India Depressed Classes Conference*. Nagpur.

——. 1979. *Dr. Babasaheb Ambedkar: Writings and Speeches*, Vol. 1, ed. Vasant Moon. Bombay: Department of Education, Government of Maharashtra.

——. 1987. *Dr. Babasaheb Ambedkar: Writings and Speeches*, Vol. 3, ed. Vasant Moon. Bombay: Department of Education, Government of Maharashtra.

——. 2002a. *Dr. Babasaheb Ambedkar: Writings and Speeches*, Vol. 18, ed. Vasant Moon. Bombay: Government of Maharashtra.

——. 2002b. *The Essential Writings of B.R. Ambedkar*, ed. Valerian Rodrigues. New Delhi: Oxford University Press.

——. n.d. *Rise and Fall of the Hindu Woman*. Hyderabad: Dr. Ambedkar Publications Society.

Bahishkrut Bharat. 4 November 1927.

——. 3 February 1928.

——. 3 June 1928.

——. 4 January 1936.

Bandyopadhyay, Sekhara. 2004. *Caste, Culture, and Hegemony: Social Domination in Colonial Bengal.* Thousand Oaks, CA: Sage.

Burton, Antoinette. 1994. *Burdens of History: British Feminists, Indian Women, and Imperial Culture, 1865–1915.* Chapel Hill: University of North Carolina Press.

————. 2003. *Dwelling in the Archive: Women Writing House, Home, and History in Late Colonial India.* Oxford: Oxford University Press.

Chakravarti, Uma. 1998. *Rewriting History: The Life and Times of Pandita Ramabai.* New Delhi: Kali for Women.

————. 2003. *Gendering Caste: Through a Feminist Lens.* Calcutta: Stree.

Chandra, Shefali. 2012. *The Sexual Life of English: Languages of Caste and Desire in Colonial India.* Durham, NC: Duke University Press.

Chowdhury, Indira. 1998. *The Frail Hero and Virile History: Gender and the Politics of Culture in Colonial Bengal.* London: SOAS Press.

Cohn, Bernard S. and Ranajit Guha. 1988. *An Anthropologist among the Historians and Other Essays.* New York: Oxford University Press.

Crenshaw, Kimberlé. 2003. Demarginalizing the intersection of race and sex: A black feminist critique of antidiscrimination, feminist theory and antiracist politics. In *Critical Race Feminism*, 2nd edn, ed. Adrien Wing. Albany: State University of New York Press.

Crime Investigation Department. 1953. Bombay City secret abstracts of intelligence, 28 May.

Desai, Neera and Maithreyi Krishnaraj. 1987. *Women and Society in India.* New Delhi: Ajanta.

Dube, Saurabh. 1998. *Untouchable Pasts.* Albany: State University of New York Press.

Enthoven, R.E. 1922. *The Tribes and Castes of Bombay*, Vol. II. Bombay.

Government of Bombay. 1909. *Muralis.* Proclamation of the Judicial Department. File #1559.

————. 1913. *Bills on opinions on the* muralis *to make further provisions for the protection of minors and girls.* Proclamation of the Judicial Department. File #715, part I.

Grewal, Inderpal. 1996. *Home and Harem: Nation, Gender, Empire, and the Cultures of Travel.* Durham, NC: Duke University Press.

Gupta, Charu. 2002. *Sexuality, Obscenity, Community.* London: Palgrave Macmillan.

————. 2010. Feminine, criminal, or manly? Imagining Dalit masculinities in colonial India. *Indian Economic and Social History Review*, 47(3): 309–342.

Hardiman, David. 1995. *The Coming of the Devi.* New Delhi: Oxford University Press.

Hatekar, Archana. 1999. Dalit movement and Dalit woman's question. In *Dalit Stree Asmitecha Avishkara va Disha*, ed. Vandana Sonalkar. Pune: Alochana.

Haynes, Douglas. 1991. *Rhetoric and Ritual in Colonial India: The Shaping of Public Culture in Surat City, 1852–1918.* Berkeley: University of California Press.

Hill-Collins, Patricia. 1991. *Black Feminist Thought: Knowledge, Consciousness and the Politics of Empowerment.* New York: Routledge.

Janata. 4 August 1934.

————. 4 July 1936.

————. 8 June 1940.

————. 26 March 1949.

————. 6 November 1954.

Jangalgop. 1940. Samataa mahila sainik dal. *Janata*, 13 April.

Jogdand, P.G., ed. 1995. *Dalit Women in India: Issues and Perspectives.* New Delhi: Gyan Publications.

Kamble, Baby. 1990. *Jina Amucha*, 2nd edn. Pune: Maansanmaan Prakashan.

————. 2008. *The Prisons We Broke*, trans. Maya Pandit. Chennai: Orient Longman.

Karve, Svati. 2003. *Streevikasachya Paulkhuna* (Important Achievements in the Development of Women). Pune: Pratima.

Keer, Dhananjay. 1962. *Dr. Ambedkar: Life and Mission.* Bombay: Popular Prakashan.

Lynch, Owen. 1969. *The Politics of Untouchability: Social Mobility and Social Change in a City of India.* New York: Columbia University Press.

Mani, Lata. 1998. *Contentious Traditions.* Berkeley: University of California Press.

Mooknayak. 11 September 1920.

Moon, Vasant. 2000. *Growing Up Untouchable in India.* Oxford: Rowman & Littlefield.

Nandy, Ashis. 2010. *The Intimate Enemy: Loss and Recovery of Self under Colonialism.* New Delhi: Oxford University Press.

Nirbhid. 5 January 1936.

——. 8 March 1936.

Omvedt, Gail. 1980. *We Will Smash this Prison! Indian Women in Struggle.* London: Zed.

Paik, Shailaja. 2011. Mahar-Dalit-Buddhist. *Contributions to Indian Sociology,* 45(2): 217–241.

Pandey, Gyanendra. 2013. *A History of Prejudice: Race, Caste, and Difference in India and the United States.* New York: Cambridge University Press.

Parekh, Bhiku. 1989. *Colonialism, Tradition and Reform: An Analysis of Gandhi's Political Discourse.* New Delhi: Sage.

Patel, Sujata. 1988. Construction and re-construction of woman in Gandhi. *Economic and Political Weekly,* 23(8): 377–387.

Pawar, Urmila. 1989 [2000]. *Amhihi Itihas Ghadavala: Ambedkari Chalvalit Streeyancha Sahabhag* (We Also Made History: Women in the Ambedkar Movement). Pune: Sugava.

——. 1999. Dalit chalval va dalit striyancha prashna/rajkaran (Dalit movement and the Dalit woman question/politics). In *Dalit Stree Asmitecha Avishkara va Disha,* ed. Vandana Sonalkar. Pune: Alochana.

Phule, Jotirao. 1855. Trutiya Ratna. In *Collected Works of Mahatma Jotirao Phule,* Vol. 1, trans. P.G. Patil. Bombay: Education Department, Government of Maharashtra, 1991.

——. 1963. *Mahatma Phule Samagra Grantha.* Pune: Adhikari Prakashan.

——. 1991a. *Collected Works of Mahatma Jotirao Phule,* Vol. I, trans. P.G. Patil. Bombay: Education Department, Government of Maharashtra.

——. 1991b. *Collected Works of Mahatma Jotirao Phule,* Vol. II, trans. P.G. Patil. Bombay: Education Department, Government of Maharashtra.

——. 1991c. *Samagra Vangmay,* ed. Y.D. Phadke. Mumbai: Maharashtra State Literary and Cultural Committee.

——. 2002. *Selected Writings of Mahatma Phule,* ed. G.P. Deshpande. New Delhi.

Rao, Anupama. ed. 2003. *Gender and Caste.* New Delhi: Kali for Women.

——. 2009. *The Caste Question: Dalits and the Politics of Modern India.* Berkeley: University of California Press.

Rege, Sharmila. 2006. *Writing Caste/Writing Gender: Reading Dalit Women's Testimonios.* New Delhi: Zubaan.

——. 2013. *Against the Madness of Manu: B.R. Ambedkar's Writings on Brahmanical Patriarchy.* New Delhi: Navayana.

Rubin, Gayle. 1993. Thinking sex: Notes for a radical theory of the politics of sexuality. In *The Lesbian and Gay Studies Reader,* ed. Henry Abelove *et al.* New York: Routledge.

Salve, Muktabai. 1855. Mang maharanchya dukkhavishayi nibandh (An essay on the grief of Mang-Mahars). *Dnyanodaya,* 15 February and 1 March. In *Streevikasachya Paulkhuna* (Important Achievements in the Development of Women), ed. S. Karve. Pune: Pratima, 2003.

Scott, David. 1999. *Refashioning Futures: Criticism after Postcoloniality*. Princeton, NJ: Princeton University Press.

Searle-Chatterjee, Mary and Usurla Sharma, eds. 1995. *Contextualising Caste: Post-Dumontian Approaches*. Oxford: Blackwell.

Shivtarkar, Kumari Anusuya. 1934. Mahilaa Vargane Kay Karawe? (What should woman class do?) *Janata*, 14 April.

Sinha, Mrinalini. 1995. *Colonial Masculinity: The 'Manly Englishman' and the 'Effeminate Bengali' in the Late Nineteenth Century*. Manchester: Manchester University Press.

——. 2006. *Specters of Mother India*. Durham, NC: Duke University Press.

Sonkamble, Chandrakanta. 2002. Interview with the author. Pune.

Spivak, Gayatri Chakravorty. 1988. Subaltern Studies: Deconstructing Historiography. In *Selected Subaltern Studies*, ed. Ranajit Guha and Gayatri Spivak. New York: Oxford University Press.

Times of India. 3 March 1930.

——. 17 June 1936.

Zelliot, Eleanor. 1994. *Dr. Babasaheb Ambedkar and the Untouchable Movement*. New Delhi: Bluemoon Books.

Part II
The paradox of education

5   Education and life in the urban slum

Dalit women gained immensely from Dalit radicals' modern rhetoric and discourse of education, social and moral reforms, yet in actual practice they had to struggle on a day-to-day basis against the interlocking technologies of caste, class, gender, sexuality and education. Both in their home villages as well as in the urban spaces of Pune and Mumbai, many first-generation Dalit learners had to fight numerous and intricately braided battles as they sought to enter the formidable fortress of government municipal schools to seek formal education. While Pune was the firmly rooted capital of Brahmani culture, Mumbai rocked as a cradle of cosmopolitanism.

This chapter is devoted to the historical, lived, and everyday experiences and subjective realities of women who attempted to exercise the theoretical 'right of all' to education. By uncovering how caste is again and again reconstituted in the city, I challenge the concept of city as liberatory and democratic both in the Dalit and non-Dalit imaginary. The modern rhetoric of both the colonial government as well as Dalit radicals emphasised formal education as a 'magic wand' for social, economic, cultural, religious and emotional emancipation. This process involved two sets of multi-pronged battles for women: gender discrimination within the family and the difficulties of migration, segregated housing, spatial inequality and low-quality schooling in the public domain.

Some scholars have recorded romantic laments over the fall of the bourgeois Puneri *wada* (literally the traditional Brahman home; also a way of living) and the emergence of the colonial ward. Yet we barely know how Dalits articulated historical discontinuities and continuities across heterogeneous times in their everyday lives. Apart from Zelliot's article 'The history of Dalits in Pune', there is a significant lack of documentation on the urban history of Dalits in modern Pune and Mumbai. Some urban geographers, anthropologists and sociologists have traced Dalit workers' lives in the two cities. Instead of simply locating them in the urban histories of these cities, however, this and the following chapters will document Dalits' everyday lives in these spaces to unravel their emergent historical subjectivities. As such, I dwell on both the opening of opportunities, hitherto unexplored ontological hurts and continuous humiliation, as well as the politics embedded in the process of education in the cities. This chapter reconstructs first-generation Dalit women's practical difficulties in accessing education resources, especially in Pune.

The first section of the chapter deals with Dalits' migration and their initial struggles to settle in the city and serves as a background to understand the circumstances in which Dalit girls began to acquire formal education. Most poor migrant families settled in slums, at building construction sites where they attempted to find work, or beneath road bridges or overpasses. They fought fierce battles for their everyday survival and at the same time struggled to educate their children. Dalit migrants were rebels who broke their ties with the traditional village social/caste structure and moved to cities to found new lives, and to fashion themselves and their communities amidst new oppressions. I chart their competing battles through the lived experiences of the Dalit women of the first generation who moved from the villages into the city *jhopadpatties* (slums) and were caught in a vicious cycle of poverty, lack of education and low-paying occupations, yet who worked strategically to achieve their own form of modernity.

The second section analyses the segregated urban spatiality of Pune and Mumbai to uncover how Dalits' social and educational subordination was reinforced by spatial markers. On the one hand, the flight to the city anchored a promise of emancipation; on the other hand, the reproduction of segregated living spaces in urban areas once again excluded Dalits from the commonweal and renewed their oppression. The third and final section continues to work through the multiple battles inside and outside the home as well as in the schools in slum areas.

The first stage of struggle: migration to ostensibly emancipatory urban spaces

Most Dalits who migrated from rural areas to Pune during the early decades of the twentieth century were illiterate or poorly educated at the time of their migration. The colonial ethnographer Enthoven reports complaints that the Mahars had been so depleted in numbers by emigration to the cities that there were inadequate staff for the village's requirements (Enthoven 1922, 417). We have very few accounts of their lives, but their daughters recounted their minor and major obstacles in obtaining any education in the villages from which they had come. Many never even considered going to school. Lakshmi Shinde,[1] a first-generation woman, reported, 'My father told us that he faced a lot of hardships; times were difficult then. He used to work on the farm in some village in Solapur. He came to Pune later. He did not know school. He never told us anything about it' (2000). Lakshmi's father did not think about education. By contrast, however, Lalita Naik's father wanted to attend school but never had the opportunity. Lalita[2] paraphrased his story in an interview:

> I was full of curiosity and remorse when I saw these Brahman boys walk to school. I did not have any such luxury. I had to work in the fields, watch cattle, collect firewood, and help my father and mother with all jobs, including the village *taraalki*.[3] I used to keenly observe these Brahman boys going

to school whilst I sat under a tree with my cattle. I almost ignored my herd in order to watch the boys. They were nicely dressed in white shirts and *dhotar* [dhoti], with black *topis* [caps] and bags hanging on their shoulders. They used to carry books, usually in a bag. I used to wonder what this was all about. What was school? Why was I not allowed in school? Why did I have to look after the cattle while they attended school? Why did my parents not send me to school? What did they do at school? What is reading like? What do they read? What does the teacher teach about? I used to see them all play during their recess from my faraway shady tree.

(Naik 2001)

Lalita's father thus reflected deeply on his exclusion from school and expressed his desire to enter its unfamiliar space and participate in the learning process. In order to follow his 'deviant' desire, he sat outside the school every day and wrote in the mud whatever he understood from the echoes of the teacher's voice bellowing from the confines of the classroom. The 'falling words' of the teacher were like those of God, who would impart knowledge in order to open the eyes of Dalits. The master inside the school enjoyed 'symbolic' power; Lalita's father found legitimacy even in his murmurs. The micro-operations of power thus led to the reproduction of conditions of inequality, in that the upper-caste Brahman teacher was an intellectual, a spiritual *deva* – rather, a *bhudeva*, a God descending from heaven to earth to impart knowledge to the 'untouchable', 'ignorant', 'stupid' body.

With little or no education, many Dalits migrated to the city from the end of the nineteenth century. According to the 1912 account of H.H. Mann, an English agriculturalist, there were between 7,000 and 8,000 Untouchables in Pune, then a city of 111,381 people. However, he deals with Poona city, not the suburban areas that housed Dalits (Mann 1967, 180). Pune's population increased from around 250,000 in the 1930s to 500,000 in 1954. Dalits became an increasingly major element of that population beginning in the 1970s. Their share of the city's total population increased from 6.63 per cent in 1971 to 9.87 per cent in 1981, 15.78 in 1991, and 25.42 in 2001 (Census of India 1991, 66–67; 2001, 420).[4] This huge increase came about largely through migration from rural areas due to droughts in large parts of Maharashtra during 1966 and 1967 and again in 1972 and 1973. The incoming migrants lived, for the most part, in the rapidly growing slums; by 1976, more than a quarter of a million people lived in shanty and squatter settlements. By 2001, the city had a total Scheduled Caste (SC) population of 125,127 (Census of India 2001, 420). Some women remembered their villages and their flight to the city. Gangabai Kuchekar,[5] an old and partially blind woman, narrated her journey:

I remember that I was married and had two children then. We came to this place in the 1960s for employment because there was no work in our village. We came to Poona and lived in a slum near the Holkar Bridge. Then we moved to the bridge near St. Mira's College. After that, when the

Yashwantnagar slum [near Netaji High School, Ganesh Nagar] was allocated [to Dalits], many of our [Mang] friends moved here, and we joined them.

(G. Kuchekar 2004)

The Holkar Bridge is beside the bungalow where Elphinstone, the cautious colonial educator, once resided. Many poor, homeless Dalits found shelter under the city's bridges. Even with recent rapid developments and flyover bridges sprouting all over the city, construction workers and other poor people huddled under the bridges they were building; these became temporary residences until they could find better places to live. Many families in the city bought polythene sheets at *juna bazaar* (cheap markets) or collected them from garbage dumps and forced them into the cracks on the underside of the bridge to make a canopy under which they could set up their hearth and home. Their pots and pans lay around, equally exposed to the sun and rain. Women covered in grime cooked on makeshift coal or kerosene stoves; smoke rings curled up to the railway line above the bridge. Couples chatted while children played or snuggled into their polythene home cocoons. Of privacy there was none, and there was no dichotomy between the home and the world. The *ghar*, home, was indeed *baher*, in the outside, open world.

Rani Kamble remembered her father's migration to the Tadiwala Road slums, immediately north of Pune Railway Station:

He told us that this area belonged to the Mahars. He came here from the nearby village of Shirur. They were many children and there were constant fights amongst my grandfather's two wives. There was hardly any food to eat. So one day my father left home and came to Pune with his friends. He started with loading and unloading goods and other odd jobs at the railway station. Later on he found employment with the railways and became a gangman. He was then gradually promoted and became a clerk.

(R. Kamble 2001)

Thus poverty and hunger drove Rani's father to Pune. Like other illiterate or low-literate Dalits, he was readily absorbed as a menial labourer into the railways. Railways, ports, industries and mills provided new opportunities of employment and livelihood to Dalits, but they rarely made it to the supervisor ranks; they were mainly lower-level apprentices, temporary labour, or at most clerks. The structures of caste feeling were firmly rooted in the city. While poverty and bickering drove Rani's father to the city, Kirti's father moved to Pune for education and employment. He reported:

Yes, there were a handful of children in our family. But my father also had some land, which my younger brother is cultivating today. Of course, the land is divided among the brothers, and we do not have acres and acres like our neighbours, the Marathas. Most importantly, I do not remember my father ever using his feet for walking, because he owned a *ghodi* [pony]. He always had his *phetaa* [turban] tightly wrapped around his head and looked magisterial riding the *ghodi*. He also enjoyed some authority in the village and was held in esteem even by the Marathas. I went to school and was educated until the seventh grade in Taakali. I then studied until the tenth grade at a school in Sangamner town. But after my father passed away when I was fourteen or so, I had to earn and support the family as well. I was not very interested in farming and left it to my other brothers. What I was interested in was seeking an education and good employment, so I left the village and came to Pune in the 1960s, just like Kirti's maternal uncle. We were fortunate to have my stepsister married to a clerk in the railways. Both of us used this family connection and found shelter at her place. She lived in the quarters beside the Railway Station. She supported us immensely in the initial years. I worked very hard and took classes at the night school. I later managed to enrol in the Agriculture College and graduated with a B.Sc. in Agriculture. While I was studying, I also had to work because I had to earn my living as well as send some money to my mother and brother in Taakali. I worked odd jobs during those times: I played the drums or clarinet in brass bands, helped with *pandals* for marriage and other festive occasions, and also helped my brother-in-law with some account-keeping at his *usaachya rasaacha dukaana* [sugar cane juice shop]. I am very proud of myself and my accomplishments, and so are my village and community.

Thus, many Dalits migrated to and continued to reside in Pune. Kirti's father found employment with the state's Agricultural Department and was gradually promoted as *saaheb* to a Class-One Officer position towards the end of his career. Although he continued to dwell in the city, he found a home in Yerawada, a Dalit slum on the margins. *Jhopadpatties* sprang up rapidly in Yerawada and the state government's vacant land was immediately taken over by squatters, especially following the industrial growth of the mid-1960s. In Pune in 1971, the SC comprised 6 per cent of the population and 38 per cent of the shanty population (Bapat 1980, 190). These were mainly first-generation city inhabitants.

Kirti's father also decided to reside in Yerawada, for several reasons. First, he found a cheap home in a chawl in a Buddhist community, Siddharthanagar (named after Prince Siddhartha, Gautam Buddha), which was home to many poor and low-income families. Significantly, and as the name explicitly suggests, Siddharthanagar housed many Mahar-Buddhists; Mangs also found homes in Yashwantnagar, and Kaikadis and Wadaris lived in the deep interior of the Yerawada slum. In this manner, various migrants depended on their caste, village and kinship networks to seek housing and employment in the city. They lived in affinity groups and preferred social cohesion. Because of this, they actually *collaborated* in the *construction* of caste in urban slums. This may seem a negative outcome; however, as Meera Jangam mentioned, caste connections also functioned positively, as an informal welfare system to which participants could turn in times of distress. Meera and her husband actively organised the Matang community in order to support children's education, start sewing and computer classes, educate individuals on state support for SCs, and engage in effective environmental and hygienic management in their settlements.

Yerawada was on the Pune–Nagar highway, and this prime location allowed Kirti's family to travel frequently to their village. Her father was the first Dalit person from his village to attend college and seek his Bachelor of Science degree. This was a rare achievement for a Dalit man in the 1960s. Sovani's study testifies to this; there was only one male Dalit college graduate in Pune in the late 1950s. Hence, as Sheetal recounted, everyone praised her father for his accomplishments and called him 'Master'. This was a symbolic recognition of his education and status, as he was not an educator to be called 'Master' in the traditional sense of the term.

Women generally followed the men to the cities. Kausalyabai Kuchekar, a waste-picker, reported that she came to the city after her marriage in Nasik in the late 1950s. Her husband brought her to the Yashwantnagar slum in Yerawada, and she continued to live there and collect *kaagad-kaach-patraa* (scrap paper, glass and tin) as far back as she could remember. She clearly remembered that poverty drove her to find some means of livelihood, so she began collecting *kaagad-kaach-patraa* in big polythene bags. She slung them over her shoulders and the weight caused her to droop as if she was always-already bending in obeisance to one and all as she roamed every street of the Yerawada slum to pick all the saleable items from the garbage heaps by the roadside or homes and sell them to the *sheth* (merchant). After all these years of slouching and back-breaking labour, she was delighted to mention that only five years before I spoke with her she could finally afford to buy a *haatagaadi* (handcart) to collect her *maal* (merchandise) of scrap items. Much had transpired along her journey from the polythene bag to the *haatagaadi:* the city had changed, her children were married, and her husband, who had been employed, had no work, not even casual; he stayed at home permanently. She had to singlehandedly run the household and educate her youngest daughter.

Unlike Kausalyabai, Surekhatai mentioned that her profession of *tamaashaa* (folk theatre) brought her family to Pune; Urmilatai reported that her marriage to Harishchandra Thorat, who worked in Mumbai, enabled her migration. Most of them continued to live in the cities, but they also maintained their affective and, to a lesser level, economic ties with their villages. They visited regularly, supported their relatives' education, and engaged in social activities there. However, their stories also underscored their complicated relationship with the city.

A tale of two cities in one: Dalits and Brahmans in modern urban landscapes

The politics of the socio-historical cartography of Pune and Mumbai have permeated into the everyday lives and mental worlds of its residents. This section investigates the spatial markers of social subordination that reinforced inequality/ inequalities in the cities. Of course, Pune and Mumbai share their segregated structure with other metropolises like Kolkata, Chennai, Delhi and Bangalore.[6] Yet studies on such residential segregation are rare. This section unravels the different mentalities as well as the mysterious, concentric inner and outer rings of Pune. For colonial officers as well as for Indians, the public domain had not acquired the same sense as in the West, so there was spatial segregation: a fundamental dividing line between the core and margins.

Pune has been considered the social, educational and cultural capital of western India by Dalits and non-Dalits alike.[7] Its language, intonation, accented Marathi, culture and food habits were considered unique and at best Brahmani; many non-Punekars were and are in awe of Punekars. This is a testament to Brahman hegemony in Pune, which unlike Nagpur did not nurture a Dalit movement. In 1937, Dalits comprised about 9.2 per cent of Pune's population, while the Advanced Castes like Brahmans and Chandraseniya Kayastha Prabhus comprised 19.2 per cent (Omvedt 1974, 202). Even in 1952, there were 16,755 Brahmans as opposed to 578 Chambhars, 133 Dhors, 1,100 Mahars and 261 Matangs in Pune (Gadgil 1945–52, 42). These relative numbers clearly indicate both the Brahman and Brahmani nature of the city to Brahmans, non-Brahmans and Dalits alike. Hence, many Dalits have always-already taken pride in their Puneri Marathi. Non-Puneri Dalits and non-Dalits alike sometimes shy away from or even avoid talking to Puneri Dalits in the latter's *shuddha* (pure, here 'cultured') language. Some Dalits thus participated in consolidating Puneri Marathi as a form of cultural capital.

The map in Figure 5.1 clearly reveals caste clusters in two concentric circles of Pune city: Mahar, Matang, Chambhar and Dhor as well as Brahman *wadas*; Chambhars' Jawahar Nagar; Matang *vasti* near Parvati; Matang-Mahar and Buddhist *wadas* in Kirkee, Yerawada and Dattawadi; and Bhamburdas' Ashanagar and Wanowari were and are located on the margins of the city and in the outer rings. Unlike them, however, by making its location the centre and heart of Pune city, Sadashiv *peth* continued to maintain its historical and cultural hegemony. Yet this supremacy was not absolute, and non-Brahman and Dalit radicals consistently tried to create cracks in Brahmani spatial inequality. Phule set up schools in Bhokarwadi, Ganj and Kasba, which bordered Sadashiv *peth*. Lahujibuwa Mang worked at his *taalim* (gynmasium) in these spaces.

Chitpavan Brahmans dominated the inner core of Pune; their parts of the city included the Sadashiv, Shaniwar, Narayan and Shukrawar *peths*, which formed the robust heart of Pune city. Although Kasba was the earliest *peth*, Sadashiv *peth*,[8] built by the famous Madhavrao Peshwa,[9] became the most prestigious and prosperous of the *peths* in Pune. It was and is the social, educational and cultural *polis* around which the city has grown over three centuries. Chitpavans easily exchanged their traditional scholarly and priestly vocations for arms and played a significant role as money movers and power brokers in eighteenth-century Pune (Gokhale 1988, 315–316). Madhavrao made great efforts to provide them with the basic infrastructure for a comfortable living, with a good water supply, markets and venues for cultural practices. As such, Sadashiv *peth* is replete with most of the esteemed, prestigious, quality schools; theatres like the Bharat Natya

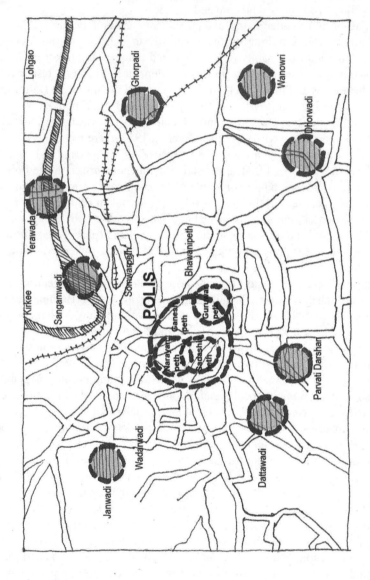

Figure 5.1 Pune city (map by author).

Mandir and Tilak Sabhagruha (for Marathi plays and talks); the Bharatiya Itihaas Saunshodhak Mandal (Association for the Investigation of Indian History), Tilak Maharashtra Vidyapeeth, Asthtanga Ayurvedic College, Maharashtriya Mitra Mandal, and many small music schools and social and cultural centres. Some upper castes were also involved in reinforcing *sanskruti* culture by conducting weekly classes in temples to teach Sanskrit *shlokas*, Hindu prayers, and good manners and habits to children.

The Deccan Education Society and its New English School were inaugurated by Brahman social reformers, including Tilak, Agarkar and Chiplunkar in Sadashiv *peth* in 1878. Tilak and other Chitpavan Brahmans like Madhav Ballal Namjoshi were charter members of the faculty. They were passionate about this work: in 1919, referring to his comradeship with Agarkar, Tilak said,

We were men whose plans were at fever heat, whose thoughts were of the degraded condition of our country, and after long thought we came to the conclusion that *the salvation of our motherland lay in the education, and only the education, of the people.*

(Basu 1974, 213, emphasis added)

Moreover, other highly regarded old schools were founded in the early nineteenth century, like the Ahilyadevi High School, Nutan Marathi Vidyalaya, Gopal High School, Renuka Svarup High School, the famous Dnyan Prabodhini, and many more are found in the core of the city – in and around Sadashiv *peth*. Yet, as I have analysed in Chapter 3, Tilak also reserved these efforts for Brahmans because he believed in segregated learning for members of different castes.

Since the seventeenth century, Chitpavan Brahmans alone have dominated Sadashiv and Narayan *peths* and given Pune its unmistakable Puneri Brahman stamp and conscience. The use of the term *Puneri* is intriguing: when one anonymous Dalit teacher started teaching at a college in Mumbai, her Brahman colleague Phadke said to her, 'You come from Pune but you are not a *khari* [true] Puneri' (Anonymous 2002). I want to emphasise the rude rub in this term 'true Puneri', which clearly alludes to a Sadashiv Pethi Brahman; certainly all non-Brahmans and Dalits are excluded from this historical *kharepanaa* (truth).

Sadashiv and Narayan *peths* thus became the citadels of the orthodox Puneri Brahmans. Sadashiv *peth* became a synonym for orthodox Brahmanism, while Narayan Peth enjoyed prestige because it housed the *Kesari* newspaper office and became the organising centre for Tilak's party. The *Kesari* group harboured an air of political arrogance: as their Brahman critic D.R. Gadgil aptly described, 'they felt that whatever they did was toward the country's welfare' (quoted in Omvedt 1974, 202). High-caste society was also fluid in that it participated in activities of trade and business rarely prescribed by heredity. This Brahman arrogance and cunning politics strategically excluded the lower castes from the *polis*. Of course their labour was required, and they were essential to the economy and society, but they were kept at a distinct distance in the outer ring of the surrounding *peths* like Kasba, Somvar, Mangalvar, Budhvar, Guruvar, Bhavani and

Nana. Nana, Somvar, Guruvar, Bhavani and Ganj housed the artisan castes, Mangalvar the Mahar and Mangs, and Ghorpade the Chambhars. Dalit settlements were mainly found in the peripheral areas of Yerawada,[10] Vishrantvadi, Vadgaon Sheri, Dhorvadi, Kondhava and Hadapsar. In these places, they huddled together in very overcrowded conditions.

The spatial hierarchy of Dalits' home villages was thus reproduced even in the cities and they were pushed to the margins. They resided in areas closer to their workplaces: in and around the police/army barracks of Vadgaon Sheri, the Research and Development Institute and Mental Hospital area of Vishrantvadi, the airport area of Lohegaon, the Southern Command military area of Mundhva, and the Kirkee ammunitions factory. In 1818, with the establishment of Poona Cantonment – or Camp, as it was and still is famously called – many Dalits served the British as menial labourers, house servants, butlers, and keepers of horses and donkeys. Due to their employment their localities grew around the British Army: areas near Ghorpuri, Vanavadi (Wanowrie), Camp, Khadki (Kirkee) Cantonment and Solapur Bazar, as well as two Modi Khanas. K.N. Kadam (2003) recounted his days at the prestigious St Vincent's Boys' School in the Camp area. Kadam mentioned the historic reason behind his success: his grandfather served as a butler and his family owned many horses and buffaloes. Hence they could afford, and also had the courage to enrol him in, St Vincent's, a premier education institution in Pune. It is important to note that 'many "butler's sons" considered themselves superior to lads from the village' (quoted in Zelliot 1994, 29). Yet this group produced one eminent leader: Shivram Janaba Kamble.

After the Panshet Dam flooded in 1961 and submerged Dalit settlements in Mangalvar *peth* and Bhamburda, there were about twenty-eight Backward Class registered housing societies (Brahme and Gole 1967, 103–104; see also Zelliot 2000, 223). The construction of these post-flood societies was very slow due to faulty infrastructure; nonetheless, the colonies scattered in different areas of Pune had comfortable houses surrounded by trees and flowers and were very well kept. I interacted with some Dalit women at the Parnakuti and Ambedkar Housing Societies, to the north of Deccan College. Most importantly, the clean, well-maintained Ambedkar Society, which housed middle-class and lower-middle-class residents, was surrounded by *jhopadpatties* like Lakshminagar and Siddharthanagar.

Dalits also resided in the fallow lands of Chaturshringi, left for the Untouchables, and within some dry lands in Ashanagar, part of what was then known as Bhamburda (currently Shivaji Nagar), another old Maharwada, which were given to these Dalit communities during the flood relief operations in the 1970s. These settlements were often insalubrious, with a very low quality of housing and unhygienic conditions. The poor housing created ongoing health problems for urban Dalits. While some Dalits rented, many second- and third-generation residents owned their houses in slums or in lower-middle-class housing schemes. They migrated and continued to live in the city, and gradually accumulate resources to buy homes, even if they were in slum areas. Many Dalits lived in small one- or two-room tenements, especially in Mangalvar, Ganj and Ganesh *peths* and the Parvati *paayatha* (foothills).

Dalits were thus on the boundaries of the *polis* and of Pune's community. The dominant castes looked upon them as resources – and, at the same time, as threats who could suddenly subvert upper castes' hegemonic rule at the centre. With the dawn of modernity, Dalits fought for their rights during the colonial period. In post-colonial times they have become 'potential equals', yet they were and are 'different'. They certainly lived in the emancipatory, modern city; they were supposedly equal, but have continued to live separately and on the margins. Dalits at the periphery were thus not included in the social, educational, economic, cultural and political life of, and did not have access to resources of, the Sadashiv *peth polis*. Although the city offered and opened up many avenues of emancipation, spatial inequality has continued to affect Dalits negatively.

During Peshwai's Brahman *raaj* of the seventeenth and eighteenth centuries, Dalits were confined to a specific social and cultural space. Ambedkar articulated how hegemonic classes pushed the 'broken men' (Dalits) dwelling in the *gaothan* (main village) to the *gayaraan* (forest or fallow lands) (Ambedkar 1990, 274–275). He contradicted Gandhi's belief in 'village republics', arguing that villages were in fact strongholds of social discrimination. Hence, he emphasised Dalits' flight to the city in the hope that urbanisation would open up hitherto unavailable opportunities and that the anonymity it offered would enable a liberating experience for them. This was Ambedkar's rationale, yet his dream went unfulfilled and the promise of the city was broken. For him (as Marx would argue, for the labouring classes), theoretically, the modern, urban space would enable Dalits to break down the village hierarchy of spaces and experience equal treatment and a sense of justice, to be judged by their capacity and not their caste. In practice this had its potentials as well as its limitations. Due to spatial inequality, Dalits struggled for their right to the city. There were limitations to Dalits' sense of belonging to the *polis* and they made efforts to reclaim it. They were thus spatially and emotionally barricaded from the city of 'haves'. Dalits were populations on the periphery, as against the citizens in the *polis*.

Generally, however, geographically, culturally and economically disadvantaged Dalits had to travel long distances to get to the schools in the heart of the city, and even with extensive transport systems such travel was not easy for Dalit children in terms of time, convenience, safety and cost. Women often spoke longingly about the schools in the hub of the city, which excluded them from historical time. Dalits' living has always been delineated by space: where they live, where they may go, where they may sit, and so on. This spatiality fed into other educational problems. The dominant classes socially and culturally constructed space. Educational space was not devised with them in mind; their sufferings did not end.

Prakshoti Pawar is a second-generation educated woman whose parents were a working couple interested in developing interest in extracurricular activities for their children. Prakshoti certainly appreciated their efforts, but complained that:

> attending hobby classes is a challenge because they are conducted in the heart of the city, which is so far from this place. How can a girl cultivate

hobbies when she is asked to get home early? I am not allowed to indulge in any partying, something that I love. But I will allow this freedom to my children.

(P. Pawar 2002)

Prakshoti's family lived in the Maharashtra Housing Board, a subsidised industrial housing scheme just beyond the Yerawada slum constructed by the state government after it forcibly cleared some slums. The state resettled these inhabitants and built new apartments for the benefit of the salaried middle class. However, to gain the best education and cultural capital and be in the company of middle-class, upper-class and upper-caste friends, Prakshoti and her brother had to travel frequently to Sadashiv *peth*, the *polis*. Travel taxed not only their purse but their time. Infrastructural impediments like changing buses added to their difficulties. Prakshoti also expected her parents to accept 'that' Puneri culture. She complained that, unlike her brother, she had to return home early: *saatchya aat gharaat* (get home before seven/dark), as the saying goes. She described the problems Dalits faced in integrating with the inhabitants of the *polis*, the strangeness of the *peth*, and consequently the construction of their social, educational and cultural exclusion.

In a similar vein, one Dalit woman mentioned her experiences of living away from the *polis* in the Siddhartha Nagar slum of Yerawada: her family moved out of the slum and into a flat just on its margins because they could afford it; although they believed that they had thus escaped the slum, they had escaped it only to a limited extent. Difficulty of transport was and is just one hurdle for Dalits on the periphery to be included in the best available social, cultural and sports facilities located in the *polis*. It was difficult to find a rickshaw to take them home in the evenings because no *rickshavaalaa* (rickshaw driver) would agree to enter Yerawada slums after dark. To the rickshaw driver's question, 'Where exactly do you want to go in Yerawada?' the family provided landmarks: 'It is just Nagar Road, Kataria hospital', or 'just the *chowk* after the Bund garden bridge'. The *rickshavaalaas* flatly refused to drive passengers into the interiors of the slum.

The urban landscape of Mumbai also bore the scars of caste-based segregated housing.[11] Kusumtai Gangurde underscored the Brahman, Muslim and Maharvaadaa elements in the city:

I remember when my family migrated to the city. It must have been in the 1950s. We lived in the Ghatkopar chawls. The Brahman *wada* was a separate enclosure. The chawl also had Kunbis, Muslims, Mahars, and Chambhars living in their own spaces. The areas were demarcated along caste lines.

(Gangurde 2006)

Kusumtai underlined caste housing in the cosmopolitan city's Bombay District Development Board and Bombay Port Trust chawl. Caste communities settled together and also supported other caste members migrating to the city. I reiterate that on the one hand these caste politics and processes constructed and strengthened caste groups; on the other, they were important for a community ethos. How could Dalit migrants find homes in the elite Colaba town area or the western suburbs of Mumbai? Because of this difficulty, as well as a considerable housing shortage and higher rents, they resided in Central Mumbai chawls in Worli, Dadar, Lal Baag, Wadala, Parel and Ghatkopar. Only very recently did Kusumtai's family move from Ghatkopar chawl to one- or two-bedroom flats in Borivili.

Even Mumbai's Dalits reproduced the vicious caste segregations within the community. A Buddhist family mentioned that while the Marathas felt superior to the rest, among the Dalits, the Konkani Mahars felt superior to the others. According to them, the most important reason was that Ambedkar was 'authentically' Konkani because his family hailed from Dapoli in the Konkan region. Thus they were the 'actual heirs' of Ambedkar (Gangurde 2006)! Mumbai's chawl dwellers resided in seven- to eight-storey buildings, at times surrounding a common *maidaan*. These chawls, which housed many Dalits and other lower castes and classes, were poorly lit, ill-ventilated, and barricaded with grilles, a constant reminder of their use as colonial prisons. They smelled of dampness and were breeding grounds for many diseases, most prominently tuberculosis and asthma. As social scientists have reminded us, the surroundings also stank due to residents' garbage heaps; one had to carefully avoid stepping on refuse while walking between chawls. (Residents are improving these conditions, though the job is still underway.)

Many reformers, scholars and lay women and men alike have decried the increasing filth in the city or the public domain. As Dipesh Chakrabarty argues, this could be due to their concerns with modernity. A clean city or public domain may be a bourgeois prerequisite; however, in the context of India, Dalits were and are excluded from such common rights of human beings. This contest, then, may not be just 'between the bourgeois order of the middle-class and those [Dalits] who flout its rules', as Sudipta Kaviraj (1997, 83) argues. Scholars who argue that dirt survived in public domains as a way of showing that Indians refused to be disciplined by (Western) modernity have paid little attention to homeless and migrant Dalits who have been treated as filth.

On every level inside the chawls, a long, dark corridor separated small cubicle homes on either side. The corridor space was bustling at all times and was used equally by everyone: women, men, children and the elderly. Children played and the elderly spent their entire days at the doors, while women cleaned rice, lentils and grains and attended to other daily chores. Men in general were absent during the daytime because they were at work. After evening tea, everyone geared up again: the women cooked dinner and helped with the children's homework until the men got home. Pressure-cooker whistles competed while appetising smells of curries and seasonings wafted through the corridors. Unlike the women, the men spent most of their evenings in the open: walking or chatting at the *paar* (parapets) and beyond, and playing cards or their favourite musical instrument, the banjo. But after-dinner walks were very common and families, groups of men and women, and couples took leisurely strolls in adjacent streets, sat by the fenced police *maidaan*, and shared their day-to-day lives, hopes and futures.

The rise in the city's population also increased congestion and overcrowding in Dalit areas. It was common for seven or eight people to live in one room of less than 300 square feet, unlike the Brahmans, Jains or Parsis in Pune, or the Gujaratis in Mumbai. Dalits also had a limited water supply; most adults used the municipal water tap and public latrines and toilets, and kids defecated in the open in allocated spaces in the slums or sometimes in a *maidaan*. Water waste was a problem; pipes would burst or water taps could not be properly controlled. Suvarna mentioned fights over water in Pune:

> We depend on water from the corporation tap near the *maidaan* and the public toilet. We drink water from the tap behind the toilet. There are four taps and as far as I remember people stood near one tap and pushed their vessels to fill water. Of course it was on a first-come-first-serve basis, but still it led to many physical and verbal fights. Nanubai, our neighbour, was the strongest on both fronts and we fear her even today. These days, most women stick to their number in the line to fetch water. And the area is cleaner than it was previously. The local Bauddha corporator has built better taps for us.
>
> (S. Gaikwad 2006)

Thus the right to the city was and is compounded by the right to water, housing, health and hygiene. Suvarna smilingly continued: 'I will not forget that my height has been stunted due to carrying many pots of water on my head, both in the morning and evening' during her laborious daily task of fetching water before and after school hours.

Very few families had independent bathrooms. Instead they had a *mori* or *nhaani*, a small corner of the house with a three-foot wall or *padadaa* (cloth curtain) to block the view. It was usually used as a sink. Utensils were cleaned there or outside the door, and it was also used as a toilet-cum-bathing space. Every house in Dadar's Naigao chawl also had a *mori*. The chawls also had two communal toilets on either side of the corridor on each floor, one for women and the other for men, used by about twenty families. Suvarna's Pune experience was reproduced in Mumbai chawls, where the toilets and drinking water taps were also in the same space. Dalit housing in the slums of Nana, Mangalvar and Kasba *peths* in the heart of Pune likewise faced water and toilet facility problems. Much of the housing was substandard, but there were also many *pucca* houses with tin roofs. Some Dalits also possessed electronic equipment such as televisions, tape recorders or refrigerators.

After 1947, Pune started to become a major industrial city, its development boosted by the construction of the Bombay–Pune Highway. Factories sprouted in the Hadapsar belt, Nagar Road and the Kothrud area. The population of Pune increased from 588,545 in 1951 to 721,698 in 1961, due largely to the increase in commercial activity. Post-independence Pune witnessed the Dalit Buddhist conversion movement of 1956, increasing jobs and education facilities, the benefits of the reservation system, and another wave of migrants, especially following the droughts of 1960 and 1970. The industrialisation of the city also led to problems of housing, sanitation, livelihood and education. 'In 1984 there were 340 slum pockets housing 33 per cent of the population', most of which was Dalit (Bawa 1987, 246, quoted in Zelliot 2000, 223). According to Bapat's study of Pune's slum housing, 'Backward Classes constituted 38.18 per cent of the 605 households.... The Buddhist population was 10.25 per cent of the sample' (Bapat 1980, 202). As the next section will show, Dalits were entangled in a vicious circle of living in slums and seeking low-level education.

The second stage: first-generation education in *jhopadpatti* schools

By the time of independence in 1947, Dalits had in most cases won their struggle for the right of entry to educational institutions and of girls to be educated. This was a first-stage struggle. The battle now moved on to its second stage: taking advantage of whatever education was available. Even after the right to education was won, rural children – particularly girls – still found it hard to attend school. D.R. Gadgil's study of education in the late 1930s reveals some interesting facts (Gadgil 1945–52, 286–287). Fergusson College of the Deccan Education Society educated fourteen Dalit boys out of a total of 1,370 students. There were no Dalit girls. However, Zelliot (2000, 221) mentions that she was 'told by a Buddhist woman that she did attend Fergusson in this period but not under the caste name of Mahar'. There were three male Dalit engineering students out of a total student enrolment of 201; no Dalits attended B.J. Medical College. The highest education level for Dalit women was high school; there were only fourteen Dalit female students out of a total of 2,395. It is worth reproducing Gadgil's figures of 1938–39 (1945–52, 286–287), as I have done in Table 5.1.

Even in Sovani *et al.*'s study the proportion of Brahmans receiving education at different levels was far higher than among Dalits or Marathas. For example, four Dalit men had received an eleventh-grade education, as compared to 157 Brahman and fifty-eight Maratha men. Only two Dalit women received the same, as compared to 108 Brahman and four Maratha women (Sovani *et al.* 1956, 38–39). Moreover, the school hierarchy ranked Maharashtra's municipal schools the lowest in the graded system. The school structure coincided with the state's caste and class architecture. Dalits sent their children to the schools that were available because they lacked the money, the time, the influence or the knowledge to send them anywhere better. These schools were characterised by absent teachers, bad teaching, easy progress from one class to the next, little or no facilities for students or teachers, and poor teaching aids. They did offer some educational amenities like bags, shoes, uniforms, books and meals. However, as we will see, few Dalit women knew about these or availed themselves of them.

Table 5.1 D.R. Gadgil's (1952) study of Dalit education in the late 1930s

Category of institution	Backward Class boys	Backward Class girls	Total student enrolment
Arts colleges			
Fergusson	14	0	1,370
S.P.	9	0	881
Wadia	6	0	412
Professional colleges			
Engineering	3	0	210
Agricultural	1	0	174
Law	14	0	363
B.J. Medical College	0	0	303
High School for Boys	153	0	7,811
Middle School	54	4	383
High School for Girls	0	14	2,395
Training College (Men)	41	0	278
Training College (Women)	0	6	98
Seva Sadan Training College	0	2	68
V.J. Municipal Tech	5	0	61
Tailoring Colleges	6	0	79

The municipal schools had very poor physical infrastructure. Most of the time they had dilapidated buildings, leaking roofs and mud floors, a depressing atmosphere, few basic amenities (for example, no toilets for girls) and a less-than-adequate number of teachers. Hirabai reported: 'The classroom was dark and dusty. Many a time the ground was also unkempt, damp, strewn with fire-wood and bugs and ants crawling around' (H. Kuchekar 2002). The bad atmosphere in municipal schools was not conducive to study. Many boys in the slums did not take their studies seriously: second-generation slum dwellers like Vaishali Chandane, Lakshmi Shinde, Nanda Kamble and many others complained about their ill-disciplined brothers (Shinde 2000; N. Kamble 2001; Chandane 2001).[12] These boys were tempted by unskilled labour jobs which earned them easy money. Very few of them aspired to study and advance themselves. They therefore took odd jobs with irregular pay. They were not much interested in schooling and indulged in harassing teachers and female students. They were also often addicted to smoking, drinking, gambling and other vices. Parents failed to control their sons and protect them from this '*kattaa* culture'.[13] Boys were generally found loitering around such *kattaas* and *chaavadis* (gathering places) in groups, chatting, smoking or chewing *paan* (betel leaves) – rarely during the daytime but mostly in the evenings and at night-time. Boys indulging in antisocial activities were picked up by the police and either returned to their homes in the mornings or left in prisons. Girls and women were very familiar with such *kattaas* and they consciously and strategically avoided such male-dominated, gender-specific spaces. Many Dalit parents imprisoned their girls inside the four walls of the house to protect them against exposure to the *kattaa* culture. Most men generally respected women students, but some men harassed them.

Researchers point out that location, physical facilities, teachers, examination policies, hours of instruction and curricula all contributed to gender differentials in enrolments. These supply factors, like demand factors, often have a different impact on parents' decisions about educating girls than on their decisions about educating boys. All other things being equal, female enrolment should be inversely related to distance: that is, the shorter the distance to school, the greater the likelihood that girls will attend (Khan 1993, 229–230). Yet, as noted above, even when they were admitted to school, Dalit students often had to sit in distinctly separate spaces far from the teacher, or even in the corridor or on the verandah. Meena Mahajan's mother Parvatibai, who did not have much time to talk to me because she had to attend her vegetable stall, recounted that she had never been to school, but she remembered her brother sitting in the school corridor while the teacher taught.

> The Brahmans sat first, then the Maratha, then Chambhar, Mahar, and Matang in the dust at the doors of the school, outside.... *Kai aaiku yenaar o yevhadya laamb, tumhich saangaa kasa shikaayacha ann kaay shikayaacha? Mulinna tar baaher jaayalaa manaai, ghar kaam phakta!* [How could a student listen from so far? You tell me. What knowledge was to be sought and how were we to seek it? Girls were not allowed to go outside; they were to engage only in housework!].
>
> (P. Mahajan 2002)

Parvatibai thus once again demarcated the 'caste-rows' – rows in the classroom along caste divisions. She also suggested that the inscription of 'feminised' domains of the 'private' by some Dalit parents did not allow Dalit girls to be educated. Even the idea of going to school was in most cases beyond their imaginations. Moreover, Parvatibai pointed out that the social hierarchy was crystallised in the education system. Students in the classroom were strictly categorised along caste lines that also decided their capabilities and their rank: the highest caste would be the first-benchers, who were the most 'intelligent', thus reproducing the social hierarchy. The lowest castes were the last in – or outside – the classroom. Thus schools, within and without classrooms, were arranged in order to perpetuate social divisions; there could be no infiltration on an individual or a collective scale. Moreover, when the Dalit bodies were made *visible*, the upper-caste pupils perhaps felt more privileged and thus able to further denigrate Dalit students.

First-generation Dalit learners reported that the school they attended was the *only* one available. Many parents did not pay much attention to the quality or medium of the school. They were happy that they could at least send their children to *some* school; the excitement of entering the citadels so long denied to them was the stronger motivating force. According to Sheela Nikam (2005):[14]

There was only one school in my village. It went until fourth grade and after that children had to go to some town for further education. This long distance and the parents' poverty discouraged the children. The girls were more affected as they were not allowed to travel so far. They were made to stay home after grade four or seven.

Thus girls could only attend schools nearby. The parents, particularly the mothers, were anxious as to their safety if they had to travel far. In addition, they wanted the girls home early so that they could help with the housework. Physical distance thus mattered significantly.

Despite this, village children often had to walk for miles, crossing rickety, swaying, river bridges, to get to school. In rural areas, children seemed to accept long walks to school as a natural part of life. This is the case even today in some remote parts of India, where there are few or no other modes of transportation. City children, however, were not used to this and complained about the long distances to school. Many children enjoyed their walks to school, running along roads, playing pranks, and stealing mangoes, guavas and berries on the way. This was more fun than the actual school, as Draupadi Nagare[15] recounted: 'Many a time I missed school because I did not like it much. It was far, and I did not like studying. I loved to play with my friends. I was not very interested in school and in studies' (2004). Even Jyotsna Rokade[16] was happier playing with her friends than attending school (2004). Some girls found the alienating curriculum, absent teachers and boring lessons with difficult mathematics obnoxious. Urmilatai[17] added, 'No child wanted to scratch his [or her] brains learning the tables or the additions and multiplications. They all wanted to play in the mud, herd cattle, and bathe in the rivers, which were more fun—no hard [mental] work was needed' (U. Pawar 2004). Perhaps this was why Dalit radicals focused on cultivating the habit of serious learning, which was more important to the oppressed community.

While some found school boring, others continued their journeys. In her autobiography, Shantabai Kamble writes of her trip to the technical school:

> I passed Class 6. For Class 7, I had to go to Pandharpur or join the technical school with the boys. I had no money to go to Pandharpur and Master Patil doubted I could cope with the boys. However, after a few months, Guruji Kamble enquired about me and made me join the technical school. I was the *only* girl in the school. I felt left out. I engaged in all the jobs the boys did. At the end of the year, I had to go to Pandharpur to take my exams. When the results were out, my cousin and I had passed the exams.
>
> (S. Kamble 1986, 26, emphasis added)

Shantabai was the only Dalit girl in her primary school in the early 1940s, as well as in the technical school. The upper castes refused to send their girls to the technical school, where they would be required to work alongside boys on 'male' jobs such as ploughing, sowing, reaping and carpentry. Even the teachers discouraged girls in this respect, and as a result upper-caste girls went to the high school in Pandharpur. Secondary education called for travel to towns, which the Dalit parents could barely afford; only a small minority of Dalit girls (like Kamble) reached that level.

Many more opportunities opened up when Dalits migrated to the cities. This process of migration also occurred at a time when education was opening up for Dalits in the early decades of the twentieth century. Despite this, most of the first-generation learners said that there were very few Dalit girls in their schools. For example, even in the late 1940s, Baby Kamble, Shantabai Kamble and Rukmini Ghangale were the *only* Dalit females in their classes, because few Dalit parents supported education for girls. They often believed that education was the business of Brahmans and not of Mahar or Mang girls. Shantabai was allowed to attend school because she could thereby obtain a small scholarship of three rupees. Every resource was important to poor households.

Yet, like some upper-caste elites, some Dalits sought to limit women's education. They emphasised masculine and bourgeois values: that girls should be educated only up to a particular level or that certain subjects were not suited for girls. Alaka Kale[18] said, 'Though my father was an officer, he thought that science and commerce were not for girls. A girl should study until matriculation and if she progresses ahead at all, arts is the stream for her' (2002). The transnational gendering and feminisation of certain types of studies has been commented on widely by various scholars, including Bourdieu (Bourdieu and Passeron 1977, 77–80),[19] For example, teachers commonly believed girls to be less capable than boys in mathematics; consequently, they failed to use teaching techniques that might improve girls' achievement in that subject. Most of the time girls were channelled into domestic science, handicrafts and biology, while boys went for chemistry, mathematics and vocational subjects. Alaka's father's standpoint embraced this 'feminised' curriculum emphasised by some upper-caste nationalists who believed that arts, drawing, painting and crafts were the most suitable subjects for women.

In a few cases, mothers joined fathers in underscoring such prejudices. They did not support higher education for women, especially in streams of education that were traditionally 'masculine'. Mothers had different kinds of fears regarding higher education. They argued that many Dalit boys rarely studied; they saw them loitering around the slums. Therefore, they were concerned that if their daughters studied too far ahead or in traditionally 'male' subjects, they would surpass the boys in their community, thereby eliminating their chances of marriage. These mothers preferred to have uneducated or undereducated married daughters than educated 'spinsters'. Some mothers opined that daughters should get married while still studying and continue their studies from their marital homes.

Dalit fathers simultaneously encouraged and limited their daughters' aspirations. Some also reproduced Victorian bourgeois and upper-caste agendas of 'masculine' and 'feminine' education. Yet, at the same time, many Dalits diverged from the upper-caste model and supported non-traditional subject areas as well as higher education for women. Shantabai Kamble, for instance, pursued her technical training at school. Dani and Pawar were successful postgraduates. Unlike upper castes, Dalit radicals, in their newspapers as well as in specific caste-*panchayat* newsletters, regularly and widely advertised Dalit women's educational achievements in the public arena. But this was not an easy task.

Some women complained that their teachers did not teach them properly; they just passed on their limited knowledge. The teachers typically acted arrogantly towards the pupils: when they asked questions, they insulted and shouted at them, discouraging any queries. The girls learned the texts without understanding the content. Snehlata Kasbe (2003)[20] said:

> I disliked geometry. It was in the ninth grade when we were taught some geometric theorems. The teachers just copied them from the books to the board, one after the other, and told us to copy them in return.... Nobody asked as to how the teacher derived the proof. They were scared or even uninterested. Also, the teachers did not explain it well. So nobody dared to ask questions. I asked once, but, with the response I got then, I never dared to ask anything after that. They did not reply properly, only insulted us. No one asked any questions and we learnt everything by rote. We just scraped through the subject most of the time.

Snehlata and other respondents underscored the power relationship in the classroom. The teacher's gaze was positioned on the classroom, minutely observing the students. Moreover, no questions or comments were entertained. Even if someone gathered enough courage to ask a question, he or she was rudely talked down. This was generally applicable to all students; however, in the case of first-generation Dalit women, the demeanor of the Brahman and other upper-caste teachers led to further smothering of Dalits' attempts to interact and question. They were immensely humiliated in a public space which was supposed to be liberatory.

Government incentives and impediments

Their flight to cities did not bring a considerable change in the conditions of the poverty-stricken Dalits. The Dalits were immigrants and strangers; they had nothing but their labour and the capacity forced upon them by social and economic exigencies. Gadgil's 1936 survey projected that Dalits would advance in the 'lowest' professions, clerkships and supervisory manual labour (Gadgil 1945–52, 77). The parents were not sufficiently educated to get white-collar jobs. They lacked the ability to pay school fees or to buy uniforms or books. In most cases these girls were able to enter the portals of education only when free schooling was available to them.

In an attempt to increase literacy after Indian independence, the Five-Year Plans and budgets allocated large sums to the education sector. Tuition, uniforms, meals, milk and other necessities were made available at subsidised rates or even free of charge. In most cases the parents of the first-generation learners were illiterate and had no understanding of the educational process. Despite this, many recognised the importance of education and accepted that their daughters should attend such free schools (M.B. Chitnis 1973, quoted in Joshi 1986, 43–45). Free education was provided even at college level. Urmilatai reported:

It was only when I came to Mumbai that I felt that I was so close to the college. It had an evening programme; I did not have to pay any fees like the others. So I told myself to avail myself of this significant opportunity. Earlier, when I was in my village, I did not want any of this. But when I was in Mumbai, working, I understood the importance of higher education and the concessions given. We have free scholarships that have come to us on their own, so why not use them prudently?

(Pawar 2004)

Only a few, however, took advantage of the various other concessions that were available on paper. Snehlata said that her school was a *zilla-parishad* (district government) school up to Class 7, and later she went to the Gram Shikshan Sanstha. She continued, 'I got a uniform, meals, milk, and books till Class 4 only. We did not have to pay any fees' (Kasbe 2003). Sometimes these government-provided amenities proved to be the only attraction for increasing student attendance. 'We went to the school just to get the sweet powder', said Meera – not the books or the teaching. Such cases were, however, very rare; the majority failed to make good use of the opportunities available. Indeed, most of the informants said that they were unaware of them. Some reported receiving them in particular classes, but this was very limited. Hardly any received scholarships. Ratnaprabha Pawar[21] said that the teachers did not tell her about any scholarships or qualifying exams for them (2002). Parents' failure to take advantage of these concessions often had a very detrimental effect on children's education. Few Dalits could afford to buy textbooks, shoes, pencils and bags. Many women talked about their parents' inability to meet these indirect costs; they sought small loans to make up the difference.

These stories clearly point to a failure of execution in education projects. It is probable that the available funds were in many cases appropriated corruptly. High-caste people continued to complain about the concessions bestowed upon Dalits, but it was questionable whether many of these benefits reached them at all. Indeed, the whole issue of concessions was and is a sensitive one for both Dalits and non-Dalits. They are much contested – historically, sociologically and politically – and are an emotional issue for all.

Urmilatai (2004) reported that she received free textbooks until Class 4:

We always bought third- and fourth-hand books, whatever we could get for studies; with whatever we could understand before, after, under, and amidst the graffiti. All this was bought at the cheapest available rates as my mother could not spare much money. There were all kinds of pictures in the book:

animals, humans, trees, glasses, goggles, names of girls and boys, messages of love, poems, criticisms, filthy language … all kind of things were written there.

This was the shabby state of the books that Urmila used. The actual text often had to be discerned from the available *dnyanasaagar* (ocean of knowledge). Urmilatai also used old exercise books and textbooks: 'I used *vahya* [exercise books] made of the old papers and did not trouble my parents for newer ones' (2004). This was the best that Dalit parents could provide for their daughters. Yet, since they could not buy books, some girls kept away from school; Snehlata, for example, remarked, 'I did not like to go to school much because I could not afford to buy the textbooks and exercise books' (Kasbe 2003). Snehlata's comment was reinforced by Meera and others (Jangam 2004; B. Kale 2002). Meera Jadhav's sister also dropped out of school because her father could not support the cost of books for three daughters. Not all girls were equally encouraged to seek education. Meera was favoured over others because she achieved good grades and showed an inclination to become an officer, unlike her sisters. When her two younger sisters failed to perform at school, they were heaped with insults and abuses as well as beatings (*phatke*). Rita (2003) reported:

> Instead of understanding my difficulties with studies, my family blamed me. Relatives joined my parents and call me a dullard. They pointed to my knees and called them my brains and said that they did not work and hence I was not fit to study ahead. I also thought that this was probably true, and dropped out of school.

Thus the parents engaged in 'blaming the victim' (Ryan 1976) and discouraged Rita and Sheetal, and some girls lost interest in studying further.

In some cases Dalit fathers could not afford to send their children to the schools of their choice, but still encouraged their daughters' education. One father took out a loan to support his daughter's education. Meena[22] talked about what her father, who worked at Lohegao Airport, had to do to make ends meet and send her to a good private school: 'He had two jobs. Sometimes he had to take out loans to pay off my fees. But he wanted me to be an officer and so he sent me to this school' (2001). Such extreme poverty was more prevalent among first-generation learners. Because of their education and employment, the second and third generations were often well settled and searched for better options. Some were unaware of the financial hardships their mothers had faced. They wanted better education. They wanted to attend English-medium and convent schools – and some of them did. However, once they had started their uphill journeys, they encountered other restrictions.

Dress was another concern. Bharati was ashamed of going to school: 'I used to also feel ashamed of my dress and got a lot of beatings from my teachers. He said *our* clothes were always dirty' (B. Kale 2002, emphasis added). The teachers and the sub-staff of peons and others also commented on the students' lower-caste backgrounds, poverty and dirty uniforms: the centuries-old, stereo-typed markings of the 'dirty' Dalit life. These girls felt ashamed to attend schools that mocked their pasts and presents. However, Bharati was a rare woman who continued her education despite these insults.

Champabai (2002)[23] never had many exercise books:

> I used a slate till Class 7. Most of our caste children had only textbooks. We didn't know exercise books, pens, or pencils at all. I scribbled all my home-work and even the classroom study on one slate. And I remember we used to write everything in just one book, all subjects in one book. My mother bought books very rarely and my father did not pay much attention. He did not know much about my school or my schooling. He never bothered to inquire about it. This was the case with most of the parents of the lower-castes.

Unlike Champabai, many women never had books. Snehlata remembered the used-book auction that was held after exams (Kasbe 2003). She informed their parents about the quoted price, but since it was too high for the family, they could not buy any books for her that year.

Some women also emphasised that they could not attend college due to finan-cial hardship, or they had to choose 'easier' subjects. Some subjects required regular attendance and experiments. A lecturer who funded her own education said that 'the university was too far. Economic problems crept in the way. I liked psychology but I could not afford to attend the practicals regularly, so I chose political science, which did not have that condition' (J. Gaikwad 2002). Thus financial hardship influenced Dalit girls' ability to pursue the courses of their choice.

Statistically speaking, educational enrolment and the gap in education between boys and girls has been narrowing since independence; the disparity is less at the lower primary level and increases at the next two levels (Table 5.2). In 1961 there were 11,703 Mahars as compared to 26,479 Matangs in rural Poona district. Out of these, 9,495 (about 81.13 per cent of Mahars) and 22,864 (86.34 per cent of Matangs) were illiterate (Census of India 1961). Until 1981, 46.67 per cent of Mahars (21,773 out of 46,650) and 65.42 per cent of Matangs (53,260 out of 81,412) were illiterate, out of a total SC illiteracy rate of 54.43 per cent in Pune district (Census of India 1981a). In the case of SC students, the disparities have been similar, though they continue to be greater than among the general population. Nonetheless, by the 2000 to 2001 school year, the difference had diminished considerably. Yet these numbers fail to reveal anything about the quality of the education received or the multiple and complicated difficulties Dalit women faced in their education (Table 5.3).

Table 5.2 Nationwide enrolment by stages of all categories of students by gender (in percentages)

Year	Primary (1–4)			Middle/upper primary (5–8)			Higher secondary (9–12)		
	Boys	Girls	Total	Boys	Girls	Total	Boys	Girls	Total
1950–51	72	28	100	84	16	100	87	13	100
1960–61	67	33	100	76	24	100	79	21	100
1970–71	63	37	100	71	29	100	75	25	100
1980–81	61	39	100	67	33	100	69	31	100
1990–91	59	41	100	62	37	100	67	33	100
2000–01*	56	44	100	59	41	100	61	39	100

Source: National Informatics Centre (2006a), Karlekar (1983, 194). Both the census figures and Karlekar provide numbers in lakhs; I have calculated the percentages for clarity purposes.

Note
* Provisional.

Table 5.3 Nationwide enrolment by stages of SC students by gender (in percentages)

Year	Primary (1–4)			Middle/upper primary (5–8)			Higher secondary (9–12)		
	Boys	Girls	Total	Boys	Girls	Total	Boys	Girls	Total
1980–81	65	35	100	73	27	100	75	25	100
1989–90	62	38	100	67	33	100	74	26	100
2000–01*	57	43	100	61	39	100	63	37	100

Source: National Informatics Centre (2006b).

Note
* Provisional.

The home environment

Many Dalit girls lived in poor home environments that were not conducive to education. Subsistence and indebtedness were perennial problems, and the home could hardly provide a space where difficulties pertaining to homework or school could be solved.[24] Meera stated:

> My father was a drunkard and beat up my mother. My mother used to run to her aunt's place along with her children to protect herself from her drunkard husband. It was difficult to attend school. I never studied at home. There was no space at home. Whatever was taught was only at school. I also did not like to study at home because of some comments people made. Our relatives used to visit us sometimes. If they saw me with a book at all, they used to ask me what future I had with those books. We were to sell *kaagad-kaach-patraa* [paper-glass-tin-rags], they said. Why study then? They also

told my mother that I should not be educated much and suggested that she stop my schooling. But my mother did not listen to them.

(Jangam 2004)

Conditions at home were so miserable, she added, that she attended school whenever it was possible. She said that whenever she was with her grandmother's sister, who lived in the slum near the school, she went to school. Later, when they had a permanent *patraa* (thin tin sheet) house in that area, she continued her schooling. Dalit girls like Meera had nobody to ask them about their education, to talk to them or guide their studies. The lack of physical space at home made the school seem very spacious in comparison, so they engaged in studies only at school. What learning did they acquire in such circumstances?

Some parents were either not educated or had no time to help and encourage their daughters in their studies. They believed that it was the teacher's job to teach, and their child's job to study. This was a striking contrast with upper-caste/middle-class families, as well as middle-class Dalit families, in which parents gave constructive support to their children's education, as I will show in the next chapter as well as in Chapter 8. Many parents were not competent enough to guide their children.

Male Dalit students were often involved in physical labour outside school hours during the daytime and had time to study only at night. This, however, was difficult. Most families had just one small kerosene *batti* (lamp) at home, if any. They certainly could not afford electricity. I often heard stories of studying under the street lights in the evenings and at night. Men's autobiographies and narratives often mentioned street lights, which were the ultimate source of light to study at night after a laborious day's work. The repetition of the story in the community symbolised as well as strengthened the difficult circumstances that Dalits faced in order to seek knowledge and education. Since they could not afford lamps and light at home, they were driven to squat on the streets to study. Of course, due to strict moral norms, girls could not do this.

Dalit parents who did take some interest in their daughters' education had in many cases imbibed some of the prevailing high-caste attitudes towards learning: for instance, that learning could be acquired through formulaic verbal repetition, reminiscent of the *shlokas* chanted by Brahmans. They also believed that education could be forced upon reluctant children through strict discipline, including physical beatings, to make them memorise their lessons. Rani thus recalled:

My mother used to work outside. As soon as she came home in the evening, she would get ready to sit near the stove. She used to make us sit near the *chul* [a mud stove] beside her. She used to *bhaakri thaapaayachi* [make bread] with one hand and stir the curry with the other. And her mouth used to work too. She always used to ask us to read the lessons aloud. She said that the louder we read the lessons, the better we would memorise them, so we had to read aloud.

(R. Kamble 2001)[25]

In this manner, the easier lessons were memorised in the mother's presence. The father had little time to spend on children's homework.

Some parents kept their daughters away from school during family functions like marriages and festivals. Bharati discussed how her parents encouraged absenteeism by producing fake medical certificates that excused her from school (B. Kale 2002). The girls were engaged in housework during such occasions. The household was the mother's domain; mothers mostly socialised and restricted their daughters owing to the gendered nature of childrearing roles.[26] Mothers, not fathers, were responsible for the safety of their children in private and in public. Many times, their fears resulted in the end of education for girls after Class 4 or 7. Elder daughters suffered particularly badly. In most cases the eldest daughter in the family was raised to assume the role of a mother so that she could stand in whenever the real mother was away from home. Their studies tended to suffer particularly badly as a result. These were times when the eldest daughter had nobody to whom she could direct her questions. In such circumstances the eldest daughters barely studied or just managed to scrape through each class. Meera's mother was educated only until Class 3, when she was forced to quit in order to assist her mother and look after her younger siblings (S. Gaikwad 2004).[27] Therefore, these daughters had a particular disadvantage even after they started their schooling.

Many Dalit parents barely had the time or confidence to approach the high-caste teachers, while high-caste parents met the teachers at school regularly to check on their children's progress. A few mothers, like those of Urmila Pawar and Lalita Naik (2001), visited the schools and boldly faced the teachers. In her interview, Urmilatai (2004) mentioned her brave mother, who warned the teacher that if he verbally abused her daughter in the future she would definitely question him. Lalita Naik's (2001) mother frequently met with teachers to monitor her children's progress. However, other parents hardly bothered. Dalit parents could not generally afford extra tuition. Students attended extra classes mainly for difficult subjects like English and mathematics. Most Dalit girls had to try to scrape through these subjects without extra help, though a few, like Borade (2002) and Kumud Pawde (2005), said that their teachers did give them some extra readings to study for their scholarship exams.[28]

The lower-class Dalits lacked an English-speaking culture, in contrast with middle-class Dalits (as I will examine in the next chapter). Although they aspired to listen to their children speak English, few lower-class parents supported this education. Most of the women I interacted with felt that the lack of English-medium schools had hindered their careers. With English, they said, they would have been more confident, outgoing, bold and outspoken. They also believed that English enabled significant prestige and a sense of superiority, which they lacked. Snehlata reflected that an English-medium school would have made a world of difference:

> If I had gone to an English-medium school it would have made *khupach pharak* [a big difference] to my life. I would have been able to converse

with you in fluent English. I would have been able to attend the parent-teacher meetings for my eldest son and talk to his teachers. I never did that. Besides this, students in an English medium are very confident and also do well in life. The Marathi-medium students lack this confidence. They waste a lot of time in building it. Everything is different about English school; in Marathi schools half the time is spent coping with so many problems and complexities.

(Kasbe 2003)

Snehlata therefore directly connected the English language and English schools with self-confidence. That self-confidence, she believed, was missing in many Dalits. The next chapter will address this issue in further detail.

By contrast, the slum dweller Meera had other concerns. A prestigious English-medium school would call for material accessories that she could not afford. She continued:

If I had been in [an English] convent school, I would have been a different person. They are all rich people there, and I would have wasted my life demanding things [that my parents could not have afforded]. I would have spoken very good English, but I would not have understood real life. Here, staying in this environment ... and fighting for a good living gives me immense confidence and authority; there I would have lacked it. It is very different to rise from zero to a well-established background.

(Jangam 2004)

To Meera, in contrast with life in middle-class apartments, the slum environment demanded a different struggle. She had different opinions on instruction in English for herself; importantly, though, she strategically enrolled her children in good English-medium schools.

The 'privilege' of jhopadpatti schools

Grinding poverty, increasing unemployment and community distress all restricted the kinds of support and recognition that parents could allocate to their children's education. Dalit girls who were in the first generation of learners were *highly privileged to go to school under any circumstances.* Whatever the quality of the school, the fact that they could enter a school at all was most important. Kamal Jadhav (2001) commented: 'The standard and medium of the school did not matter at all. We could attend school; that was more than enough.' Champabai Bhalerao (2002) poignantly remarked:

We went to the nearest available school and were *privileged to get whatever we could,* compared to our cousins in the village. They remained illiterate and continued with the small farming. At least we could study a little and get our children educated. My father could afford to send me to school because he did not have to pay any fees. If he had to pay them, perhaps I would not have been able to attend at all. In those times nobody knew about the benefits of education.

Champabai added that the main pressure for children to attend school regularly did not come from the parents but from the school: 'The peons used to come from the school and drag the children there. If a particular child was registered in school but did not attend, then the peons used to come and take that child to school.' Draupadi Nagare (2004) and others reiterated this. When the missionaries and leaders like Phule tried to start schools in the nineteenth century, they followed a similar strategy: they grabbed children and brought them to the school. The peripatetic missionaries exhorted Dalits to send their children to school, and Lahuji Mang and Ranba Mahar helped Phule in his endeavours. This practice continued in the post-independence period: government workers searched for children and took them to school because the state's education agenda was unfinished.

Some girls saw their schools as an escape from their homes in the slums. School provided a break from their household duties. Often, it was the friendships and games rather than the curriculum that provided the attraction. These Dalits lived huddled in slums, in small, cramped 'matchbox' houses with few windows and poor ventilation. Sometimes ten individuals lived in a single room. These girls had no playgrounds. Lakshmi Shinde (2000) mentioned that at times some NGOs, like the Deepgruh Organisation in the Parvati slum, had *baalvaadis* (play schools) for small children and held classes for the students for a minimal fee. However, few children received even such minimal training. The plight of Dalit girls was formidable. Again, the unsafe environment of their *vasti* called for parents to constrain girls, but the school was one free space where they could play unreservedly. It was the main motivation for Jyotsna:

> I went to school because I could play with my friends there. Studying was a small part of this. You know the atmosphere in Yerawada ... and so I liked to play when I was at school. All of us walked together and it was fun being with my friends, playing and studying together.
>
> (J. Rokade 2004)

Thus, for Jyotsna, school also became a safe space to play and have fun with friends.

Many informants complained that their teachers did not teach them properly. Jyotsna commented: 'The teachers in municipal schools were very casual. They were not regular, did not teach properly. There was one teacher for four classes. They were constantly chatting with other teachers, leaving the students to scribble something in their tattered books' (J. Rokade 2004). In many cases, they did not consider low-caste pupils 'worth teaching'. They took little interest in pupils' progress; they merely advanced them a grade automatically, year by year. Draupadi, Sandhya's mother, said of her experience at a government school: 'It was just pushing from one class to the other. No grades or marks, *dhakalat jaayacho* [we were pushed from one class to the next], no standards' (Nagare 2004). There was no discipline, no proper teaching. Teacher turnover was high: they wanted to get away from the low-status slum schools as soon as they could.

Jyotsna, who attended the Netaji High School, complained that her teacher did not teach properly:

> Sometimes, if they were new, they were not able to teach properly. Some weren't bothered as to whether the class understood their lessons or not. Some of the college teachers were irresponsible. They sometimes did not complete the syllabus for a subject. They also did not know much, could not explain well. So we had to join [private tutoring] classes.
>
> (J. Rokade 2004)

The Gramscian and Freirean concepts of 'banking education' underscore the deposition of knowledge by the teacher alone, as Jyotsna describes here. The teacher was always-already on a pedestal, delivering funds of knowledge to the student below him or her; it was never the other way around. The teacher was also not accessible to the student. In this manner the teacher always remained a teacher and the student a student.

Ambedkar argued that teachers were in fact *saarathi* (guides) and were thus essential agents in the process of socialisation. They had a significant role to play in the future of a child. In a similar vein, commenting on the role of the pedagogue, Emile Durkheim stresses that 'such a person was essential for the socialisation of young minds into the collective representations – the dominant norms – of a particular society' (Durkheim 1956, 1961). Working on the child's qualities of habit, discipline and suggestibility, the teacher would develop 'a number of physical, intellectual, and moral states necessary for good citizenship'. John Dewey (1916, 39; see also Dewey 1910) also states that:

> Education is an endless experiment wherein educators aid students in creating ways and means of actively transforming themselves to secure the most complete and effective adaptation. They should educate the individual's creative and artistic ability as well as their ability to engage in critical inquiry and if necessary, carry out the reconstruction of the existing social order to evolve a better society.[29]

Yet, most often teachers and students do not share a common value code, be it in India,[30] the UK or the US for that matter. Many studies have brought to light that there is a need for teachers to appreciate the fact that a culture which is different from their (middle-class) culture is not necessarily inferior or in need of reform. Ray C. Rist (1977) and William Ryan (1976) argue that race and ethnicity are crucial variables in a teacher's assessment of students. These works highlight that teachers' expectations of students are influenced by non-academic factors and that when teachers have high expectations, students become high achievers.

Teachers decide on their expectations based on factors such as caste, class and gender, and make decisions about each child's education based on those expectations.

A study by Jane Torrey of a Harlem ghetto found that teachers were systematically imposing white values, culture and language upon black children.[31] Children who were unable to adapt to this essentially alien culture were treated as potential failures. Teachers who were primary agents in the process of superimposing a new culture believed that speaking and understanding the language of whites and adopting their social manners were essential for the child's general advancement. In the Indian case, teachers also rewarded the 'good' language style of students from a considerably privileged upper-caste background.[32] Teachers and parents have often disciplined children to use the upper-caste 'cultured' speech (for example, *ho* instead of the lower-class/caste *ha* for 'yes'). Thus, Dalit language and culture are different from the 'standard'; Dalits are constantly erasing such *ha* vocabulary.[33] One Dalit writer, reflecting upon his school experiences, remembers how a Brahman teacher thrashed him hard to make him pronounce the word *vyombi* ('fresh raw wheat from the fields') correctly. He continues:

> I used to follow my cousin to school. I did not have clothes to attend school. My mother asked someone for a set and I wore that. I had a feeling of inferiority when I went to school with the well-dressed students, so I used to sit in a corner. I had a Brahman teacher. Whenever he was angry he used to call us *dhedgya, maangatya*.[34] If we did not wear caps, he used to yell, 'you *haraamkhor* [bastard], are you Ambedkar's heir? But that won't work here.' He used to use bad words and cane us thoroughly. He used to also derogatorily address us as '*dhedraaje* [King of Dheds], *maangraaje* [King of Mangs].' All the children laughed at us. We were tortured immensely when he used such caste names for us. He used to ask us to leave the class for want of a *topi* [cap]. He used to beat us up thoroughly; some Dalit boys left school due to this.

(Quoted in Wagh 1986)

The upper-caste teachers thus used all sorts of physically and psychologically corrosive language against Dalit pupils, in the process encouraging many to drop out of the educational process. They caned them frequently and disciplined them in the Brahmani 'cultured' speech. While some students dropped out, many Dalit students continued to endure the insults and to educate themselves to whatever extent possible.

Significantly, the curriculum also selectively depicted the world of the dominant and strong, thus ignoring the marginalised. Marginalised people internalised and evolved complex cultural strategies to ignore and forget pedagogic knowledge presented to them at school – 'certified degrada'.[35] Geeta Nambissan reported that Scheduled Class/Scheduled Tribe students found their language and culture to be different from the standard (Nambissan 2000). The practice of differentiation and discrimination against the SC (and other subalterns) across a range of social institutions and practices, including curriculum and distribution of knowledge, continues through the system of education.

A study by A.B. Wilson and J.W.B. Douglas in the United Kingdom finds that neatly dressed children and those whom the teachers felt came from 'better' homes tended to be placed in higher academic streams than was warranted by their measured IQ (Karlekar 1983, 205). In an analogous manner, in the Indian context, many teachers placed the children from upper-caste and middle-class backgrounds in higher academic levels and Dalits in lower levels. Even if Dalit children were neatly dressed, there was no equal chance of their being treated well. Their neat, clean uniforms were not enough to *erase* their 'dirty' backgrounds; even Ambedkar faced severe social discrimination in education and employment.

Robert Rosenthal and Lenore Jacobson, in their provocatively titled work *Pygmalion in the School* (1993), systematically dwell on the teacher's attitude, which makes or mars students. It is worth quoting them at length here:

> Even before a teacher has seen a pupil deal with academic tasks she is likely to have some expectation for his behaviour. If she is to teach a 'slow group', or children of darker skin colour, or children whose mothers are 'on welfare', she will have different expectations for her pupil's performance than if she is to teach a 'fast group', or children of an upper-middle-class community. Before she has seen a child perform, she may have seen his score on an achievement or ability test or his last year's grades or she may have access to the less formal information that constitutes the child's reputation.
>
> (Rosenthal and Jacobson 1993, viii–ix)

Therefore, the teacher's expectations, however derived, could serve as an educational self-fulfilling prophecy.

Teachers' stereotypes and ignorance of Dalit culture, low expectations and negative labelling were exacerbated by structural inequalities of caste, class and gender, the intransigence of social attitudes, and the implicit ideologies that supported all of these. This was always-already deeply contested territory. In India, the caste system indirectly constrained the educational opportunities of lower-caste children despite constitutional guarantees of equality. Some scholars have argued that teachers may unconsciously treat low-caste children differently from other children or have reduced expectations of them (Khan 1993, 226). My evidence showed, however, that the teachers often discriminated consciously.

There was also another problem. Lakshmi (Shinde 2000) stated that in some cases, lower-caste pupils got back at the high-caste teachers by adopting a *goondaa*-like personality. She reflected, laughed and continued:[36]

> The few upper-caste teachers were scared. This was because the school was located in a slum dominated by Dalits and the number of lower-caste

teachers in the school was higher than the 'other' caste. Occasionally, the students behaved very arrogantly in the presence of the teacher. I used to sometimes walk out of class when I did not like it. The teacher did not say anything. They were easily scared by the presence of boys from my *vasti* who were *goondaas*.

This was the municipal school atmosphere in a few slums. Some boys did not allow teachers to teach in class. They harassed them. It appears that in some cases the school itself was under the students' control.

Meera said that she did not have a teacher for mathematics because '*pora tiku deta navhate ek hi shikshak* [the boys did not allow any teacher to settle down in the school for a long time]' (Jangam 2004). The majority of students suffered due to this misconduct by a few boys. The schools in the *vasti* were sometimes an *addaa*[37] for miscreant men. Many of them were victims of such misconduct and were further attracted to antisocial behaviour, which turned them into juvenile delinquents. This picture is rampant in subaltern ghettos all over the world.

Dalit women also had to face sexual harassment in school. Parents often complained about insecurity for girls attending schools. Instances of abduction, rape and molestation of girls dampened the enthusiasm of parents and female students in pursuing education beyond a certain age; thereafter they remained bound to their homes. Parents were hesitant to send their daughters to schools that had only male teachers. Nearly all committees and commissions that have looked into illiteracy have recommended increasing recruitment of women teachers.

Misbehaviour by teachers was also responsible for the large number of girls dropping out of the education system around puberty. Sometimes girls had to grant sexual favours in order to get their work done. Even non-Dalit girls were sexually abused, but Dalit girls faced a double oppression due to their caste. Moreover, they have been historically treated as 'public' property with loose sexuality, and hence faced deeper and different difficulties due to the double burden of their caste and gender. Yet no Dalit women spoke openly about eve-teasing or sexual harassment to me, except for Meera. The other respondents simply denied it, stating that it was not of great significance for them, or kept silent. Perhaps they purposefully maintained silence on this sensitive issue. Such silence and ignorance is often a defence for women who feel that they would invite trouble and even shame on themselves if they spoke out. Dalit girls at times felt helpless against masculine forces and learned to be conveniently oblivious to such comments. They knew that the wider society placed Dalit women's sexuality on the lowest grade and equated them with sexually touchable and 'loose' women like *muralis* or *jogtinis*, as analysed in Chapter 4. Dalit radicals continued to fight against such social constructions, caste differentiation and stereotyping. Meera was an exception to the rule. She reported:

When I was in Class 7, I used to go to this Bhujbal class for maths. We had a teacher who liked me very much. I did not like him at all. He used to get closer at times, but one day as we stood together he suddenly bit me on my cheek. I told my mother, who complained to the higher authority, and that was the end of the teacher's career in Bhujbal. He was sacked. After that I did not go to any class as such.

(Jangam 2004)

Instead of maintaining silence, Meera's bold mother complained to the authority and later stopped her daughter from attending the class. Due to this experience Meera grew so apathetic towards classes that even during School Secondary Certificate examinations, when most of the students went for extra coaching, Meera opted to study on her own.

Many upper- and lower-caste teachers knew that they could get away with such behaviour because they were teachers and girls were students over whom the former could exercise power. However, not all teachers were bad; there were a few idealistic ones who went out of their way to help their Dalit pupils. The most famous example was that of Ambedkar's Brahman teacher, who gave Ambedkar his last name. Ambedkar's family name was Sankpal, but in order to avoid its low-caste connotation he took his village name – Ambavade – so it became Ambavadekar. However, his Brahman teacher, who was named Ambedkar, showed great concern for the young boy and also provided him with a daily lunch to spare him the long walk to his home. In honour of this teacher the boy registered his name as Ambedkar.[38]

Some women mentioned teachers who took an interest in their progress and advised them about further opportunities. Poonam Rokade (2004),[39] now an engineer, praised her teacher:

During my school, my teacher did help me in mathematics. He spent some extra time on my coaching and did not charge me any fees. The engineering syllabus was tough and I felt like dropping out at times. I repeatedly failed in one particular subject and I could not figure out the reason. I thought it was caste discrimination. However, one day, I gathered the guts to face the teacher of that subject and asked him the reason for my failure in his subject alone. He was [an upper-caste] Maratha named Chavan. He explained that my method of writing answers was faulty. He also advised me to solve previous years' exam papers and get them reviewed by him. I followed his advice and succeeded.

A few teachers were innovative and implemented changes for the interest and benefit of the students, asking them to teach the class or to help other students. Such tendencies were nonetheless the exception rather than the rule.

Caste discrimination and humiliation in schools

Mohammad Talib (1998, 199–209) has described the experience of working-class children in a school located in an urban village on the southern outskirts of New Delhi. He observed that teachers would always say, 'This child was deficient in the *ruchi* [interest] necessary for aspiring education of any kind' (200). One student he quoted said, 'My teachers have always told me so. They told me that my head does not contain brain but *bhusaa* [dry grass]. They said so because I do not understand the lessons in the class' (203). Convinced, he dropped out. Such qualitative information is relevant to understanding Dalits' reasons for dropping out of school, rather than just blaming them for their non-attendance in schools. Such children are often persuaded by their upper-caste teachers to believe they lack the aptitude for education.

The humiliation faced by Dalit girls at school was the rule in most cases.[40] Monica Sathe[41] was troubled because, despite earning higher grades, her teachers encouraged the 'others' (upper-caste students) and not her. She stated, 'In my case they never acknowledged that I was doing well. I did not like it, but still I studied to prove myself' (2005). Hirabai Kuchekar (2002) was reminded of a Brahman teacher during Class 7: 'He was really harsh. He asked me, "What are you going to do with education?" He further continued, "These people will never improve. You will never understand this maths; it is not meant for you"'.

Shalini Moré (2002) and Nanubai Pagare (2004)[42] did not want to speak about such experiences, while Nani (Bhalerao 2000) and Draupadi Nagare (2004) simply denied the experience vociferously and said that none of 'that' existed. Interestingly, they did not want to name 'that' as caste experience because they were not very comfortable speaking about it. Thus women were intensely troubled and chose to even erase the use of caste in their vocabulary and reduced it to 'this' and 'that' categories. Certainly, I do not deny that some have escaped caste discrimination; however, such narratives in particular create conditions for the 'unspeakability' of caste. I interpret their silence as a result of being so damned by the obnoxious caste system and the sentiments enveloping it that they refused to remember their past, and to relate to their 'Untouchable' background.

In municipal schools with majority lower-caste pupils, however, there was no discrimination among pupils. Suvarna Kuchekar[43] reported:

> I did not face *anything* in school as it was a corporation school dominated by backward children. The teachers also, even if from the open category [upper-caste], did not practice caste discrimination.... My friends also know my caste and are fine with me. They come home with me and I to go their places, and we are quite close. I have never hidden my caste.
>
> (2002, emphasis added)

When there were a number of high-caste children, however, the humiliations could come from them also. Bharati complained, 'Children teased me a lot. They wanted me to maintain a distinct distance from them because I belonged to a *dirty* caste. They hid my bag and stole my only pen. So I did not like to go to school' (B. Kale 2002). Ratnaprabha Pawar (2002), now a teacher, recounted:

> when we sat on the benches the 'other' girls very overtly or even covertly and neatly tucked in their skirts, so that they would not touch mine. They

also met in separate groups also and stayed away from other castes. I never had friends from the upper castes as such.

In this manner, caste-based friendship was practised in the schools. Jyotsna Rokade (2004), Ratnaprabha Pawar (2002), Hirabai Kuchekar (2002) and others were familiar with such impenetrable caste groups. Many upper-caste children had been well socialised by the parents and teachers and practised whatever had been preached to them, leading to such discriminatory practices towards their classmates. Yet there were other upper castes who befriended Dalits and helped them. Vasant Moon's friends provided him with food, clothes and books (Moon 2001).

Some sought to hide their caste background if at all possible. Meena Mahajan[44] said:

> In school I told my friends I was a Maratha. I had a terrible complex. I thought that 'they' would not talk to me if I revealed my caste. Once, when I was in Class 10, one teacher loudly asked me, *'Tu Hindu-Mahar naa ga?'* ['You are a Hindu-Mahar, right?']. I felt so bad I stood with my head down. I was the only one in that class. I also never gave my address as Mangalvar Peth, as it is a Mahar *aali* [ghetto]. I do not tell my caste openly even today. Why tell if it is not required? I declare that I am a Brahman.
>
> (M. Mahajan 2002)

Meena's testimony brought out the ways in which Dalits sometimes try to 'pass' as upper caste. Dalits could be identified due to some stereotypical markers; their place of residence, as dealt with earlier, was one such marker. In this instance, to hide her markings, Meena concealed her home address. Another way of doing this was to speak in public in a prestigious nasal-toned Marathi, a Marathi very different from the one they spoke in private in the precincts of their homes. Meena was also fortunate to share an upper-caste last name, Mahajan, so nobody could discover her actual background.

The municipal Marathi-medium school is at the lowest level in the school hierarchy. Most Dalit students from these schools had low aspirations; this was true for most of my interlocutors during their school days. They were first-generation learners who were grateful to at least attend school, which their parents could not. Most of them suggested that they never thought about their careers or futures. It is only the second- and third-generation learners who talked about this vociferously. Most of the first-generation learners were married off very early, before they started making use of their education for employment. They did not dream of anything to begin with, and by the time they started doing so their dreams were shattered.

Most of the first- and some of the second-generation respondents were transferred from one class to the other. They wanted to make use of their education for employability, and teaching provided the best opening in this respect, as the basic qualification was to pass Class 7. Hence everybody in the community, including Ambedkar (see Chapter 4), insisted that girls must be taught until matriculation so that they could apply for teaching posts. Further, teaching was popularly seen as a suitable occupation for women. Most of the women I talked to stated that as girls they had the desire to become teachers. Snehlata Kasbe reported: 'I used to look at my teachers who moved around the class with a stick. I also wanted to imitate that. I thought the profession *commanded more respect*' (2003, emphasis added).[45] Nonetheless, there were others who took on different occupations, becoming clerical staff, nurses, officers, doctors, police, and so on.

Dalit women's experiences thus questioned the very nature of egalitarian citizenship promised by the state. Dalit radicals, as discussed in Chapters 1 and 2, expended their energy to bring Dalits into the ambit of education, equality, social justice and citizenship. Yet, in practice Dalit women continued to face numerous difficulties exercising their rights. Although the practice of untouchability had visibly declined in the cities, some villages still support the practice in contemporary times.[46] Dalit women agreed that caste discrimination had lost its overt sharpness in the city to a large extent; however, they did suffer from it in many minor forms. Most significantly, they reported that despite these difficulties they were better prepared to challenge any discrimination. Certainly, the process of education, though intimidating and humiliating, also prepared them to fight social injustice, inequality and poverty.

Conclusion

In pre-colonial and colonial times, the Brahman Peshwa and colonial Raj suppressed Dalits' demands for rights to the public space. Because, in the modern vocabulary, public space was linked to universal citizenship, when Dalits were denied public spaces they were denied citizenship. This chapter sought to explicate Dalit spatial exclusion in Pune. Moreover, several studies, like those of B.V. Shah (1964), Chatterjee (2000), Suma Chitnis (1981) and Kakade (1979), have argued that neither students nor their relatives experienced caste discrimination or ill treatment associated with their caste status. However, perhaps these scholars failed to pick up on casteism in their studies since, though some Dalits could talk about the discrimination they faced, many others would prefer to remain silent and not talk about such practices. Opposing scholarly claims, the Dalit women I spoke with argued that, though subtly at times, caste continued to be a source of oppression in modern cities. Free access to education was ineffective unless Dalit women were welcomed in schools.

This chapter has examined the matrix of interconnected struggles of social, cultural, economic and spatial inequality that reinforced educational impediments for Dalit women. Following the promises of Dalit radicals' methods rooted in modernity, many Dalits abandoned their stigmatising traditional occupations and migrated to the liberatory city, which was ostensibly modern and hence caste-free. Yet Dalits' oppression was renewed through various avatars: problems of migration, segregated housing, food and water scarcity, sanitation, spatial inequality, and low-quality education. Thus, although they lived in the city, they hardly belonged to it; they were always-already on the margins, socially, spatially, educationally and culturally. They were 'equal' but 'different', and hence continuously coerced to accept living on the periphery. Many Dalits accepted their place. Yet many others consistently struggled against such constraints, coerced and disciplined themselves, and appropriated rationalist modernity in strategic ways to refashion themselves and their futures. The next chapter continues the herstory of Dalit women's multiple and intimately braided struggles as they sought to escape the slum and advance to 'middle classness'.

Notes

1 Lakshmi is a young, smart and successful Matang businesswoman. She lives in the Parvati slums and handles a number of small businesses. She has special employment schemes for women: making flowers, costume jewellery, and so on.
2 I have known Lalita since my childhood. I remember her with her eyes turned towards the ground, a bag on her shoulder, limping to her office.
3 The caste-based labour of Mahars, such as watching the village, dragging carcasses, deciding boundaries, and so on.
4 There was a phenomenal rise of 41.48 per cent in the urban population of Pune district between 1961 and 1971 (Census of India 1981b, 7).
5 Gangabai Kuchekar is a Matang woman from Yashwant Nagar-Yerawada slum and Meera Jangam's co-sister's (husband's brother's wife's) mother.
6 A recent study (Viththayathil and Singh 2012) has highlighted residential segregation along caste lines in India's major metropolitan cities of Delhi, Mumbai, Kolkata, Chennai, Bangalore, Hyderabad and Ahmedabad
7 During my historical fieldwork, many Dalits acknowledged my *shuddha*, Puneri Marathi and were in awe of it.
8 This Peth/Kasba is named after the famous Sadashivrao Bhau, who presumably died fighting the Third Battle of Panipat.
9 Madhavrao Peshwa is said to have brought the Chitpavan Brahmans from Konkan and resettled them in Sadashiv Peth area of Pune. He is noted for his experiments, such as building underground water channels from a small dam on the Parvati hill to Sadashiv Peth. Most *wadas* in this area have their own wells and *houds* (water tanks) for a constant supply of clean water. This Chitpavan-dominated patch signifies and exercises Gramscian 'hegemony' for any Punekar. 'Commonsensically', a Sadashiv Pethi Brahman is famous for his thrift, connivance, grammatically 'pure', nasal-toned Marathi and other similar features of highest Brahmanhood.
10 Siddhartha Nagar is in Yerawada. Siddhartha is the princely name of Gautam Buddha and Siddhartha Nagar was dominated by Buddhists.
11 Nandini Gooptu's study (2001, 146) also shows how untouchable migrants from rural UP to Kanpur found homes in the socially segregated ghettos.
12 Lakshmi Shinde, Matang, Class 12, self-employed; Nanda Kamble, Buddhist, BA, nurse; Vaishali Chandane, Buddhist, advocate. I interviewed all three in the Parvati slum.
13 *Kattaa* is a Marathi word meaning 'parapet'. In Marathi, *kattyavarchi pora* (boys on the *kattaa*) has a negative connotation.
14 Sheela Nikam, Buddhist, Class 3, is president of the Hawker's Union in Borivili, Mumbai. Sheelatai talked to me for at least four hours. She would not let me go and insisted that I stay at her place that night. She had a lot to tell me. She also gave me a copy of her autobiography in process, *Mazhya Jivanacha Pravaas* (*The Journey of My Life*).

15 Draupadi Nagare, Buddhist, Class 7, housewife, Ramtekdi, Pune. She is about eight years old, and we fondly called her *Tai*.

16 Jyotsna Rokade, Buddhist, Masters in Commerce, Sales Tax Officer, Vishrantvadi, Pune. I had to interview the working women on national holidays. They saw to it that they finished all their housework and were free to talk to me whenever I went for the interview. I followed the Rokades from their house in Mundhwa to Vishrantwadi and of course to Yerawada.

17 Urmila Pawar, Buddhist, MA (Marathi literature), Borivili, Mumbai.

18 Alaka Kale, Buddhist, MA, Lecturer, Karve Road, Pune.

19 For Bourdieu the traditional division of labour assigns to women familiarity with things of art and literature. See Bourdieu (1984, 57).

20 Snehlata Kasbe, Matang, BA, Senior Officer, Pune Station, Pune.

21 Ratnaprabha Pawar, Matang, Class 12, diploma in education, municipal school-teacher, Bibwewadi, Pune.

22 Meena Ranpise, Buddhist, MA, lecturer, Sinhagad Road, Pune.

23 Champabai Bhalerao, Buddhist, Class 7, housewife, Yerawada, Pune. She felt hon-oured to be interviewed and was interested in telling me about her past life, Nana (her husband) and her managerial skills.

24 Most informants from the slum agreed that they did not have enough room at home. See also Nambissan (2000), Talib (1998) and Muralidharan (1997).

25 Alaka and Rani Kamble are Matang sisters. Alaka has a BA and is job-hunting, while tutoring from home. Her sister Rani also has a BA and works at Dapodi-Pune. I inter-viewed the sisters at their home in Tadiwala Road slum in Pune. Alaka wanted to work for the community.

26 Carolyn Steedman (1986, 106) writes about how women/mothers socialise little girls into accepting restricted futures, forcing them into familiar and genteel ways and fitting them for self-abasement. However, we should also note the parents' concern for the security of their daughters.

27 Mrs Gaikwad, Matang, Meera Jangam's mother, Class 3, works at a preschool in Yashwantnagar slum.

28 Mrs Borade, Buddhist, Class 9, conducts sewing classes in Dapodi, Pune; Professor Kumud Pawde, Buddhist, MA (Sanskrit), retired, lives in Dhantoli, Nagpur. I spent a whole afternoon with Kumudtai; her interview was full of personal stories and social activism. We talked while her sisters cooked some spicy Nagpuri mutton curry for us. I stayed for lunch and enjoyed the company of this erudite feminist.

29 Phule and Ambedkar understood the critical responsibility of teachers and hence wanted to do away with the Brahman teachers who harassed the Untouchables.

30 I have already discussed works by Nambissan, Talib and Murlidharan in the preced-ing pages. All of these scholars suggest that the school curriculum does not resonate with working-class/Dalit students.

31 I draw upon works which deal with the failure of schools to make connections with the lives of working-class children. Such studies helped me understand a parallel process of education in India, where teachers imposed Brahmani norms. See Torrey (1973) and Steedman (1982, 2–3). bell hooks remembers that she was mainly taught by white teachers whose lessons reinforced racist stereotypes. 'For black children, education was no longer about the practice of freedom. Realizing this, I lost my love for school' (hooks 1994, 3).

32 See also Pierre Bourdieu's most insightful ethnographic observations about French schooling. He shows how French schoolteachers reward good language style, especially in essay and oral examinations, a practice that tends to favour those students with considerable cultural capital who in general are from privileged family origins (Bourdieu 1977; 1997, 75–78). I return to this argument and expand on this debate in Chapter 8.

33 My experience, observation and fieldwork testify to this social fact. Carolyn Steed-man (1986, 38) also offers an analysis of what happens when one changes social

class, as well as when one is in a middle-class school. Her voice changed and her Lancashire accent began to disappear.

34 These are slurs for Untouchable castes, like *Mhardey* for Mahars, *Dhedgya* for Dheds, *Mangtya* for Matangs, and so on.

35 The pioneering research of scholars like Talib, Muralidharan and Nambissan underlines my conjectures and my argument that the curricula do not resonate with Dalits. Their contentions regarding the disjunction between the contents of school textbooks and the culture and environment of lower-caste children resonate with the Western postulates I delineated earlier. In the lower-caste (SC) context, Talib (1998, 200, 203–205) observes that the life of the oppressed, such as the quarry workers' children, does not find expression in the life and thoughts of the privileged in society, who thus ignore them altogether.

36 *Goondaa* means a ruffian.

37 The term *addaa*, a place for youth to congregate, has positive and negative connotations. Here I have used it in a negative sense, as a place that brought together miscreant youth.

38 Many Dalits have grown up with these stories, but see also Omvedt (2004, 4–5).

39 Poonam Rokade, Buddhist, engineer, Mundhawa, Pune.

40 In what follows, I have drawn upon Philip Corrigan's work (1991), which is very Foucaultian, also discussed in Chapter 1. In his scholarly paper Corrigan demonstrates the way students' bodies are taught and disciplined. He also argues that the school system works to arrange and reflects a series of rewards and punishments, in which, of course, punishments can be rewards and vice versa. Gore (1998) engages with a similar argument.

41 Monica Sathe, Matang, Masters in Social Work, Karve Nagar, Pune.

42 Shalini Moré, Buddhist, MBBS, Sinhagad Road, Pune, owns two clinics. Nanubai Pagare, Buddhist, literate, housewife, Yerawada, Pune, is Lalita Naik's mother.

43 Suvarna Kuchekar, daughter of Hirabai Kuchekar, is a Matang with a BA in commerce and was searching for a job.

44 Meena Mahajan, Buddhist, Class 12, housewife, Ghorpade Peth, Pune.

45 Some Dalits thought that at least the 'divine' profession of teaching would bring them respect.

46 A recent study by G. Shah *et al.* (2006, 65) reveals that untouchability is present in 80 per cent of rural areas.

References

Ambedkar, B.R. 1990. *Dr. Babasaheb Ambedkar: Writings and Speeches,* Vol. 7, ed. Vasant Moon. Bombay: Department of Education, Government of Maharashtra.

Bapat, Meera. 1980. *Shanty Town and City: The Case of Poona, Progress in Planning.* London: Pergamon Press.

Basu, Aparna. 1974. *Growth of Education and Political Development in India, 1898–1920.* Delhi: Oxford University Press.

Bawa, Vasant Kumar. 1987. *Indian Metropolis: Urbanization, Planning and Management.* New Delhi: Inter-India Publications.

Bhalerao, Champabai. 2002. Interview with the author, 20 May. Yerawada, Pune.

Borade, Lata. 2002. Interview with the author, 15 July. Dapodi, Pune.

Bourdieu, Pierre. 1977. *Outline of a Theory of Practice*, trans. Richard Nice. Cambridge: Cambridge University Press.

——. 1984. *Distinction: A Social Critique of the Judgment of Taste.* Cambridge, MA: Harvard University Press.

——. 1997. *Culture and Power: The Sociology of Pierre Bourdieu*, ed. David Swartz. Chicago, IL: University of Chicago Press.

Bourdieu, Pierre and Jean-Claude Passeron. 1977. *Reproduction in Education, Society and Culture*. Thousand Oaks, CA: Sage.

Brahme, Sulabha and Prakash Gole. 1967. *Deluge in Poona: Aftermath and Rehabilitation*. Poona: Gokhale Institute Studies No. 51.

Census of India. 1961. Maharashtra, Vol. X, Part V-A, tables for SC-ST in Maharashtra, Vd. 4326–12a. Bombay: Government of India.

——. 1981a. Series 12. Maharashtra, Part (ix) ii, special tables for SC (4–6).

——. 1981b. *District Census Handbook 1981, Pune*. Bombay: Government of India.

——. 1991. Series 14. Maharashtra, Part VIII (1): SC-1: Distribution of SC population by sex for each caste, 66–67. Bombay: Government of India.

——. 2001. Ward-level primary census abstract for slum areas of million-plus cities, 420. Bombay: Government of India.

Chandane, Vaishali. 2001. Interview with the author, 10 August. Parvati, Pune.

Chatterjee, S.K. 2000. *Education Development of Scheduled Castes: Looking Ahead*. New Delhi: Gyan Publishing.

Chitnis, M.B. 1973. An educational, social and economic survey of Milind College students. In *Milind College Annual*, Vol. 10. Aurangabad: Milind College.

Chitnis, Suma. 1981. *A Long Way to Go: Report on a Survey of Scheduled Caste High School and College Students in Fifteen States of India*. New Delhi: Allied Publishers.

Corrigan, P.R. 1991. The making of the boy: Meditations on what grammar school did with, to and for my body. In *Postmodernism, Feminism, and Cultural Politics: Redrawing Educational Boundaries*, ed. Henry A. Giroux. Albany: State University of New York Press.

Dewey, John. 1910. *My Pedagogic Creed*. Chicago, IL: Flanagan.

——. 1916. *Democracy and Education: An Introduction to the Philosophy of John Dewey*. New York: Macmillan.

Durkheim, Emile. 1956. *Education and Sociology*. New York: Free Press.

——. 1961. *Moral Education*. New York: Free Press.

Enthoven, R.E. 1922. *The Tribes and Castes of Bombay*, Vol. II. Bombay.

Gadgil, D.R. 1945–52. *Poona: A Socio-Economic Survey*, Part 1 of two volumes. Pune: Gokhale Institute of Politics and Economics.

Gaikwad, Jyoti. 2002. Interview with the author, 20 May. Ramnagar, Pune.

Gaikwad, Sheetal. 2004. Interview with the author, 1 August. Yashwantnagar, Pune.

Gaikwad, Suvarna. 2005. Interview with the author, August. Pune.

Gangurde, Kusum. 2006. Interview with the author, June. Mumbai.

Gokhale, B.G. 1988. *Poona in the Eighteenth Century: An Urban History*. Delhi: Oxford University Press.

Gooptu, Nandini. 2001. *The Politics of the Urban Poor in Early-Twentieth-Century India*. Cambridge: Cambridge University Press.

Gore, Jennifer. 1998. On the limits of empowerment through critical and feminist pedagogies. In *Power, Knowledge, Pedagogy: The Meaning of Democratic Education in Unsettling Times*, ed. Dennis Carlson and Michael W. Apple. Boulder, CO: Westview Press.

hooks, bell. 1994. *Teaching to Transgress*. New York: Routledge.

Jadhav, Kamal. 2001. Interview with the author, 16 September. Pune.

Jangam, Meena. 2004. Interview with the author, 5 August. Pune.

Joshi, Barbara, ed. 1986. *Untouchable! Voices of the Dalit Liberation Movement*. London: Zed Books.

Kadam, K.N. 2003. Interview with the author, 12 June. Ambedkar Colony, Pune.

Kakade, S.R. 1979. *A Study of the Integration of the SC in Indian Society: A Case Study in Marathwada.* Ph.D. thesis. Pune: University of Pune.

Kale, Alaka. 2002. Interview with the author, 1 July. Karve Road, Pune.

Kale, Bharati. 2002. Interview with the author, 18 June. Pune.

Kamble, Alaka. 2001. Interview with the author, 30 October. Tadiwala Road, Pune.

Kamble, Nanda. 2001. Interview with the author, 10 August. Parvati, Pune.

Kamble, Rani. 2001. Interview with the author, 30 October. Tadiwala Road, Pune.

Kamble, Shanta. 1986. *Majya Jalmachi Chittarkatha,* 2nd edn. Pune: Sugava.

Karlekar, Malavika. 1983. Education and inequality. In *Equality and Inequality: Theory and Practice,* ed. Andre Beteille. New Delhi and New York: Oxford University Press.

Kasbe, Snehlata. 2003. Interview with the author, 10 September. Pune Station, Pune.

Kaviraj, Sudipta. 1997. Filth and the public sphere: Concepts and practices about space in Calcutta. *Public Culture,* 10(1): 83–113.

Khan, Shahrukh. 1993. South Asia. In *Women's Education in Developing Countries: Barriers, Benefits and Policies,* ed. Elizabeth M. King and M. Anne Hill. London, and Baltimore, MD: World Bank.

Kuchekar, Gangabai. 2004. Interview with the author, 23 July. Yashwant Nagar–Yerawada, Pune.

Kuchekar, Hirabai. 2002. Interview with the author, 8 January. Pune.

Kuchekar, Suvarna. 2002. Interview with the author, 8 January. Sinhagad Road, Pune.

Mahajan, Meena. 2002. Interview with the author, 29 April. Ghorpade Peth, Pune.

Mahajan, Parvati. 2002. Interview with the author, 29 April. Mangalwar Peth, Pune.

Mann, H.H. 1967. The Untouchable classes of an Indian city (Poona). In *The Social Framework of Agriculture,* ed. Daniel Thorner. Bombay: Vora and Company.

Moon, Vasant. 2001. *Growing Up Untouchable in India: A Dalit Autobiography.* Lanham, MD: Rowman & Littlefield.

Moré, Shalini. 2002. Interview with the author, 1 June. Sinhagad Road, Pune.

Muralidharan, V. 1997. *Education Priorities and Dalit Society.* New Delhi: Kanishka.

Nagare, Draupadi. 2004. Interview with the author, 11 September. Ramtekdi, Pune.

Naik, Lalita. 2001. Interview with the author, 22 May. Ramtekdi, Pune.

Nambissan, Geeta. 2000. Dealing with deprivation. *Seminar,* 493, September.

National Informatics Centre. 2006a. Nationwide enrolment by stages of all categories of students by gender (in percentages). Table 15. Available at www.education.nic.in/statscontents.asp (accessed 14 June 2006).

National Informatics Centre. 2006b. Nationwide enrolment by stages of SC students by gender (in percentages). Table 16. Available at www.education.nic.in/statscontents.asp (accessed 14 June 2006).

Nikam, Sheela. 2005. Interview with the author, 22 October. Borivili, Mumbai.

Omvedt, Gail. 1974. Non-Brahmans and nationalists in Poona. *Economic and Political Weekly,* 9(6/8): 201–216.

——. 2004. *Ambedkar: Towards an Enlightened India.* New York: Viking Press.

Pagare, Nanubai. 2004. Interview with the author, 20 May. Yerawada, Pune.

Pawar, Prakshoti. 2002. Interview with the author, 10 April. Pune.

Pawar, Ratnaprabha. 2002. Interview with the author, 10 April. Bibwewadi, Pune.

Pawar, Urmila. 2004. Interview with the author, 5–7 September. Borivili, Mumbai.

Pawde, Kumud. 2005. Interview with the author, 16 October. Dhantoli, Nagpur.

Ranpise, Meena. 2001. Interview with the author, 12 May. Sinhagad Road, Pune.

Rist, Ray C. 1977. On understanding the process of schooling: The contribution of labeling theory. In *Power and Ideology in Education*, ed. Jerome Karabel and A.H. Halsey. New York: Oxford University Press.

Rita. 2003. Interview with the author.

Rokade, Jyotsna. 2004. Interview with the author, 15 August. Vishrantwadi, Pune.

Rokade, Poonam. 2004. Interview with the author, 15 August. Mundhawa, Pune.

Rosenthal, Robert and Lenore Jacobson. 1993. *Pygmalion in the School: Teachers' Expectations and Pupils' Intellectual Development*. New York: Irvington.

Ryan, William. 1976. *Blaming the Victim*. New York: Vintage Books.

Sathe, Monica. 2005. Interview with the author, 30 July. Karve Nagar, Pune.

Shah, B.V. 1964. *Social Change and College Students of Gujarat*. Baroda: University of Baroda.

Shah, Ghanshyam, Harsh Mander, Sukhadeo Thorat, Satish Deshpande and Amita Baviskar. 2006. *Untouchability in Rural India*. New Delhi: Sage.

Shinde, Lakshmi. 2000. Interview with the author, 9 October. Parvati, Pune.

Shukla, Sureshchandra and Rekha Kaul, eds. 1998. *Education, Development and Underdevelopment*. New Delhi: Sage.

Sovani, N.V., D.P. Apte and R.G. Pendse. 1956. *Poona: A Re-Survey, the Changing Pattern of Employment and Earnings*. Pune: Gokhale Institute.

Steedman, Carolyn. 1982. *The Tidy House*. London: Virago.

——. 1986. *Landscape for a Good Woman: A Story of Two Lives*. London: Virago.

Talib, Mohammad. 1998. Educating the oppressed: Observations from a school in a working-class settlement in Delhi. In *Education, Development and Underdevelopment*, ed. S. Shukla and R. Kaul. New Delhi: Sage.

Torrey, Jane. 1973. Illiteracy in the ghetto. In *Tinker Tailor: The Myth of Cultural Deprivation*, ed. Nell Keddy. Harmondsworth: Penguin.

Viththayathil, Trina and Gayatri Singh. 2012. Spaces of discrimination: Residential segregation in Indian cities. *Economic and Political Weekly*, 58(37): 60–66.

Wagh, Vilas, ed. 1986. Dalit Madhyam Varga. *Sugava*, special Deepavali issue, November–December.

Zelliot, Eleanor. 1994. *Dr. Babasaheb Ambedkar and the Untouchable Movement*. New Delhi: Bluemoon Books.

——. 2000. The history of Dalits in Pune. *Journal of the Asiatic Society of Bombay*, 74: 211–239.

6 Modern middle-class Dalits

Seeking education and escaping the slum

Many Dalits militantly asserted their traditions, language and culture; at the same time, ambiguity and cultural anxieties found deep roots in the minds of some Dalit elites who were *becoming* 'modern'. As a result, the latter constantly combated their past and present identities to deploy 'technologies of the self' to transform and refine themselves, and to fit more easily into the rhythm of urban Brahmani cultural hegemony. For example, many second- and third-generation Dalit women developed 'cultured' *shuddha* Marathi: the Brahmani 'ho' instead of the lower-class 'ha' for 'yes'; the nasal instead of the flat-toned *aani-paani* (Paik 2009, 192). As such, many Dalits spoke two different Marathi dialects – informal and formal. The Marathi spoken inside the home, the 'mother's breast milk', was distinctly different from that used outside – the 'tinned formula' (Illich 1981, 32). Most women with whom I interacted represented both.

This chapter examines what may be broadly categorised as the experience of emerging *modern middle-class* Dalits. They are sometimes depicted as a new type of caste ('Dalit-Brahman') in India: one that may be entered through achievements in education and employment (Wagh 1986, 1994; Beteille 1970; Dushkin 1999). In this way, some Dalit-Brahmans believed that they could – at least to some extent – escape their caste by becoming middle class. Following Dalit radicals' rhetoric, modern Dalits did not believe in inherited privilege but sought to make their destiny through their own merit, and to improve and advance themselves and their families, communities and nation.

This chapter focuses on the intentional *generative* practices, the varied and complicated processes through which many Dalit women and men continuously and consistently sought to escape from the circuitous predicaments of the slum, poverty, low-level education and social exclusion in order to appropriate modernity. Another aim of this chapter is to reveal the processes of accessing such modernity by investigating how the teachers and lower-middle-class, elite parents practised the dictum of the classic Marathi proverb '*chaddi lage chham chham, vidya yeyi gham gham*', which means 'the harder the stick beats, the faster the flow of knowledge'. Here, I extend the meaning of the proverb to untangle the processes through which Dalit parents and teachers sought to discipline Dalit girls and women into 'doing well' in order to radically *remake* themselves and *fashion* their present and futures.

To Dalits, their entry into a modern middle class was a *generative* moment of history itself. It was almost a moment of emergence. At times Dalits conflicted with the upper-caste social and mental hegemony, yet they used these forces to produce new reversals and energies in order to transform their worlds. In the process, they created unintended and unexpected results; however, they also suffered multiple ruptures, displacements and fissures of consciousness itself. Dalits' 'will-to-power' to affirm, for example, not consuming *tupa*, displaying their caste surnames with increasing pride, or donning full, starched cotton saris and sleeveless blouses to mark their elite status is a generative activity which affirms the *generativity* of life itself. Dalits' will-to-power is a newly developed sensibility, indeed a political strategy, that resists the ruling classes' normative and hegemonic ideals and structures.[1] Yet the monster of caste continued to haunt Dalits.

Dalits marginalised by the dominant, upper-caste social and cultural hegemony have had very little or no say in the construction of their socially acknowledged identity. Hence, many lower- and middle-class Dalits struggled to sanitise their language, dress, names, and so on (Paik 2011). Significantly, however, many Dalits also resisted this Brahmani sterilisation and strategically chose to converse, for example, in the foreigners' English language, which was powerfully prestigious all over the world. (My conversations with Dalit Buddhists in the US uncovered a collective 'thumbs up' regarding the use of English in public and private conversations.) Most significantly, it was a language of modernity and hence a form of cultural capital for Dalits, as discussed in more detail in Chapter 2. It acquired a different connotation in the Dalit discourse. Dalits and non-Dalits alike upheld and celebrated this linguistic colonial gift – yet to Dalits it had a *different* and *deeper* significance.

By adopting English language, dress and manners, a twentieth-century Dalit man could claim recognition and respectability as a *saaheb* (respectable European officer) in order to participate in the modern institutions of abstract equality (citizenship, democracy, civil rights), as well as for concrete gains. By speaking in the tongue of the powerful coloniser they sought to gain respectability, which was fundamental to their everyday human dignity and human rights as Dalits because it supplemented abstract equality and refused to be defined by its terms. Women also remade themselves internally, by fortifying inner resources of *pratishtha* (honour), *svaabhimaan* (self-respect), *svaavalamban* (self-reliance) and *dhaadas* (daring), and externally, for example, through an itinerant, performative body politics of donning full saris, hitherto a privilege of the powerful upper-caste women. Out of these double-headed struggles emerged their personhood, which was significant in constructing their individual and collective agency. Thus, struggling against their past and a complicated 'Untouchable' pathos was a fundamental battle for many Dalits as they attempted to subvert old definitions with new consciousness and creativity, a process which Margo Perkins (2000, 30) has rightly called 'rewriting the self'.

Middle-class Dalits who held a comfortable status in society faced peculiar challenges – in a way a 'double consciousness' – over different markers such as food, language, dress and locality that marked their Untouchable background. Each of these markers cause(d) social-psychological violence to Dalits as they sought to discipline themselves. Historians have yet to investigate these deeper emotional histories as they shaped Dalit women's everyday experiences. The processes of everyday negotiation with Dalit markers and of overcoming their Dalithood involved various strategies: some resisted radically, some were silent, and others 'passed' as upper castes. The latter faced a constant danger of being 'caught'. Moreover, this suffering, telling and showing took place within a crucible of social, historical, intellectual and political relations. This speaking and writing was also a doing, a form of action and agency – 'one that [was] already a moral practice and a way of life' (Butler 2005, 126). In many instances, many Dalits successfully overcame their dilemmas and radically recovered their self-hood in the 'third combat stage', as Frantz Fanon brilliantly captures it (1963, 159). Many others clearly continued to struggle with their 'appropriate' place in the 'modern' society. I narrate such a complicated *aesthetic of the Dalit self* here.

This chapter is divided into four sections. The first outlines different strategies which Dalit parents adopted to discipline their daughters. They often used the *chhadi* (stick) discursively as well as in actual practice to inculcate habits and to educate. I also uncover gender discrimination in schooling options within the Dalit community. The second section deals with Brahman hegemony. The third section is devoted to the reservation system and the stigma which Dalit students experienced. The fourth section discusses how educated Dalit women's lives began to play out. The conclusion brings together the many different stories and their varying outcomes for middle-class Dalits who appropriated and exceeded modernity to serve their purposes, and who sought to fight interlocking technologies and radically refashion their individual selves and futures.

Chhadi lage chham chham, vidya yei gham gham (the harder the stick beats, the faster the flow of knowledge)

Western ideas and practices penetrated Dalit mentality and life from the mid-nineteenth century onwards; however, as I have revealed, Dalit radicals did not import them directly. Instead, they twisted and turned them to their own ends. Dalits sought to gain respectability and status like that of the higher colonial officers. In the process of 'becoming' modern, many Dalits deployed the *chhadi* both metaphorically and in actual practice. At one level, especially externally, the policing of middle-class Dalit girls paralleled that of the upper castes. Yet, at another, interior level, deeper emotional and socio-psychological processes shaped the lived and everyday experiences of Dalit women who attempted to *escape* their Dalithood.

Ambedkar provided one important motivation for these struggles. He stood as an ideal for what an educated woman or man could achieve. Social aspirations and economic advancement also inspired struggle. In many cases, Dalits sought encouragement from direct or even indirect political engagement in the Ambedkar and post-Ambedkar Dalit movement. No Dalit-Buddhist woman who talked to me mentioned being inspired by Gandhi, Nehru or Indira Gandhi. They unanimously underscored the essence of Ambedkar's ideals, as laid out in previous chapters. Ambedkar was and is the rallying point for many Buddhists and other Dalits. A few Matangs and Chambhars looked upon Indira Gandhi and the Communist leader Annabhau Sathe as ideals. The Dalit responses in Mumbai and Pune to my questions (posed between 2000 and 2006) about the meaning of Ambedkar (and also to Zelliot's question a decade ago) were all in personal terms: 'inspiration, courage, identity and a surprising one, peace!' (Zelliot 2001, 138). Thus, 'there are many meanings to Ambedkar: inspiration for the educated, hope for the illiterate, threat to the establishment, creator of opportunities for Dalits and discomfort for the elite' (ibid., 140). Ambedkar donned Western dress and insisted on the use of the English language in schools, but he also argued for making Sanskrit the official language of India. Moreover, he was equally adept and regularly wrote and spoke in Marathi, Hindi and English. He was well versed in Pali and Sanskrit.

Many Dalits followed Ambedkar's advice and migrated to the city; although the city was liberatory in many ways, it also confined the Dalits to the slums, as Chapter 5 showed. Many Dalits aspiring to improve and make it on their own sought to break away from the slum, which became a metaphor for the Dalit, in order to appropriate a certain modern middle-class status and respectability. While upper castes were naturally and always-already endowed with bourgeois subjectivity, Dalit women were excluded endlessly from it. Challenging some scholars who have taken pains to show how peasants, lower castes and Dalits were untouched by and in fact resisted modernity, I uncover how Dalits indeed consistently and strategically appropriated modernity; they embraced and resisted it, at times, for their own ends.

In the process, however, many middle-class Dalits developed a 'double consciousness' that engendered *dual* personalities, and therefore many conflicts and contradictions in the Dalit psyche (Du Bois 1994, 2). One of these has to do with the split, divided, or double consciousness of the colonised. W.E.B. Du Bois (1994, 2–3) pointed out this peculiar sensation:

> This double-consciousness, this sense of always looking at one's self through the eyes of others, of measuring one's soul by the tape of a world that looks on in amused contempt and pity. One ever feels his two-ness. The history of the American Negro is the history of this strife – to merge [the] double self into a *better and truer self.*

It was in and due to the constant shuttling between the two worlds of this divided subjectivity that doubly colonised Dalits sometime attempted to 'hide their identities' or overcome their Dalithood in a number of ways: by moving to different neighbourhoods or changing their food habits, comportment, language and names (Paik 2009, 2011).

In some cases, escape from the slums could be physical, as to army life in a cantonment, to a better neighbourhood or to a mission school. Many Dalit children found shelter and schooling opportunities with Christian missions and their agents, who readily adopted and admitted them to their schools. Christian mission schools could be found, for example, in Pune, near the Dalit *vastis* in Vadgaon Sheri, Yerawada, Kirkee, Shastri Nagar and in the Cantonment area, as analysed in Chapter 5. It is obvious that the missionaries targeted lower castes residing on the margins of the city as well as those lower castes employed with the British in the Cantonment area. Christian missionaries, along with some Brahman, non-Brahman and Muslim reformers, were the pioneers of education in India. Despite their efforts to enter education in western India since the early nineteenth century, very few first-generation women were admitted to the missionary schools. One reason for this may be that when the independent Indian government started engaging with the planned economy and concentrating on education, the mission schools began to wane.

Another possible reason, as second-generation learner Sandhya *akkaa*[2] pointed out, was that slightly more well-to-do Dalit parents did not want their children to be converted to Christianity (S. Meshram 2004). The missionaries had converted many Dalits to Christianity by giving them an alternative to Hinduism, along with food, education, medicine and moral support. When the missionaries started proselytising in the early nineteenth century, they received immense support from the lower castes. Their schools proved popular because they provided free food, uniforms and boarding facilities to the Untouchable children. The question of fees did not arise. Poor Dalits could not afford these amenities; many did not mind converting to Christianity. Many Mahars and Matangs turned to Christianity for their deliverance. There were Dalit conversions in great numbers in Aurangabad, Ahmednagar, Srirampur, Rahuri and other places in Maharashtra. These places were mission stations, the base of missionaries. They had some prestigious missionary schools, libraries and well-equipped mission hospitals. Ahmednagar was a strong centre of missionary activity, along with Poona and Bombay (Church Missionary Society 1926).

Baby Jagtap, a mission-educated woman who studied at the Shirur Hostel, remembered her difficult circumstances and legitimised her father's actions:

> We were very poor and did not have enough to eat or [clothes to] wear. So when my father came to know about the Christian mission hostel he immediately admitted us there. I liked the atmosphere at the mission because the conditions at home were not very comfortable. I made good friends at the hostel and the Christian sisters [nuns] were very good. So I preferred to stay there. Life was very disciplined. We got up in the mornings, had a common assembly, and then entered classes. The sisters were very loving. They taught us well and did not discriminate, as in my earlier school. They also took up our studies in the evenings and helped us understand.
>
> (Jagtap 2002)[3]

Baby was grateful to the missionaries and mentioned their strict disciplinary life. It was rare indeed to come across a mission-educated girl student. There is less information on the girls in the missionary boarding-schools or Phule's schools, such as what they studied, to what levels, or what happened to them after they completed their studies. Nor is there much information on the girls educated and housed in hostels by the non-Brahman leaders and Ambedkar. Suffice it to say that some girls did attend schools.

Parents moving into middle-class occupations and locales greatly facilitated education. These socialised parents attempted to discipline their children, inculcate good behaviour, encourage better study habits, coach them, and sometimes coerce them to succeed in their studies and in life in general. Manini, Malavika and their brother[4] were under constant pressure to perform better. Both of the sisters emphasised that their parents coerced them to pursue science education when they themselves did not want to (Pawar and Pawar 2004). The parents did the same with their son. They wanted their children to be doctors. When I asked their mother about this, she said:

> There was no doctor or any other professional of that high rank in my family or my husband's. Most of them were in clerical services or were teachers. Both of us, my husband and I, were earning well and we thought that we could afford good educations for our children. We wanted our children to avail themselves of this opportunity and do their best. As students in rural areas we had no facilities or choices, but we could provide unlimited opportunities to our children. With this thinking we resolved to make them doctors or engineers and so we pushed them toward that. However, we did not take into consideration our children's choices. Also we did not think about their non-English background and how they would have to fight the English-speaking world. Those were different times, but we acted in a craze.
>
> (U. Pawar 2004)[5]

Thus, elite Dalit parents wanted their children to attain heights unknown to the community or the family in the past or present and expected better performance. Yet, in the process of seeking individual and social respectability and honour, they failed to take into consideration the choices or particular talents of their children, thus forcing their own aspirations onto them. The two sisters were critical of their parents' failed strategy and vowed to discuss career options with and allow good choices for their own children.

Many lower-middle- and middle-class Dalit parents generally emphasised a 'respectable' middle-class lifestyle; they wanted their children to be well behaved. They also wanted the dominant castes to know that their children came from 'good' homes, that they themselves were people of good character.[6] In this way, they sought to counter the many negative stereotypes about Dalits. A respectable demeanour was seen to be necessary for girls to ward off dangerous attention from males. Many middle-class Dalits tried to portray a good image, rather their best one, to the upper castes in the hope that they might be accommodated within the hegemonic structure of power. This strategy was also important for building their self-confidence and self-respect. In the process,

Dalits went beyond their individualistic concerns to embrace the needs of their larger community.

Hence middle-class Dalit parents, following Ambedkar, argued that strict discipline was required both to train Dalits for success in education and to work on building their *svaabhimaan* (self-respect). Parents often cited examples from their own lives to teach their children. To inculcate discipline they sought to embody the old Marathi proverb, '*chhadi lage chham chham, vidya yei gham gham*'. Fathers, and sometimes mothers, often used corporal punishment to compel their children to attend school and study hard, whether they wanted to or not. Urmilatai thus stated (Pawar 2004) that in the beginning she did not like school, but still attended it because she was afraid of her father. Her parents often beat the children with a stick, building a psychology of fear in them. Nonetheless, after her father's death she continued to attend school, feeling that she should fulfil his dreams. She said, 'I started looking seriously at school only after his death. I just thought I should follow his advice, as he used to thrash us to make us attend school' (2004). Kamal said, 'my father saw to it that I was never at home or never missed school' (Jadhav 2001). In such an atmosphere it was seen as a moral failing to express any dislike of school. Although Ivan Illich (1971) has rightly criticised this disciplinary attitude towards education,[7] Urmilatai's attitude reveals a certain ambiguity on the issue. She abhorred the discipline, yet understood her father's deeper motives. Amita[8] also spoke about her father's expectations and ideals which, above all, encouraged her to attend school regularly (Pillewar 2005). In a similar vein, Dr Jyoti Kadam (2002)[9] recounted her school days:

My mother taught us in our initial years of school. She taught us till she could cope with alphabets, small words, and maths tables. However, in higher grades, my father took over. I was generally good at studies but, when it came to maths, I was slightly scared. I solved easy problems or those I could handle well and strategically skipped others I found difficult. Due to this erroneous habit, during one of the tests in seventh grade, I failed in maths. I was ashamed of my schoolwork for the first time. My teachers and classmates were certainly shocked at my score. Nobody could believe it and they shot all kinds of questions at me. When my father saw this, he was very angry and resolved to look into my maths skills. For the first time, he made me work late in the night to practise maths. We solved different difficult arithmetic problems. However, we only did this the night before exam; I wished I had told him the truth earlier. Anyway, the wooden *patti* [measuring scale, also used for beating] rapped endlessly on my arm and thigh until I found out the actual arithmetical logic of solving the problems. This was the first time that I, a first-ranker, had to take physical beatings for my studies, and I learnt a lesson for life. After that episode, I started to look at the root of any problem to be solved. This training has gone a long way in shaping my present and future. The teachers did not take pains to make me understand maths but my father did.

Thus, most second- and third-generation learners appreciated their parents' interest in their education and were prepared to excuse the harsh methods often used to make them study.

There existed among such Dalits a general belief in the importance and utility of education. Dalit radicals' promises and efforts for education and self-fashioning had penetrated deeply. The children came to share their parents' desire for a good education. They believed that education strengthened opportunities for employment. It placed them in a good position compared to their parents, who made efforts to encourage their children. Some parents and students believed that children who did not attend formal school were failures; children aspired to succeed in life by attending school.

One second-generation respondent suggested that competition, the race to come first in class and having an edge over the others was a great motivating factor. Dr Jyoti said,

> I was told at home that I had nothing else to fall back upon but education. I was also good at studies and it was always at the back of my mind that that I had to stand first in the class. My parents insisted upon it and it also came from within me. I did not want to lag behind the others. I wanted to score the best grades and stand first in every test and in every class.
>
> (Kadam 2002)

Thus, while some children and parents enjoyed the rigorous routine and worked for the best academic performance in the classroom, many students were unable to withstand parental pressure. But they certainly understood that the struggle to acquire a higher social status engendered a ruthless race.

Significantly, many elite Dalit parents, like their non-Dalit counterparts, funded and encouraged extra coaching. The privatisation of education led to rapid commercialisation; coaching classes became an essential, thriving business in India. Many teachers had virtually stopped teaching in colleges; they compelled students to attend their private coaching classes instead. In urban and rural areas, almost all middle- and lower-middle-class students enrolled in some class or other. By providing vacation courses as well as regular batches and crash courses, coaching centres large and small catered to all who enrolled and paid fees. Education was thus increasingly privatised and became contingent upon the availability of monetary resources. In general, Dalits could not afford to attend such classes; some poor families had to struggle to accumulate financial resources because their children were otherwise unlikely to achieve good results.

Besides parents, other family members such as grandfathers, uncles, aunts and siblings also played a significant role in ensuring that children studied diligently. The feminist Jyotitai Lanjewar reflected: 'My grandfather used to take us to school. He sat till the school was over and brought us back home. He taught us at home. He told me to appear for Class 5 exams and later admitted me to high school' (Lanjewar 2005). In such cases, the home became a learning-friendly environment. Sandhya's uncle and siblings helped her with her studies

(S. Meshram 2004). This inculcated the habit of regular reading. First-generation pupils in municipal schools rarely read anything beyond their textbooks. Indeed, some Dalit parents actively discouraged wider reading habits, believing that schools offered the 'ultimate' knowledge and anything besides that was an irrelevant waste of time. Kamal, a second-generation respondent, said that her father reprimanded her when she tried to read story-books: 'We were to engage in studying school textbooks *only*' (Jadhav 2001, emphasis added). Sandhya, however, remembered that her uncles obtained books and discussed them with her and her siblings at home (S. Meshram 2004). Such actions inculcated and nurtured reading habits in some children. For most, however, reading was confined to newspapers, some Marathi magazines and light books. Reading serious novels and more intellectually demanding books was a rarity. Lengthy books aroused fear and awe. Some Dalit women were involved in other activities, such as sports, singing or playing the guitar (Pawar and Pawar 2004; Waghmare 2004). Swati[10] was a rare woman who played cricket during her school and college days in the 1980s. Every Sunday, on her way to practice, she donned her freshly ironed white shirt and trousers, and proudly carried her cricket equipment on her shoulders. She also practised regularly with her father. Thus many well-to-do parents attended to the overall development of their children. Such extracurricular activities barely existed for first-generation learners. In this way some second- and third-generation Dalit women learners acquired interest in activities outside the curriculum to a greater or lesser extent; some turned it into a habit (see Chapter 8).

Some parents realised that involvement in such activities might give their children an extra edge in their school careers. They encouraged them to participate in crafts, dancing, music, drawing and sports, and to take pride in their achievements. Urmilatai Pawar took immense pride in her activities as a student in Ratnagiri:

> I was very bold and smart during my school times, *very unlike the rest of the Dalits*. I used to read stories and whatever I could lay my hands on. I got them from the school library. Mumbai made a big difference to my life, and I started reading more after coming here. In school I participated in plays. I once played the role of a king. It was very *unlikely* for a Dalit girl to get *that* kind of role. But I got it because I was a good performer and singer too.
>
> (U. Pawar 2004, emphasis added)

Here Urmilatai participated in the Brahmani and colonial discourse about the negative stereotypes of Dalits being 'passive', 'stupid' or 'shy'. Hence she was continuously struggling to set herself apart as a 'non-Dalit'. Such were the predicaments of Dalits who wanted to claim a Dalit identity while at the same time distancing themselves from the mass of their community. At the same time, it is important to note that Dalits were *not* as a rule granted leading roles in the theatre; Urmilatai was rightfully proud of her efforts and achievements. She continued to recount her daughters' attainments:

I wanted them to do something else; not the usual rut of everyday school and college. Something to relax, and engage in.... My younger daughter is a Kathak dancer and has performed on stage a few times. The older one is a Sangeet Vishaarad [a higher degree for singers] and is still learning ahead; she also conducts classes for beginners.

(U. Pawar 2004)

Second- and third-generation learners wanted their children to engage in different activities and to learn hitherto unavailable arts and culture. They were thoughtful of their daily grind and wanted to enjoy leisure (as Ambedkar had once suggested [1997]) and to advance intellectually. One Dalit activist family encouraged their only daughter's hobbies of modelling and theatre as well as her aspirations to be a director.

Most first- and second-generation learners were educated in municipal schools. Only a few from the second generation and more from the third generation studied in better-quality institutions. Most women reported that the quality of the private schools was far better. The private school system was also characterised by less caste discrimination, more attentive teachers and competition for quality; they considered government schools highly discriminatory, of poor quality and lethargic. Historically, teaching there was dominated by Brahman or other upper castes like the Marathas, who discriminated against lower castes. Because these teachers were initially recruited by the government, caste discrimination was reinforced in these schools. Some Dalits were thus prepared to find the money to pay for private or English-medium schools that were less dominated by upper castes because their experience had shown that private schools run by Parsis, Sindhis and foreigners did not bother much about caste or the purity-pollution taboo.

This was the experience of Nani, a first-generation learner from Mumbai, who had an Israeli teacher:

I do not remember anything really significant when it comes to caste. My teacher was an Israeli. I played with her children and she treated me like her child. We were at her house the whole day. The other castes were also there, but there was nothing like caste discrimination. At that time Ambedkar's struggle was going on strong and everybody was aware of it. So maybe they knew that it would be very harmful if they behaved that way.

(Mokal 2000)

According to Nani, there was sufficient awareness in the society to prevent open discrimination. Yet this is not entirely true. As my historical fieldwork reveals, in 2006 a prestigious convent school in Pune advertised the SC background of some students in a list pinned on a wall beside the classroom door. Nobody entering the classroom could ignore it. The SC students did not receive any concession in tuition fees, yet their caste background was unnecessarily made public by the private school apparatus.

Medium of instruction: Marathi or English?

In India, the British promoted English education from the 1830s onwards as a means to inculcate 'civilisation' – what we nowadays describe as 'modernity'. English education and modernity were in practice interlinked in India. The English language is the mark of the progressive, cosmopolitan Indian and of course also a matter of prestige. Aparna Basu has underlined the ways in which Western/English education was an important determinant in the growth of a nationalist politics in Bombay and Bengal (Basu 1974, 191–192). From Tilak, Chiplunkar and Agarkar to Phule and later Ambedkar, English education was a doorway to Western ideas that sharpened their political insight. Tilak spent the first eleven years of his public life spreading English education, since he believed that the English language was 'the milk of the tigress' and that if the youth of the country were fed on this strong diet, India's liberation could not be delayed (quoted in Basu 1974, 213). Yet, as noted earlier, Tilak would not allow English education for girls.

Gandhi also saw the benefits of the English language, but he did not want Indians to become its slaves. In a similar vein, M.R. Jayakar argued that English education was seen to foster in young men a 'haughty spirit ... producing graduates who would not be "cringing, devoid of self-respect, ignorant of their cultural heritage and indifferent to the humiliating inferiority" which faces them on all sides' (quoted in Basu 1974, 214). By contrast, Ambedkar pleaded for the 'retention of English as the medium of instruction in colleges and universities at any cost' (*National Standard*, 4 July 1953) – and rightly so, because Dalits' struggles and strategies to attain *maarnyachya jaaguu* (effective positions) in, for example, the state legislatures would otherwise be futile. At a speech delivered at Aurangabad's Milind College campus, he argued:

> English is the richest of all languages. I do not believe that any other language in India, including Hindi, can be used instead of English in schools and colleges. English would be the medium of instruction in PES [People's Education Society] colleges. Hindi lacks literature and depth, both of which the English language possesses. To enrich Hindi, a Hindi academy consisting of eminent men should be started and a vocabulary should be prepared.
>
> (*National Standard*, 4 July 1953)

Thus, for Ambedkar, the English language, unlike Hindi, would not only enrich Dalits but also inculcate self-respect, confidence and prestige. His rhetoric penetrated deeper, and many first- and second-generation women affirmed their leader's reasoning.

English-medium schools in India were mostly patterned on the English public schools model; this continues to be the case even today (Chanana 2001, 269). These schools were known for inculcating a high degree of sophistication. Zweig (1964, 10) has commented on such education in the British context:

> What was, in my view, important and interesting was to ascertain which of the students came from famous public schools.... One could immediately

notice the polish of these boys, their greater self-confidence, their characteristic manner of speech and dress ... and their wider interest in the arts and
public affairs.

This was also very true of India, where English education was the passport to
better colleges and universities, and later jobs. Most of these private schools
charged high tuition fees, so attendance was restricted to families that could
afford them (quoted in Chanana 2001, 269).[11] This in itself barred such esteemed
and expensive institutions to the large majority of Dalits.

Nonetheless, many Dalits aspired to provide English education for their children. In an article in the *Times of India*, the sociologist-historian Gail Omvedt
reports the increasing use of English among Dalits, arguing that they preferred it
because 'the vernaculars have been colonised by Sanskrit for thousands of years'
(Omvedt 2006). She noted that some Dalit activists and publicists were even
starting to fetishise English. The Dalit activist and writer Chandrabhan Prasad
began celebrating Thomas Macaulay's birthday every 25 October – Macaulay
being the British colonial ruler who is more than anyone else associated with
propagating English education in India. Condemned for this by mainstream
nationalists, Macaulay has become an unlikely hero to the Dalits. Prasad stated
during this celebration that all Dalit children should hear their 'A-B-C-D' right
from birth and went on to claim that 'English *the Dalit goddess* is a world power
today; it is about emancipation, it is a mass movement against the caste order....
It is a key to the world stock of knowledge and the wealth and success that
depends on it' (Omvedt 2006).

Another reason for preferring English-medium schools has been that Marathi-
medium schools also tended to be dominated by Maharashtrian Brahmans.
Kamal, a first-generation learner who studied in a Marathi-medium school,
emphasised that she purposefully admitted her children to an English-medium
convent school of the highest quality. She reasoned:

> In Marathi-medium schools, even the highly prestigious ones, caste discrimina-
> tion is practised, and I did not want my children to face *that*. Hence, I put them
> in English-medium schools and moreover in convents, where *this* does not
> exist. We also want them to be prepared for a competitive future, and English-
> medium instruction is also good for developing a well-rounded personality.
>
> (Jadhav 2001, emphasis added)

Kamal emphasised that Marathi-medium schools reinforced caste distinctions;
she wanted to keep her children away from such humiliating treatment. Significantly, she did not use the actual Marathi word *jaatiyata* for caste discrimination, instead referring to it in casual terms such as *hey aani tey* (this and that). By
using banal vocabulary she also sought to mitigate the problem of social discrimination; for many modern Dalit elites, like some upper-caste elites, it seemed
derogatory to their background to talk about regressive caste and untouchability
practices. As modern subjects, they wanted to emphasise mastery and merit

rather than fatalism. Modern Dalits believed in carving out their own futures, yet many were inhibited by the caste virus that infected their everyday lives and future opportunities. Non-Dalits turned the language of merit around to make Dalits feel as if they were 'meritless' people who now sought the state's concessions and affirmative action benefits.

Kamal also regretted not attending an English-medium school: 'If I had attended an English-medium school, I could have even attempted the national-level Union Public Service Commission exam. I would not have limited myself to the state level Maharashtra Public Service Commission exam' (Jadhav 2001). She believed that her lack of English education had made it impossible for her to have any chance of gaining entry to the highest cadre of the administrative service, the Indian Administrative Services. While several informants voiced their anguish about not being able to study in English, others believed that even an English-medium school did not have much effect in the long term. They argued that Marathi schooling was as good as the English medium, at times even better. Snehlata Kasbe said:

> I do not think it would have made a big difference if I had studied in a convent. I have always been confident. If I was there, I would have worn short clothes and spoken in *fluent* English, which is many times grammatically wrong.
>
> (Kasbe 2003, emphasis added)

For Snehlata, instruction in English brought merely a superficial veneer of Westernisation, with sometimes farcical language skills. Such Westernisation could always be achieved later in life. Yet Sandhya and Snehlata agreed that the education they had was the best.

Nonetheless, for some women, the Marathi medium in itself stigmatised pupils. While some Brahman elites always-already sought pride in their Brahmani Marathi *maayaboli* (mother tongue), and purposely enrolled their children in prestigious Marathi-medium schools like Hujurpaagaa and Dnyan Prabodhini in the polis of Pune, Dalits were struggling to seek self-respect and prestige, which was granted to them by the foreigner's modern English language. It was in English that they found linguistic emancipation. Most Dalit women who had attended only Marathi-medium schools increasingly felt that English-medium school would have positively affected their life and careers. They believed that English brought prestige and a sense of superiority, which they had always lacked. Malavika and Manini also complained of their mothers' wrong decision to admit them to a Marathi-medium school. It was the root cause that led to their uphill battles, which could have been easily avoided (Pawar and Pawar 2004).

Some second-generation Dalit girls who attended Marathi-medium schools were not content with their quality of education. However, it was hard for a person trained in a vernacular medium and with lower social and cultural capital to succeed in such prestigious institutions. Many Dalit students felt inferior in such cosmopolitan colleges, which drew students from different religious, class and occupational backgrounds. They often possessed an ingrained inferiority complex of belonging to a lower caste. This hardship was made worse by the fact that they had been instructed in Marathi. Their experiences in vernacular-medium schools sharpened this inferiority complex and made life difficult for them. This situation was immensely complicated by the crystallisation of gender discrimination. Indeed, Dalit girls were rarely able to move successfully from a Marathi- to an English-medium educational institution.

Many second- and third-generation learners affirmed that speaking English meant confidence, boldness, and being outspoken, outgoing and respectable. They declared their desire to achieve specific emotional and psychological gains in order to refashion themselves. English-educated elite students thought highly of themselves. They knew their advantage compared to those who did not understand the language or who struggled to learn it. Many children were no doubt able to rattle off some English poems or songs at the insistence of their parents, but without prolonged English education they lacked the confidence that impressed everybody around in the slum or in middle-class neighbourhoods, nationally or internationally.

Deploying a Dalit modern self was important for self-respect and prestige. Hence, parents desired their children to stick to their books, insisted on formal education and English-medium schools, and nagged their children to practise the language at home and to speak in English, especially in the presence of outsiders. It did not stop at that; many children were made to address their parents *only* as 'Daddy' and 'Mummy'. Some were also coaxed to recite English rhymes and poems at formal and informal gatherings. Several, like Kumud Pawde, a first-generation scholar, expressed their affection for English (Pawde 2005). Some second- and many third-generation women found the language less difficult because they were mostly educated in semi-English schools that had a good culture of English teaching; they found it easier to instruct their children in English as well. They were better prepared to remake themselves and their futures.

However, an insidious hierarchy was embedded in the education system, stretching even to the reputations of different English-medium schools. Most of the students studying in convent schools – the highest in the hierarchy – looked down upon students who attended private, government or any other schools. Students from certain 'better' convent schools, like St Anne's, Bishop's, St Mary's, Cathedral or Bombay Scottish, were supposed to have higher standards compared to others, such as Mount Carmel, Rosary or St Felix. These educational hierarchies further reinforced a socio-economic hierarchy. Sociological reports underline that upper-caste/class pupils attended convents and private schools and lower-caste/class pupils government-run municipal schools (Velaskar 1998). Most significantly, gender discrimination animated parents' decisions regarding school selection.

Gender discrimination

Dalit men were both dominated and dominating within their communities and families. Ideologically as well as in actual practice, the state, family and school apparatus thus converged on the feminisation of education. In some cases fathers enrolled their sons in convents while sending their daughters to Marathi-medium schools. Sandhya went to a Marathi convent school while her brothers were admitted to prestigious and expensive convents like St Vincent's (S. Meshram 2004). Christian missionaries ran both schools, but there was a difference in standards, status and prestige. The traditional mission school did not charge anything for Sandhya's education; it concentrated on teaching and speaking in vernacular Marathi. Historically speaking, the mission schools adopted Marathi as the chief medium of instruction because '[students'] attainment in their own vernacular was so limited' and 'English was [also] to be taught only to the more accomplished students' as 'almost a reward for merit in other studies' (Chandra 2012, 53–55). Her younger brother Pramod went to the highly prestigious St Vincent's School, the top convent high school for boys. St Vincent's charged enormous fees and taught only in English. Sandhya's youngest brother Sachin studied in another convent, St Ornella's High School. It is significant to note that Sandhya's father aspired to educate only his sons in good convent schools. He managed to afford the high fees for his two sons, but not for his only daughter. Sandhya felt neglected and tormented by her past as she spoke about it, even after decades. She was forty-five years old and mother to a twenty-year-old, yet she could not forget her parents' discriminatory attitude, which she felt had blighted her life.

Jyotsna Rokade agreed: 'I was admitted in Netaji High School in Yerawada, whereas my brother attended St Vincent's High School. My parents paid great attention to his schooling and his higher education' (J. Rokade 2004). (Jyotsna's father and brother attended St Vincent's High School, the most prestigious school in Pune.) She continued that she always wanted to study at Wadia College, which attracted a cosmopolitan crowd, but her mother sent her to Garware College, a Marathi-medium institution. This may have been because her mother wanted her to be in the company of upper castes from the polis in order to Brahmanise her. Jyotsna's mother – Sulochana Kadam – was silent when Jyotsna and I pointed out how she had supported her son as opposed to her daughter (Kadam 2004).[12]

Ignoring our comments, Kadam continued talking proudly about her son and his intelligence. There was none of this for Jyotsna, who became very angry when I posed this question and looked at her mother in annoyance; she was almost on the verge of tears. She was questioning her mother's past behaviour, while her mother just ignored her and stared into space. However, after a few moments Jyotsna realised that there was no use getting angry over the matter; it was all in the past. Her mother's actions could not be undone. She told me that she had ensured that all her own children were educated in good convents and especially that her daughter had equal opportunities. Moreover, she was rearing her granddaughter as she would a male child.

The privileging of boys over girls and of the mother–son bond, which at times dissolved the mother–daughter tie, deserves a special mention. Several mothers did not pay enough attention to their daughters' education or development, as compared to their sons'. Girls often suffered compared to boys, even in middle-class Dalit families. Some educated parents believed that their daughters should attend school only up to a certain level and then seek employment. This was not only for their daughters' economic independence of them, but also to help the parents in financial terms.

As discussed in Chapters 3 and 4, choice of studies was a factor in this nexus of caste and class. Kamal, from the lower class, was discouraged by her upper-caste teacher, who asked her, 'What are you going to do with this maths train-ing?' Poonam, on the other hand, received discouragement from her family (P. Rokade 2004). Despite her brilliant performance in her studies, her father held a very low opinion about her calibre and her aspirations. He did not want to spend money on giving her a science-based education and asked her to take up arts or commerce, which would cost him less money and was deemed more suitable for women. He also believed that the disciplines of science and engineering were for men, and that they were no good for girls. Poonam's mother supported her deci-sion to take up the subject of her choice. Alaka also reported that her father con-sidered arts, drawing, painting and crafts best suited for girls (P. Rokade 2004; Kale 2002).

In a few cases, women themselves actively precipitated such prejudices. While the first-generation learner sought to build a masculine Dalit womanhood by fusing masculine attributes like daring, resoluteness and self-reliance into the feminine, as discussed in Chapters 3 and 4, some elite Dalit men and second- and third-generation elite Dalit women, like their upper-caste counterparts, sought to embellish middle-class feminine virtues and wanted their daughters to fit that model. There was convergence as well as contradiction among upper-caste and some Dalit elites' politics of resolving the 'woman question' and con-structing the 'new woman'. New modernity and bourgeois 'middle classness' called for policing and domesticating Dalit women and reproducing upper-caste norms, and some Dalits seemed to perfect Victorian and Brahmani femininity. Middle-class patriarchy and matriarchy sought to make the housewife a linchpin of domesticity and demanded that daughters be *gruhinis* (genteel, ladylike). Yet, as explained earlier, this was not an automatic or pure imitation; Dalits certainly departed from Brahmani strictures on education and gender forms. Dalits' restrictive processes also had a deeper value of constructing their self-respect, morality and respectability, and erasing the socially dominant image of an 'unruly' or 'vulgar' Dalit woman. These strategies cut the vital cords of Brahm-ani norms and made them Dalit.

Nonetheless, some mothers insisted that their daughters engage in housework: cleaning utensils, washing clothes, rolling out chapattis, decorating the home, and learning arts and crafts to please their future husbands. Alaka laughed sar-castically when she remembered her mother's training:

> She asked us to do housework first and study later. We had to get up early mornings to study and do housework, which was equally important. She wanted us to be equally capable on all fronts. She said, '*gol polya laat*' [roll

out *round* chapattis]. [She laughed heartily and continued.] It was difficult to roll *gol polya* in the beginning, and my *laatane* (rolling-pin) went all over the *polpaat*, stretching the *kanik* [dough] into all shapes *but* round. Then I cleverly devised a technique and used the steel *taat* (plate) to cut out the perfect *gol*. [This disciplining] has had such a deep effect on me that even when I want to roll the triangular North Indian *paratha*, I can only make perfectly round *polis*.

(Kale 2002, emphasis added)

Most of the time it was the mother who produced a 'cultured' woman by making daughters serve the household; they were mainly responsible for cultivating the necessary bourgeois feminine virtues. This was an essential struggle for the excluded Dalits to join the mainstream. Note also Alakatai's use of middle-class 'cultured' speech: *kanik* and *polya* instead of the lower-caste *malalele gavhaacha peeth* (kneaded wheat-flour dough) and chapatti.

Housework was as integral to the female subject as the kitchen was to the home. Despite plans for higher education, employment, and perhaps marriage, traditional norms of domesticity were important for newly emerging middle-class Dalit women. In addition, strong patriarchal forces required disciplining daughters to be suited to nurture the future generation. Second- and third-generation women were entering lower-middle-class spaces and, though they gained from entering the public domain and citadels of education, they were also restricted to an extent by these new constructions of femininity.

Moreover, in practice, only knowing how to perform mundane domestic tasks was not enough; these women had to learn to do them well. Many parents emphasised achievement in both the public and private spheres, and saw domesticity as a complement to success in the public domain. Furthermore, Dalit parents believed and hoped that, along with these behavioural conditions, formal education would help to place their daughters beyond some of society's dangers. These parents, like any other lower-class/status parents, did not want their daughters to end up in menial jobs but in comfortable lives.

Fathers did not generally interfere in these 'private' affairs. Men have usually been in the public domain, leaving the private life to their women. Yet not all fathers fell victim to this generality; some understood that housework interfered with their daughters' studies and insisted that they should *not* be made to work at home. Kamal's father always reminded his wife that 'Kamal had a lot to study, and she should not be asked to engage in domestic duties' (Jadhav 2001). Kumud Pawde also smiled sarcastically when she reflected on how her mother instructed her to be a 'decent' woman, good at domestic work: 'She stood for independence of women, but running a household efficiently needed some good training' (Pawde 2005).

But Kumudtai's father fought with his wife, arguing that Kumud could pick up these skills later in life from her in-laws. She needed to study during her school days, he said. But Kumudtai's mother was scared that Kumud would appear to have 'failed', so she made her work. Such housework apprenticeship was for girls *alone* because they bore the burden of the family's honour. Fathers and brothers rarely helped with domestic tasks. Mothers were left alone with only the daughters to help them. Because of this, most of the girls hardly had time to study; they were exhausted after school and housework. Some could not complete their homework, and then feared attending school the following day because their teachers would beat them. Other girls used housework as an excuse not to attend school and eventually dropped out. Many families believed that girls' 'brains were in their knees', perhaps because their round knees resembled a skull – or because so many household chores required them to be on their knees.

While Meena's father encouraged her education, he completely neglected her younger sister Kamla's education; Kamla reported that her parents and teachers jointly emphasised that she was not 'interested' in anything to do with school. Perhaps Meena's father could afford to educate only Meena. When Meena reciprocated positively with high grades and became 'teacher's pet', she was encouraged to the detriment of her younger sisters. The latter were neglected, dropped out of school, and began to blame themselves for not 'being able to study like their *hushaar* [intelligent] sister, Meena'.

Brahmani hegemony

Historically speaking, many Dalits radically resisted Brahman dominance across time and space. Yet, as many other Dalits constantly negotiated with Brahman superiority, they appropriated certain values and practices and made them Dalit. While this everyday negotiation may be read as Dalit resistance, in the process many Dalits were also vulnerable and tended to delegitimise their own culture because they were overpowered to a large extent by Brahmani hegemony in terms of food habits, dress, greetings, language, tradition and culture. Through multiply complicated processes, Dalits expressed their desires, fantasies and emotions and sought self-refinement. Sandhya's son Chetan,[13] who was studying genetics, stated emphatically: 'Things can be learnt only from the Brahmans. They tell you how to live, how to fight and progress in life. I will only marry a Brahman girl, even if I have to undergo a second marriage' (C. Meshram 2004).

Gramsci's (2005) and Bourdieu and Passeron's (1977) analyses of how the dominant classes exercise this power in society through their hegemony in such arenas resonate in the Dalit case.[14] Dalits negotiated these dominations in everyday practice in different ways, and theoretical conceptualisations and political consciousness emerged out of their historical and lived experiences. Uppercaste hegemony was extended and its symbolic power executed through 'pedagogic actions' that incorporated the education system, along with other systemic agencies (Bourdieu and Passeron 1977). Eventually, the prevailing common sense marginalised, illegitimated, suppressed and annihilated the lower classes. As Bourdieu argues,

> The sanctions, material or symbolic, positive or negative, juridically guaranteed or not, through which Pedagogic Authority is expressed, strengthen and

lastingly consecrate the effect of a Pedagogic Action. They are more likely
to be recognized as legitimate, i.e., have greater symbolic force.

(Bourdieu and Passeron 1977, 10–11)

The historical Brahman hegemony in social and cultural domains was reproduced in pedagogic practices. Bourdieuian reproduction denies agency to Dalits;
the everyday annihilation of their culture is nonetheless a reality in their day-to-
day lives.

Nonetheless, history has been witness to how many Dalit radicals either
gradually developed cracks in or openly subverted upper-caste hegemonic ideology and practices. At the same time, however, many other Dalits were co-opted
by hegemonic structures that gave them a sense of cultural unworthiness and
denigrated their achievements, even if they at times did not consider the
dominant culture to be the legitimate culture. These complicated emotional
upheavals animated the lived and everyday experiences of some Dalits. They
disparaged their own medicinal knowledge, artworks, traditions, culture and
crafts, and imitated so-called 'purer' and 'softer' forms of language, dress, food,
occupation, culture and pedagogy. For example, in terms of food, elites preferred
varan/dahi/tupa-bhat (dal/curd/ghee-rice) or inculcated the Brahmani habit of
consuming *tupa* and abandoning *bombil-bhaakri* (dry fish-bread). While some
elite Dalits found the pungent smell of *bombil* extremely nauseating, others
experienced a waft of *bombil* and *sukat* (small dry fish) as particularly appetising. In other words, *bombil-bhaakri* was a delicacy for lower-class Dalits that
the elites disparaged. These contrasts put Kamal in a predicament that forced her
to skip a school picnic. She was scared that, unlike her upper-caste classmates'
mothers, her mother could not afford a packed lunch for her – and if she did,
Kamal could not show to or share her *bombil-bhaakri* crumbs with anybody but
her caste-girls.

Some elite Dalits also preferred to eat softer wheat *polis* rather than crusty
bhaakri. They turned up their noses to record their disapproval of the low-class
term chapattis and insisted on calling them *polis*. Even *chahaa* (tea)-chapatti was
a coarse, low-class breakfast because elites ate a variety of foods to start their
day: *pohe, sabudana khichadi, uppit, thaalipitha* with *loni* (butter) or *shira*.
Interestingly, with the popularity of naturopathy and similar practices, the
process of refining food habits seems to have come full circle with the elitist
emphasis on coarse but fibrous and nutritious *bhaakris* over fattening, simple
carbohydrates like white rice and wheat. Deeply embedded in such discourses
was the socio-psychological violence that undermined Dalit identity. Second-
and third-generation Dalits could choose from a variety of foods, while previous
generations had been blighted by hunger and poverty. However, some elite
Dalits found it very difficult to break their traditional food habits. For example,
one Dalit family continued to eat *kutakes* (pieces of dried *bhaakri*) roasted with
a little oil, chili powder and salt. They could afford fresh *bhaakri*, but to enjoy
the traditional taste, some women made extra *bhaakris* and allowed them to go
stale in order to make *kutakes*. Dalit radicals also urged people to abandon

markers of untouchability such as the consumption of beef; while many low- and middle-class Dalits gave up eating beef, some consumed it secretly, and others openly. Some could not resist *mothyacha* (cow, literally 'big animal') mutton and relished *paatal* beef *rassaa* (thin curry) and *kheema*. One anonymous woman recounted:

> Sundays were a feast in my family. My father used to buy lots of fruits, vegetables, lemons, fresh coriander, fish, and beef at the cantonment market. I clearly remember visiting this market with butchers sitting in a line with carcasses of goats or lambs covered with flies hanging in front of them. My mother would start her Sunday cleaning the meat and vegetables. She used to pressure-cook the beef and prepare a variety of dishes: curry, *biryani*, mutton fry, and so on. I remember the big aluminium *paatela* (vessel) to cook the meat and the *biryani*. The first course was meat fry and *bhaakris*. The second course was *biryani* and sometimes beef *rassaa* (curry). There was a good amount of food and the feast extended to the next day, too. My mother would not have to cook that day. It was a relief from drudgery! Some relatives gave up beef and others consumed it. One of my grand-fathers gave it up in the name of Khanderao, while others said it was not meant for us. After moving to our new apartment on the fringes of Mahar-wada, we significantly cut down on beef, because beef is 'polluting' and we did not want to identify ourselves as the 'polluted' ones. Cooking beef can be a very smelly affair, and it was difficult to keep it secret. One day, I dis-tinctly remember my mother carrying the kerosene stove up to the building terrace to cook some beef stew. Soon she realised that it was counterproduc-tive; in the open air the smell wafted around in all directions,, and it seemed to be the fastest way to inform the entire building of our dinner menu. She scurried back home and resumed the job after making sure all the windows were closed. Whenever she would get a chance, mother would cook beef at an aunt's place.

Thus Dalits had different eating habits, but entering the middle classes brought about certain restrictions in some food items. In addition, while the middle class enjoyed thick *rassaa* full of coconut and other spices, in the lower-class house-hold the *rassaa* was particularly watery, since it had to feed the many hungry mouths.

Yet Dalits also perceived Brahman food habits – their vegetarianism (though Ambedkar argued that historically the Brahmans were beef-eaters),[15] consump-tion of *tupa*, ghee, the food item centrally associated with Brahman culture and diet, and culinary skills – to be matchless. Nonetheless, by attacking the cultural hegemony of Brahmans, Dalits also critiqued the ideological moorings of the caste system, as conceptualised and constructed by Brahmans, and found a way out and up from under. The famous Dalit activist and bureaucrat Vasant Moon had a desire for *tupa* as a child, but by the time he became a bureaucrat and could afford to buy it, he had already lost his craving and taste for it. The long stretch of time between his craving and his ability to satisfy it resulted in the destruction of desire itself. The extinction of desire, which suggested a temporal and symbolic rupture, was very significant for Dalits, who had once sought to rise up from within caste structures by attempting to perfect Brahmanhood. By questioning the cultural construction of the desire for *tupa*, thereby combating their assimilation of obvious Brahmani ideas and practices, they radically refashioned themselves.

From these deeply complicated transformations emerged a new militant and political Dalit consciousness and strategy. While many middle-class Dalits radically asserted a Dalit personhood, calling on their tradition of radicalism, past struggles and history, other middle-class Dalits had a split consciousness in this respect. On the one hand, they knew that their Dalit identity had economic and political benefits; on the other hand, they wanted to erase the cultural markers of such an identity. For example, some Dalits shed their last names, which signified their Dalit origin, and took up the *kar* suffix, which is associated with the upper castes. An example is the Nagare family. Some Nagares are Christian converts from Ahmednagar District (commonly known as 'Nagar' District) who have changed their last name to 'Nagarkar'. This is the way last names were generally constructed, namely by using place names. Some Kambles and Salves changed to 'Punekar' or 'Karmarkar', while Sankpals changed to 'Ambavadekar'.[16] However, at the same time, many Dalits took pride in and asserted their caste surnames: for example, Waghmare, Somkuvar or Pagaare.

Many Dalit girls attempted to 'mingle' to whatever extent possible with girls from upper and lower castes inside and outside schools. It was difficult for them not to compare themselves with the upper-caste communities in terms of dress, food, housing, clothes, shoes, and so on. While Kamal avoided upper castes, many girls tried to imitate Brahman habits and characteristics in their everyday living. Brahmani hegemony dominated every miniscule aspect of their history, culture, language and education. Brahman dress codes, standards of hygiene, even sari-draping styles were thought to be the best. Kamal said: 'We liked to dress up like them. *Ti brahmanan saarkhi saadi nesaayachi* (we wanted to drape our saris like the Brahmans did)' (Jadhav 2001). She did not, however, question why this Brahman style of draping a sari was supposed to be the best.

On the one hand, as Ambedkar rightly and forcefully noted, 'Brahmin enslaves the mind and Bania the body' (Ambedkar 1991, 217). I am concerned with this mental enslavement of the Dalits. However, Ambedkar's and Dalits' insistence on adopting Brahman sari styles consequently broke the deeply embedded caste hierarchy of Maharashtrian sari-draping. By draping saris like upper-castes, Dalits could transcend their Dalithood and gain respectability. Thus, when most women drape saris in a similar style, caste loses its power to divide or create differences. Dalit and non-Dalit reformers practised a similar strategy of homogenising and democratising when they equivocally supported Shudras and Dalits donning the sacred thread from the beginning of the twentieth century. Yet, as Dalits discovered the potential of political activity, they avoided attempts at higher ritual status.

Perhaps to undo these differences between upper and lower class and castes as well as to appropriate Brahman speech, many Dalits also imitated Brahmani *shuddha* Marathi, the 'correct' and 'cultured' tone of speech. (Of course, I do not deny the colonisation of Brahmani Marathi.) Some first-generation, and most second- and third-generation Dalits, spoke in a sanitised Puneri or Mumbai Marathi during our discussions. This 'public' Marathi was different from the one they spoke in 'private' (for example, in their kitchens). At the same time, a Dalit (Mahari/Mang) tone intruded into Dalits' *shuddha* Marathi. One woman recounted that because she lived in the Brahman-dominated Kothrud area of Pune and had acquired a Puneri–Brahmani Marathi, her friends (both upper caste and Dalit) refused to believe that she was Dalit (Anonymous 2010). Refining one's language required immense practice and inculcation of a habit, but, once achieved, there was barely any difference among speakers from different castes.

Caste discrimination

Some teachers made a point of identifying Dalits in front of the whole class. One anonymous woman reported:

> I myself experienced this form of routine humiliation. I studied from classes three to ten in a small English-medium school in Pune which at times practised overt caste discrimination. A clerk came twice a year into my class and commanded: 'Will the SCs stand up? I have to check the list.' The few SC students in the class stood up and the rest of the class looked at us. I felt like burying myself and vanishing away when I saw him approach the class. I simply half-stood, shifting my body weight from one leg to the other, with my head hung, pretending to work on something in my books. I felt deeply insulted, but I could not voice it. Why could I not voice it? It was because the system has trodden me down so much that I felt that this was just a minor incident. I had to be prepared for other similar – and perhaps worse – experiences. I wondered to myself: 'Why does he have to come twice a year to do this marking? The official school records have our names while we continue to study in the school, so why can't they devise some discreet way to record our concessional status instead of making us stand in class for three whole minutes?' However, I remember that while I stood with my head hung, my fellow SC classmate stood erect and looked at the clerk with an emotionless face. He was not embarrassed about his background and appeared to be oblivious to the denigration involved.
>
> (Anonymous 2001)

Thus, while this Dalit woman silently endured, others were resilient and radically claimed their Dalithood. Although in colonial times such women were few and far between, much has changed in post-colonial times, and many second- and especially third-generation women refuse to be cowed.

Like Urmilatai, Hirabai Kuchekar (2002) referred to the common social stereotype of the lazy and dirty Dalit and said that she continued to suffer such slurs from her upper-caste friends. Some respondents refused to discuss questions of caste or discrimination (see Chapters 1 and 5). However, I reiterate the complexities of investigating the silences around not only difficult memories but the everyday living of Dalits. Many women attested to casteist verbal abuse. They faced caste discrimination to some extent in their workplaces, but reported that relations between the upper and lower castes had improved.

Kumud Pawde narrated a school incident when her upper-caste friend's mother advised her daughter not to play with Kumudtai or to touch her, because Kumud was a Mahar (Pawde 1995). Another friend introduced her as a 'Kunbi'[17] to her grandmother, who had rigorous rules of *sovale*, the taboo of purity and pollution. Kumudtai also writes about the immense hurdles she faced when she attempted to learn the 'sacred' Sanskrit language. However, undeterred, she achieved her master's degree and went on to become a professor of Sanskrit (Pawde 1995, 21–31).

Janhavi Chavan[18] said that her friends who belonged to 'other' castes expressed negative opinions about SCs and about affirmative action (2001). Almost all of the respondents agreed about the prevalence of an immanent tension when discussions touched issues of caste or positive discrimination among friends belonging to mixed castes. She continued to report that caste was never much of an issue in her friendships and that most of her friends were good to her. Meenakshi Jogdand[19] reported:

> I was always surrounded by Marwaris, Brahmans and Marathas [upper castes]. I felt shy about disclosing my caste. I had an inferiority complex about it and wanted to hide it. *Chehera padato tyancha* [they frown, lose interest] when I mention my caste. Being fair in complexion, they did not expect that I would be a Matang. When the ladies in the train asked me my caste, I told them that I was a Maratha [upper caste]. However, more recently, I have started revealing my *khari jaat* [true caste identity]. I am happy to work in this [Siddhartha Cooperative] bank of SCs. The atmosphere is different here. Sometimes I am happy that I belong to this caste because I get concessions.
>
> (Jogdand 2002)

Meenakshi expressed her relief with regard to concessions, yet noted that she had hidden her caste and 'passed'. She was not the only one. Even as Meenakshi remarked on 'passing' as a Maratha and her split consciousness as a Dalit, she was working on constructing her identity in the midst of Dalit co-workers at her workplace.

Her experience resonated again when one anonymous Dalit woman reported:

> During college, I made immense efforts to hide my caste. I was always with upper-caste friends. When they expressed their disgust at affirmative action measures, I was mute. I discreetly found means to fill in the fee concession

forms required for SCs. I also hid behind the garb of my last name, which is not a caste-specific one. When I interacted with Brahmans, many times they thought that I was from an upper caste, to some extent because of my deceptive colour and the sanitised, Brahmanised Puneri Marathi language I spoke. Only in recent years, due to higher education, reading, and attending Dalit events, have I developed the self-confidence and boldness to claim my Dalit identity with pride.

(Anonymous 2001)

Although higher education intimidated some Dalits, it also allowed and helped others to reflect on their history and identity, and to shape their consciousness, as this woman did, in order to refashion themselves. After a long socio-psychological and political battle, Dalits were embracing their true selves.

The peer group was an important motivation in every student's academic life. Amita described how she and her friends studied together (Pillewar 2005). Sometimes they all gathered at her place to study. She noted that they were all Dalits. I asked her: did these girls make any friends from the other castes? The schools catered to other classes and castes, but did the children mingle? She replied that, especially in the Marathi-medium and municipal schools, caste communities tended to band together. Dalits felt most comfortable with other Dalits; they lacked the confidence and courage to face the upper castes. Some of them selected streams and subjects on the basis of what their friends had chosen. They refused to change their institutions for this reason. The upper-caste pupils excluded the Dalits for different reasons. Thus, in this instance, schools did not function as 'melting pots', as some scholars argue (Muralidharan 1997). Of course, caste differentiation was not rigid, but there was a tendency for caste-specific peer groups to develop. The organic caste system was to an extent reproduced and crystallised in the state's education apparatus. This was compounded by the fact that most first-generation parents did not allow their daughters to socialise with or visit friends. However, this began to change for second- and third-generation women, who reported having friends from other communities, particularly during their college days. A few of them were fortunate enough to be included in the peer groups of knowledgeable and influential people.

Some girls attempted to distance themselves from their castes because they were ashamed of their caste backgrounds and of people from their community. Lalita Naik reported:

I have *nehamich* (always-already) preferred Brahman friends. My brother *always* had Brahman friends. They came home but my brother never went to their place. He picked up a lot from them. I also liked Brahman friends, because my mentality and the mentality of the other Backward Caste students did *not* match, I did not like their thinking and behaviour, and I looked down upon them. In my school and college I had some *other* friends who liked me because I was clean.

(Naik 2001, emphasis added)

Thus, some Dalits, like Lalita, strongly believed that people from their own caste were 'backward' and unlikely to help them improve their lives. These Dalits from the lower and middle classes entertained a 'blaming the victim' (Ryan 1976) attitude and maintained a distinct distance from the community. They attempted to befriend Brahmans even if they practised segregation. In this manner they sought to escape from the community and drifted away from it. While many Dalits fought their assimilation of Brahman hegemony and returned to the embrace of the community, at the same time others were entrapped by its encircling tentacles and were also torn by the calisthenics of identity. Thus, many Dalit women experienced a real 'double consciousness' (Du Bois 1994) and attempted to escape the constellation of humiliation and hurt to shape themselves.

The stigma of reservation

The term 'scholarship' often aroused mixed feelings in both Dalits and non-Dalits. There is a vast amount of literature on and around affirmative action for Dalits (see, e.g. Dushkin 1979, 1999; Shukla and Kaul 1998; Kurane 1999; Chitnis 1981; Galanter 1984; Beteille 1992; MacMillan 2005); however, I am concerned here with the socio-psychological violence caused by such policies. For many Dalit girls, reservations meant the concessions they had secured as their *right* after Dalit radicals' numerous battles with upper-caste hegemony. Yet they were also troubled by the negativity associated with the discourse of 'concessions', 'affirmative action' and 'compensatory discrimination'. Along with other markers like food, language and dress, Dalits were *marked* by reservations. Some Dalit elites affirmed that such concessions stigmatised them; they were caught in a bind of seeking and not seeking reservations. Dalits were ambivalent towards reservations because they marred them psychologically, like other denigrating social practices. Although beneficial, reservations also brought many problems.

Positive discrimination definitely helped Dalits to advance in material terms. It certainly brought about a complete change in their economic as well as social status. Like Ambedkar and other non-Brahman and Dalit radicals, many women wanted reservations because they felt that the community was like a lame horse that had just begun to regain its strength and needed the *malidaa* (medicine, literally 'molasses') of positive discrimination (see Chapter 2). Yet some middle-class Dalit women emphasised that reservations were a Dalit signifier and to some extent also encouraged laziness in Dalits.

The irony of the situation was that even when some Dalits attempted to do away with reservations, the state apparatus and 'significant others' did not allow them to do so. One middle-class Dalit signing up for the UPSC exam did not want to avail himself of the lower fees meant for the SCs because he could afford to pay the entire amount himself. He maintained his Dalit identity while ticking the 'SC' box on the form, but paid the full sum required of an 'open-category' (upper-caste) candidate. However, a few days later, he received a letter from the board instructing him to pay the lower fees meant for the SCs. He was compelled to maintain his Dalit status even when he wanted to do away with its economic benefits. Certainly the disciplinary and systemic state apparatus did not allow Dalits to entertain any fantasies that they were 'normal' citizens; unlike 'open' (upper-caste) persons, they were tightly tied to their 'closed' Dalit status, at all costs.

Poor teaching

Many Dalit girls complained that they were taught poorly. Others said that their schools were boring and they preferred to play at home. Some second- and third-generation respondents disliked traditional teaching methods and wanted more interaction with their teachers. However, the teachers did everything possible to maintain their position on a pedestal. Perhaps misguided, they refused to befriend the students and made efforts to cultivate a strict disciplinarian image in order to command respect, much like family elders.

Some Dalit girls also never received encouragement for their efforts. Very few felt strong enough to fight for such recognition in class. Kumud Pawde was, however, fortunate in this respect. She stated: 'One sir [teacher], Gadgil, in the 5th class, knew I was good at English. He always said that "a Mahar girl was going ahead and" – pointing to upper-caste students – "you are the *gotay* [stones] of the Narmada [river]." I gradually progressed to Class 8' (Pawde 2005). In this instance the teacher underlined the progressive reputation of the Mahars and asked the 'others' to overtake this Mahar girl.

Some girls mentioned that they were bored with school life. They disliked it because it became a routine. Kamal said: 'I did not find any subject utterly boring or interesting. I just knew that there was no way out' (Jadhav 2001). Sometimes even the very sincere and studious students became bored and did not do well in higher classes. They just wanted to scrape through their exams. Thus the education system broke the backs of students; they felt overburdened and came to hate the sight of books.

Furthermore, due to poor teaching, students developed a dislike for a particular subject or a certain teacher and then the entire school or college. They carried this dislike for the rest of their lives. For example, Jyotsna stated that 'some students developed a dislike towards certain difficult subjects like mathematics. But it became a *mendhyanchi* [herd] mentality that a certain problem was very difficult' (J. Rokade 2004). However, there were exceptions. A second-generation postgraduate, Amita, liked school: 'I liked the vibrant atmosphere with friends and teachers. In this environment I could learn more than by staying at home. I participated in plays and entered all competitions' (Pillewar 2005). The question was how far this environment was available to Dalit girls. Amita's was a rare case.

A few students from the second and third generations found the schools to be a fertile ground to nurture their talents. Some girls were fortunate to find better school environments. They enjoyed the attention they received at school. Such encouragement is essential for a student to advance. Some girls were good at studies and sought the attention of the teachers. Amita continued:

> My performance was excellent and my teachers were good. I did well in exams and my teachers *kautuk karayachya* [praised me]. I liked it. There was not much thinking as to why I was actually pursuing an education. Only that it was 'good'. So many things happened there, teachers were good, we engaged in sports and other activities, and so I liked it. I was treated well and, obviously, I wanted more of it. That was another motivation. I was good at studies and other activities and so they liked me. They also encouraged me. They gave me the opportunity to perform at cultural events. My teachers nurtured my talents.
>
> (Pillewar 2005)

Such encouragement by teachers of Dalit students was rare. If the teacher was unable to provide such an invigorating environment, some students became disinterested in lessons. They expected teachers to solve their difficulties and make teaching more than mere textuality. Amita believed that at times the students felt that they were smarter than the teachers, and so did not like the classes. They wanted the teacher to suit their requirements – if she did not, she was no good.

The fruits of education

Many middle-class girls pursued higher degrees and a few also attended university; many others were married off early and thus had no careers. Most of the informants were forced to leave school when 'good' marriage proposals came their way. The parents did not want to give those up. Deepa Mohite said, 'My parents saw this boy when I was in Class 9 and got me married before the exams. They are responsible for my state. I am a widow; I lost my husband after two years of marriage and have a daughter to support.'[20] Such women had had to look for employment in order to raise their children. Many parents had no high aspirations for their daughters and merely wanted them to study up to basic SSC (Class 10), enrol in a professional course, and start earning. They were either pressed financially or no longer wanted to shoulder the burden of a daughter's education. Rather, her earnings should contribute to the family income.

There were, however, a significant number of Dalit women of the second and third generations who made good use of their education. In some cases this was because their fathers encouraged them to succeed. Meena Ranpise stated: 'My father wanted me to join the defence forces or to go for UPSC/MPSC. He gave me money to buy books and whatever I required' (2001). It seems that Meena's father was very influenced by his work environment at Lohegao Airport and wanted his daughter to become a high-level bureaucrat. Meena was the only one who was highly educated in the family of three sisters. Her sisters dropped out on the way due to 'lack of interest in education', as they put it. Some mothers,

Figure 6.1 Dalit women led by Kusumtai Gangurde (centre) demonstrating against the increase in fuel prices (courtesy of Kusumtai Gangurde).

Figure 6.2 The author with Mayor Rajnitai Tribhuwan in the latter's office at the Pune Municipal Corporation (photo provided by author).

like Poonam Rokade's, also guided their daughters' careers towards male-dominated fields like engineering (P. Rokade 2004).

A few girls studied independently and never relied on anyone. They devised strategies for themselves. Dr Swati said, 'I preferred to do it all on my own. I did not like to learn things by heart. I preferred to start from scratch and that is the way I understood it well' (Waghmare 2004). Others took up professional courses after leaving high school and practised them. Sandhya *akka*, a social worker, replied:

> During my school days I came across some BC parents dragging their dirty children to school. I made a wry face at the sight. I realised that these children were mistreated due to this. I wanted to know more about the status of my community and understand the social milieu, so I took up social welfare. I wanted to work for the distressed.
>
> (S. Meshram 2004)

A few, like Sandhya, were influenced by circumstances and situations that shaped their careers as social activists.

Chhaya Bahule,[21] who worked at the mental hospital in Pune, reflected:

> as a child I watched my mother and aunt who were nurses. I liked their white uniforms and also liked to serve. Later I expressed to my mother my desire to be a nurse. However, she disliked it and so I entered accounting. And here I am.
>
> (Bahule 2001)

A few respondents who were tired of studying voiced their concerns about earning money. Prakshoti Pawar[22] was one such case. She said, 'I wanted some short course which would give me the opportunity to earn a handsome salary in less time. I thought an MBBS degree was time-consuming, so I took up engineering. I had no internship. I was tired of studying' (P. Pawar 2002). Prakshoti was a rare girl to have attained her Master's degree in business administration; she was working with the reputable Mahindra and Mahindra group.

It was mostly at college level that my interlocutors developed their aspirations. It was at this later stage of their education that they started reading newspapers and magazines and interacting with the public, and became inspired to work in a particular field. Some of them were fortunate enough to be surrounded by influential and knowledgeable people who could guide them accordingly. However, while some respondents could advance towards their dreams, there were many others who could not do so. Shilpa Pagare (2001)[23] stated:

> I wanted to teach and become a teacher but there was no one to tell me how to go about it. I had an elder brother but I could never talk freely with him. He was very strict. We all held him in awe. He thought that I should be a graduate and then hunt for a job. Maybe he did not like teaching.

My Brahman friend immediately did her D.Ed. and is a headmistress now. I later got married, then children ... and I am at home.

Poor Dalit girls often lacked guidance. Others could not pursue their dreams because they would have had to travel far or reside in places away from their homes. Their parents did not allow this. A few girls chose courses along with their friends, then found it difficult to complete the course and failed.

Once married, it was hard for women to pursue a demanding career. Nonetheless, it was not uncommon to find husbands supporting their partners' educational and career advancement. In one interesting case, the mother-in-law provided the support and encouragement. Sadhana Kharat[24] said: 'I am still studying. My mother-in-law told me to pass my SSC and also advised me to study further. She shares the housework with me. So I am in my third year of college because of her' (2002). In some cases, educated husbands took the initiative and compelled their wives to study. Jyoti Lanjewar, a professor of Marathi, remembered that her husband did not allow her to sleep if she had not completed her lessons (2005). Sometimes these women, along with the educated partners who encouraged them, felt the need to improve their educational qualifications. Mrs More was one such woman. She continued her education after her marriage and children, and eventually became a teacher. She retired as a headmistress. The next chapter deals with the pleasures and pains of Dalit women in employment.

Conclusion

This chapter examined the social and cultural anxieties of middle-class Dalits. While many Dalit radicals resisted upper-caste hegemonic structures and produced cracks and crevices in them, there were many other Dalits who negotiated on an everyday basis, were co-opted, and as a result reproduced some Brahmani ideologies and practices inside and outside their homes. However, this emulation was not automatic; it involved many negotiations, for a number of reasons. In emulating Brahmani food habits, nasal-toned Marathi, rituals and rites, Dalits imitated but also subverted them by making these practices Dalit. Some became strict vegetarians, while others ate all kinds of meat, including that of the cow and buffalo. These processes were deeply complicated. They were becoming everyday affairs, and some Dalits navigated them easily. On the other hand, they caused anxiety to many Dalits struggling for self-refinement, self-improvement and self-advancement who were continuously on guard to sanitise their language, change their first and last names, move to caste-neutral neighbourhoods, eat *tupa* with *varan-bhaat* or *dahi-bhaat* instead of non-vegetarian foods, and so on. They constantly felt that the sword was hanging over their heads and feared that their caste would be exposed. At the same time many Dalits, after a long socio-psychological journey, emphasised their tradition, caste background and culture and aspired to work on their futures radically and to found new subjectivities.

Thus, while many low- and middle-class Dalits adorned their living-rooms with photographs and statues of Ambedkar and Buddha or volumes of Ambedkar's speeches and writing, others did away with these artefacts and adopted Ganesh and Sarasvati idols. In the realm of education, refashioning themselves and their futures involved disciplining Dalit girls. However, this policing departed from the upper-caste, elite strictures because Dalits were attempting to inculcate a new, hitherto absent cultural capital and the habits necessary to build a 'modern' Dalit future. This chapter has looked at the complex everyday emotional strategies Dalits have deployed in specific circumstances. These negotiations shaped their political strategy, mentality and identity. Dalits' conflict with mainstream, normative, hegemonic orders caused difficulties for many of them, but also created a field of force that produced new historical forms and a proliferation of historical experiences. Many Dalits suffered ruptures and fissures of consciousness itself; yet these forces also enabled them to affirm the generativity of life itself – to express their interests, desires, pleasures and thoughts, and to develop productive political strategies and practices. Study circles, education, employment, participation in *mahilaa mandals* (women's groups), attending speeches by Dalit leaders and engaging in extracurricular activities were some of the ways in which they sought to refashion themselves. The next chapter analyses women's continued encounters with modernity by entering the public sphere and seeking paid employment.

Notes

1 I am indebted to Nietzsche, Deleuze and Foucault for their meditations on the 'subject' and the 'will-to-power' here. See Butler (1987, 181, 21–12).
2 Sandhya Meshram, Buddhist, Master's in Social Work, Ramtekdi, Pune.
3 Baby Jagtap, Matang, class 12, typist, Sinhagad Road, Pune.
4 Manini and Malavika are Urmila Pawar's daughters. Manini Pawar has a Bachelor's in Science and is a *Kathak* dancer. She is also interested in other arts and crafts. However, she is working at a laboratory to earn her living. Her elder sister, Malavika Pawar, has a Master's in Sociology and a Bachelor's in Education. Mala (as we all call her) is an accomplished singer.
5 When Mala and Manini criticised their mother in her presence, their mother (Urmilatai) simply left the room. However, she explained the reason later on.
6 Stephanie Shaw makes a similar argument in the case of African American women. See her insightful work on 'middle-class' African American women (1996, 15–23).
7 Bourdieu and Passeron (1977) and Willis (1977) also write critically about this disciplinary aspect of the education system.
8 Amita Pillewar, Buddhist, Master's in Social Work, works as a researcher with the National Institute for AIDS Research and lives in Karve Nagar, Pune. She helped me with two interviews in Pune.
9 Dr Jyoti Kadam, Buddhist, doctor (MBBS), Dapodi, Pune.
10 While Mala and Manini were engaged in singing and dancing, Dr Swati Waghmare, Buddhist, doctor (MBBS), was a cricketer. She lived in the Yerawada slum and later moved to middle-class apartments in Vishrantwadi.
11 Original in Myrdal (1968, 1707). Myrdal engages in similar arguments about English public schools. However, I am merely referring here to highly prestigious private English schools.

12 Sulochana Kadam is Jyotsna Rokade's mother. She has a Bachelor's in Science. She had served in higher positions and was a state government employee.
13 Chetan Meshram, Buddhist, second-year undergraduate in genetics, Ramtekdi, Pune.
14 I would like to point out that I grew up observing these issues. My observations are reinforced by Gramsci and Bourdieu.
15 Ambedkar has analysed the question: 'Did the Hindus never eat beef?' According to him, 'that the Hindus at one time did kill cows and did eat beef is proved abundantly by the description of the Yajnas' in the various Vedas, Brahmanas, Sutras, and so on. 'The scale on which the slaughter of cows and animals took place was enormous.' See Ambedkar (1990, 323–328, 334–349).
16 This was the change Ambedkar's father made (Paik 2011).
17 Kunbi and Maratha are touchable upper castes.
18 Janhavi Chavan, Buddhist, Bachelor's in Computer Science, works with a firm in Yerawada, Pune.
19 Meenakshi Jogdand, Matang, Bachelor's in Commerce, works as a cashier in a bank. Bhavani Peth, Pune.
20 Deepa Mohite, Matang, failed in Class 9 and now works as a maid.
21 Chhaya Bahule, Buddhist, Class 12, clerk, mental hospital, Pune.
22 Prakshoti Pawar, Buddhist, Bachelor's in Engineering and MBA.
23 Shilpa Pagare, Lalita Naik's elder sister, Buddhist, Class 10, Yerawada, Pune.
24 Sadhana Kharat, Buddhist, third-year undergraduate student and housewife, Bibwe-wadi, Pune.

References

Ambedkar, B.R. 1990. *Dr. Babasaheb Ambedkar: Writings and Speeches*, Vol. 7, ed. Vasant Moon. Bombay: Department of Education, Government of Maharashtra.
——. 1991. *Dr. Babasaheb Ambedkar: Writings and Speeches*, Vol. 9, ed. Vasant Moon. Bombay: Department of Education, Government of Maharashtra.
——. 1997. What Congress and Gandhi have done to the Untouchables. In *Hind Swaraj and Other Writings*, ed. Anthony J. Parel. Cambridge: Cambridge University Press.
Anonymous. 2001. Interview with the author, 20 December. Mumbai.
——. 2010. Interview with the author, 28 June. Mumbai.
Bahule, Chhaya. 2001. Interview with the author, 1 June. Mental hospital, Pune.
Basu, Aparna. 1974. *Growth of Education and Political Development in India, 1898–1920.* Delhi: Oxford University Press.
Beteille, Andre. 1970. Caste and political group formation in Tamil Nadu. In *Caste in Indian Politics*, ed. Rajni Kothari. New Delhi: Orient Longman.
——. 1992. *The Backward Castes in Contemporary India.* New Delhi: Oxford University Press.
Bhalerao, Champabai. 2002. Interview with the author, 20 May. Yerawada, Pune.
Bourdieu, Pierre and Jean-Claude Passeron. 1977. *Reproduction in Education, Society and Culture.* Thousand Oaks, CA: Sage.
Butler, Judith. 1987. *Subjects of Desire.* New York: Columbia University Press.
——. 2005. *Giving an Account of Oneself.* New York: Fordham University Press.
Chanana, Karuna. 2001. *Interrogating Women's Education: Bounded Visions, Expanding Visions.* Jaipur: Rawat.
Chandra, Shefali. 2012. *The Sexual Life of English: Languages of Caste and Desire in Colonial India.* Durham and London: Duke University Press.
Chavan, Janhavi. 2001. Interview with the author, 21 May. Yerawada, Pune.

Chitnis, Suma. 1981. *A Long Way to Go: Report on a Survey of Scheduled Caste High School and College Students in Fifteen States of India*. New Delhi: Allied Publishers.

Church Missionary Society. 1926. *The Mass Movement in Western India: A Survey and Statement of Needs*. G2 I 3/0, Document #11. London: University of Birmingham, Church Missionary Society Records.

Du Bois, W.E.B. 1994. *The Souls of Black Folk*. New York: Dover Press.

Duskhin, Lelah. 1979. Backward Class benefits and social class in India, 1920–1970. *Economic and Political Weekly*, 14(14): 661–667.

———. 1999. Scheduled Caste politics. In *The Untouchables in Contemporary India*, ed. Michael Mahar. Tempe: University of Arizona Press.

Fanon, Franz. 1963. *The Wretched of the Earth*, trans. Constance Farrington. New York: Grove Press.

Galanter, Marc. 1984. *Competing Equalities: Law and the Backward Classes in India*. Berkeley, CA: University of California Press.

Gramsci, Antonio. 2005. *Hegemony*. New York: Palgrave Macmillan.

Illich, Ivan. 1971. *Deschooling Society*. New York: Harper and Row.

———. 1981. *Multilingualism and Mother Tongue Education: Taught Mother Language and Vernacular Tongue*. Oxford: Oxford University Press.

Jadhav, Kamal. 2001. Interview with the author, 16 September. Pune.

Jagtap, Baby. 2002. Interview with the author, 5 February. Sinhagad Road, Pune.

Jogdand, Meenakshi. 2002. Interview with the author, 13 March. Bhavani Peth, Pune.

Kadam, Jyoti. 2002. Interview with the author, 11 June. Dapodi, Pune.

Kadam, Sulochana. 2004. Interview with the author, 15 August. Pune.

Kale, Alaka. 2002. Interview with the author, 1 July. Karve Road, Pune.

Kasbe, Snehlata. 2003. Interview with the author, 10 September. Pune Station, Pune.

Kharat, Sadhana. 2002. Interview with the author, 10 April. Bibwewadi, Pune.

Kuchekar, Hirabai. 2002. Interview with the author, 8 January. Pune.

Kurane, Anjali. 1999. *Ethnic Identity and Social Mobility*. Jaipur: Rawat Publications.

Lanjewar, Jyoti. 2005. Interview with the author, 10 October. Ambazhari, Nagpur.

MacMillan, Alistair. 2005. *Standing at the Margins: Representation and Electoral Reservation in India*. New Delhi: Oxford University Press.

Meshram, Sandhya. 2004. Interview with the author, 11 September. Ramtekdi, Pune.

Mohite, Deepa. 2001. Interview with the author, 22 May. Ramtekdi, Pune.

Mokal, Nani. 2000. Interview with the author. 20 May. Pune.

Muralidharan, V. 1997. *Education Priorities and Dalit Society*. New Delhi: Kanishka.

Myrdal, Gunnar. 1968. *Asian Drama: An Inquiry into the Poverty of Nations*. New York: Twentieth Century Fund.

Naik, Lalita. 2001. Interview with the author, 22 May. Ramtekdi (Swami Vivekanand Nagar), Pune.

National Standard. 4 July 1953.

Omvedt, Gail. 2006. Why Dalits want English. *Times of India*, 9 November.

Pagare, Shilpa. 2001. Interview with the author, 20 May. Yerawada, Pune.

Paik, Shailaja. 2009. *Chhadi lage chham chham, vidya yeyi gham gham* (The harder the stick beats, the faster the flow of knowledge). *Indian Journal of Gender Studies* (June).

———. 2011. Mahar-Dalit-Buddhist. *Contributions to Indian Sociology*, 45(2): 217–241.

Pawar, Manini and Malavika Pawar. 2004. Interview with the author, 5–6 September. Borivili, Mumbai.

Pawar, Prakshoti. 2002. Interview with the author, 10 April. Pune.

Pawar, Urmila. 2004. Interview with the author, 5–7 September. Borivili, Mumbai.

Pawde, Kumud. 1995. *Antahsphot.* Aurangabad: Anand Prakashan.

——. 2005. Interview with the author, 16 October. Dhantoli, Nagpur.

Perkins, Margo. 2000. *Autobiography as Activism: Three Black Women of the Sixties.* Jackson: University of Mississippi Press.

Pillewar, Amita. 2005. Interview with the author, 30 July. Karve Nagar, Pune.

Ranpise, Meena. 2001. Interview with the author, 12 May. Sinhagad Road, Pune.

Rokade, Jyotsna. 2004. Interview with the author, 15 August. Vishrantwadi, Pune.

Rokade, Poonam. 2004. Interview with the author, 15 August. Mundhawa, Pune.

Ryan, William. 1976. *Blaming the Victim.* New York: Vintage Books.

Shaw, Stephanie. 1996. *What a Woman Ought to Be and to Do: Black Professional Women Workers during the Jim Crow Era.* Chicago, IL: University of Chicago Press.

Shukla, Sureshchandra and Rekha Kaul, eds. 1998. *Education, Development and Under-development.* New Delhi: Sage.

Velaskar, Padma. 1998. Ideology, education and the political struggle for liberation: Change and challenge among the Dalits of Maharashtra. In *Education, Development and Underdevelopment*, ed. S. Shukla and R. Kaul. New Delhi: Sage.

Wagh, Vilas, ed. 1986. Dalit madhyam varga. *Sugava*, special Deepavali issue, November–December.

——. 1994. *Ambedkari Prerana Visheshank-Dalitanna Brahmani Saunskrutiche Akar-shan* (Dalit Attraction for Brahman Culture). Pune: Sugava.

Waghmare, Swati. 2004. Interview with the author, 12 November. Vishrantwadi, Pune.

Willis, Paul. 1977. *Learning to Labour: How Working-Class Kids Get Working-Class Jobs.* Farnborough: Saxon House.

Zelliot, Eleanor. 2001. The meaning of Ambedkar. In *Dalit Identity and Politics: Cultural Subordination and Dalit Challenge*, Vol. 2, ed. Ghanshyam Shah. New Delhi: Sage.

Zweig, Ferdynand. 1964. *Student in the Age of Anxiety.* New York: Free Press.

7   Dalit women in employment

In general, secular education had an instrumental value for many Dalits; yet, while Dalit women understood and appropriated modern education's material and symbolic benefits, they achieved immense social, economic and psychological gains from entering the public domain and disrupting dominant discourses regarding their education and ensuing employment. Upper-caste women and men certainly recognised the importance of education for higher-level employment, which is why they strategically excluded Dalits from spheres of influence and advancement.

Dalit women played a variety of roles; they were not just wives and mothers working inside the homes. They also had to work outside the home to meet their personal and family needs. This chapter investigates the complications associated with Dalit women's experiences seeking employment and employability. By pushing them into the public sphere, modern technologies of education and employment opened up new opportunities for Dalit women even while thwarting them due to the reproduction of caste, class and gender prejudice. In the past, Dalit women had interacted to various extents with women and men from different classes and castes, but new experiences of employment radically catapulted them to newer heights: they could even engage with upper castes on potentially equal terms. What was the workplace atmosphere like for newly educated Dalit women? How did caste manifest itself in employment enclaves in the cities? Did employment bring greater emancipation for Dalit women within the home? How did it change middle-class Dalit wives? Did Dalit women achieve more equal status with their male counterparts as a result of higher education and employment?[1]

I attempt to answer the above questions in this chapter by investigating the patterns of Dalit women's financial hardships, their experiences at work, and their balance between private and public, familial and employment responsibilities, which Urmila Pawar (2004) has termed *taarevarchi kasarat* (a balancing exercise).[2] Women in particular pointed to this exercise when they described their precariously entangled battles on personal and professional fronts: between their families and jobs, between the daily grind of caring for the home and employment outside the home, and between handling the domestic and disrupting dominant discourses in order to carve out a space and status for themselves in the public domain.

Table 7.1 Student enrolment in Training College of Mumbai, 1924–25

	Brahman and similar castes	Marathas and similar castes	Untouchable and similar castes
East	123	142	7
Middle	219	293	35
South	9	31	4
Total	351	466	46

Source: *Bahishkrut Bharat* (3 June 1927).

Attitudes towards female employment

The material benefits of education were significant in advancing Dalits' struggles for individual and collective social status, intellectual strength and capabilities. Ambedkar analysed how, compared to non-Dalits, Dalits were negatively affected in terms of prospects and economic opportunities. He continued:

> It is notorious that a DC worker is shut out from many vocations by reason of the fact that he is an Untouchable, [for example] cotton mills and railways. No one can deny that his destiny is to work as a gang man. The same is the case in railway workshops. We must uproot Brahmanism, this spirit of inequality, from among the workers if the ranks of labour are to be united.
>
> (*Times of India*, 14 February 1938)

Ambedkar thus argued that even highly qualified Dalits could not obtain high-level jobs due to predominant practices of untouchability. Even in 1920s Pune, when the Teachers' Training College trained between 300 and 400 students, only two Dalits were among them (*Mooknayak*, 28 February 1920). As a result, among other resolutions passed at the Akhil Bhartiya Bahishkrut Parishad (All-India Conference of the Excluded) held on 1 June 1920 in Nagpur, Dalit radicals underscored the increasing enrolment of Dalit students in male training colleges (*Mooknayak*, 5 June 1920). Dalits also demanded that the minimum age limit for government jobs be increased by three years for Dalits. The annual report of the Education Department included a caste breakdown of the enrolment of students in the Training College of Mumbai Province for the 1924–25 academic year (*Bahishkrut Bharat*, 3 June 1927), shown in Table 7.1.

Drawing upon these statistics, Ambedkar contended:

> According to the annual report of Bombay Presidency's Education Department, Brahmans constitute nine per hundred of the population, Marathas fifty-seven, and Untouchables and 'others' were twenty-three. Per population figures, Brahmans should have secured seventy-six, Marathas 510, and Untouchables 267 seats in the training colleges. The figures clearly reveal that Marathas and similar groups did not face such a big loss; however,

it seems that Brahmans have *gilankrut* [swallowed] the *saaraa hissaa* [entire share] that actually belonged to the Untouchable classes. In my opinion, this is extremely contradictory. Thousands of businesses and occupations are open to the touchables. They can fill their stomachs in any manner they desire.

(*Bahishkrut Bharat*, 3 June 1927)

Thus Ambedkar argued that there was a discrepancy between Brahmans' representation in the population and the resources and rewards upon which they drew. The statistics also reveal that Marathas and other similar castes were taking over Brahmans and would pose a threat to Dalits. He further emphasised that:

the teaching profession was suitable to Dalits because there was no other profession as *saadhaa, sopaa, susaadhya* [simple, easy to accomplish or attain, readily procurable and practicable] as that of teaching. Yet, to be denied even entry to it is the height of injustice. This is injustice on the lines of occupation, but even in terms of the social, the predominance of Brahmans in teacher-classes instead of Untouchables is very unpropitious. This is because teacher education is a *saarathi* [guide]. Who should be a teacher is the most important question in seeking the welfare of society. How long can we afford to continue the utter destruction of society by giving the reins of education to those [Brahmans] who treat others as less than animals, pour scorn on other at all times, and always doubt others' wisdom or understanding! If school was only to teach the Marathi alphabet, it would be a different matter. But schools should mould children's minds, should actually perfect them toward social beneficence. *Shalaa haa uttam naagarik tayaar karny-acha karkhaanaa aahe* [schools are the workshops for manufacturing the best citizens]. Hence, the more intelligent the foreman of a workshop, the better the goods it produces will be. Schools are not a Hindu restaurant [that] will succeed with the appointment of a Brahman cook. Even if everybody eats food cooked by a Brahman, nobody in contemporary times will do with education bestowed by Brahmans. So, the government should think about this comprehensively and provide seats to Untouchables in the Training College in accordance with their populational representation. Because you could not bring about improvement, will you also not give *nyaya* [justice]?

(*Bahishkrut Bharat*, 3 June 1927)

To seek social justice in education, Ambedkar drew upon a wide repertoire of constitutional tactics to generate pressure on the government from inside and outside the Bombay Legislative Council. He strongly advocated 'progress' and confirmed his commitment to the improvement of Dalits, yet he also regularly questioned whether the colonial state was living up to its avowed ideals of democracy and fairness – for example, in the realm of education and particularly teacher education. Because they had a fundamental role to play in these complex battles, Ambedkar advised women to educate themselves and to seek employment as teachers. A seventh-grade education was the minimum criterion to enter Teacher Training College, and some Dalit women trained as teachers, as did Shantabai Kamble in 1942. Many Dalit and non-Dalit women also favoured teaching because it allowed them the flexibility to successfully handle their private and professional lives. They could better train their children and future generations.

In the case of women in general, the feminist sociologist Karuna Chanana observes that there has been no observable shift towards equalising educational opportunities among women, with those from lower social and economic strata continuing to remain either unrepresented or underrepresented in the sphere of higher education (Chanana 2001a, 267–268). Studies by several social scientists in different parts of India reveal that it is usually the children from the higher castes who are able to take advantage of higher educational opportunities to gain worthwhile employment (Chanana 2001a, 265; Shils 1961; Mishra 1961; Kamat and Deshmukh 1963, 5–6; Shah 1964, 19–22; Parekh 1966, 56; Naik 1965, 22, 108). Many have, however, sought to downgrade the importance of caste per se. Moreover, Chanana (2001a) argues that the significance of caste as a determinant of educational opportunity has been overemphasised. She draws upon the works of M.N. Srinivas (1962), Andre Beteille (1965) and M.S.A. Rao (1957) to support her thesis.[3] She states:

> By and large, the lower castes are poor, and it is their poverty, rather than caste status, which tends to bar them from enjoying the fruits of new educational opportunities. Caste is, thus, important as an expression of the inequalities in the economic structure.
>
> (Chanana 2001a, 265)

Although it is obviously true that poverty limits employment possibilities, I shall in this chapter question the pronouncements of leading sociologists that caste has not played a significant role as a determinant of opportunity. I have already discussed in the preceding chapters Dalits' difficulty in accessing quality educational institutions. The discrimination practised in classrooms by school staff and students alike is a clear indication that caste was also a significant factor in impeding Dalits' progress. Very rarely did the congruence of caste, rank and class work in Dalits' favour. Furthermore, many women were often silenced by the caste monster, unable to voice their experiences of oppression.

Some elite, upper-caste reformers, like Gandhi and Nehru, were interested in education for more than its immediate benefit in terms of employment. Even Ambedkar (along with other Dalits) shared his educational and civilisational anxieties, yet material gains from formal education were more important to Dalits. Upper-caste elites seemed to be less troubled by material acquisitions, perhaps because they always-already possessed them and sought to contain them in their particular social environment. Hence, they emphasised that education should actually take one closer to one's Maker (Gandhi 1986, 312). However, for Dalits the question was whether their social and material circumstances would allow them the leisure and luxury to develop themselves as well as engage with their Maker. For these reasons Ambedkar, like his teacher Dewey, sought to eliminate educational distinctions such as the dualism between labour and leisure (liberal education), and constructed a combined course of intellectual and practical studies. For Ambedkar, this resolved the problems of education in a democratic society (Dewey 1916, 185). In order to ensure better employment opportunities, Ambedkar (like the African American leader Booker T. Washington) also stressed the need for technical education and hands-on training so that Dalits in general, and women in particular, could seek different kinds of employment.

Most of the Dalit women with whom I interacted wanted to be employed because they clearly understood the connection between their incomes and the family's economic survival. Historically, Dalit women had always engaged in work in the public sphere as well as domestic labour, so employment in the public domain, outside the home, was not new to them. In the past, however, such manual work was a mark of their degraded feudal status. In contrast, upper-caste women's physical labour was confined to the private space of the home and subsequently within the limits of respectability. Upper castes viewed the 'public' (low-class and -caste) woman to be inherently dangerous, unruly and coarse; she was seen to embody an irresistible sexuality that supposedly ensnared (high-caste) men. This upper-caste anxiety fed into the Hindu elite nationalist discourse that placed the ideal, upper-caste, middle-class woman within the family home. Dalit parents and daughters were aware of the historical, social, economic and sexual exploitation of Dalit women in the public domain and did not want this fate for themselves. Hence, they sought to acquire whatever formal education was available to them to break away from traditional caste-based labour in the villages. As a result, as I explained in Chapter 6, some Dalits negotiated with modern discourses, transformed them, and, taking into consideration their specific political and social circumstances, became intensely involved in self-disciplining and self-refinement. Moreover, while first-generation learners sought whatever education and employment was available, many second- and third-generation middle-class women reported that employability for a stable economic status was the major reason they sought education.

Following her seventh-grade education, the feminist Shantabai Kamble interviewed for a teaching position and was appointed to teach the second grade in Kurduvaadi's girls' school on 16 January 1942 (S. Kamble 1986, 77). Her husband had married another woman, so Shantabai decided to leave him and took up employment. Most significantly, her father and brother supported her decision and helped her in her new position. She enjoyed teaching at the school, which paid her fifteen rupees a month (ibid., 85). Kamble eventually became headmistress of a girls' school in Dighanchi (115).

Clearly, there is a chance that someone with a higher level of formal education will find a prestigious as well as a profitable occupation, *ceteris paribus*. However, all things were not equal for Dalit women, very few of whom, historically, could attain higher education. A few years' attendance at a primary school would hardly produce the qualifications needed for better and more prestigious forms of employment. Many women with whom I interacted belonged to the lower-middle class or middle class and found mostly lower-category jobs: clerks, municipal teachers, nurses, and so on. In fact, several Dalit women noted that low levels of education could fetch better employment opportunities, for example, in the case of *jhaaduvaalyaa* (sweepers). While many first-generation women disapproved of such a strategy, many second- and third-generation women struggled to attain a comparatively higher level of education. For all intents and purposes, I am discussing the effects of secondary- and tertiary-level education here.

Many employed women from the first and second generations managed to reach the seventh grade and find employment as teachers. The second and third generations of learners were more likely to take their studies a little further and even graduate. Only a few pursued postgraduate work, and there were scarcely any professionals among them: three doctors (two with MBBS – Bachelor of Medicine, Bachelor of Surgery – degrees) and two engineers. None had obtained a Ph.D.[4] Most women emphasised that their education was a means to achieve economic security, social prestige, good marriage proposals and companionship. Unlike the students in Chanana's study of two Delhi colleges, these Dalit women were not seeking higher education so as to have a 'good time' or 'because everyone got the same college education after schooling' or even as something to do while 'waiting to get married' (Chanana 2001a, 274–276). Most of the first- , second- and third-generation learners mentioned the financial hardships they had faced in the process of their education. Most agreed that they sought education and then a good job basically to break free from the clutches of financial hardship. They mentioned their difficulties in obtaining satisfactory employment despite having the necessary qualifications.

Many single as well as married women sought employment. While financial hardship and career-making were reasons mentioned by some single women, married women reported the changing attitudes of their husbands towards their entry into employment as well as the necessity of having a second earner in the family. They all agreed that their employment contributed immensely to their family's financial stability; financial considerations thus influenced and determined life choices. Second-generation learner Gitanjali Rithe,[5] working with the (Buddhist) Karuna Trust,[6] reported:

> Yes, women must be employed. Employment provides a new opportunity; it bestows a different status, prestige, and most importantly independence, which are crucial [for women] in order to have a stand of their own in the family and society. My family does support my employment because I am bringing in money. Nobody will deny *lakshmi* [wealth]. It has changed me and I have also started understanding more after interacting with people and being in the public. My formal education has helped me get this job and also to gain status in other people's eyes.
>
> (Rithe 2001)

This submission resonated with most women's experiences. At times, proponents of patriarchy (female and male) deployed misplaced pride and emphasised keeping women away from paid employment as a mark of high status. Yet many Dalit women emphasised the significance of *lakshmi* and their consequent bending of patriarchal norms. Women's market labour lifted the family above the poverty line and men increasingly encouraged women to seek higher education and employment, even if the prime motive was to stabilise the *saunsaraachaa gaadaa* (family cart) effectively. In the process, however, they responded to their immediate economic circumstances and reinforced an instrumental attitude towards education, which was primarily important for gaining employment (regular employment, if possible). Yet, some second- and third-generation learners emphasised their intellectual advancement through education.

Sociological studies on employed women have revealed that, although education and employment have propelled many women out of the domestic sphere, neither has brought about radical changes in societal attitudes, particularly those of men (Chanana 2001a, 341; Mies 1973). This finding resonated to an extent in the Dalit communities I interacted with. Prakshoti Pawar, an unmarried engineer from the third generation, said that Dalit men often practised gender discrimination and wanted them to change their perspective towards their educated and employed wives. She stated: 'Dalit men must understand the hardships of these employed women. They have to change', adding, 'I would like to marry a man who will be on par with me and understand me. If I cook for four days, he should cook for three days, at least' (P. Pawar 2004). While Prakshoti emphasised gender equality when I interviewed her on a Sunday afternoon, her father and brother were watching television and her mother was listening to us while working in the kitchen. Unlike the male members of the family, her mother effectively combined manual work both inside and outside the home. Prakshoti's comments were a reflection on her mother's hard life and continuing low status, and the male family members' negligence of such unpaid domestic labour. Although Prakshoti enjoyed her work and was independent, self-confident and assertive, her case reiterated how the traditional norms relating to feminine and masculine duties continued to exist in many Dalit households.

Another such case was Hirabai Kuchekar (2002), who obtained a good job as a result of her education. She emphasised that women had to manage everything and work hard to get out of the mundane daily rut. She and her daughter revealed that they did not enjoy equal status with their male counterparts (H. Kuchekar 2002; Suvarna Kuchekar 2002). They felt that their employment was taken for granted; there was nothing special or unusual about it that would command any special status or respect within the family. The pair had to take care of the household while employed outside, while the males of the family were engaged only with their employment and in paid labour. Thus, elite men wanted to associate with women who were educated and employed. Although women gained new experiences in the process of their education and employment, their oppression was also reinforced in a different way. Prakshoti's and Suvarna's mothers, like many other non-Dalit mothers, fulfilled their 'natural' roles first and their employed roles also first. This is not a Dalit-specific problem; however, it was prevalent in many Dalit families. Educated and employed women had to take care of their 'natural' roles as well as their newly constructed position, yet few Dalit women were prepared to voice their grievances about this within the confines of the family. They expected a negative response and some feared maltreatment if they voiced their opinions. Being accultured to accept their *baaichi jaat* (woman's caste) in life, they were themselves unsure whether they even had a case to make. Sometimes when I was talking to the women in the presence of their husbands or in-laws, they felt unable to voice their opinions. At least two women directed me to change locations during our conversations: we relocated from living rooms to their intimate bedrooms when we came to such discussions.

Homemaking, housekeeping and childrearing were always-already considered 'feminine' jobs that women had a duty and an obligation to perform in addition to any outside work. Shantabai Kamble writes in her autobiography:

> My mother used to work in the fields the whole day and come home in the evenings. We used to all sit outside waiting for her because she would get the begged bread and would also cook something. After wiping her face with a little water, she used to sit at the *chul* [hearth] to make *bhaakris*.
>
> (S. Kamble 1986, 26)

Shantabai's mother had no respite and slogged like a 'bullock', both inside and outside the house, from birth to death. In an insightful article entitled 'Women as bullocks', Sharon Kemp discusses the lives of rural women in Gaothan, a Maharashtrian village. In this survey, the women constructed three models of their everyday lives:

> Two of these were women as wives and women as mothers. However, the third was women as bullocks. Women said, 'We work like bullocks'. Moreover, they said, '*baikanna ani bailana jasta kam astana pan nav matra purusache hote* [women and bullocks do more work, but the man is named or praised]'.
>
> (Kemp 1998, 217)

Kemp commented that women were thus regarded 'like an oil presser's bullock. Nothing else! Eyes covered by blinders, work all the time. No rest. No one to say you are tired' (218). I extend the image of the menial work of the bullock to the Dalit women in the city, where they were expected both to labour within the home and to supplement their family income through outside employment.

Not all women preferred to be employed in public; Deepa Mohite (2001) preferred to work outside the home in order to escape the torment of her in-laws' authoritarian dictates and constant nagging. Baby Jagtap (2002) reported that her in-laws initially did not support her employment. However, later, when they actually observed the benefits of her income to the family, they agreed. She was of the opinion that if the family had sufficient resources, she would not have gone outside the house to work. In some cases, educated Dalit women have refused to marry husbands who would not support them in their work. Dr Swati Waghmare (2004) reported that some Dalit men who were interested in marrying her suggested that she would not be able to practise medicine in her clinic after marriage. Swati readily rejected such offers. This case suggests how some middle-class Dalit men wanted to marry women who would conform to the model of elite domesticity. Patriarchal norms would not allow the woman to work outside the home because she might become domineering, assertive, or very 'free' in her behaviour with other women and men. Such idioms would also not tolerate the family surviving on a woman's income. In general, however, this attitude has shifted across time; many men prefer working women who could share financial responsibilities in addition to the traditional work of looking after the home and bringing up children. Some argued that work actually enhanced women's courage and confidence in the outside world as well as the family's prestige, and provided women with a purposeful activity.

Education and employment: individual and community struggle

In general, there is in India a political idiom of helping in the uplift of one's own community. Communities believe in helping their own and will put great effort into achieving this and they view education as benefiting the community as a whole. Some examples of caste movements for such ends are those of the Namashudras of Bengal, the Nadar/Shanars of the Tamil South, the Ezhavas of South India and the Jatavs of North India (Hardgrave 1969; Lynch 1969). The Ambedkar movement was also in this vein.

Some Dalit women did indeed deploy such language of 'uplifting the community'. A few women from the first generation and the majority of women from the second and third generations did think beyond the immediate goal of education as employability and talked of education for the community. I noted this community consciousness and commitment to serving the community in the voices of Dalit women mostly from the lower-middle and middle classes. Stephanie Shaw rightly pointed out a similar dynamic among Black women who saw education as for the race, to uplift the race (Shaw 1996, 68–76, 81). Black parents had a much grander mission than white parents, she says: 'They were not educating individuals but manufacturing levers' (ibid., 68). Shaw focused not on what the schooling process represented for the student and the subsequent personal advantages it might bring, but on its potency for the community at large. Altogether, the schooling process provided especially effective reinforcement for family and community attitudes towards what a woman ought to be and do. The school programmes meshed perfectly with the expectations of the family and community, and served mightily to accomplish them.

The community ethos propelled Dalit women's education. A few Dalit women from the first generation and most from the second and third generations

said that an educated woman need not be employed if she was financially comfortable. Rather, they suggested that educated women should serve the community and help to uplift the Dalits. For example, Alaka said that she was using
her employed position to serve the community. She continued:

> If they are financially comfortable, they can work for the community. I came
> to teach at the high-school level as a means of employment and also as a
> means to engage with the youth. Teaching is immensely satisfying when I
> interact with students and can attempt to understand their difficulties, their
> future goals, and advise them accordingly. I take efforts to encourage stu-
> dents, especially from the Dalit background, to read, write, discuss, and
> work harder toward improving themselves. I conduct extra lectures toward
> these activities and I am enthralled by the response.
>
> (Kale 2002)

Thus Alakatai contributed to strengthening the future Dalit generation through
her teaching.

Even women who were not formally educated turned what little training they
had back into the community. Sheelatai Nikam, who attended school only up to
Class 3, eventually became leader of the Hawkers' Union in Mumbai. She
started by selling lunches, then sold snacks and savouries, and owned two large
food stalls on Fashion Street, a flea market in Mumbai's Fort area. Later on, she
became very active in organising women selling items on the footpaths of
Churchgate, Mumbai. She also fought the state government to get a quota and a
part of the sellers' market reserved for women from all castes. Sheelatai sent
petitions to the Central Railway Minister to reserve food stalls for women on
every railway platform in the country. She spoke of her dream of establishing an
organisation called Mata Ramabai Ambedkar Pratishthan (Mother Ramabai
Ambedkar Foundation) to provide work for all women, irrespective of caste
(Nikam 2005).[7] She was also planning to buy land with the help of a cooperative
society, where she could establish a shopping mall with food stalls and other
shops run by economically and socially disadvantaged women. In the process,
they could gain financial independence.

In a similar vein, Shantabai Kamble, the headmistress of a girls' school,
started *praudhavarg* (adult classes) for women in her Bauddhawada (S. Kamble
1986, 115). Her husband led adult classes for men. There were about forty
women in Shantabai's class who were reading, writing and learning to sing
songs and make speeches. She continued to exhort the community to educate the
children; they should become doctors and lawyers, she insisted (152).

Sheelatai could not talk about the effect of her education because, even
though she had an opportunity to study with her mother, a teacher, she did not
study beyond the third grade (Nikam 2005). She mentioned repeatedly that she
did not like her studies. Furthermore, she recalled an event when she was asked
to speak and share a stage with other Dalit women activists. She noted the con-
descending attitude of the educated, middle-class, so-called 'feminists' from

Dalit communities who left the stage on her arrival. 'These women,' she said, 'were not interested in talking to an uneducated woman.' Significantly, the disparaging attitudes of Brahmans towards Dalits, of Dalit men towards Dalit women, and of mainstream feminists towards Dalit feminists were mapped onto the behaviour of educated middle-class Dalit women towards uneducated Dalit women. For some middle-class Dalits, the mere achievement of formal education was a primary factor in deciding to whom one would speak. Modern education was a significant factor in creating dissension among Dalit women. Sheelatai's humiliation on stage mirrored the experience of the ways upper-caste, elite women occluded Dalit women with little or no education, as Chapter 3 explained.

Unlike the first-generation learners, many second- and third-generation women were aware of the existing facilities and possibilities for Dalits and acted accordingly. Sandhya Meshram talked about her social work:

> I sought employment after I had finished my Master's in Social Work. I wanted to work for *aaplaa samaaj* [our community]. My employment experience has been wonderful; it has been emotionally satisfying working on so many projects in the slums.
>
> (Meshram 2004)

Many Dalit women like Sandhya *akkaa* purposefully opted for a Master's in Social Work in order to serve the community. In this manner, women were also nurturing a collective consciousness. This collective consciousness, which seems to be a given, always-already endowed in Shaw's work, at times had to be 'consciously' built into the lives of many Dalits. Dalits were growing critically conscious about the community and working towards its advancement.

In a similar vein, Meera worked for *her* Matang community by helping students seek school admission, fetching caste certificates, completing paperwork for the illiterate to obtain funds from the state, and so on, free of cost. She was also involved in obtaining small loans for Matang women from the Anna Bhau Sathe Pratisthan (Foundation) (Jangam 2004). In order to do this, she got to know the 'right' people as well as the 'right' modes of operation. Although diverse Dalit castes have (and do) imagined themselves as and lived as a common community, dissent has also been real at particular political conjunctures. Meera noted that Buddhist organisations in her slum took care of Buddhists as well as others, to an extent; however, there was no such network for the Matang community. Hence, she focused on Matang women. Sudha Bhalerao (2004) also underscored a family metaphor and mentioned that she would support 'AP', *aaplya paiki lok* (our community people). Of course, she did not mention Dalit castes per se. Thus there was a tendency towards nepotism among some Dalits, with Buddhists supporting Buddhists and Matang supporting Matang, Chambhars, too, supported their immediate community, in the process confining privilege to caste locations. At the same time, they also produced social welfare networks upon which their community could rely.

In general, however, community work was not considered a particularly high priority among many elite Dalit women; at least, it was not stated as such. Ambedkar propounded that Dalit education should also lead to the uplift of the community. However, in practice, the voices of many Dalit women demonstrated that 'the uplift of the community' was not their primary goal in pursuing education. It was the persistence and pervasiveness of caste discrimination, their experiences as Dalits and as women, their process of education, and their consciousness through critical thinking that led these particular women to speak about and to act on behalf of their social responsibility.

Liberating the self

Some Dalit women wanted a better and more liberated life. Many second- and third-generation learners wanted to be engaged creatively; they were assertive and insisted on their independence. Amita Pillewar, a socially committed woman, stated:

> Employment and moving in the public is necessary because it bestows independence, confidence, and information. One is engaged. One must use education to look at oneself and change oneself. We should also see that change in others. My family always supported employment. But my married sisters are at home because their in-laws do not support it.
>
> (Pillewar 2005)

Reinforcing Amita's views, Nanda Kamble said that Dalit women should be actively engaged; even if only signing up for occasional technical courses, anything was good to keep them busy and independent. She continued: 'It is no use sitting at home and cooking for the family, we must do something and be away from that routine and it will help us economically also. My family supported me and the income helps enormously' (N. Kamble 2001). Hirabai Kuchekar stated that while education was a primary factor in her pursuit of employment, even entry into the public domain made her confident, bold and assertive. She was almost a *new* woman (2002). Women thus articulated how the 'public' was responsible in shaping their emotionally contoured political practices and overall lives. Gitanjali Rithe stated: 'Education and employment made me know the outside world. I interact with so many people and learn so much every day' (2001). Lalita Naik, a banker, was of the opinion that her education and then her job had greatly improved her confidence (2001). She had been disabled and diffident, but education and a good job brought about a major change in her psyche and personhood. This was the result of Dalit radicals' thorny struggle for entry into the public sphere.

Ratnaprabha Pawar added that she was happier working outside the home because it was torture staying at home with her constantly complaining in-laws, nagging husband and demanding children (2002). She found solace in her workplace as she interacted with her colleagues and focused on her daily duties.

However, she pointed out that it was not her education, but more her diploma in education that helped her find the job. Many Dalit women reinforced Ratnaprabha's views. It was technical training that helped them secure employment, not the process of education per se.

Self-employment and subversion

I came across a few women respondents who were self-employed. For them, education had provided only a base to initiate some income generation; personal initiative was vital. Indu Gade[8] was one such person. She was a farmer's daughter who migrated with her husband to Pune. She had been educated up to the seventh grade and wanted to go on to do a teacher's diploma. However, because of her husband's job transfers, she was unable to pursue a career in teaching. Instead, she stayed at home raising her daughters until they started school. She continued:

> After my daughters started attending school, my husband said that I could do something instead of *just sitting* at home. He knew the art of bookbinding and so we bought a shop here. I sat there during the daytime and took orders for binding books. He worked on the orders after he was home from his day job. We also needed to earn some extra income to educate our children well. Being away from our in-laws, there was no question of their objection to my self-employment. However, even if they did, we would have continued with our plans. The shop has helped a lot financially and also helped me develop myself. I have improved a lot because of it. *My language has changed a lot and must change if we want to [interact and engage] with better people and excel.* Why stick to something which is not going to benefit you at all and is going to be harmful in life? It is of no use. I interact with so many people and have developed good managerial skills with that. I spend my income on my family.
>
> (Gade 2002, emphasis added)

Thus, in the case of Indutai, her husband motivated her to engage in some activity because according to him and her she was *just sitting* at home. Of course, her domestic labour counted for little: it had no value in his or her eyes and was unpaid. Indu's husband's encouragement of her active involvement was also financially driven. Yet the very act of allowing his wife to present herself in public, to interact mainly with men and to handle monetary affairs indicated the sudden 'freedom' granted to Indutai. She stated:

> Many agree with the saying: *vyapaar karaavaa Marvaadyani, Maharani naahi* [Marwaris (a thrifty business community) alone are fit for business, not the Mahars (who are a low caste)]. On the contrary, if you look at my case, a Mahar, or even lower, a Maharin [female Mahar] was doing business.
>
> (2002)[9]

Thus women constantly challenged dominant upper-caste, normative and hege-monic discourses in theory and practice, and gained immensely as a result. Indutai was in a small business, something not allowed to Mahar males; females were further marginalised. Nevertheless, Indutai's case was a rarity.

Like Indutai, Lakshmi Shinde owned several small businesses in the Parvati *jhopadpatti*. Lakshmi, a smart young Matang woman, owned two big Tata Sumo vehicles in which she gave guided tours (Shinde 2000). She was also engaged in employing slum women in a cottage industry involved in embroidering saris and decorating them with beads, glass work or small, shiny *tiklis* (bindis). Moreover, Lakshmi helped her brother in his social activities by focusing mainly on women's issues. She talked to me while feeding her four-month-old baby, because she had no time later. Her mother owned a small spice-grinding mill located inside their small house, and the family lived in this spice-congested space. Lakshmi's education and business success were instrumental in making her courageous and confident. She added that the 'real world was outside, out there' and not inside the home, so it was important to break the barriers of con-fined spaces.

Another successfully self-employed Matang woman was Meera Jangam (2004). She operated from Yashwant Nagar slum in Yerawada, where she owned two cooking-gas agencies. She also planned to start a sewing class and a com-puter class for girls, and had allotted a room in her new house for this project. On the whole, the less educated appeared more likely to take the path of self-employment. Boradetai,[10] who ran a sewing class, reported that education did not help her much; it was her engagement and activities outside the home that helped her advance (Borade 2002). Boradetai and some others did not particularly think that education was a key to their self-employment. Yet they agreed that their education did provide them with the necessary confidence to run a business, as well as the basic skills of literacy and numeracy. Of course, illiterate and unedu-cated people who had never stepped inside a school carried out their small busi-nesses like hawking in a very successful manner. Their education took place on the job. Nonetheless, education clearly helped many women to build a better busi-ness, to prevent themselves from being cheated, to maintain their accounts, and so on. As Baby Jagtap stated (2002), a job gives women the opportunity to make good use of their education – even, presumably, if that education was fairly basic.

Some illiterate Dalit *tamaasgirs* (folk performers, dancers in this case) made a living from the folk art form of *tamaashaa* dancing. As revealed in Chapter 4, and historically speaking, although Dalit radicals celebrated the *jalsaa* (folk drama), from the early twentieth century they also sought to discipline the 'immoral' lives of *muralis* (women wedded to the god Khandoba) and *tamaas-girs* in Maharashtra because the women represented 'backwardness'. They sym-bolised Dalits' degradation and were objects of exploitation and sexual possession for men of all castes and hence had to be 'cleansed' and their 'deviant' sexuality curbed. In this manner the politics of caste, gender, sexuality and moral reforms complicated modes of political participation and of subject formation in a colonial context. Yet in post-independence times, *tamaashaa* has been retrieved as an 'icon' of Marathi identity and sanitised for middle-class consumption in contemporary Maharashtra. Although degraded as a lower art form, the state of Maharashtra and its agents (the Ministry of Culture in particular) appropriated *tamaashaa* and *tamaasgirs* to represent 'authentic' Maharashtrian *sanskruti* (culture). Thus, the state apparatus has once again co-opted Dalit social actors even as it bestowed upon them rewards, titles and prizes.

Tamaashaa was a highly stigmatised occupation due to the potential for sexual abuse by clients. The danger continued for some performers, as was made clear by Mangalatai Bansode, the eldest daughter of a famous *tamaashaa* dancer – Vithabai Narayangaonkar – from Narayangaon near Pune. Mangalatai reflected:

> In the beginning I was scared to face the audience. However, gradually I learnt to handle the public. *Hey lok cheshtaa kartyat, maskari kartyat, pan kunibi haat nhai laavalaa ajoon … mee kadak bai haaye* [The audience makes fun of me, ridicules me, but nobody has so far touched me physically, because I am a very strict woman]. *Mee ek lakh deto, don lakh deto, zhopaayaa ye … ashe mhas prasang hote* [they offered me one or two lakhs to sleep with them for one night, there were many such incidents]; but, I never gave in and just continued with my *tamaashaa*. My family has been attacked; I have faced caste discrimination in my village. My husband has acted like a coward at times, but this is life.
>
> (Bansode 2004)[11]

This was the life of a *tamaashaa* dancer: insecure and unstable, oppressed by the intersecting entanglements of caste, gender and sexuality; however, the caravan was always on the move. Due to her engagement with the *tamaashaa*, Mangalatai was always-already a promiscuous Dalit woman for men of all castes: higher, lower and middle. She continued:

> The political parties dominant in the village, *sarpanch*, *patil* [headman], the landlord who gives us this place to put up our stage, and the police – all torture us. Anybody can come and bully us, kick us. We are so helpless … *hittha log haagatyat titha aamhi khaato* [people defecate here and we eat our food in this very place and dance here]. Despite all this, I have to continue with this life, for I have 150 people to feed. We have to keep everybody happy in this line [of *tamaashaa*], and I have been tolerating these people since I was 9. I just smile at them and get away. Sometimes the public gets mad and political party people are a great nuisance. They start shouting from the gates, *aamcha paksha, aamhala sodaa, vis maanasa sodaa* [ours is the ruling party now, give us free entry, let our twenty men enter for free]. How do we live in such circumstances?
>
> (Bansode 2004)

Mangalatai argued that Dalit female dancers were at everybody's mercy: upper- and lower-caste men as well as the major and minor politicians. She complained that the state's stricter rules were ruining the art of *tamaashaa*; however, she was a competent businesswoman who controlled her empire astutely and wisely. Although the performative art form of *tamaashaa* was exploitative, ironically, it was also financially empowering for the Bansode family – including its male members – as well as others who were dependent on them, such as those employed in the troupe.

Tamaashaa has been a contested performative practice for the government, social scientists, Dalit and non-Dalit social activists, and *tamaashaa* artistes themselves. Feminists in particular are embroiled in a dilemma about whether professions and practices that have historically been linked with prostitution should be scrapped or supported. Some argue that prostitutes, bar girls, dancers, and the like should be respected as professional 'sex workers'. Yet they fail to take into account the fact that these stigmatised professions have been historically associated with particular low castes as well as being gendered. *Laavani samaraadni* (Laavani Empress)[12] Surekha Punekar, hailing from Pune, has gained a very high reputation for her art in recent years. She recounted her overlapping and complicated struggles to build her career in *tamaashaa*:

> My maternal grandparents were in *tamaashaa*. My father was a *hamaal* [coolie] at Pune Railway Station. He continued with his *hamaali* during the daytime and engaged in *bailgadicha tamaashaa* [the bullock cart *tamaashaa*] at night. Once the bullock cart met with an accident and I got a deep cut on my leg. During those time there was only *zhaadaa khaalchaa* [under the tree] *tamaashaa*, there was no proper stage. *Tamaasgirs* also did not get any income out of the art that you come across these days. I was introduced to the stage when I was only 8 years old. I liked to dance and sing. My father taught me to sing well. He did not allow me to sleep and *phatke dyayache aavaaj chadhavanya sathi* [beat me to sing in a high pitch]. I stood on a chair and sang.
>
> (Punekar 2002)

Surekhatai took physical beatings from her father in order to help her family earn a living because she knew there would otherwise be no food at home. Hunger was common, she reported:

> We went from village to village to perform. When we got to the village we first begged for *bhaakri* and *kaalvan* [bread and curry], and then after collecting everything ate together at a *chaavadi* [village common hall] and performed at night. After three or four months we got home for Divaali and worked at *dhunya bhaandyachi kaama* [washing clothes and utensils] in about ten to twelve households. We never had food to eat in our home. I remember *maajhe garibiche divas* [the days of my poverty]: sometimes we got only black tea [because there was no money to buy milk] and *batar* [hard bread].
>
> (Punekar 2002)

In this manner, Surekhatai was afflicted by hunger and poverty during her child-hood. Poverty was further compounded by illiteracy. Surekhatai was not sent to school because her migratory lifestyle could not allow this luxury. She reasoned:

> My parents were alcoholics. Because my father was *kalechya naadaat* [engrossed in the art] he did not send me to school. We were six siblings. I must say that while my parents sent my sisters to school to be educated until the third grade, I never got such an opportunity. I don't know the reason – my mother said she didn't know.
>
> (Punekar 2002)

Although schooled in the art of *tamaashaa*, Surekhatai was denied formal educa-tion. She was also dominated by her older sister and mentioned that it was only after she abandoned her sister's *phad* (makeshift *pandal*, and here business) that she started her own *tamaashaa phad*. She did well for four years.

Surekhatai's social and sexual labour of the *laavani* constituted a kind of 'body politics': she boldly evoked the erotic through her body, for example, winking with her left eye, making other lewd gestures by using her body in a sensual manner, or singing lustful or passionate songs like *pikalyaa paanaache deth kiti hirvaa* (a mature leaf is very green or full of juice, but here meaning 'body') or *yaa raavji, kaay saangaa tumchi marjee* (come guest, let me know your desire), with themes that were flirtatious and sexually motivated, in order to 'seduce the public', who would then literally throw money at her or at times offer it with 'respect' for her abilities. *Tamaashaa* dancers were on the lowest rung of the ladder of sexuality and outside the dominant discourses that strength-ened the connection between chastity and caste. As the feminist scholar Gayle Rubin has argued, discourses of 'sexual morality [have] more in common with ideologies of racism than with true ethics [because they] grant virtue to already dominant groups' (1993, 15). Thus, upper castes re-signified Dalit women's morality to amplify upper-caste morality and caste power. The women were in constant and potential danger of being violated physically and faced many other *vyaap* (stressors), as Surekhatai recounted:

> I got an opportunity to perform at Rangbhuvan and Nehru Center in Mumbai and my career took off from there. People talked about my singing and *adaakaari* [gestures]. *Tamaashaa* has changed its form over the recent years and become more lewd and raunchy, because the public is not the same as earlier. Today you find a lot of money and less of the art form; the clothes and *adaakaari* are changing immensely, and if this is the state of the art today, what will happen to future dancers? I struggled immensely from 1998 to 2003. I have also acted in movies. However, all this hard work got to me, *itkaa vyaap jhaalaa malaa, gharchaa vyaap, satat vyaap* [I was and am totally stressed, stress of the home, always stressed].... I developed dia-betes; however, I continued my *ghode-daud* [horse-race] for seven years. I used to fall sick but I worked undeterred. I got my brother and sisters

married. I got my cousins married. Everything is settled now. I have earned up to 80,000 rupees for a show, when things were fine. However, I am in debt today and have to start afresh.

(Punekar 2002)

Surekhatai reflected on the changing nature of *tamaashaa* and argued that its public performance was becoming more vulgar. She continued that she had done her best to use her talents for the betterment of the community at large:

I perform *laavanis*. Some of them are very famous.[13] I engaged in a few song-in-drama performances. Along with a *dholakivaalaa* [drum player] and *petivaalaa* [harmonium player], I visited villages and performed *daaru bandi, hundaa bandi* [anti-liquor, anti-dowry] and *AIDS virodhi* [anti-AIDS] government programmes and earned an honorarium. I travelled to villages for this. I performed not only for men but also women [because women never attended and I wanted them to do so]. I also won a prize of two lakhs at the 1998 Laavani Mahotsav [Great Laavani Festival].

(Punekar 2002)

Surekhatai was actively involved in social activism. She also seemed sensitive to gender discrimination because, while men watched Dalit women dance on the *tamaashaa* stage, they would not allow *their own* respectable women to watch these shows. She thus questioned the double standards of some men who constructed hierarchies in caste, class and sexuality. Surekhatai decided to perform 'special' *tamaashaa* shows *only* for women. During such events, she herself stood at the doors of the public halls to welcome the women who came to watch her dance. During these 'ladies' nights out', women immensely enjoyed themselves and transgressed gendered boundaries, for example, by whistling like men. In this instance, for once, the *tamaashaa* theatre, typically a masculine space, engendered a liberatory possibility for many women.

Both Mangalatai and Surekhatai were introduced to the stage by their parents. They continued to be the breadwinners of their families, both before and after marriage. Moreover, the fact that they were married and donned thick gold *mangalsutras* (the chain of black beads worn by married women as a sign of wedlock in a Brahmani tradition) had an immense significance for them. One obvious reason was that such marriages were outside the norms of conjugality and were not monogamous: *tamaasgir* women were not bound to the monogamous strictures of marriage and they may have had 'open' marriages. The *tamaashaa* stage was their school, on which their parents, like schoolteachers, subjected them to *phatke* (beatings) to discipline them and teach them to sing and dance. Their perpetual life-on-wheels provoked desire and derision, and forced them to travel from village to village to perform their art and earn their livelihood.

Perhaps their lack of education did not affect them greatly in financial terms; however, they often spoke longingly about the school which did not include or welcome them. They were already earning good money. Although exploitative, *tamaashaa* was their business, and it successfully fed the numerous families dependent upon it. These women were of instrumental value to their families; though kicked by one and all, they handled their affairs efficiently. They felt gnawed at not only by others outside the family, but by their own parents, siblings and children. Through their personal initiative, they had launched small businesses and opened up opportunities for themselves. However, this was also possible because of the sexual labour of the Dalit women who played a key role in this industry. Traditionally, these are despised and lowly occupations, and such women have to struggle constantly to preserve their honour within and outside the Dalit community and to enhance their social status. Although Maharashtrians sanitised the art form and attempted to bring it into the mainstream, the majority continued to look down on it. Men from all castes liked to watch the women dancing or even engage in sexual adventures with them, but continued to despise them as 'public prostitutes'. As a result, Dalit women continued to battle the entanglements of overlapping patriarchies, caste, class, education or its lack, gender, sexuality, moral norms and labour to earn their livelihoods, fill their stomachs, and maintain their integrity and selfhood.

Discrimination, reservations and employment

Dalit women had the advantage of reservations for certain positions, but there were not enough positions to provide jobs for more than a few. For a long time, 70 to 80 per cent of all seats were in the 'open' (not reserved) category, and the upper caste, which constituted 15 per cent of the population, benefited the most. What is more, more than 88 per cent of the reserved seats for Dalits in the public sector remain unfilled or are filled by other castes, as are 45 per cent of such positions in the state banks. A close examination of the caste composition of government services, educational institutions and other services reveals an 'unacknowledged reservation policy' for upper-castes, particularly Brahmans, insidiously built into the system (National Commission on Dalit Human Rights 2006). According to the National Commission on Dalit Human Rights (NCDHR) (2006):

> Of the total Scheduled Caste reservation quota in the Central Government, 54% remains unfilled, according to the National Commission for Scheduled Castes and Scheduled Tribes's report. Brahmins comprised 70% of the Class I officers in governmental services, though they represented only 5% of the population in 1989. At universities, upper-castes occupy 99% of the teaching posts in the social sciences and 94% in the sciences, while Dalit representation is a lowly 1.2 and 0.5 percent, respectively.

Dalits tend to be placed in lower positions. Historically speaking, in 1928 there were no Depressed Classes even as clerks in the government service (Ambedkar 1928). Even in 1942, the communal proportion in the Indian Civil Services reveals 363 Hindus, 109 Muslims, nine Parsis, eleven Sikhs, and only one SC candidate (Ambedkar 1991, 418). The trend continues and Dalits are restricted to lower cadres. The NCDR went on to note that: 'As of 1.1.2001 the position of the SCs in Central Government Services are as follows: SCs in Group A constitute 11.21%, group B 12.43%, group C 16.24%, group D 17.55% and the lowest category 60.45%' (National Commission on Dalit Human Rights 2006). Dalits are thus concentrated in the lowest categories.

In a nutshell, reserved posts were often not filled, and those employed in such positions often suffered the pangs of caste and class discrimination. While reservations have helped Dalits enter the colleges and universities of their choice, it has not benefited them to the expected extent in the field of employment. On the whole, they had to gain such positions through their own initiative and by demonstrating their calibre. The situation was particularly difficult for Dalit women, who did not get any additional official provision along gender lines and had to compete with Dalit men. Poonam Rokade mentioned her struggle to enter the job market following the successful completion of her engineering degree. She was aware that she had to compete with Dalit men for any reserved posts. She stated:

> If you are facing competition, you have to take into consideration the requirements of the jobs. You should also make constant efforts to improvise and have an edge over other candidates. The best will be selected if the candidates do not use their influence [i.e. nepotism]. It is a cutthroat competition and we [Dalits] have to make greater efforts when we are racing with other [non-Dalits] candidates. Reservations helped us enter the colleges, but we have to struggle and prove our mettle to fetch good jobs. My father did not support me earlier; he did not think much about it. However, today he proudly talks about me being an engineer and an officer with the MSEB [Maharashtra State Electricity Board]. I am the only woman engineer in my department.
>
> (P. Rokade 2004)

Poonam thus emphasised fierce competition not only with 'other' candidates but within the Dalit community itself. This gives the lie to those upper castes who raise a hue and cry over supposed 'falling standards' due to reservations. Compensatory discrimination allows Dalits to enter higher education; however, unless they show their competence, take initiative and work hard, they cannot, as a rule, take advantage of their education in the public sphere of employment.

Once employed, Dalit women were also discriminated against in various ways – some subtle and covert, some overt, as Shantabai Kamble experienced at the Women's Training College in 1950. She reported:

> The Women's Training College was very friendly. We studied in a competitive manner. The college did not believe in untouchability. However, I had one experience. All girls at the college took turns in serving food. Badve [a Brahman girl student] from Pandharpur joined us later on. Overall, the mention of [the last name] Kamble suggests the caste. One day Pramila

Kamble and I were to serve food.... When I served *polyaa* [chapattis] to Badve, she refused to take it from me. She also did not take the *bhaaji* [vegetable] from Pramila. However, when another girl, Mhetre, took to serving *polyaa*, Badve took *polyaa* from her. All Untouchable girls understood this. After experiencing Badve's [practice of untouchability] for four to eight days we came to the conclusion that she practised untouchability. Pramila Kamble, the house leader, complained to Mrs Atre, the lady superintendent. Atrebai called Badve and said to her, 'Badve, you are a teacher and you believe in *ashprushyataa* [untouchability]. You are from Pandharpur [the holy land of God]. The fact that you are Badve ensures that everybody at home practises *sovale* [the ideology of purity-pollution]. But that will *not* work here. You leave our college. We will *not* keep you here. Go to Pandharpur and practise your purity-pollution.' After Atrebai reprimanded Badve severely, she folded her hands to seek apology and agreed *not* to practise caste discrimination and untouchability again. After this, even if she did not want food, was not hungry, she still took food if we served her.

(S. Kamble 1986, 96, emphasis added)

When Shantabai faced caste discrimination she was supported by Atre, a Brahman woman, who was the reformer Pralhad Keshav Atre's wife.

But not all women were fortunate like Shantabai. Many women mentioned the prejudice in attitudes and actions, the pointed and queer questions and abusive and insulting language, sarcasm and slurs on appropriate behaviour, and hidden agendas that they suffered in the process of trying to find employment. A famous Dalit economist reported that though he was nationally and internationally renowned for his work, he suffered from prejudicial practices – the torment of being a Dalit. Upon noticing the images of Ambedkar and Buddha in his office, his surprised higher officer said, 'Oh! I did not know [that] you are a Buddhist.' After this the officer's attitude towards him changed (personal conversation, 12 September 2006). Even Ambedkar, who attained higher education at numerous world-renowned institutions like Columbia University and the London School of Economics, could not escape these denigrations on his return to India (Ambedkar 1992, 667–91). What can we say about ordinary Dalit women? Lalita Naik reported:

They have troubled me and also said that I am a BC and do not know my job. They envied my promotion and said '*kaanaa maagun aali aani tikhat zhaali* [a substantial achievement despite entering the competition late]'. However, over the years, I gradually learnt to handle such derisive comments ... *mee jashaas tase vaagate* [my behaviour answers 'tit-for-tat'], though no one had dared to trouble me. *We* should be taking pride in what we are; why deny our identity? That is *our* past on which we have built *our* present, struggling at every step and we are successfully building *our* futures.

(Naik 2001, emphasis added)

Women like Lalita were aware of Dalit women's difficulties in employment, especially when they were recruited or promoted as SC candidates. The non-Dalits insulted them at every step. Although slightly vulnerable in the beginning, Lalita and other women learned to fight the insults heaped upon them. In the process, they also built their consciousness and brought about a significant change in themselves and the community around them. As I revealed in Chapter 6, during her school days, Lalita strategically avoided Dalit girls because she thought they could not provide her with the 'proper' cultured living her Brahman classmates did, and of course, she did not want to be identified with Dalits; however, after spending long years on her higher education, she gained employment. Lalita's exposure to social, political and ideological debates in the public domain brought about an enormous change in her. Instead of erasing her identity and hiding her Dalit past, she took pride in her Dalit history, tradition, culture and present in order to build a robust future. She reiterated Dalit radicals' agenda of building and uplifting the community.

Some Dalit women adopted an aggressive attitude towards caste issues. Sudha Bhalerao (2004) asserted that she had never tried to hide her caste. Rather, she continued,

> I have given many facilities to our caste people. I have helped Dalits seek jobs; I have given concessions when they are late to the office. I agree that I am biased towards them. I am just protecting them the way Brahmans do their kin, so what is wrong with it?

Thus Sudhatai made some individual attempts to 'protect' her Dalit colleagues.

Generally, upper castes have used their privilege and power even over reserved posts. They have also deployed 'merit' criteria to challenge Dalits, though scholars and social scientists have contested the politics of meritocracy. This has led to much controversy. The upper castes claimed that standards were being compromised for the sake of political correctness. As a result, institutions they dominated devised a range of ways to avoid having to make such appointments, leaving the reserved places unfilled. After a reserved post was advertised three times and the institution had still failed to get a reserved-category candidate, the post automatically became 'open category'. These legalities have led to some tortuous internal politics. Meena Ranpise was suspended for a while when she was serving as a part-time lecturer. She reported:

> They wanted a person from the open category. However, I fought back. Things are fine now. My colleagues speak against affirmative action and also argue that all SCs are unworthy of the jobs they get. The upper castes are good at *kaavaa karne god bolun tey kaam karoon ghetaat* [cunning, they get the work done using sweet talk]. I lack these qualities and I should pick them up to ensure success in the future. I do face verbal abuse, but that is for all, not for me specifically.

> (Ranpise 2001)

Meena mentioned the malpractices involved in reserved and open positions. She also pointed out the verbal abuse to which non-SCs subjected the SCs, including blaming Dalits for failing to 'make it'. She wanted to learn the 'sweet' and 'nice' ways of 'others'.

Kumud Pawde similarly wrote a heart-wrenching tale about her efforts to learn Sanskrit and later to get a job as a Mahar teacher of Sanskrit. As a Mahar, she was ridiculed, excluded and discouraged from applying for jobs; she remained unemployed despite attaining a Master's degree in Sanskrit, hitherto the purview of the upper castes. When she eventually found employment, it was because she took her Maratha husband's last name – Pawde – and discarded her Mahar last name, Somkunvar (Pawde 1995, 30–31).[14] Seematai Kuchekar (2002) also pointed out the social stereotype of 'lazy' Dalits her upper-caste colleagues used to taunt her with as well as others. Although marked by slurs regarding their Untouchable background, due to political and cultural change over the years, some women (e.g. Urmila Pawar, Seema Kuchekar, Lalita Naik and others) learned to fight for justice. However, many were also silenced and did not want to talk about such experiences.

For Dalit women, their caste was compounded by their gender. The Dalit assistant commissioner of police Kamal Jadhav faced such discrimination in her employment. She reported:

> The higher officers from other [non-Dalit] castes favour their own candidates, so I could not get a promotion for a long time. They spoiled my confidential report, and that affected my service record. Since we belong to lower-caste backgrounds we have to work harder to prove ourselves, our aptitude. Otherwise they always call us names. Sometimes even our community does not understand our problems. I used to commute daily and the officer from our caste complained that I was not punctual. He also tried to transfer me to police stations in slums or ones with fewer facilities. However, I have learnt to respond to such discrimination.
>
> (Jadhav 2001)

Kamaltai reiterated the predominance of patriarchal norms, which re-signified that women did not have the calibre and commitment required for masculine jobs like police work. This was precisely the phenomenon that most second- and third-generation Dalit women have experienced. They described their painful stories and ended with a sense of accomplishment, confidence and courage to stand and fight any oppression. Through their everyday struggles for justice and power under the domination of the colonial and post-colonial state and upper castes, they constituted themselves as the significant agents of social change. They thus engineered and propelled the Dalit movement. In the process, they refashioned themselves and worked collectively to uplift and improve future generations.

Gender discrimination was prevalent. Rampant sexism would not allow Dalit (and non-Dalit) men to cooperate with Dalit women, who were becoming their competitors. Like other men, many Dalit men considered themselves to be 'primary' earners who had to strive to earn a living and to look after their families. They were of the opinion (as the trade union debate goes) that the Dalit women seeking employment and increasing competition for them were actually secondary earners whose income was used to accumulate the family's durable goods. Hence, many were very agitated over the reservations granted to women (33 per cent of the whole). Unlike the second- and third-generation learners, first-generation women did not have to deal with such intensely gendered and sexist politics.

Some Dalit men often expressed displeasure if their wives tried to apply for higher positions, or preferred them to forgo promotion. I interviewed one Ambedkarite who is the leader of the SC-ST teachers' union at a college in Pune. On being asked about his wife's profession and advancement, he replied:

> I am happy that my wife is working with a good bank. She is doing well; however, I do not approve of her promotions, advancing ahead at the cost of my family. I am a staunch Ambedkarite and believe that my wife should take care of the family first.
>
> (Anonymous 2002)

Reinforcing his wife, another such 'Ambedkarite' stated:

> I had already talked to my wife about her present employment and her promotions when I proposed to her. I did not and do not support her promotions, as that would call for transfers to different places [even remote places] in the state. I want my family to be together, not scattered. Hence I will not support her promotions. [Pointing to me, he further said:] At least you are working for a cause, you are doing your bit; my wife does not even read anything, she does not have to do an M.Phil. or a Ph.D. for that matter, so why bother? We are happy the way we are.
>
> (Anonymous 2006)

Of course, this story resonates in non-Dalit households as well. What is important is the use of the 'Ambedkarite' label to justify patriarchal and selfish beliefs and motives, which called for holding back women, without taking into consideration the opinions of their wives. By contrast, Phule and Ambedkar expended their energies to fight against such private patriarchies. Especially in the second case, the man controlled his wife's bank account but never showed his own account to her. Nor did the wife have any courage to ask about it; that would be blasphemy.

Trends in Dalit women's employment

My research uncovered some dominant trends in the employment of Dalit women. Most of them were clustered in low-paid and low-status occupations like teaching, nursing and clerical jobs. A few were lecturers at city colleges. Teaching, being a feminised occupation, was very popular among the women with whom I interacted. It was also easy to be a primary school teacher after some training. Women preferred teaching due to its convenient schedule for family life.[15] The community supported such employment of women due to the myriad benefits mentioned above. These women reported that only a few families were not very supportive.

The rule of 'the higher the occupation, the fewer the women' resonates in the Dalit case.[16] Very few Dalit women have entered medicine, business management or other high-status jobs, or gained top positions in their institutions. Of the women with whom I spoke, only two were in the police; one was a police officer and the other an assistant commissioner of police. This is a reflection of the limited employment opportunities open to women.[17] The circularity of low-quality municipal school education, lower levels of education and lack of access to employment equally contributed towards keeping Dalits stuck in lower jobs. Post-independence Bombay Presidency made immense efforts to uplift Dalits in multiple ways, including economic, social, education and employment opportunities, but Dalits faced numerous hurdles in attaining higher education, higher positions and well-paid jobs.

Women were additionally constrained by their preferences, lack of career orientation and commitment, and the discriminatory practices and recruitment policies followed by employers in the public and private sectors. Perhaps the increase in the general level of education of women or efforts at equality have not led to greater employment among women. 'Even while formal discrimination tended to disappear, informal policies and practices continued to persist' (Chanana 2001a, 340).

Very few of my Dalit interlocutors had career goals. Sandhya Meshram (2001), Dr Jyoti Kadam (2002), Dr Shalini Moré (2002), Meenakshi Jogdand (2002) and others were happy with their jobs and thought that it was enough to take care of their families financially. Moreover, men's careers were highways steadily rising and falling towards retirement, while women had to limit themselves due to their home responsibilities, childbearing and -rearing, and in-laws. 'Women are like *trishankus* bound between their careers and households and may be reluctant to devote the necessary time and energy to their career', Chanana writes (2001a, 356).[18] Many had lost interest in venturing into new arenas and seemed reluctant to forge ahead. Nonetheless, a few second- and third-generation learners had definite career goals and were doing well. Chanana argues that this was evident from media reports on women in top positions in the corporate world, which indicated that women had the drive and the capacity to push to achieve top positions. However, such women were exceptions (ibid., 367). Dalit women were further exceptions, shackled by both their caste and their gender.

Conclusion

Dalit womanhood was constructed in specific social and historically contingent circumstances; Dalit women were not just wives and mothers but had to enter the new labour market and work for family and personal needs. Employability to achieve a stable economic status was the major impetus for getting girls educated. Most of the first- , second- and third-generation learners with whom I spoke aimed for economic gain; however, some second- and third-generation learners also aimed for intellectual advancement through education. Education for the earlier generation was about jobs above all, whereas with the middle classes it was also about prestige and respectability. Nonetheless, except for a few women in elite professions, by and large most educated middle-class women were restricted to lower-grade, 'pink-collar' professions, for example, as nurses, secretaries, typists, receptionists, clerks and primary schoolteachers. They remained in Class 4, the lowest level of public employment, and could not effectively influence any decision-making. Although some had prospects for promotion thanks to reservations, they also faced verbal abuse from non-Dalits and 'soft' discrimination from Dalits themselves.

A few Dalit women trained themselves in different skills like typing, shorthand and computers. Moreover, they enrolled themselves in the government employment exchange. They argued that it was not so much education as employment that had helped them most of all in their lives. Formal education and the ability to earn an independent income thus did not necessarily bring about a drastic change in the domestic status of Dalit women. Rather, they had to labour twice as hard to maintain their position in the family. Yet the process of disrupting hegemonic discourses and practices opened up new possibilities even as it set limitations on women's individual agency. Nonetheless, many women, including some second- and third-generation learners, had thoughtfully and carefully carved out their careers. Thus there were some significant changing trends among the three generations of women.

Many women went silent when I asked about discrimination and experiences of untouchability; some expressed their agony in the face of caste discrimination in the workplace. They often said that they did not find a 'suitable' or 'healthy' atmosphere in their workplace, even given their newly acquired education. Often, there was no 'touch-me-not-ism' or overt discrimination; however, there was ample subtle discrimination and verbal abuse. It was more so with the Dalit women entering the 'middle classes'. Employment brought about many changes in the mental and physical make-up of most Dalit women: their rustic language changed to the more prestigious, 'cultured', nasal-toned Marathi; their mannerisms with outsiders and guests changed; sometimes their last names changed; and most of the times their locality changed. Many did not want to be associated with their stigmatised background, increasingly attempting to wipe the past away and mingle with the general population. Even so, there were many others who proudly proclaimed their background. Many women eventually learned to stick up for themselves, gained self-confidence and daring, and became resilient.

This chapter has highlighted changing trends among the three generations of women. Unlike that of upper-caste women, Dalit women's education was not necessarily connected with the requirements of a marriage market. Rather, education was the key to self-development, which was to be generated out of a stigmatised selfhood, and education was to be an important tool for income generation. Within the Dalit community, compared to the first-generation and most of the second-generation women, some second- and most third-generation learners had greater financial independence. Some men said that they wanted the women of their families to progress and cooperated with them in achieving this. However, this cooperation rarely materialised in everyday practice. The educated, employed woman could still be highly exploited in the home and subjected to male brutality. Yet renegotiation over duties and obligations actually occurred in the bedroom, kitchen, and during evening walks, as I will show in the next chapter, which deals with the *taarevarchi kasarat* of Dalit women within the confines of their private homes.

Notes

1 Karuna Chanana (2001b) argues that:

> experts of women's studies as well as women themselves have often taken the view that their education and employment are fundamental to their enjoyment of equal status [or equality and status]. This is because most of them assumed that better education and employment gave women an earning capacity which in turn enhanced their social status.

2 *Taar* is a metal wire, *varachi* means above and *kasarat* means exercise, hence *taarevarchi*, the balancing exercise. The phrase originates in street displays by the nomadic Dombari community, in which a metal wire or rope is tied between two tall bamboo poles that are placed in the ground at a distance of fifteen to twenty feet apart. The height of the wire can be anywhere between twenty and twenty-five feet. Children (mostly girls) and women perform the feat of tightrope walking on this wire, with or without a long bamboo balance pole in their hands. The father or husband normally plays a drum below. Perhaps, like the upper castes who make Dalits dance to their tune, Dalit men in turn make Dalit women dance to their music.

3 In what follows, I am principally drawing on Chanana's pioneering work on Indian women's education (2001a).

4 Only one, Professor Jyoti Lanjewar, had a doctorate. She is a feminist writer from Nagpur who is doing a commendable job for women through the Republican Party of India in Maharashtra (10 October 2005).

5 Gitanjali Rithe, Buddhist, Master's in Commerce.

6 The Karuna Trust, based in England, is a Buddhist NGO which has done some admirable work in the slums. It has a well-established network in Maharashtra. In the Dapodi slum, I visited Karuna's office, which runs programmes like *baalavaadi* (preschool), tailoring classes for girls and women, and a small clinic.

7 Sheelatai was very excited about this project and also offered me a significant role as chair in the management of the *pratishthan* on my return to India.

8 Indu Gade, Buddhist, Class 5, self-employed, Aundh Road, Pune.

9 Such stereotypical norms prevail in a society where a particular caste is associated with a particular occupation.

10 Lata Borade, Class 9, conducts sewing classes. Dapodi, Pune.

11 Mangala Bansode, illiterate, Matang *tamaashaa* dancer. I am grateful to Mangalatai for looking after me when I was in the village in Nagar. I thank her for her generous hospitality. She took care that I could rest amidst her troupe and talked to me at length despite her many duties. We kept shifting places for our talks in case her husband or sons overheard us. Mangalatai offered me lunch: the best *methichi bhaaji* (a vegetable dish made from *methi* leaves) and *bhaakri*, cooked on an open *chul* (hearth).

12 *Laavanis* are often bawdy or even erotic songs sung with gestures.

13 Some, like '*Ya Ravaji*', '*Pikalya Panacha, Deth Kiti Hirava*', and so on, are available on CDs sold in the market.

14 Kumud Somkuwar, after marrying Motiram Pawde, became Kumud Pawde. Changing one's name after marriage is gendered and patriarchal: only women's last names are automatically changed to the husband's last name, never the other way around. However, recently there have been some changes in this trend. Some feminists take the first names of their father and their mother as a last name; others take only their mother's first name as their last name (e.g. the notable activist writer Lata Pratibha (mother's name) Madhukar (father's name)). A friend who attempted to change her name and adopt her mother's first name was prevented from doing so by her mother, who said that such an act would signify that she had no father. Thus, the presence and name of the father is very significant.

15 I agree with Karuna Chanana's findings about the most noticeable trends in women's employment. The highest proportions of employed women are teachers. 'Their percentage of distribution in this and other professions in 1966 was: teachers, 74.70%; nurses, 7.10; clerks, 11.80; typists, 1.70; physicians, 1.00; and other professions, 2.45' (quoted in Chanana 2001a, 337).

16 David Reisman puts it very aptly: 'Women are clustered either in low status occupations or in the lowest rungs of the prestigious professions.' It is worth quoting Reisman's opinion about American women here:

> The rule is a simple one: the higher, the fewer.... Once they qualify, the higher-the-fewer rule continues to apply; the higher in terms of rank, salary, prestige, or responsibility, the fewer the number of women to be found.
>
> (Quoted in Chanana 2001a, 337)

Even Stephanie Shaw (1996, 130) points out that Black women were not an exception to this rule, and they were/are found in feminised professions, as nurses or librarians. Moreover, their commitment to providing a service and their skill in doing so determined their status as public sphere workers.

17 Chanana (2001a, 340) makes a similar argument.

18 I am once again drawing on Chanana's work (2001a, 2001b). She is of the opinion that women do not want to aim single-mindedly for top jobs. This is true of even highly educated professional women such as doctors and university professors. As a matter of fact, most of them are reluctant to describe themselves in career terms and continue to look upon themselves primarily as housewives and/or mothers. This is one of the reasons why they are reluctant to take on additional responsibilities that require investment of time and energy beyond the time limits defined by their jobs.

References

Ambedkar, B.R. 1928. Motion submitted to the Legislative Council, Bombay, on behalf of the Bahiskrita Hitakarini Sabha (Depressed Classes Institute of Bombay) to the Indian Statutory Commission, Damodar Hall, Parel, Bombay, 29 May.

——. 1991. *Dr. Babasaheb Ambedkar: Writings and Speeches*, Vol. 10, ed. Vasant Moon. Bombay: Department of Education, Government of Maharashtra.

——. 1992. *Dr. Babasaheb Ambedkar: Writings and Speeches*, Vol. 12, Part V, ed. Vasant Moon. Bombay: Department of Education, Government of Maharashtra.

Anonymous. 2002. Speech, Fergusson College, Pune, 7 February.

——. 2006. Speech, Yerawada, Pune, 2 July.

Bahishkrut Bharat. 3 June 1927.

Bansode, Mangala. 2004. Interview with the author, 1 and 15 September. Nagar and Pune.

Beteille, Andre. 1965. *Caste, Class, and Power.* Berkeley: University of California Press.

Bhalerao, Sudha. 2004. Interview with the author, 1 October. Pune.

Borade, Lata. 2002. Interview with the author, 15 July. Dapodi, Pune.

Chanana, Karuna. 2001a. *Interrogating Women's Education: Bounded Visions, Expanding Visions.* Jaipur: Rawat.

——. 2001b. Educated working women in India: Trends and issues. In *Interrogating Women's Education: Bounded Visions, Expanding Horizons.* Jaipur: Rawat Publications.

Dewey, John. 1916. *Democracy and Education: An Introduction to the Philosophy of John Dewey.* New York: Macmillan.

Gade, Indu. 2002. Interview with the author, 15–16 March. Aundh Road, Pune.

Gandhi, M.K. 1986. *Gandhi on Education: The Moral and Political Writings of Gandhi, Volume 1: Civilisation, Politics, and Religion*, ed. Raghavan Iyer. Oxford: Clarendon Press.

Hardgrave, Robert. 1969. *The Nadars of Tamilnadu: The Political Culture of a Community in Change.* Berkeley: University of California Press.

hooks, bell. 1994. *Teaching to Transgress.* New York: Routledge.

Jadhav, Kamal. 2001. Interview with the author, 16 September. Pune.

Jagtap, Baby. 2002. Interview with the author, 5 February. Sinhagad Road, Pune.

Jangam, Meera. 2004. Interview with the author, 5 August. Pune.

Jogdand, Meenakshi. 2002. Interview with the author, 13 March. Bhavani Peth, Pune.

Kadam, Jyoti. 2002. Interview with the author, 11 June. Dapodi, Pune.

Kale, Alaka. 2002. Interview with the author, 1 July. Karve Road, Pune.

Kamat, A.R. and A.G. Deshmukh. 1963. *Wastage in College Education.* Study #43. Poona: Gokhale Institute of Political Science and Economics.

Kamble, Nanda. 2001. Interview with the author, 10 August. Parvati, Pune.

Kamble, Shanta. 1986. *Majya Jalmachi Chittarkatha*, 2nd edn. Pune: Sugava.

Kapur, Promilla. 1970. *Marriage and the Working Women in India.* New Delhi: Vikas Publications.

Kemp, Sharon. 1998. Women as bullocks: A self-image of Maharashtrian village women. In *Images of Women in Maharashtrian Society*, ed. Anne Feldhaus. Albany: State University of New York Press.

Kuchekar, Hirabai. 2002. Interview with the author, 8 January. Pune.

Kuchekar, Seema. 2002. Interview with the author, 8 January. Pune.

Kuchekar, Suvarna. 2002. Interview with the author, 8 January. Sinhagad Road, Pune.

Lanjewar, Jyoti. 2005. Interview with the author, 10 October. Ambazhari, Nagpur.

Lynch, Owen. 1969. *The Politics of Untouchability: Social Mobility and Social Change in a City of India.* New York: Columbia University Press.

Mehta, Rama. 1975. White collar and blue collar family responses to population growth in India. In *Responses to Population in India: Changes in Social, Political and Economic Behaviour*, ed. Marcus F. Franda. New York: Praeger.

Meshram, Sandhya. 2004. Interview with the author, 11 September. Ramtekdi, Pune.

Mies, Maria. 1973. Class struggle or emancipation? Women's emancipation movements in Europe and the US. *Economic and Political Weekly* (15 December).

Mishra, B.B. 1961. *Indian Middle Classes: Their Growth in Modern Times.* London and New York: Oxford University Press.

Mohite, Deepa. 2001. Interview with the author, 22 May. Ramtekdi, Pune.

Mooknayak. 28 February 1920.

———. 5 June 1920.

Moré, Shalini. 2002. Interview with the author, 1 June. Sinhagad Road, Pune.

Naik, J.P. 1965. *Educational Planning in India.* Bombay: Allied Publishers.

Naik, Lalita. 2001. Interview with the author, 22 May. Ramtekdi (Swami Vivekanand Nagar), Pune.

National Commission on Dalit Human Rights. 2006. February. Available at http://ncdhr. org.in/.

Nikam, Sheela. 2005. Interview with the author, 22 October. Borivili, Mumbai.

Parekh, R.D. 1966. *Non-Urban Graduates of Gujarat.* Ahmadabad: Gujarat University.

Pawar, Prakshoti. Interview with the author, 10 April 2002. Pune.

Pawar, Ratnaprabha. 2002. Interview with the author, 10 April. Bibwewadi, Pune.

Pawar, Urmila. 2004. Interview with the author, 5–7 September. Borivili, Mumbai.

Pawde, Kumud. 1995. *Antahsphot.* Aurangabad: Anand Prakashan.

Pillewar, Amita. 2005. Interview with the author, 30 July. Karve Nagar, Pune.

Punekar, Surekha. 2002. Interview with the author, 20 September. Kasba Peth, Pune.

Ranpise, Meena. 2001. Interview with the author, 12 May. Sinhagad Road, Pune.

Rao, M.S.A. 1957. *Social Change in Malabar.* Bombay: Popular Book Depot.

Rithe, Githanjali. 2001. Interview with the author, 12 June. Ambedkar Society, Pune.

Rokade, Jyotsna. 2004. Interview with the author, 15 August. Vishrantwadi, Pune.

Rokade, Poonam. 2004. Interview with the author, 15 August. Mundhawa, Pune.

Rubin, Gayle. 1993. Thinking sex: Notes for a radical theory of the politics of sexuality. In *The Lesbian and Gay Studies Reader,* ed. Henry Abelove *et al.* New York: Routledge.

Shah, B.V. 1964. *Social Change and College Students of Gujarat.* Baroda: University of Baroda.

Shaw, Stephanie. 1996. W*hat a Woman Ought to Be and to Do: Black Professional Women Workers during the Jim Crow Era.* Chicago, IL: University of Chicago Press.

Shils, Edward. 1961. *The Intellectual between Tradition and Modernity: The Indian Situation.* The Hague: Mouton.

Shinde, Lakshmi. 2000. Interview with the author, 9 October. Parvati, Pune.

Srinivas, M.N. 1962. *Caste in Modern India and Other Essays.* Bombay: Asia Publishing House.

Times of India. 14 February 1938.

Waghmare, Swati. 2004. Interview with the author, 12 November. Vishrantwadi, Pune.

8 Education, marriage, children and family life

The history of the family is central to social history. Specifically, Dalit family life shaped and was in turn transformed by wider social and political reforms and particular intellectual, emotional and cultural contexts. Dalits' struggles with upper castes in the public sphere were reproduced in their intimate familial relations because Dalits were dominated and dominating at the same time. Thus marriage cannot be treated in isolation, because it is embedded in and interlocked with specific social, cultural, religious and economic contexts. This chapter once again breaks down the artificial distinctions between the public and private spheres, this time in terms of marriage and the family, by illustrating how the public realm continuously penetrated the private and vice versa.

Dalits' novel imagination of *family* helped to constitute the ideologies, structures and boundaries of the emerging 'middle class'. In this chapter, I trace the crafting of women's subjectivity, the community's anxiety around respectability during its passage to modern middle-class status, and the contradictory outcomes this had for women. By shifting the focus from the external processes shaping gender and community to more intrinsic ones that operated within the households of Dalits, this chapter illustrates how the interlocking technologies of family and political, economic and social relations indeed constituted each other. Building on Chapter 4, I demonstrate how the expectations of the community and the wider public entered into the family home, directing and sometimes also constraining marital conjugal relationships and conduct. I outline how and why the family and marriage became a site of struggle for Dalit women and men. In accordance with changing social, political and economic forces, the colonial state and reformers felt the need to reassemble patriarchies in the early twentieth century. Both external forces in society and internal, familial processes led to the conflict between traditional authority structures and patriarchies and reformulations of Dalit women's position.

Kumud Pawde was very straightforward about her marital relationship; she chuckled and said with delight, 'He did not accept me; I accepted him' (2005). By contrast, Hirabai Kuchekar (2002) was very shy. Some Dalit women who had struggled very determinedly throughout their lives melted instantly when the conversation turned to their marital lives, but many of them were also understandably reluctant to air their dirty laundry in public. They remembered their weddings, reflected on their marital relationships, and narrated their stories of their daily grind. Marriage proved a difficult realm of study. It was not easy to recover the *kharepanaa* (truth) about marital history and intimate conjugal relations. The conversation aroused very different emotions: joy, sorrow, compromise, adjustment, rebellion and peace.

Although Dalit male reformers challenged caste structures and Brahmani patriarchy, they also embraced some patriarchal norms and reproduced gendered idioms, as previous chapters have demonstrated. Women and men embraced the ideals of modernity and traversed the democratisation of education, proper marriage and conjugal relationships, and modern motherhood. Restructuring the family with women as companionate wives, good mothers and class socialisers was important to them. Yet in Ambedkar we come across some novel and radical notions of gender and conjugality. He emphasised a new form of life for women and articulated a *double task* – both individual and collective. Women were to be fully autonomous human subjects and choose their partners; at the same time, conjugality was also intricately linked to the interests of the community. Thus, he and other Dalit radicals transcended the false dichotomies of the private and public and instead saw both as imbricated in the same total context.

According to Dalit radicals, women and men were to be helpmeets to one another. As such, they were to carry out their domestic and community roles in equal measure. Yet there were some constraints, because Dalit radicals, including Ambedkar, displayed patriarchal anxiety and made family the primary concern of women. In this manner, the family thus became a major site of conflict as Dalits entered the middle-class private sphere. Certainly, Dalit women were not enjoying 'more freedom', as some elite feminists would like to believe.

In this chapter, my first aim is to explore the most intrinsic constellation of deeply intimate practices in educated Dalit women's lives: marriage, companionship and the language of romantic love, as well as contradictions around gender. Second, I investigate their intense struggles to nurture in their children certain talents and experiences. I thus uncover the ways which Dalit women intended, insisted on, and engaged in the process of concertedly cultivating new cultural capital and activated a habitus. They formed a set of cultural repertoires about how their children should be raised. This chapter will explore why education, which at one level successfully contributed to Dalit women's emancipation, also turned into a mixed blessing. It seeks to illustrate how education also socialised many Dalit women to be more obedient and dependent. It further isolated them from their own families as well as from the lower classes. Yet in thinking about their marital relationships during our conversations, many of the Dalit women with whom I spoke sharpened their criticality and opened up different choices for themselves. Some experiences are threaded through the lives of all married women; nevertheless, there were Dalit-specific problems.

To untangle the complicated familial lives of Dalit women, this chapter is divided into three sections. The first section illuminates male Dalit leaders' ideas about the intimate: marriage and childrearing. I deal with their most radical techniques, which foregrounded women's problems, such as childcare, and preserved their human dignity. The second section delves deeply into the actual experiences of educated Dalit women, who attempted to connect with their leaders' ideas, continually resisted patriarchy, and at times accepted their subordinate position by performing a *taarevarchi kasarat* (balancing act). The final section focuses on Dalit women's struggles in constructing cultivated childhoods. In line with the modern ideals of education, women were significant social and potential cultural transmitters for future generations. They strove to build social and cultural capital afresh for their children.[1]

Rethinking intimacy, family and marriage

By interlinking issues of sexuality, caste, class, gender, race and education, Dalit activists differed from colonialists, nationalists and 'liberal feminists', and aligned themselves with post-colonial feminist theorists of 'intersectionality'. Although, to an extent, Dalit radicals embraced Victorian and Brahmani ideals of womanhood, they also radically departed from them. Hence, from the beginning of the twentieth century, they made determined efforts to school Dalit girls, looking upon them as individual and collective historical agents. Their educational rhetoric penetrated deeper. By educating themselves and instilling ambition in their children, Dalit women shaped their political consciousness and built their own *svaavalamban* (self-reliance), *pratishtha* (honour and dignity) and *aatma vishvaas* (self-confidence), as well as that of the Dalit community as a whole. With this *double task*, women were to be very much in the public political space, provide leadership to the community, and enjoy freedom at home. Although at times treated as 'ornaments of the community' (Ambedkar 1936), Dalit women had a real and explicit political value, not merely a symbolic one.

In this manner, Dalit spokespersons went beyond the instrumental value of women's education. Their agenda for educating women severely critiqued the nationalist and women's movement programmes, which saw women as 'helpmeets' for the new class of Indian men who were also responsible for nurturing the private, spiritual space (Chakravarti 1998; Chatterjee 1989). The 'new woman' paradigm of Hindu reformers, confined to Brahman women, failed to incorporate the social, political and educational struggles of Dalits, particularly Dalit women.

However, Dalits, including Ambedkar, also wanted women's roles to be central to family life. He intricately intertwined the Enlightenment concepts of individual rights, companionate love and domestic management with normative Indian ideals of devotion to family, thus producing a dyadic Dalit couplet. These struggles led to changes in marriage forms through which non-Brahman and Dalit leaders in Maharashtra and south India sought to modernise their communities. They used new models of family and marriage (for example, the *Satyashodhak* marriage form) in order to discuss their ethico-political personhood (Rao 2005; Hodges 2005). These alternative forms also provided an idiom of frugality as against wasteful expenses. But these norms of democratisation rooted in modernity – the French Revolution and Western European industrial-isation – though very productive, were not beneficial to all. These norms were twisted and turned by Dalit families who struggled with the ideas of individual and the family. Many families did not champion the value of independent, auto-nomous, rights-oriented women.

Dalits politicised the practice of marriage and discussed it in public pro-grammes. By challenging caste orthodoxy as well as Dalit patriarchy, Dalit spokespersons reimagined and commented on the private lives of Dalit women as being based on mutual desire. In this manner, they sought to emancipate Dalit women both in the political, private and public spheres. Ambedkar even ceased to consider marriage compulsory, though he delayed it rather than completely ruling it out. He argued that intermarriage was the only way to annihilate caste, because it could break down the relationship between the maintenance of caste purity and the control of women's sexuality. During the Mahad Satyagraha of 25 December 1927, he forcefully articulated that inter-caste marriages could lead to the establishment of true equality:

> It is a common experience that inter-dining has not succeeded in killing the spirit of caste and the consciousness of caste. I am convinced that the real remedy is intermarriage.... Where society is already well-knit by other ties, marriage is an ordinary incident of life. But where society is cut asunder, marriage as a binding force becomes a matter of urgent necessity. The real remedy for breaking caste is intermarriage. *Nothing else will serve as the solvent of caste.*
>
> (Ambedkar 1979, 67, emphasis in original)

Thus breaking the caste rules of kinship, along with emphasising the sexual underpinnings of caste society, was important to Ambedkar. Radical inter-caste marriages based on choice were one way to completely transform Hindus and challenge the centrality of caste practices. Yet, as noted in Chapter 4, Ambedkar was not the first one to broach the topic.

Many second- and third-generation women, including Sheela Nikam, Kumud Pawde and Prakshoti Pawar, supported inter-caste marriages. Kumudtai affirmed:

> We also believe in inter-caste marriages and in national integration. We our-selves have set an example for our children. One *suun* [daughter-in-law] is a Gujarati Bania. Amit's wife was his classmate in engineering, she is a Bud-dhist. Another son got in touch with a Khatri from UP. When she was here she bowed to all with her head covered by her *pallu* [veil]. My mother-in-law is a Maratha and this girl gets along very well with her.
>
> (Pawde 2005)[2]

Similarly, Sheelatai (Nikam 2005), who had a low level of literacy, had allowed her son to marry outside the community. She reported:

My eldest daughter-in-law is a Maratha and she wanted to have this Ganapati portrait in the living room. I allowed her despite my Buddhist faith and all the taunting from Dalits. I don't say anything to them, but make them realise that they cannot force others and they are mistaken.[3]

Thus, Kumudtai and Sheelatai were successful in limiting endogamous marriages. Yet they also illustrated that most inter-caste marriages were hypergamous and only rarely hypogamous: they were between Dalit men and upper-caste women, rarely the other way around. While these Dalit families vehemently transgressed caste discipline and questioned its power, many others could not bring themselves to be so radical. They insisted on endogamous and intrareligious marriages: while marriages between Mahar Hindus and Buddhists were acceptable, marriages with Mahar Christians were not. In this way, they marginalised Dalit Christians. (A quick glance at Buddhist matrimonial columns provides good evidence.) Moreover, some women also complained about other limitations: for example, the social exclusion of their mixed-caste children.

However, like some upper castes, one reason why some middle-class Dalit women aspired to higher education was indeed to fetch 'good husbands'. Their understanding of what constituted a 'good' marriage was often informed by a belief that Brahman households provided a model for 'egalitarian' and 'liberal' practice. They contrasted the oppressive patriarchy of the Dalit home with that of an idealised 'Brahman' family life.

Yet, as history has shown, upper castes and Dalits borrowed heavily from each other in social terms. They were involved in sanskritisation and Dalitisation at the same time. There were vibrant discussions on marriage among Dalits that also addressed the strain of weddings on financial resources. Sitaram Namdeo Shivtarkar, president of the Bahishkrut Samaaj Parishad, held in Belgaum district in 1929, argued:

> Dalits are spending enormously on marriages. Many times they are in debt and each caste leader should work and stop these practices. The age of marriage should be fixed at a minimum of twenty-two for boys and sixteen for girls.
>
> (Quoted in Pawar and Moon 1989, 88)

He continued, 'Also, instead of spending on ostentatious weddings, we should spend it on our children's education. Like some bad customs, we also have good customs of divorce and remarriage. Some upper-caste Hindus are now finding these useful' (*Bahishkrut Bharat*, 29 March 1929).

Thus, Shivtarkar underscored marriage reforms, arguing, most importantly, that Dalit customs of divorce and remarriage established the autonomy of Dalit women in comparison to upper-caste women. Such social practices also underlined Dalit egalitarianism. On the one hand, unlike upper-caste women, Dalit women could divorce and remarry; on the other hand, Brahmanical values held widow remarriage in disrepute and, when they remarried, they occupied a lower status and were excluded from inheritance rights. In fact, liberal reformers like M.G. Ranade intervened to uphold Brahmani caste practices and promote greater social conservatism. Shivtarkar noted that caste Hindus were resorting to adopting certain non-Brahman practices, like divorce, which they had earlier deliberately negated.

Moreover, Shivtarkar's financial lament was echoed in M.G. Bhagat's sociological study of Dalits in early 1930s Mumbai. He found that Dalits did not have a permanent source of income; their monthly income averaged less than ten rupees, which was far below the average standard of living. They were so poor that they were forced to resort to begging, yet they borrowed money for extravagant weddings and were mostly in debt. Money-lenders exploited them thoroughly (Bhagat 1935, 63–77). Dalit wedding celebrations were grand feasts because people could enjoy them only occasionally. Yet, according to Shivtarkar, spending on education was more important than luxurious weddings and the feasts that followed.

Like the *Satyashodhak* and Self-Respect marriages, Dalits questioned elaborate Brahmani rituals and decided that their weddings were to be performed using simple rites, conducted by their own priests. They thus expelled the Brahman priest. These attempts to challenge the Brahmans' sacerdotal power continued through folk performances and publications as well as political gatherings, and instilled great confidence in the Dalit community as a whole.

The Mahar Panch Committee, after considering the problematic customs of dowry and incurred debts, resolved that marriage expenses should not exceed a maximum of sixteen rupees (Pawar and Moon 1989, 89). The custom of dowry, which was reinforced by the Brahmo Marriage Act of 1873, affected not only the upper castes but also some Dalits. Although almost all educated women understood the thriving wedding industry, with its ensuing waste and financial pressures, they were complicit in the transactions of the marriage market. Many emphasised that they did not give or take any dowry: they only 'gifted' the groom a gold chain or wedding ring or some cash. Dowry, instead of the earlier bride-price and exchange of gifts, once again became customary as Dalits spent money on their sons' education and sought to recover these expenses from the bride's family.

Another immoral practice Dalits shared with upper-caste Hindus was that of child marriage. In a speech at Elphinstone College, Mumbai in 1938, Ambedkar advised Dalits to stop this practice. On 20 July 1942, he attended the All India Depressed Classes Women's Conference (Mahilaa Parishad) at Nagpur (under the presidency of Mrs Donde) and attacked it again, emphasising the significance of women's organisations and testifying that women were very active in the Dalit movement (Ambedkar 2002, 425).

Ambedkar, like Periyar, was confident that women would have to emancipate themselves. He had a sharp awareness of the moral and material pressures in women's lives, as well as of gendered practices in the community to select brides and bridegrooms. By constructing the husband as sexual partner, enforcing the equality of husband and wife, and promoting companionate marriages, Ambedkar argued for Dalit women's individual subjectivity.

Considering the domestic and social circumstances of women, he was not arguing for abstract or 'modern' principles of equality or rights, but for more concrete changes. He objected to the normative position accorded to women in the family and underscored that 'women have been denied the right [to determine their marriage and the age/time for it] and the right to choose their husband too'. He opined that 'a woman is an individual and she has her own rights which have to be respected' (Ambedkar 2002, 89). He also pointed out that 'parents always take into consideration the man's opinion of the woman he wants in his life; however, nobody bothers about the woman, and many a times beautiful girls have been made to tie the marriage knot with ugly men' (Ambedkar 2002, 89; Pawar and Moon 1989). Ambedkar was distinctive because he commented on Dalit women's choice, individualism, personal freedom and autonomy. Nonetheless, Dalits have in general taken a long time to come around to such a view. Very few first- and only some second-generation educated women enjoyed the right to choose their partners. The trend nonetheless changed with many of the second- and third-generation learners, who were granted more freedom to choose their husbands.

In this manner, marriage became a site of propaganda for social reformers attacking the caste hierarchy and restrictions on women's sexuality. Very few male radicals granted partnership and agency to women in general and Dalit women in particular. Denying that marriage was a sacrament to be encumbered with religious rituals, they deemed it a contract that involved mutual consent and could be ended by divorce, and argued that both men and women could remarry. By contrast, conjugality in both the Brahman and Victorian senses was based on the apparent absolutism of one partner and the total subordination of the other. Just as the king reigned over his dominion, so the head of the household (*kartaa*) ruled over his family. Although nationalists tied intimate conjugality to the nationalist agenda, leaders like Gandhi and Ambedkar undermined this Hindu ideal by bringing women out into the public sphere of politics. Ambedkar, unlike Gandhi, argued for woman's equality with men and for conjugal relationships based on equality. For him, like Phule and Periyar, marriage could also be inter-caste. By contrast, Gandhi could not accept such inter-religious or inter-caste marriages; however, later on he adopted a radical practice of participating in inter-caste marriages alone.

Unlike upper-caste reformers, who suggested early marriages for girls, for Ambedkar, marriage was a 'liability'. At the Mahilaa Parishad held in 1942 in Nagpur he said,

Don't be in a hurry for marriage, it *hinders* a girl's progress. Marriage is responsibility. It involves economic responsibility and unless the couple is ready for this, *tyanchyaavar lagna laadu nakaa* [don't thrust marriage upon them].

(Ambedkar 2002, 426, emphasis added)

Ambedkar was thus not opposed to marriage, so long as it was entered into at a relatively mature age so as not to impede a girl's educational progress. He also expected a relationship of friendship and equality in married couples. He continued:

> The most important thing is that after marriage every girl should assist her husband like a friend. However, she should underscore *samataa* [equality] in their relationship and *gulaamaasaarkhi vaganyas tine khambirpane nakaar dyavaa* [refuse forcefully to act like a slave]. If you act on this advice you will attain high *maansanmaan va kirti* [respect and honour]. Further, you will also improve the honour, prestige, [and dignity] of the Dalit classes.
>
> (Ambedkar 2002, 427; Pawar and Moon 1989, 89)

After marriage a woman and man were to be friends and equal partners, like comrades in organisations. This was immensely relevant to improving the dignity and pride of women and the community. Yet there were limitations, because the woman was to responsibly assist her husband. Further, *she* was to befriend *him*, and with these actions she was burdened with the improvement of not only her honour and dignity but that of her husband and of the Dalit community as a whole.

Figure 8.1 Organised Buddhist women dressed in white at the Dhammadiksha Suvarna Jayanti Bauddha Mahila Sammelan (Buddhist Women's Conference to commemorate and celebrate the golden jubilee of the conversion to Buddhism), Nagpur, 10 October 2005 (photo by author).

Ambedkar embraced Buddhism at a meeting in 1956, in which he gave twenty-two vows to the Buddhists, and his fight against atrocities towards women was also reflected through the prism of neo-Buddhism. The principles of freedom and access to knowledge for women embedded within it played a significant role for Dalit women. Domestic violence was intertwined with the alcoholism that was widespread among Dalit men, and one of the Buddhist vows, 'I shall abstain from alcohol', brought new hope to Dalit women. Ambedkar asked women not to feed their spouses and sons if they were drunkards. He said that Buddha gave equal status to women alongside men and was a pioneer in the cause of women's liberation: 'Manu, in fact, was responsible for the degradation of women' (Ambedkar 1965, 18; see also Ambedkar 1987, 429–437). Dalit-Buddhist women reinforced Ambedkar's call at the Dhammadiksha Suvarna Jayanti Bauddha Mahila Sammelan (Golden Jubilee of the Conversion to Buddhism, Buddhist Women's Conference), held in Nagpur on 10 October 2005. They praised the gender equality of Buddhism and invited Buddhists to live up to this humanitarian ideal, given that many women were still terrorised by domestic violence within their families.

Most significantly, by granting women choice with regard to marriage and its timing, birth control and family size, Ambedkar sought to make them autonomous. As a Labour Minister he argued in favour of maternity benefits. He also argued in his 1936 Independent Labour Party (ILP) election manifesto that overpopulation was the major cause of poverty in India. The ILP was perhaps the only party that incorporated this view into its election manifesto.[4]

Ambedkar's views on birth control, like many of his positions, conflicted with Gandhi's. While Gandhi did discuss contraception he was opposed to any artificial means of birth control, thus emphasising his faith in self-control. Some members of the Hindu Mahasabha, Muslims and Catholics – though not Christians in general – also opposed birth control, but radicals like R.D. Karve, Ambedkar and Periyar analysed the issue in materialist socio-economic rather than moral terms. Family planning and contraception were not for population control alone: they protected the woman's health and granted her some measure of leisure from domestic drudgery. Ambedkar (1997, 290) believed that every individual should enjoy leisure time in order to make possible a life of culture. Significantly, by 'lessening toil and efforts necessary for satisfying physical wants' (291), a Dalit could live worthily. Ambedkar thus placed great confidence in the masses, asserting that, though illiterate, they were intelligent enough to understand their own interests. Women could thus stop toiling ceaselessly and contribute to constructing culture.

On 10 November 1938, in the Bombay Legislative Assembly, Ambedkar steered an unofficial resolution regarding measures for birth control. In a December 1938 speech to the students of Elphinstone College, he argued:

> Several of you might get married. But what are you going to do after marriage? A heavy responsibility rests on your shoulders. I had a very poor childhood and my parents gave birth to fourteen children. I went to Elphinstone barefoot and

used my father's torn coat. I hold my father responsible for all this misery. Now this responsibility rests on you as well as on women. You should see that what I say is meant not only for males but also for females. This is a matter of social welfare and you should think deeply about it. How far will you provide education and other facilities to five or six offspring? So you should consider that leading a brutish life is against humanity.

(Quoted in Mangudkar 1976, 63–64)

Ambedkar argued for smaller families that provided personal freedom to women. He also explained the inverted ratio between the size of a family and its poverty and argued that large numbers of children in a family hindered Dalits' progress: 'Those who marry should remember that producing many children is a *dushta krutya* [evil act]. Every parent is responsible for providing *chaangali paristhiti* [better circumstances] to their children' (Ambedkar 2002, 427). Hence, he underlined that Dalits should strive to have healthy children. He argued that the survival rate of children (and women) was more important than the birth rate (Mangudkar 1976, 63), and that birth control would go a long way in improving the health and financial conditions of the Scheduled Castes. Moreover, he affirmed women's autonomy by defending the lawsuit of R.D. Karve, a birth control advocate and sexologist.[5]

Many first- and second-generation Dalit women understood the challenges of raising children and, in contrast with their parents, restricted their numbers of children. The Meshram, Waghmare and Ranpise families all had only one child, but many Dalits, like non-Dalits, continued to prefer male children, a quest that led to higher birth rates. There were some exceptions. For example, Kumud Pawde wanted a daughter: 'In those days it was all right to have more children. I was craving a daughter, and I could have her only after three sons, so four children for me' (2005).

Ambedkar argued with men for ignoring the feelings of women and emphasised women's personal freedom. When his party worker in Solapur announced that he was going to marry for a second time at the age of fifty-six because he and his first wife could not have children, Ambedkar responded, 'You cannot produce a child, if a fault lies with you. If your wife thinks of marrying another man for this, will you tolerate that? A woman also wants a child, like you; her desire is probably stronger' (Pawar and Moon 1989, 91). Ambedkar thus gave absolute priority to conjugality over maternity and emphasised women's need for autonomous self-development. He emphasised complete equality between women and men, with relations between them to be entirely voluntary and therefore open to change. Through a programme of reform of property, marriage and divorce laws, Ambedkar sought to question the prevailing Hindu law (embodied in the Hindu Code Bill of the 1950s), which was patriarchal and denied women certain fundamental rights. He strongly advocated gender equality, but faced opposition from many who could not subscribe to the idea of women's rights to property and divorce, the abolition of caste in the matter of marriage and adoption, and the prescription of monogamy.

Simultaneously, however, Ambedkar also emphasised a woman's central role in *her* family life and *her* support to her husband. On the one hand, this focus on the family confined women largely to the domestic sphere and controlled their emancipation. On the other, it led to the reformulation of the reproduction of social relations, which involved women as key players. Thus, unlike upper-caste reformers, Ambedkar did not then create a dichotomy between the social and political and confine women to the social. Instead, for Dalit women, the social penetrated formal and informal political struggles; women annexed new arenas of life. Yet this strategy created paradoxes for women within the movement. Through education, Ambedkar sought to link the emancipation of Dalit women with the internal transformation of the culture and ethos of the family.

His agenda of 'modernisation', or rather democratisation, was slightly limited, but his critique was very pointed and his efforts were effective. Most importantly, Ambedkar had progressive ideas on gender and agreed with many modern feminists' conceptualisations. Paradoxically, however, he could not escape the Victorian-Brahman image of the traditional 'power' and 'purity' of womanhood, as exemplified by the mother situated in the home environment. He was trying to grapple with many dynamic processes; he argued for women's autonomy and at the same time contained their full emancipation. His radical views operated within certain middle-class boundaries, yet even this limited liberalism was a boon to many Dalit women. Although he challenged patriarchy, patriarchal values lay dormant within the movement and even the radical Dalit Panthers could not strike at the roots of its ubiquitous structure. To further grasp the shifting, complicated and dialectical relationship between Dalit radicalism and the woman question, I will turn now to analysing the actual everyday experiences of Dalit wives.

Shifting femininities and masculinities: Dalits' contradictions around gender

Once I got to know my interlocutors, after weaving through their school and college experiences, parental stories and jobs, I delved into their experiences of marital life and childrearing. Men generally looked down upon women; they dominated them in order to exercise power they may not have been able to exercise elsewhere. By restricting women they reconstituted the existing system and reinforced gender discrimination and gender-differentiated family roles in which women were largely restricted to the home. It was difficult to discuss these questions in the presence of their in-laws and husbands. We talked about these relations only after we had reached a certain level of comfort, especially towards the end of our dialogues. Sometimes it took me several hours and, at times, several meetings to obtain such information; only then could I enter such sequestered spaces in the ideas, actions and lives of Dalit women.

One woman could not control her tears. Her husband was encircling us to check whether his wife abused him verbally in the course of the interview. She could not speak freely in his presence and decided to take me to her bedroom in order to talk to me unhindered. Other women suggested that discussion of marriage was out of bounds, citing in a critical tone the autobiography of Urmilatai, who had described her wedding night (U. Pawar 2004). They condemned her for her lack of propriety and discretion, and suggested that she had described the wedding night in order to gain popularity. Nonetheless, Urmilatai told me that she was not ashamed of what she had said or written.

A few women shared their fantasies about marriage and men. These conversations were very rare, though, and women did not openly express their love. Manini Pawar, a second-generation woman, could not control her emotions and spoke at great length about her expectations of her marriage, the tensions within the couple's romantic love, and her disappointments (Pawar and Pawar 2004). Like others, she was struggling to lead a peaceful, healthy and happy married life.

Manini's sister Malavika had a 'love-marriage': she was involved in a relationship with her present husband before they were married. She talked about the alternative marriage which her parents, who did not approve of her relationship, or even the idea of a love-marriage, wanted to force upon her – though later on they had to accede to Malavika's wishes. Although the community harboured some rigid rules of endogamous marriage, caste and religious rules were sometimes broken. Women made critical choices through inter-caste and inter-religious marriages. Malavika reported that it was quite difficult to adjust to her north Indian in-laws; yet, in contrast to her parents' relationship, she has a friendly relationship with her husband. Like many second- and-third-generation learners, she emphasised more egalitarian gender relations and the flexibility of domestic duties. Malavika continued:

> I do find a lot of difference between my parents' married life and mine. There was a lack of friendship in their relationship. I think it was that generation, those times, when the love relationship was ironed out. However, on the whole, I do think that my parents did have a good relationship. My father was less educated than my mother. They had ego problems. Unlike us, they never sat calmly together to handle any problems. Husbands dominate universally; *purushpradhaan sanskruti aahech* [patriarchy is a prevalent phenomenon]; but at least my husband sits with me and makes efforts to make me understand.
>
> (Pawar 2004)

As with other second- and third-generation women, for Malavika conjugality was predicated on equality between partners. Ultimately, however, she blanketed her real emotions and said she was 'fine' with her in-laws and her husband. She accepted her subordinate position as might any other woman. Not many women aimed overtly to subvert gendered relationships inside the family. During our conversation Malavika attended to her unending domestic labour by working swiftly and adroitly that evening and the subsequent morning: cooking, cleaning, and managing her kids, her computer and the maid.

In contrast to Malavika's love-marriage, Manini had had an arranged marriage:

> It was rosy in the beginning as it always is. However, I realise how I slog every day. He does not offer any help with housework; now it is difficult to end these bad habits because I have encouraged them. I always compromise because I do not want any fights. In my childhood I did not understand the gravity, sensitivity and intensity of this relationship. I blamed my mother then. However, I understand it when I face it and have to live it, *prakar-shaane jaanavata malaa* [I feel it poignantly]. But I still want to be with him.
>
> (Pawar 2004)

Manini was trying to perform her *taarevarchi kasrat* by balancing her hobbies, job, husband and home. Her prime responsibility was to run the household, because her husband was a freelancer with no regular income. She was always concerned about the health and well-being of her family. One woman reported that her husband also did not like her mixing with other men (Anonymous 2004). While men were free as birds[6] and could easily mix with other women and at times even make sexual overtures, patriarchy regulated women's movement in the public as well as the private sphere. Sexual and caste purity were to be maintained *mainly* by women.

Significantly, all the educated Dalit women with whom I spoke were married to educated Dalit men. As a rule, the husbands were better educated than their wives. Although they were possibly misguided, some Dalit parents believed that their daughters' marriage to educated and employed Dalit men would bring prosperity to them. Modern, middle-class Dalit men sought educated, sufficiently trained women to nurture their progeny. Therefore, education and employment were prime factors for many Dalit women's successful marriage bids, and this was also a big step for these families towards acquiring middle-class status. My second- and third-generation interlocutors fit mainly into this category.

Maya (Mane 2005),[7] Manini, Malavika, Urmilatai, and many others agreed that education served as a good qualification to find educated and well-employed men. It did provide them with a sense of independence and autonomy, and helped them to challenge their parents, in-laws or husbands – to an extent. Nonetheless, they had to contend with similar forces of domination inside and outside the home. Others agreed that men helped with domestic chores as well as with tackling in-laws. Although it was no easy task, many women developed self-assertion to some extent.

By contrast, other women argued that education did not play a constructive role in marital life. Women were to become genteel *gruhinis* alone; education was to facilitate such a transformation among 'unruly' Dalit women. But some women did not agree with such an elite ideal. Shantabai Bhalerao reported: '*Patishi patale nahi* [I could not get along with my husband] because he wanted *phakta gruhini* [only a ladylike wife]' (quoted in Hatekar 1999, 74). Her marriage had thus broken down. Some women believed that uneducated couples got along better than educated ones. Dr Shalini Moré (2002) thus stated:

> I do not think education plays any role in marital life; it is basically your understanding, your sharing and cooperation that matters. Were my parents educated? No. My husband comes home, relaxes, watches the TV, and at times we go out. I think that a woman must be very understanding and adjusting if she wants her family to be happy and do well. She is the one responsible for it.

Thus she underlined that by being moderate and compromising, a woman played a central role in a marriage. Higher education made this harder, because women believed in their ideas and wanted to act on them but ultimately failed to do so.

While Shalini had some share of love, Sheela Nikam's husband totally deprived her of it. She thus showered all her love on her children, her *chaaphaa* (jasmine) tree and most significantly her association with the *ferivaalya* (hawkers) (Nikam 2005). For Sheelatai the discussion of her social projects was more exciting than her married life. She went silent when I asked about her husband. Only after we had spent several hours talking about her career as she advanced from *bhaajipoli vaali bai* (lunch-box maker) to president of the Hawkers' Union of Mumbai did she confide in me:

> I do not have time to cry for Sheela Nikam. I feel for the *chaaphaa* tree that is alone, he [the tree] is alone today. He wanted me to take care of him. I have something of a companion in life for once.... If it was any male, people would have called me names. I always feel departed from him, he was something to me, *tyacha tharatharana, paavsaat bhijana* [his shivering, his drenching in the rain]; he was like a yogi standing there all alone. It was awful to see him in the blazing sun, at times only very red flowers, at times, leaves, small leaves, no flowers.... He was beautiful in that too, just blooming.
>
> (Nikam 2005)

The *chaaphaa* tree was Sheelatai's lover. The gender-neutral tree became a masculine figure – *he* stood tall and firm and battled the rain and cold, *he* blossomed when he was happy, to make her happy. She broke down in tears while talking about her companion, whom she loved deeply.

Some Dalit women re-inscribed the existence of the vices of polygamy. Men sometimes married for a second time if the first wife was barren. To an extent, previous divorce practices were contained as Dalits became upwardly mobile. Emphasising their respectability meant that many Dalit women remained married for life, whereas men were free to take more than one wife if they had the means or inclination to do so. The indissolubility of a monogamous marriage was, in effect, binding on the women alone; they had limited alternatives.

Chitratai's husband was *absent*, because he had left her and married another woman. However, her middle-class status did not allow her to discard her *mangalsutra*. She also donned it for her safety, both inside and outside the Dalit community. Thus the black-beaded necklace acted as a shield for women, helping them to avoid sexual advances from men. The size and length of the necklace also mattered (as it did to the *tamaashaa* dancers in the previous chapter). Chitratai (not her real name) continued to be regarded as her unfaithful husband's property. She became very emotional as she continued:

> Every man has two women in his life: one is the actual wife and the other is the dream woman. He always has a Madhuri Dixit [a popular female Bollywood star] in his mind. This someone is whom he likes. He does not talk to his wife, though. That is his goddess. That cannot be spoken, but he is so happy with her in his own mind. Yes, women have it too. And if men go to the bar, nowadays the employed women can go to hotels. Again, a woman has *maryaadaa* [limits], a man does not. My husband drank liquor; I was beaten up and kicked even when I was pregnant. Later, when my children started growing older, I had an attack of tuberculosis and had surgery. My husband was already with another woman by then and he still lives with her. They have children too. He visits us sometimes, but there is nothing between us.

> (Chitratai 2005)

The middle-class Hindu ideal of marriage, the unacceptability of divorce and the agony of perpetual oppression by men thus affected many women.

The matter often became more complicated once a woman was married and living with her in-laws. Notions of the correct role of the family man, the use of respectful terms for husbands – *aaho* (the respectful 'you') – impregnated the private sphere of the home. Meena Ranpise thus said that although her husband helped her in the kitchen, her in-laws did not know this, because they would never approve of the man working in the kitchen or even helping his wife. By contrast, however, other second- and third-generation women sought divorce if their marriages were not successful. My interaction with a Buddhist elder who ran a marriage bureau revealed that many divorced Buddhist women were seeking men. They were becoming more assertive and prioritising their individuality before their families. Marrying a second time was not a stigma to them.

Many women were very happy that they had found me to talk to about their lives. They narrated their suppressed lives, their beatings, their everyday fights and resistance. Wife-beating and terrorisation of women repeatedly emerged as important issues. Physical violence within the family played a key role in keeping women oppressed and exploited. It was routine in the lives of many women, though not everybody provided details. Meera Jangam's mother, for example, had her share of problems: a drunkard for a husband and beatings every evening, after a miserable day spent scavenging in street garbage for *kaagad-kaach-patra* (scrap paper, glass and tin pieces that could be sold, recycled or used) (Gaikwad 2004). Despite labouring daily for their families, such women did not receive any love, understanding, care or warmth. They silently endured the beatings – but sometimes they did hit back. At times the husbands got very violent and almost killed them. Even the pioneering feminist Babytai Kamble recalled that '*maarhaan, bhaandan, radaarad, aani upaas, hey aamche rojache khuraak* [beatings, fights, crying, and starvation were our everyday nutrition]' (quoted in Hatekar 1999, 74).

Taking into consideration their violent lives, many Dalit women felt that Brahman households were 'different', that is, progressive in terms of women's rights, and hence sought to learn from and imitate them. This was surprising because many Brahman women romanticised Dalit women's lives and believed in turn that they were the ones who suffered the most oppressive forms of patriarchy and that lower-caste women had the privileges of drinking, smoking, beating their husbands and moving around freely in public. Shalini Moré (2002), Smita Khedkar (2002)[8] and others were torn between overlapping patriarchies and felt that they had much to learn from Brahmans, including their conduct in marital life. Shalinitai said:

> Brahman women are more dominating. In our families the males always say how the wives are incompetent and dependent, and discourage them. They say: *Tulaa hey samajanaar naahi, tu naahi karu shakanaar hey* [You will not understand this, you will not be able to do this]. Children listen to this and say the same to the mother. Maybe the next generation will do something.
>
> (Moré 2002)

Shalinitai was very disturbed by the treatment her sons and her husband meted out to her. She was a medical doctor like her husband and her sons, yet they little valued her labour and achievements. She, along with others, suggested that educated Dalit men should be cognisant of how they committed psychological and symbolic violence and oppressed women. As it was, Shalini's husband's and sons' discouraging treatment paralleled the behaviour of upper-caste men towards Dalit men and women, and of the coloniser towards the colonised. In this manner, wider caste and public relations were reproduced within the family. In a similar vein, Swati's mother interjected:

> With the Brahmans the situation is different. The males are dominated and they see to it that they also dominate their wives by taking them into confidence and making them do what they themselves want, in a comfortable manner, using their sweet tongue. Our males fight and their egos are very big. They will not touch housework and expect things to be done fast.
>
> (S. Waghmare 2004)

Thus, once again the Waghmare family underlined the *difference* between Dalit and upper-caste men. Some women saw Brahman women as dominating, and others saw men as dominating. They ignored, however, the ways in which Brahman women were subjected to 'softer' oppression and seemed to harbour an uncompromising belief in Brahmani values and practices, which they emphasised were more egalitarian, companionate and liberal than those of Dalit households.

Notwithstanding a few notable exceptions, even Dalit men, including some scholars at an academic conference held in 2008, harboured reverent notions that upper-caste – especially Brahman – women were 'fair', 'beautiful' and very 'articulate', and therefore attractive. Deeply implicit in this declaration was the allegation that Dalit women are dark, ugly and inarticulate. According to these Dalit men, this was the main reason for increasing sexual liaisons and marriages between Dalit men and Brahman women; they drew parallels with the increasing number of marriages between African American men and white women in the United States.[9] Most significantly, such declarations by Dalit male scholars use Dalit women as a site upon which to claim their fitness as intellectuals. Similarly to Dalit males, some African American men have expressed reverence for white women's beauty; Assata Shakur argues that Black men say that 'white women are sweeter, Black women are evil; white women are more understanding, Black women are more demanding' (Shakur 1987, 112).

The conference discussion was deeply significant due to its emergence in a particularly academic context – a setting in which 'new knowledge' is produced and Dalit lives are debated by scholars. Some Dalit men's misogynist objectification of Dalit women found its source in the larger Brahmani patriarchal structure of Indian society. It is also a common thing for men to downgrade women. It is ironic, indeed, that some lower-caste scholars with rich, progressive political histories of breaking caste codes and Brahmani hegemony once again emulated and reproduced a similar bio-genetic map of inequality between Brahman women and Dalit women. Moreover, they failed to understand that notions of 'beauty' and 'articulation' are very subjective.

By contrast, many second- and third-generation women like Amita Pillewar, Suvarna Kuchekar, Janhavi Chavan, Prakshoti Pawar, Meena Ranpise and others thought that there was no major difference between Dalit and Brahman families. Brahman families also had strong patriarchal arrangements and engaged in domestic fights, but they believed that women in Brahman households were in a more dominant position. Moreover, they agreed that as Dalits they did not have to suffer the practices of dowry, of *purdah*, of enforced widowhood like upper-caste women. Unlike Moré and others, these Dalit women did not elevate Brahman familial relationships; they did not think of themselves as lower than Brahman women in any sense.

Increasing levels of education for men and women at times had contradictory effects on marital family life. Due to these struggles and dynamic processes many unmarried second- and third-generation women hoped to find educated, understanding and cooperative companions. They reported difficulty finding such partners. In some instances, as in non-Dalit families, contradictory gendered practices prevailed in the selection of brides and bridegrooms: for a prospective bridegroom, the essential criteria were level of education and earnings, whereas for brides it was being educated and a good housewife. Dr Swati Waghmare reported:

I think that education does make a difference and significantly affects the home environment. Further, the mother's education makes a big difference. She has a voice to an extent and can influence her husband and children. There has to be an understanding between them, however. A few educated and well-settled Dalit boys proposed to me. They were doctors and engineers who wanted their wives to be at home. I was surprised with these views and I instantly refused them. But this is the mentality of some men even today. What is the use of studying, then? My degree will be wasted if I do not practise medicine. I am happy I refused that marriage proposal. I have my clinic today and I am doing very well. Yes, some families from the upper castes have a different atmosphere, *saunskaar* [cultural traits], and the parents are very cooperative.

(S. Waghmare 2004)

Swati disdainfully rejected prospective husbands and thus challenged Dalit men's attempts to restrict her public participation and their antipathy towards women as income earners. Some elite men embraced the dominant conceptions of masculinity and female respectability, in which the man was the breadwinner who decided the confines of the private and public domains. To them, the housewife was the linchpin of domesticity; women and children were 'nonworking', 'dependent' and 'to be protected'. They were still grappling with radical changes in the community.

In contrast with some middle-class Dalits who were interested in domesticating educated women, other Buddhists sought educated partners who were engaged in public employment. They also crafted their matrimonial advertisements accordingly. On the one hand, men valorised family values and preferred traditional but educated and employed women who would manage the home, look after them and their children, and nurture their families. Some of them also believed that a more highly educated and employed woman developed *shinga* (literally 'horns', a derogatory word in Marathi that actually means 'developing radical ideas'), as argued cogently by Urmila Pawar (2004). Suvarna Kuchekar (2002) argued that 'many a time male education was only on paper, in practice it did not change their mental make-up. Some men simply acquired higher degrees.' Swati's mother also approved of Dalit women's subjugation. On the other hand, there were also liberal-minded men like Sandhya Meshram's husband who wanted their wives to be companions and to work to advance their education and careers.[10] Mr Meshram said: 'I want Sandhya to enroll for a diploma or other higher education. She is working with an NGO and can still work toward achieving more' (Meshram 2002). Some men also supported women in seeking higher education and assisted them with family work.

Married life was thus an ordeal in which some men emulated Brahmani patriarchal practices and hardened gender injunctions in Dalit families. They constricted women's sexuality and movement in the public through coercion and consent. Women did not have a real share in the power in these structures; nonetheless, they agreed that the atmosphere was changing. There was also the problem of the continued stigmatisation of single women, often rejected for marriage due to their higher age. Suvarna, a lawyer, reasoned that 'people had all kinds of doubts about me; they thought that I must have some fault and hence did not get married earlier' (S. Kuchekar 2002; see also Chapter 3). Such single women of 'marriageable age' were still waiting to get married.

Similarly, even Lalita Naik took a long time to get married. She was physically challenged, with a weak left leg, and that was perhaps the reason why she married a man who was less educated than her. Here was a rare case. Overburdened with domestic labour, during our talk she was working in the kitchen while calling her daughter for a bath, asking her son if he was studying, and requesting that her husband fill the pots sitting outside her living-room with water. She reiterated that education had helped their marital life to a large extent and that her husband shared responsibilities:

> My husband helps me at times, getting vegetables, filling water in the kitchen, very rarely though. He takes up the children's studies sometimes. We also fight but then we sit and figure out what went wrong. Only yesterday we celebrated twenty years of our marriage.
>
> (Naik 2001)

Lalita's notion of shared responsibilities seemed to be occasional help from her husband. Like many other women, she did not protest. Most second- and third-generation women sought this sharing of work and romantic love. Prakshoti Pawar (2002) was looking for a good partner in life:

> I do not want a reproduction of the issues in the community in my life. My family members have a good understanding and we enjoy quite a free atmosphere. My father does help my mother to some extent. But in other SC families the males are kings, but their women are not queens.

Prakshoti, the only woman with a master's degree in business administration from a reputable institution, argued that education did not necessarily lead to a good understanding among couples; she had come across such broken upper-caste families. She rightly pointed out that female managers in the households were called 'queens' by men, but in practice were treated as maids. Women's lives and labour had lower values; this increased their isolation and dependence on men.

For example, some women worked as if they were *bail* (bullocks tied to the oil-press), both inside and outside the home. Rajnitai,[11] a Dalit mayor, recounted the routine of her domestic slavery:

> I wake up by 4 or 4.30 a.m. My husband works with the railways in Mumbai and that means he also needs to commute between Pune and Mumbai. He is a suburban guard. I start my day with cooking, washing, and bathing my mother-in-law, as she is incapable of doing it herself. I prepare my

children's breakfast and leave the house at 10 a.m. and return only at 9 p.m. My family supports me a lot.

(Tribhuwan 2005)

Rajnitai thus listed her unassisted, gruelling morning schedule in her office, located in the Pune Municipal Corporation building. She believed that her family supported and contributed to her success by allowing her to practise her vocation – an undeniable fact. At this moment, Rajnitai's male assistant raised his eyebrows and expressed his disbelief. (Men tend to view women's roles as 'nature's gifts'; every woman has to work like this and a mayor is no different, so what is the point in voicing and discussing 'womanly' duties?) The mayor was surrounded by upper-caste male assistants who dictated terms to her diplomatically. She was merely a pawn of the ruling party; upper-caste men controlled her ideas, actions and voice. Thus some Dalit women leaders, like many non-Dalit leaders, could hardly exercise their agency and power, even though they were in positions of authority.

In a similar vein, Nani laboured for her family. She agreed that women acted as maids to their husbands and in-laws. She also demonstrated her outward modesty by instantly pulling her *padar* over her head in the presence of men (Mokal 2000). Every time she encountered them she refused to face them and turned away immediately but very modestly. Nani was expected to take good care of the family and attend to all private and public activities while keeping her *padar* firmly over her head. Thus she was to be modern yet moderate, modest, devoted and simple.

Many women often supported their men's every action, if often reluctantly. However, there were some exceptions to this rule. Shantabai Kamble's parents adopted a firm stand against their oldest son-in-law. Even when Shantabai's husband wanted to marry for a second time for no specified reason, her brother and father protected her. They asked her husband to give up the second woman if he wanted to be with Shantabai. They also asked him not to trouble Shantabai (S. Kamble 1986, 60). Nonetheless, radical feminists like Urmila Pawar faced immense turmoil in their married lives. The very fact that she expressed this in a detailed written account after her husband's death speaks volumes of the silencing of Dalit women. Even Babytai wrote her memoirs in hiding, because she was scared that her husband would find out her story. These rare writers sought to reveal to Dalit men the ways in which they oppressed women. Urmilatai described the turmoil in her marriage, especially after she had secured her MA, a degree higher than her husband's. Perhaps he was uncomfortable with this and with her growing awareness of her rights:

On the one hand, he admired my writing and my public speaking skills. He often expressed this to his friends and relatives. On the other hand, these very things upset him immensely, they made him angry. This led to quarrels between us. I used to make him understand: 'See, I am also a human being, I also do a job like you. I also get tired. My work and I have some value, just as yours.' But I could feel it was all nothing to him. He used to say, 'Look at our women in the villages. They get up when the husband tells them to and sit down when he allows them to do so. Don't they manage their families well?'

(U. Pawar 2003, 206)

Urmilatai's husband wanted to maintain his traditional authority as a husband. He questioned her abandonment of the traditional domestic responsibilities and duties of Indian womanhood, to some of which he had been accustomed since his childhood. When Urmilatai's husband witnessed changes in her thoughts, he often wondered about the development process of his wife's new horns. 'These must be cut off at the appropriate time and she should be restricted', he must have thought. Secretively, however, Urmilatai rejoiced in the fact that he was too weak to do that; her horns 'had far outgrown his reach' (ibid., 209).

Urmilatai analysed her struggle to attain her fundamental rights as an individual. She was often admonished by her husband and other Dalit males when she started participating in the women's movement and the language of rights started taking root in her mind. They asked, 'Are you joining *those* women? Beware! *Those* thoughts are not at all necessary for us', meaning their family and community (209, emphasis added). She continued:

And the person would make such a face that I used to feel as if I had joined a gang of criminals. And yet I felt I had gained a new perspective on the women around me. I was becoming fearless. The women's movement had given me a clear and unbiased view of any man or woman as an individual and also provided me with the strength to observe this in actual day-to-day practice.

(U. Pawar 2003, 209)

While Urmilatai describes the exciting moments of her initiation into feminism, her husband seemed to be very agitated by her new streak of radical writings, ideologies and praxis. Her autobiography clearly illustrates the couple's journey from love to no love. It also amply reveals Urmilatai's gradual isolation from her husband. In her autobiography she refers to him by his first name – Harishchandra – after they meet and even after their marriage. Later on, however, when the gulf between them widens, she calls him by his last name: Thorat.

Urmilatai, an elite feminist, also believed that private confrontations should never be made public, thus mirroring upper-middle-class Brahman families who rarely displayed their family problems in full view. Yet some slum dwellers were less circumspect in this matter. For example, Meera's mother said that she would, if necessary, retaliate against her husband. She was not afraid of any public displays: 'We slap our husbands if they slap us; we are not like the women living in flats who tolerate all suppression. So we are happy in a way' (Gaikwad 2004). Thus the confidence and assertion of some lower-class Dalit women was remarkable as opposed to that of some educated, employed, middle-class Dalit women following their *maryaadaa* (limitations).

Like many upper-caste women, Dalit women believed that they were answerable to society. Although most of these women were at the receiving end of oppression, many, including Meera, Urmila and Lalita, had also resisted and cracked the formidable walls of patriarchy. They found the 'middle paths'[12] they needed to keep their families and individuality intact. They became confidently and thoughtfully well versed in the *taarevarchi kasarat* for their happiness as well as that of their families.

The first generation were satisfied with whatever little education they received. This limited education was indeed a privilege to them. They were also happy that they could send their daughters to school. But many middle-class second- and third-generation learners forcefully articulated their needs and at the same time understood their subordinate positions. Like upper-caste women, they were showered with gifts as well as punished by Dalit males. Yet they continued their journeys towards a certain 'modernisation', a 'middle-class' status; sought self-improvement and advancement; and had higher expectations for themselves as well as for their children. They were stretching their boundaries and attempting to redefine their futures.

Most women, as devoted wives, spoke very well of their husbands. Men feared domination from more highly educated women. However, there were some dynamic processes at work, and many ideas were gradually changing. While the first generation was happy to be educated, at times employed, and happily married, the second- and third-generation women were more vocal, but also restricted. They agreed that they could engage in companionable relationships with their husbands, however unequal. They also mentioned that their statuses were no less than their husbands', and that Dalit families were changing and granting more independence and freedom to women. All these struggles influenced their practices of childrearing as well.

Middle-class Dalits and the construction of cultural capital

There were distinct differences between the three generations of women in their ideas on rearing children. By rules of exclusion and lack of leisure, upper-caste men excluded ordinary women and Dalits from the systematic cultivation of hobbies and habits. Dalit women understood their historical and social rejection, and thus made significant efforts to change their dispositions and build a better future for their children by constructing 'cultural capital' for them. They often followed contradictory approaches to childrearing. As a result, they either embraced or disavowed their own cultural heritage, but they deliberately tried to stimulate their children's social and cognitive skills. They made sure that their children were not excluded from any opportunity that might eventually contribute to their advancement. The first-generation poor families were committed to providing comfort, food, shelter, and other basic support to sustain their children's natural growth, which they viewed as an accomplishment. They paid little attention to the deliberate cultivation of children and their leisure activities that occurred in middle-class families.

Thus, as the educated Dalits advanced towards 'modernity', they initiated their children into new and unfamiliar learning processes. This was a part of the Dalit middle classes' struggle for self-discipline: diligently accumulating assets, assembling resources, strengthening themselves and struggling to get ahead and move up. Like Ambedkar, many women, including Manini and Malavika Pawar (2004), Prakshoti Pawar (2002) and Meenakshi Jogdand (2002), talked about English-medium schools for their children, about which they expressed very high opinions. Unlike their parents, they did not depend on teachers alone and wanted to augment this education by teaching at home. By contrast, a few, like Nanda Kamble (2001), emphasised Marathi culture and vernacular education; they were an exception. Women were also looking for additional training for their children that would help build their cultural capital.

Bourdieu has extended the logic of economic analysis to ostensibly non-economic goods and services in order to establish the concept of 'cultural capital'. Cultural capital covers a wide variety of resources, including information about the school system, educational credentials, verbal facility, general cultural awareness and aesthetic preferences. In this manner, culture becomes a power resource. Working through a Bourdieuian framework allows me in turn to illuminate Dalits' struggle to accumulate 'cultural capital' (Bourdieu and Wacquant 1992, 19; Bourdieu 1997, 6–8, 75–76; 1984, 5–14; Bourdieu and Passeron 1977, 177–219). By gendering Bourdieu's concept of cultural capital, I also articulate a 'feminine' cultural capital.

Dalit women understood that the accumulation of capital in an embodied state began in childhood and would pay rich dividends inside and outside school. For Bourdieu, constructing such capital required pedagogical action and a time investment by parents, other family members or hired professionals to sensitise the child to cultural distinctions. Marginalised Dalits who neither inherited cultural capital nor possessed such agents to inculcate it had to build it from scratch. Many Dalit women boarded the school bus to access the *only* school available and did not have opportunities to accumulate capital. Even schools and family often failed to supply the required assets to first-generation women. But middle-class, better-educated second- and third-generation Dalit women deliberately pursued courses of study that would lead to higher-status occupations and pushed their children to be self-confident, independent high achievers. Nanda Kamble affirmed:

> Yes, my education will definitely help me rear my children differently. My mother could not understand anything; however, I will guide my children, tell them about different careers; give them everything I could not get.
>
> (N. Kamble 2001)

Many women referred to the deficiencies in their own education and made efforts to teach their children differently. In this, they hoped to build a 'middle-class' image for their children to give them a better start in life as well as counteract the negative stereotypes of Dalits common throughout Hindu India.

Most women reiterated the importance of a 'better' life for their children. As earlier chapters described in detail, any first- and some second-generation women had suffered from blatant social, economic and religious discrimination in municipal schools and subsequently in their employment. They and their children had been considered privileged to attend municipal schools that practised inequality and discriminated against them. Although this experience had shown them the benefits of a better education (as well as of its availability), their continuing poverty restricted them from realising such goals. Thus Hirabai Kuchekar, a Zilla Parishad clerk, expressed her concern that her lower economic status did not allow her to send her children to 'good' schools:

I have not been able to take *vyavastheet* [proper and good] care of my children due to my work. I could not send them to a *good* school, so I had to send them to a municipal corporation school, which worsened the situation. The teachers did not teach well and the student body was drawn from the surrounding slums. I was in a joint family and had to earn to take care of everyone. I had to neglect my children. I have been employed since the birth of my very first child, I had no time for my children and they have suffered due to that. They do not have any hobbies. One son sells vegetables after school and also during vacations. My eldest daughter is working.

(H. Kuchekar 2002, emphasis added)

Hirabai was thus caught up in a vicious circle of deprivation. Such working mothers could not find even a small amount of quality time for their children. They were overburdened with duties and neglected the overall growth of their children, while the men of their families were 'free as birds'.

However, many second- and third-generation middle-class Dalit women had different expectations and opinions. They were well settled socially, economically and residentially, and had better knowledge about the education system and their urban environment. Most agreed that their education, and moreover their exposure to the public sphere, had been a rewarding experience for them. Their public engagement definitely helped them to rear healthy children; they struggled on a day-to-day basis to acquire the best social, economic, cultural and religious capital for their children. Unlike their mothers, these women attended the Parent–Teacher Association meetings to check their children's progress.

Many highly educated Dalit women also attempted to *develop* a taste for sports, arts, music, dance, culture and pure sciences in their children.[13] While Draupadi Nagare (2004) was happy that she and her children could attend school, her daughter Sandhya Meshram (2001) regretted that the poverty of her family had prevented her from attending drawing classes, but she supported her son Chetan's varied extracurricular activities. Chetan's grandfather trained him to hold chalk and draw lions, rabbits and elephants on their tiled floor. They wanted to develop in Chetan a taste for art, music and science; he thus pursued genetic engineering, and his hobbies included playing the guitar, swimming and cricket (C. Meshram 2004). Likewise, Prakshoti Pawar's parents worked very hard on her behalf and sent her to dancing class. Yet they were also involved in selective gendered restrictions: Prakshoti needed to return home earlier than her brother (P. Pawar 2002). Of course, parents were also concerned about their daughters because the streets were also often full of 'loitering boys'.

Lack of information and financial status were other hurdles to acquiring the necessary cultural capital. Some middle-class Dalit families wanted to cultivate 'classical' culture in their children: for example, 'cultured' Marathi pronunciation. It is intriguing to note that Urmilatai spoke to me and to her daughter in different Marathi dialects. While sitting in her living-room, the public space of her home, Urmilatai used the sanitised and sanskritised Marathi for 'outsiders' – which in this case included me. However, in the confines of her kitchen, while speaking to her daughter, an 'insider', she used her Konkani Marathi dialect. Thus the language used outside the home was different from that used inside, which was a regional or even a social dialect. Some Dalits thus practised 'code-switching', strategically using different dialects of Marathi according to the formality of the situation and exercising their choice of language and dialect. The scholar Ivan Illich has aptly described the formal and informal forms of language as 'tinned formula milk' and 'mother's breast milk', respectively (Illich 1981, 32; Belwalkar 1998). Daya Pawar's autobiography *Baluta* likewise reveals his life and his linguistic journey from his village to the slums, and on to middle-class apartments in Mumbai. In Shantabai Kamble's narrative the rustic *gavraan* (village) Marathi dialect changes to a formal 'cultured' dialect as the author travels from her home village to settle in Mumbai. These linguistic changes certainly led to the sanskritisation of the children's Marathi language. Further, Urmilatai spoke proudly and unendingly about her daughters' accomplishments in music and dance. This rare woman reiterated the need for passion in life:

> I could not get a proper pencil [to study], but I have striven hard to provide everything to my children. Malavika is an accomplished singer and Manini is a *kathak visharad* [the highest level of achievement in *kathak* performance]. Manini takes classes in order to improve her singing and also teaches singing. I think everyone should have an art to indulge in, to forget our identity, our sorrows.
>
> (U. Pawar 2004)

While some middle-class Dalits were trained in 'classical' culture and developed a selective amnesia with regard to their own cultural traditions and art forms, others fought to make a living out of them. Meera Jangam (2004) looked to outdoor sports as hobbies. She wanted to send her daughter for karate training while her son was already playing football at school. Thus, there was a 'distinction of tastes' between the Pawars and the Jangams. While the middle-class Pawars' tastes were 'bourgeois aesthetic', the lower-class Meera spoke of the 'art of living' (Bourdieu 1984, 40–41, 47). Coming as Meera did from a lower class, her concern was to develop in her daughter the physical and mental strength to fight the adversities of her slum environment. She also wanted her son to play cricket and football instead of playing musical instruments, dancing or singing.

Another feature of the middle classes, pointed out in an issue of *Sugava*, was the marked tendency for middle-class Dalits to distance themselves from their parents and communities (Wagh 1986, 1994).[14] The authors of these articles elaborated on the changing attitudes of educated and employed Dalits. They spoke a different language, dressed and ate differently, and resided in caste-neutral neighbourhoods. For example, Meera Jangam's two children were attending an English-medium school, and she struggled to search for a house far away from her present slum because its environment was not conducive to her children's growth. Similarly, many Dalits from Yerawada slum have resettled in the Maharashtra Housing Board Colony and in some posh localities on Nagar Road, Airport Road, Ram Nagar, and so on, which housed mixed-caste and middle-class residents.

One third-generation boy did not want to be identified with his educated Dalit mother because he did not find her as 'smart' and 'active' as other, upper-caste mothers. In addition, she had the habit of rubbing roasted tobacco on her teeth, which was disgusting, he said. These informants emphasised that Dalits were 'lazy and fatalistic', so they wanted to avoid being associated with such traits or markers. In this, they revealed the extent to which they had internalised the 'dominant' viewpoint underlined by some colonial ethnographers. There was an assumption that Dalits in general were trapped in a 'backward' culture, and that the only remedy was to disavow one's caste background. Of course, many non-Dalits use tobacco; however, they would not be marked by its use the way Dalits are.

To such middle-class Dalits, *tamaashaa* carried a stigma because it was a marker of their lower-caste, unstable, fragmented, vulnerable, downtrodden, feudal status. Hence, they rejected it and instead tried to develop *new* tastes, aspiring to own the culture and elite tastes of the higher castes, such as for *shast-reeya sangeet* (classical music). Understandably, Surekha Punekar (2002), who earned her living as a *tamaashaa* dancer, did not want her children to be associated with her 'polluted' world. Uneducated but lucratively employed, this accomplished dancer sent her children away to a boarding-school at the hill-station of Panchgani in Satara district. Due to the itinerant nature of her work, she felt that she could not otherwise provide them with a stable education – or life, for that matter. She wished to keep them away from the world of *tamaashaa* – of dance and of her life.

By contrast, Mangalatai Bansode (2004) followed and wanted her children to follow their ancestral calling of *tamaashaa*. The Bansodes reported that they were following their *khaandaani* (ancestral property; in this case occupation): that *tamaashaa* was an art gifted to them by their *khaandaan*, their ancestors, and they were continuing their tradition. They glorified their status as *tamaasgirs* and their art of *tamaashaa*, and considered themselves part of a distinguished lineage in this respect. Their art-of-living was firmly rooted in their culture, which then became their art-of-aesthetic; they were nourished mentally and physically by their art form.

Although economically well-off, Mangalatai understood her oppressive occupation and social and sexual labour, and regretted that she could not educate her children because of her self-employment, which forced her to be on the move (dancing in villages) all the time. She was a very responsible woman and the primary earning member of her family. Life was never stable enough for her or her children to attend school. Her children were also not always interested in school, since they were in the lucrative business of *tamaashaa*. If education was for employment, they already had jobs. Her son, Nitin Bansode (2004),[15] talked about their business:

> I want to progress in life. I have six movies to my credit. We also have CDs of our *tamaashaa laavanis*. We earn around one to two lakhs during *jatraa* [village fair] and at other times it is around Rs.30,000 to Rs.40,000. Last year the earning was a little low due to the famine. But we normally do not get less than Rs.30,000. At times we have to spend on our own. During rains there is a loss. Again, due to the elections yesterday, less public is watching our show today, so we have to bear all these losses.

Nitin illustrated the precarious nature of his *khaandaani*, their business, which depended on public participation as well as political scenarios. Nonetheless, Mangalatai and her sons were consolidating their ancestral economic and cultural capital and ensuring their future. During our many conversations I watched live *tamaashaa* for the first time in my life and saw the mother–son duo dance and act like a couple in public. Her occupation and living demanded that this literate Dalit woman break social and cultural norms. Averagely educated, middle-class Dalit men and women would certainly disapprove of such occupations for women.

Nitin was nevertheless also in a dilemma about his children's education, because he could not pay attention to it. He simply aspired to educate them in good schools. He explained:

> I am doing well in movies, remixes, and so on. My son accompanies me on all my shows. When he will turn two or three, I will admit him to a hostel. I am in *tamaashaa*, but I do not want my children to follow me there. Everything is changing; the future of *tamaashaa* is not good. The public is misbehaving. At least now they are a little in control, I don't know what will happen in the future. I am a little confused about my children's future. Those who are studying in the village it's fine for them; however this son who is with me ... *I am confused about him*. At times I think he should perform on the stage and at the same time I say that he should attend school. If he likes this then it should be just a hobby, *but he should educate himself*.
>
> (2004, emphasis added)

Thus some uneducated Dalits were concerned and confounded by the circumstantial quagmires that bound them and their children, but they certainly believed in the promise of education.

Some Dalits elevated their educational aspirations and sent their children abroad for higher studies. By contrast, some middle-class Dalit girls *had* to acquire the feminine cultural capital of taking good care of the home: cooking, cleaning, rearing bright children, sharing, and shouldering responsibility for the whole household.[16] Rajni Tribhuwan (2005) was a homemaker overburdened with housework whose first duty was 'to take good care of [her] family members'. Like Annapurna, the goddess of food, cooking a variety of fresh food, rolling out chapattis, and washing utensils and clothes were her first priorities in life; unlike many men, she felt guilty when her public duties prevented her from fulfilling her private concerns.

Unlike Tribhuwan, Kumud Pawde, the famous Dalit feminist scholar and writer, was more worried about cultivating good habits, especially reading:

> One good thing that I instilled in my children was the habit of reading. I am happy that there was no TV or else they would have taken to that. The *vaachan sanskruti* [culture of reading] is dying out today. This is very dangerous.
>
> (Pawde 2005)

Kumudtai mentioned the rare cultivation of *sanskruti* (culture) for Dalit children. She regretted that children were getting used to 'fast' media like TV and the internet and that they did not want to read books.

The *sanskruti* of religion was another challenge. On the whole, the cultural capital that well-educated Dalits tried to acquire did extend to the sphere of religion. Here, in many cases, they sought to assert their independence and modernity as Buddhists, regarding Buddhism as an important element of their distinctive culture. Y.D. Waghmare, a Dalit Buddhist, in a short essay provocatively titled 'My children need a religion', suggested the need for such religious capital for Dalits:

> Instead of following the old, sympathetic religious values, I would support a rational, scientific, rejuvenating religion and ask my children to follow the same. Buddhism causes physical progress, the progress of the mind and speech. This is the reason that Indian foreign policy and domestic policy also follow the [Buddhist] *Panchasheel*. Despite all its virtues, Indians are shy of this religion. There is no other religion with the message of *atta, deep, bhav* [Be your own light]; why should we be ashamed of giving this religion to our children?
>
> (Y.D. Waghmare 1986, 23)

By reciting *Panchasheel* and *Vandanaa* and attending events at *viharas* with their children, many educated Dalit parents made a point of cultivating Buddhist practices in their children. They followed rational Buddhist principles to build their dignity and self-confidence. At the same time, others chose to follow the Buddha as well as Jesus Christ, Guru Nanak, Saibaba and Hindu deities (Paik 2011).

Conclusion

This chapter has tracked the anxiety and critical transformations in Dalit families over generations as they were shaped by practices and processes of modernisation. It has investigated the specific roles of the educated Dalit woman who coveted the power of agency: deploying, producing, intending, selecting, insisting, deciding as a wife, a homemaker and a child nurturer. Dalit men were dominated and dominating at the same time. Their behaviour towards Dalit women paralleled that of the upper castes towards Dalits as a whole. Dalit men subjected Dalit women to mental and symbolic as well as physical violence and cruel forms of torture. Yet not all Dalit women consented to patriarchal relationships within the home; they emphasised their self-development and self-assertion and carved out different paths for themselves. They challenged some Dalit men who emphasised a modest, mellow and modern *gruhini* model. In this case, change will not come *only* through movements for Dalit power – as is the case in the battle with the higher castes – but also through Dalit women's struggle against the men of their own community. Although constrained to an extent, many women also emphasised changing gender relationships in the family as well as flexibility in domestic arrangements. At times their husbands helped them in these critical transformations.

I have investigated how certain universalistic ideas about rights, interests and choice played out in the particular context of Dalit family life. The critical transformations in Dalit women on a social, economic, cultural and psychic level suggest momentous turbulence and contradictions: ordeal and exhilaration, despair and triumph. Such arrangements and derangements indeed exceeded norms of patriarchy and sanskritisation. Women enjoyed some authority and independence and their worth as women was substantial, as was their responsibility.

Women undertook schooling not merely for 'knowledge-seeking' or the achievement and status that higher degrees represented, per se; education was also a training ground for employment and for engaging with the wider public. Second- and third-generation learners in particular understood that education should aim not only at individual growth but at cultural growth and community uplift. Many such Dalits thus set great store by education and disciplined their children to do well in their studies overall. This in itself provided a counter to the discrimination practised in the schools; by sheer hard work and perseverance, significant numbers of Dalits were able to obtain educational qualifications and cultural capital that opened up new jobs and worlds for them. However, the picture was messier and the problem much vexed. Dalits were grappling with many dynamic processes in their social, cultural, political, public and private realms. They simultaneously embraced and radically rejected dominant practices. Women who were restricted in many ways were vocal about their subjection, though they also understood their subordinate positions. They had little power within their own communities and households. Nonetheless, many followed a middle path, becoming more independent and enjoying companionate relationships with men. Ultimately, what mattered was their ability to educate themselves in the face of indifference and hostility, and at the same time to struggle continuously against masculine control over their social and sexual behaviour. This struggle underscores their capacities for challenge and sacrifice.

Notes

1　I draw upon Bourdieu's conjectures of 'capital' (1984). I have already signalled the 'building' of this capital for Dalits in earlier chapters. Here I demonstrate this in Dalits' everyday practice.
2　Kumudtai's sons were married to Khatri, Maratha and Bania women, all touchable upper-caste women. The Nikam brothers were also married to Maratha and Brahman women.
3　Ganapati is the god of knowledge in Hinduism. A large image of him was placed in Sheela's living room. This would offend some Buddhists; however, it is not uncommon to find such pantheons of Hindu gods in Buddhist homes. Furthermore, though many Dalits have converted to Buddhism, many also follow Hindu practices.
4　This bill, which was later included in the manifesto, was presented by Prabhakar Roham in the legislative assembly (Mangudkar 1976, 15–16).
5　Scholars have neglected the history, politics and discourse of sexuality and sexology in colonial western India. Douglas Haynes has recently embarked on such a study.
6　I draw upon Sharon Kemp's paper (1998) to illustrate my point here. The rural women in Sharon Kemp's paper also call attention to the oppressive nature of their dependent status and their daily toil and drudgery. The Gaothan women Kemp interviewed compared men to birds because there are fewer sanctions that accompany their behaviour. The image of a bird with its connotations of freedom, weightlessness, and even playfulness contrasts with the stolidity of the earthbound and hardworking bullocks (i.e. women).
7　Maya Mane, Buddhist, Class 12, magician. I thank her for her generous hospitality; I interviewed her and stayed at her place that night, because it was too late to travel when we finished the interview at two in the morning.
8　Smita Khedkar, Buddhist, BA, unemployed, Pune.
9　This view surfaced once again in a recent major conference on Dalit Studies held at a leading institution in the United States.
10　Since Mr Meshram was at home that day when I interviewed Sandhya *akka*, he had a lot to say. I had to ask him to stop interrupting, as I wanted Sandhya *akka* to speak.
11　Rajni Tribhuwan, Class 10, Mayor, Pune Municipal Corporation Office, Pune.
12　My use of the term 'middle paths' here draws upon the Buddhist philosophy of the 'middle path', which propounds a balanced life between extreme austerity, and extravagance and indulgence; this is the 'Noble Eightfold Path of right outlook, right aims, right speech, right action, right means of livelihood, right effort, right mindfulness, and right concentration' (Ambedkar 1992, 238).
13　Bourdieu 1984, 5.
14　These issues focus on the emerging Dalit middle classes and their brahmanisation. The authors and editors caution Dalits to be aware of their education and cultural roots.
15　Nitin Bansode, Mangalatai Bansode's son, Class 3/4 (as he said), *tamaasgir*.
16　For an interesting overview of the debate on the ethics of care, including an analysis of the feminist debate initiated by Carol Gilligan, see *An Ethic of Care* (2003). By gendering Bourdieu's concept of cultural capital, I also articulate a 'feminine' cultural capital.

References

Ambedkar, B.R. 1936. *Janata*, 4 July.

——. 1965. *Rise and Fall of the Hindu Woman*. Hyderabad: Dr Ambedkar Publications Society.

——. 1979. *Dr. Babasaheb Ambedkar: Writings and Speeches*, Vol. 1, ed. Vasant Moon. Bombay: Department of Education, Government of Maharashtra.

——. 1987. *Dr. Babasaheb Ambedkar: Writings and Speeches*, Vol. 3, ed. Vasant Moon. Bombay: Department of Education, Government of Maharashtra.

——. 1992. *Dr. Babasaheb Ambedkar: Writings and Speeches*, Vol. 14, ed. Vasant Moon. Bombay: Department of Education, Government of Maharashtra.

——. 1997. What Congress and Gandhi have done to the Untouchables. In *Hind Swaraj and Other Writings*, ed. Anthony J. Parel. Cambridge: Cambridge University Press.

——. 2002. *Dr. Babasaheb Ambedkar: Writings and Speeches*, Vol. 18, ed. Vasant Moon. Bombay: Government of Maharashtra.

Anonymous. 2004. Interview with the author. Mumbai.

Bansode, Mangala. 2004. Interview with the author, 1 and 15 September. Nagar and Pune.

Bansode, Nitin. 2004. Interview with the author, 15 September. Nagar.

Belwalkar, Suman. 1998. Marathi language: Used at home and outside. In *House and Home in Maharashtra*, ed. Irina Glushkova and Anne Feldhaus. Delhi: Oxford University Press.

Bhagat, M.G. 1935. *Untouchables in Maharashtra: A Study of the Social and Economic Conditions of the Untouchables in Maharashtra*, MA thesis. University of Bombay, India.

Bourdieu, Pierre. 1984. *Distinction: A Social Critique of the Judgment of Taste*. Cambridge, MA: Harvard University Press.

——. 1997. *Culture and Power: The Sociology of Pierre Bourdieu*, ed. David Swartz. Chicago, IL: University of Chicago Press.

Bourdieu, Pierre and Loïc J.D. Wacquant. 1992. *An Invitation to Reflexive Sociology*. Chicago, IL: University of Chicago Press.

Bourdieu, Pierre and Jean-Claude Passeron. 1977. *Reproduction in Education, Society and Culture*. Thousand Oaks, CA: Sage.

Chakravarti, Uma. 1998. Reconceptualising gender: Phule, Brahmanism and Brahmanical patriarchy. Microform. New Delhi: Centre for Contemporary Studies, Nehru Memorial Museum and Library.

Chatterjee, Partha. 1989. Colonialism, nationalism, and colonialized women: The contest in India. *American Ethnologist*, 16(4): 622–633.

Chitratai (pseudonym). 2005. Interview with the author, 22 October. Mumbai.

Gaikwad, Sheetal. 2004. Interview with the author, 1 August. Yashwantnagar, Pune.

Gilligan, Carol. 2003. *An Ethic of Care*. New York: Columbia University Press.

Hatekar, Archana. 1999. Dalit movement and Dalit woman's question. In *Dalit Stree Asmitecha Avishkara va Disha*, ed. Vandana Sonalkar. Pune: Alochana.

Hodges, Sarah. 2005. Revolutionary family life and the Self-Respect Movement in Tamil South India, 1926–49. *Contributions to Indian Sociology*, 39(2): 251–277.

Illich, Ivan. 1981. *Multilingualism and Mother Tongue Education: Taught Mother Language and Vernacular Tongue*. Oxford: Oxford University Press.

Jangam, Meera. 2004. Interview with the author, August.

Jogdand, Meenakshi. 2002. Interview with the author, 13 March. Bhavani Peth, Pune.

Kamble, Nanda. 2001. Interview with the author, 10 August. Parvati, Pune.

Kamble, Shanta. 1986. *Majya Jalmachi Chittarkatha*, 2nd edn. Pune: Sugava.

Kemp, Sharon. 1998. Women as bullocks: A self-image of Maharashtrian village women. In *Images of Women in Maharashtrian Society*, ed. Anne Feldhaus. Albany: State University of New York Press.

Khedkar, Smita. 2002. Interview with the author, 11 February. Ramnagar, Pune.

Kuchekar, Hirabai. 2002. Interview with the author, 8 January. Pune.

Kuchekar, Suvarna. 2002. Interview with the author, 8 January. Sinhagad Road, Pune.

Mane, Maya. 2005. Interview with the author, 8 September. Goregaon, Mumbai.

Mangudkar, M.P. 1976. *Ambedkar and Family Planning*. Pune.

Meshram, Chetan. 2004. Interview with the author, 11 September. Pune.

Meshram, Sandhya. 2004. Interview with the author, 11 September. Ramtekdi, Pune.

Mokal, Nani. 2000. Interview with the author, 20 May. Pune and Mumbai.

Moré, Shalini. 2002. Interview with the author, 1 June. Sinhagad Road, Pune.

Nagare, Draupadi. 2004. Interview with the author, September.

Naik, Lalita. 2001. Interview with the author, 22 May. Ramtekdi (Swami Vivekanand Nagar), Pune.

Nikam, Sheela. 2005. Interview with the author, 22 October. Mumbai.

Paik, Shailaja. 2011. Mahar-Dalit-Buddhist. *Contributions to Indian Sociology*, 45(2): 217–241.

Pawar, Manini and Malavika Pawar. 2004. Interview with the author, 5–6 September. Borivili, Mumbai.

Pawar, Prakshoti. 2002. Interview with the author, 10 April. Pune.

Pawar, Urmila. 2003. *Aayadaan*. Mumbai: Granthali.

——. 2004. Interview with the author, 5–7 September. Borivili, Mumbai.

Pawar, Urmila and Meenakshi Moon. 1989. *Amhihi Itihas Ghadavala: Ambedkari Chalvalit Streeyancha Sahabhag*. Pune: Sugava.

Pawde, Kumud. 2005. Interview with the author, 16 October. Dhantoli, Nagpur.

Punekar, Surekha. 2002. Interview with the author, Kasba Peth, Pune.

Rao, Anupama. 2005. Sexuality and the family form. *Economic and Political Weekly*, 40(8): 19–25.

Shakur, Assata. 1987. *Assata: An Autobiography*. Westport, CT: L. Hill.

Tribhuwan, Rajni. 2005. Interview with the author, 13 November. Pune Municipal Corporation Office, Pine.

Wagh, Vilas, ed. 1986. Dalit madhyam varga. *Sugava*, special Deepavali issue, November–December.

——. 1994. *Ambedkari Prerana Visheshank-Dalitanna Brahmani Saunskrutiche Akarshan* (Dalit Attraction for Brahmani Culture). Pune: Sugava.

Waghmare, Swati. 2004. Interview with the author, 12 November. Vishrantwadi, Pune.

Waghmare, Y.D. 1986. My children need a religion. In *Sugava*, special Deepavali issue, November–December, ed. V. Wagh.

Conclusion

Modern forces of education and democracy continuously created opportunities and constraints which conditioned Dalit women's choices in the twentieth century. This book has gendered modernity and investigated the triumphs and tragedies of Dalits in modern Indian cities. It has traced Dalits' exigent engagement with the modern, a field of force in itself, as well as the maelstrom, the elation and enlargement, despair and frustrations as Dalits tore down caste structures and sought to achieve a certain citizenship and activate critical transformations of self-development. For Dalit women, entry into the modern precincts of education was a generative moment of history itself. Most significantly, they did not confine themselves to merely modernising their lives but were deeply engaged in practices of democratisation. It was indeed a moment of emergence. Dalits conflicted with the colonial power and upper-caste social and mental hegemony, yet they used these forces to generate new reversals and energies in order to transform their worlds. In the process, they created unintended and unexpected results; however, they also suffered multiple ruptures, displacements and fissures of consciousness itself, as I have shown in this book. Dalit women's will-to-power was a newly developed sensibility, indeed a political strategy, and a generative activity which affirmed the *generativity* of life itself.

After several decades of struggling to acquire formal education on a par with or even excelling that of upper castes during the colonial and post-colonial periods, Dalit women increasingly gained access to schools at the primary, secondary and post-secondary levels. Dalit womanhood was under construction in twentieth-century western India. By the end of the twentieth century, the landscape of Dalit women's education in western India had undergone transformation to a considerable extent. The category of the modern Dalit woman, though coherent in certain historical conjunctures, has been deeply marked by variations in caste practices, age, education, economic status, employability, location, subordination, norms and transgressions, all entangled and circulating simultaneously in contemporary Maharashtra.

Thousands of Dalits migrated to the cities, benefited from the modern forces of education and employment, and fought with the colonial and post-colonial states to achieve rewards and benefits in the form of reservations. In the late and post-colonial periods, Dalit women increasingly sought public education and employment. They became employed in different sectors of the formal and informal economies, as Pune became an industrial and later an IT centre, and Mumbai consolidated itself as the commercial capital of Maharashtra. Yet many Dalit girls continued to drop out of school and those who acquired education were able to seek only lower-level jobs, for example, as clerks and nurses. Historians have failed to engage with this story. By contrast, some anthropologists have investigated and attempted to trace the failing education policies of the state and the drawbacks of formal education. They have, however, mostly overlooked the roots of Dalit exclusion from education and employment throughout the entire twentieth century, focusing instead on the continuing failure of formal education policies and processes, and the increasing unemployment and underemployment of Dalit youth in north India.

This study supports the findings of anthropologists on the inadequacies and inequities of education, but it has also unravelled the ways in which education has proved to be a mixed blessing. I challenge the conventional understanding that education has had a straightforwardly positive effect, showing that while it has sometimes been a channel of upward mobility, success and self-assertion, its multiple processes have also served as a vehicle for entrenching inferior status and creating constraints, especially for Dalit women. I want to reiterate that we need to think not only of the failures of education but also of what education may have offered to Dalit women in particular historical, cultural, intellectual and political contexts. I have traced how education facilitated both new possibilities and the denial of resources and opportunities at specific historical conjunctures. Moreover, I have also paid attention to how it has framed different conversations and contradictions, politics and cultures, present and future.

The conventional emphasis on continuity in the exclusion of Dalits and the failure of educational programmes seems flawed on a number of fronts. For that matter, any analyses predicated on the assumption of continuity would be almost as inadequate as those based on an assumption of total change. Dalit women's educational exclusion and repertoire of difficulties were not a simple survival from the past, but were generated at specific junctures through interactions among Dalits and their political conflicts with upper castes, nationalists, and the colonial and post-colonial states over the course of the twentieth century. Phule, Ambedkar and many Dalit radicals struggled for civic rights and education. Dalit radicals critically engaged with methods rooted in modernity and also sought to exceed them; to them, seeking education amounted to the fight for *naagarikatva* (egalitarian citizenship) and political power as well as an opportunity for building intelligence and *trutiya ratna* (critical consciousness). The colonial state did promote Dalit women's education and attempted 'fair play'; however, it was the agency of Dalit actors that appropriated the universal value of secular education and infused it with local, vernacular Marathi and political concepts like *maanuski* (humanity), *svaabhimaan* (self-respect), *svaavalamban* (self-reliance), *dhaadas* (daring), *pratishthaa* (honour), *maanavi hakka* (human rights), *naagarikatva* (egalitarian citizenship) and *sudhaaranaa* (improvement and self-improvement). Neither the government nor upper-caste nationalists could adequately address Dalits' fundamental agenda of democratising education, which included not only the fight against the state and Brahmanical forces but also deployed the technology of the self for the radical remaking of the modern Dalit self, family, community and, ultimately, the nation. Dalit radicals' rhetoric penetrated deeply to become fundamental truth for the Dalit community and to shape Dalit women's political consciousness.

The rhetoric and practice of education: a contradiction

There was, however, a sharp contradiction between the rhetoric and the practice of secular education. This book has investigated how schools emerged not only as sites of struggle but also as part of a political process between colonisers and colonised, as well as among colonised touchables and Untouchables themselves. These doubly colonial forces created the *educational conjuncture* of the 1920s. In order to fully understand these historical contingencies, I have woven together Dalit women's struggles for civic rights, economic mobility and education – the public institutions – with private anxieties over family, gender, marriage, kinship and sexuality – the intimate lives of Dalit women. Caste, class, gender and culture are central to the history of education.

The colonial government (though incongruous and miserly at times), missionaries, and upper-caste, lower-caste and Dalit advocates of reform played creative roles in arguing for common municipal education and in making ample educational opportunities available, yet the benefits trickled down to only a few. The rhetoric of inclusion and the ostensible right for all to education turned in practice into a right merely to the right of Untouchable students to obtain segregated education. Officials of the British government and some orthodox upper-caste men often colluded and manoeuvred to restrict education only to upper-caste children, thereby emphasising Brahman exclusivity and hegemony in education. Thus the doctrine of 'separate but equal' reigned supreme. Some revivalists, like Tilak, argued for 'separate education(s)' or 'separate learning(s)' for children from different castes and genders. In many cases, school committees and upper-caste women and men did not blame poor teaching techniques, prejudiced upper-caste teachers, or the inadequate facilities available to Dalits for their underperformance, but rather the immorality, indifference, ineptitude and idleness of Dalit children. In so doing, the rhetoric of public schooling also suggested that lower castes did not need the same education as upper castes and that a 'separate education' would serve the interests of Dalits.

Many non-Brahman and Dalit radicals understood the painful but powerful paradox of Dalit education: while the colonial government and upper-caste reformers and revivalists were toiling to improve their education and making individual and collective efforts to promote *dnyanasanchay* (education preservation) within their caste and class locations, Dalit education was deteriorating at the same time. Once non-Brahmans and Dalit had grasped this contradiction they launched their staunch struggles for civic rights, including access to formal education and *dnyanaprasaar* (knowledge dissemination). They used Marathi concepts to understand their emancipation and looked upon education as a deeply democratic and political process to attain *naagarikatva* (egalitarian citizenship) and *raajkiya sattaa* (political power). Phule and Ambedkar both regarded education as a liberating force against Brahmani domination. They saw the lower castes and Untouchables as being mired within the caste system and believed that through education they would be able to develop the necessary *trutiya ratna* to assert themselves against this system of oppression. Developing such a political consciousness was particularly necessary in a context where most schoolteachers were from the upper castes. I described Phule's battle to allow Dalits any access at all to education as the first-stage struggle. I examined the ways in which Dalits have fought and won this battle and then gone on to the second stage, obtaining an education on equal terms to that of the upper castes and classes. One of the key questions I have asked is: to what extent has this whole experience brought about the hoped-for liberation of the Dalits, and Dalit women in particular, in a situation of continuing and evolving discrimination?

The changes that took place in the Dalit community were actually different from those which Ambedkar anticipated; his expectations about the transformative power of education were ultimately undermined by the complex processes and forces of history as well as by social inequalities and structures of power. Education was the first step on Ambedkar's road to political power for the oppressed, and he did his best to use his position to achieve this end. Answering his clarion call to educate was no easy task; it was a path strewn with the thorns of caste segregation, disproportionate Dalit poverty, and the struggles involved in moving to and settling in city slums and ghettos, made worse by social, economic and mental insecurity. Paradoxically, education instilled in many Dalit women confidence and pride in gaining access to a hitherto unavailable opportunity and space. At the same time it generated a fearful passivity and became an instrument in their social, economic, religious and psychological denigration. It was a rarity indeed to come across a Dalit woman who enjoyed her school experience. Dalit women were socialised to accept their place on the lowest rung on the ladder, to represent and inscribe their subordination and submission. I have drawn attention to the processes that went into the making of the 'incapability' of Dalits, rather than blaming them for their failure at school or other opportunities.

Gender and agency within the Dalit community

My study has gendered modernity. Moreover, the Dalit woman of the 1990s was very different from the one who attempted to seek education in the beginning or the middle of the twentieth century. By the end of the twentieth century, women in metropolitan cities presented themselves confidently, articulated their demands cogently, and understood the increasing pressures of political, social, historical and intellectual debates. Modern Dalit women were thus agents, deploying, producing, intending and selecting, at times directly and at times indirectly. Although they were not always as vocal, articulate, coherent or overtly political (as men may seem) and did not always follow a rational strategy, they still engaged and focused their attention towards an objective for themselves and their community. This critical fashioning of Dalit women was a product of historical processes over generations during the course of the twentieth century. There were significant connections between first- , second- and third-generation Dalit women learners during the colonial and post-colonial periods. These connections, however, were not merely ones of continuity. As this work has shown, Dalit female actors have been negotiating over many decades with state power, upper-caste women and men, and Dalit men to shape and reshape social relations, household and familial relationships, industrial economies and political conflicts. Specific historical contingencies, shifting relations among caste, gender, sexuality and class hierarchies, changing state policies, changing intellectual circumstances, and conflicts between acceptance and rejection of Brahmani normative practices have transformed the circumstances of Dalit women. Both the micropolitics and macropolitics of Dalit women's intimate lives and their connections with larger structures of the economy, politics, community, society and the nation have been responsible for shaping their consciousness.

This study has interconnected three separate strands of historiography: Dalit studies, education studies and women's studies. Contemporary scholarship, except for a few notable examples, has tended to deny Dalit women a history: histories of Dalit castes leave out issues of gender, while histories of women have not dealt centrally with caste as it affects Dalits. Moreover, even notable scholars have substituted caste for Dalits and gender for women, thus further complicating the story. Dalit studies by contrast have often tended to narrate either a triumphalist emancipation or the victimisation of Dalits. In other words, Dalit women are shown either as 'smashing the prisons' or as 'terribly thrashed', 'brutally battered' and sexually subordinated by Dalit men, upper-caste men and women, and the masculine state apparatus. Such a binary configuration of power in terms of domination and emancipation has reduced the multiplicity of power relations into two unambiguous alternatives which mask the complex and variegated nature of power. Moving beyond binary oppositions, this book has shown how Dalit women were challenged by multiple forms of power which repressed them and at the same time produced numerous possibilities for political transformation. Further, instead of focusing only on 'broken' Dalit women or the violence to which they are subjected, I have also sought to illustrate how men and women indeed supported each other in the public and private spheres.

I have thus worked upon the blind spots in the mainstream historiography of India, of Dalit studies and of the women's movement. To a great extent, mainstream historiography of both India and the women's movement has focused on upper-caste, elite women and mapped their struggles as Hindu and Indian. Several forces shaped this particular history and politics. Elite Brahman men conspired with the colonial state to restrict education to certain gender, caste and class locations, and thereby reinforced a selective dissemination of knowledge. Over time they allowed Brahman women to share their privilege. As a result, although upper-caste women initially shared their educational exclusion with Dalits and many were sympathetic, they implicitly strengthened middle-class and patriarchal values and were complicit in the elite agenda of education. Upper-caste women shared gender oppression with Dalit women, yet they implicitly allied with – and did not challenge – their caste locations and Brahman patriarchy. Even those few who did make such efforts, like Pandita Ramabai, drew largely upon Hindu nationalism's model of the elite Aryan woman, thus excluding Dalit women altogether.

This study has shifted the focus of scholarly analysis from upper-caste, Brahman women to ordinary Dalit women. By concentrating on Dalit women's lives and working from their vantage point, it has trained its gaze on the politics of Brahmani hegemonic practices, elite Hindu nationalism and liberal feminists' strategies of exclusion. In so doing, the book has illuminated the ruptures and tensions along lines of caste, class and gender in the Indian feminist movement which led to a particular politics of the women's and nationalist movements that excluded Dalit women. I have sought to document the ways in which Dalit women were excluded from the larger imagining of the nation by both nationalists and liberal feminists.

By contrast, Phule, Ambedkar and other Dalit radicals grasped the specific ways in which caste cross-cut gender, class and sexuality to shape Dalit women's oppression. They opposed upper-caste privilege and suggested a Dalit agenda of democratising education and gender relations, of liberating and shaping Dalit women's political consciousness, which lay at the conjunction of civic, political, social, cultural, legal and economic forces. Gender emerged as a fractured and unstable category because Dalit radicals like Ambedkar infused Dalit femininity with masculine attributes like *dhadaadi* (daring) and *nischay* (resoluteness), thus challenging Brahmani construction of a fickle-minded, gentle and genteel womanhood. Yet the male radicals' agenda was thwarted by ambiguities and anxieties as they dealt with issues of gender within the community.

Nonetheless, women challenged local patriarchal relations, expanded the radicals' 'feminist' discourse, and shaped their consciousness at the interstices of gender, caste, community and sexuality. Rather than prioritising one over the other, to Dalit women and men, individual, familial and community emancipation were entangled and simultaneous goals. Thus, in colonial India as now, there were multiple and historically contingent feminism(s). Dalit women's subjectivity emerged in a historical and educational conjuncture in a colonial context that precluded any subject formation. Moreover, women did not make claims for their particular caste communities and never regarded themselves as coming from specific castes (for example, Mang or Chambhar). Indeed, in specific educational conjunctures, women united disparate Dalit communities and widened the educational discourse of Dalit radicals. Feminists and other groups can certainly draw upon Dalits' political strategies in particular historical, social and intellectual circumstances.

This book has straddled history and anthropology and extended from the colonial to the post-colonial period. Studying Dalit history also means using materials that may not exist in the official archives; historians have to make extensive use of 'unofficial' or even 'unarchived' or 'trivial' sources as well as oral history, and thus engage with hitherto-unfamiliar spaces of knowledge production. Historians of India have worked on the education of Dalits in limited ways. Moreover, there has been a lack of communication between historians of education and Dalit studies; I have attempted to cross this divide. For the most part, sociologists, anthropologists and political scientists have examined the impact of education on Dalits, who have been marginalised both in terms of education and employment. However, these social scientists have not engaged in serious historical research. Inequity in schools was embedded from the start: that is, the mid-nineteenth century. Inequities of caste, citizenship and educational opportunity have their roots in the end of the nineteenth and early twentieth century.

In such historical conjunctures, schools were indeed the most local of institutions, steeped in the politics of place, claim-making, caste construction, neighbourhood, and affected by and in turn shaping the interlocking technologies of caste, class, gender, sexuality and community. Both Dalits and non-Dalits understood schools as gatekeepers of the good life: socio-economic mobility, civic inclusion, political participation and vocational opportunity. Yet much sociological analysis treats the education problems of Dalits as emerging in the present, emerging automatically either as a failure of the post-independence state or of the neo-liberal economy. But it is impossible to appreciate the expansion of educational opportunity in all its complexity without taking ideas about caste practices into consideration; we cannot fully understand the meaning of caste in modern India without examining its techniques in shaping formal educational institutions during colonial and post-colonial periods. Caste, gender, class, family and culture are central to the history of education in India.

Scholarship on Dalit history has paid very little attention to the ways in which the Dalit movement was gendered. Dalit women's daily existence is missing from most of these accounts. The occlusion of the entanglements of domestic time with time spent on political organising in women's lives suggests that Dalit history is radically incomplete. Understanding Dalit women's agency and education requires, as this study indicates, a multi-pronged analysis. Women's education was not isolated from social, economic, political and intellectual contexts; hence it was embedded in education, family, moral and gender reforms. The main modern force examined in this study has been Dalit women's agential practices of participation in the Dalit movement as Dalits fought internal and external colonialism, Brahman hegemony and the colonial state. Moreover, even inside colonialism they struggled against different social actors. Dalit women's agency, at times fractured and not fully autonomous as in the liberal narrative, was produced in specific historically contingent practices and contexts; the skills and abilities it enabled were products of a specific subordination. Women's ideas, actions and lives thus cannot fit into the usual universal paradigm of enactment and subordination but need to be located in the heterogeneity of women's efforts at the interstices of individuality, family, community, politics, affect and embodiment.[1]

This study has rejected a straightforward account of transition to and triumph of education, though it does find a gradual strengthening over time in the position of Dalit women. First-generation women mentioned that they were 'privileged' to get whatever education they could. The second- and third-generation learners also asserted that they were 'definitely in better times' than their mothers. This study has examined how education has also enabled women to fight against inequality, poverty, patriarchy and social injustice. Women demonstrated considerable creativity by articulating the Dalit agenda of education, insisting on building *svaabhimaan*, *pratishthaa* and *svaavalamban*, actively participating in the Dalit movement, and enabling the remaking of the self and the community. They thus took advantage of the changing economic and political conditions around them.

Yet Dalit women also continued to face constraints on both the domestic and public fronts, which had been refigured as significant sites of political resistance by Dalit radicals, especially Ambedkar. Women became victims of *double* patriarchy: Dalit and non-Dalit men, inside and outside the home.

Schooling: between vision and reality

There was a clear contrast between Phule's and Ambedkar's visions of how education might transform the consciousness and social conditions of Dalits, in particular Dalit women, and the reality. The modern technologies of secular education included Dalit women; however, their intimate experiences point to the reality of their exclusion and of caste practices of discrimination in schools. There have been some transformations, yet Dalits continue to face unequal treatment from upper-caste as well as Dalit teachers and peers.

During colonial times, Dalits had to fight for the right merely to attend school. By the time of independence in 1947, this battle had been largely won – Dalits were normally permitted to sit inside classrooms. Educational uptake and the resulting literacy rates were, however, very poor, particularly in the villages. But Dalits were on the move, encouraged by Ambedkar and other leaders to abandon oppressive village life and migrate to the cities, which they saw as more liberating.

Settling largely in slum locales of the city, Dalits had access to free municipal schools. Unfortunately, they continued to suffer caste-based discrimination in the cities, though in different ways than in the rural areas. The quality of the municipal schools was very low for the most part. The high-caste teachers generally had a poor opinion of their pupils and failed to speak and understand the language of Dalits. Furthermore, they imposed dominant Brahmani values, culture, language and even intonation upon children. Few Dalit pupils went beyond the most basic education; many dropped out even before achieving this. To many Dalit students, the need to earn income came into conflict with their educational aspirations. They therefore had low aims, and most left school at an opportune moment to take odd jobs with irregular payments. The unsatisfactory quality of municipal schools, the only educational spaces then available to most

Dalits, entangled them in a vicious circle of low-quality education and low-status jobs. The slum girls who studied in the municipal Marathi-medium schools were at the lowest level in the school and socio-economic hierarchies. Their parents did not prioritise their education, and they received even less encouragement at school. In this way, the education system mirrored the socio-economic disabilities which Dalits and Dalit women suffered in general.

Dalits settled mainly on the outer rings of the cities to which they migrated, reflecting their marginalised and liminal status. Chapters 5 and 6 examined the 'tale of two cities' within Pune; the two mentalities, one of the *peths* – the quintessentially Puneri – and the other of the *gayaraan* (literally 'fallow lands') Dalit *vastis* (neighbourhoods) on the margins. The best educational facilities were in the core area in the heart of the city, Sadashiv Peth. This was the 'polis', inhabited largely by the high castes; it possessed a hegemonic symbolic power in the Punekar imaginary. Dalits' exclusion from the polis by hegemonic caste and state apparatus suggested limitations to the former's claims to egalitarian citizenship. In recent years, Pune has gained an international reputation as a centre for information technology. Although this has brought about unprecedented economic growth, the effects have largely bypassed the Dalits, especially those in the slums and on the margins of the city. Nonetheless, though this urban space is thus hierarchised, it provides some opportunities for Dalits who can work within the system. If they have the means and ability, they can strive to gain access to the modern amenities of the city and its variety of schools and colleges, vocational training institutes, and employment opportunities in the business and service sectors.

In these respects, schools have operated as 'learning machines' to thoroughly discipline and rank pupils. Only those who conformed to the system and learned to negotiate their way through were able, as a rule, to achieve success on its terms. Paradoxically, however, such discipline was necessary for the Dalits if they were to have any chance of competing with or even excelling the upper castes. The pedagogic machinery thus crystallised social and political hegemony; some Dalit women and men internalised this rationality of learning and emulated upper castes. Thus upper-caste hegemony was extended and its symbolic power was executed through the education system, along with other systemic agencies.

In my historical fieldwork, I found that Dalits who had negotiated the system with some success tended to downplay the caste discrimination they had suffered. Many of my respondents of this type – mainly second- and third-generation respondents – were in fact uneasy about such a question being raised. I have discussed the phenomenon of silences and the complexities of investigating them in everyday living in a caste-riven society. When pressed, many agreed that they had in fact faced verbal discrimination and/or abuse, and had tried to counter or resist this oppression. Certainly, a range of markers in city life helped to delineate Dalits who, unlike in the villages, could not be distinguished through crude physical markers such as their form of dress, demeanour and enforced distance. Their localities on the margins of the city by contrast were an important new marker of their identity in the urban context. In the upper-caste imagination, the slums in which the Dalits lived were a vision from hell, with their window-less corrugated iron shacks, open sewers and pigs roaming the lanes. Upper castes could never envisage living in such conditions which they perceived as filthy. They abhorred, also, Dalits' eating of meat (particularly beef) and looked down on their ways of talking. They noted with disapproval Dalits' reverence for Ambedkar, their Buddhism, and so on. In schools, upper-caste teachers singled out Dalit pupils for receiving the special benefits reserved for the Scheduled Castes. These benefits were publicly displayed in periodic roll calls within classes or notices on school bulletin boards. Many Dalits who were identified in such ways were implicitly shamed before the other pupils. The state apparatus, in collusion with powerful upper-caste elites, continued to subject and vilify Dalits, and to expose them to ongoing social, physical, legal and psychological violence.

At the same time, even Dalits who had to live in the slums made the most of what little they had. Often they managed to construct relatively solid houses. They fought for and obtained a reliable water supply, electricity, and even some modern gadgets. Often they worked hard and sent their children to school. In this, they maintained what dignity they could. The slums therefore did not, on the whole, conform to the stereotypes held by high-caste people, who in many cases had never set foot inside such places.

To most Dalits in the slums or middle-class apartments, and to those from the first and second generations of learners, education was an important tool to gain jobs. All Dalits agreed with Phule, Ambedkar and other Dalit radicals about the ways in which education was a solution to all their problems. Yet their daily lives exposed the contradiction between Ambedkar's vision of the transformative power of education in terms of political consciousness and social conditions (for Dalits in general and women in particular) and the actual reality.

Most such interlocutors agreed that it was not education as such but employment that had helped them most in life. A few Dalit women had in fact educated themselves in different skills like typing, shorthand and computers without any formal support. Although this continued to be true for many second- and some third-generation learners, I found also that many of the latter valued intellectual attainment and self-improvement, which was linked in part to a desire for greater social prestige. In some cases they had attained a much higher level of formal education and on this basis were able to enrol in the government employment exchange to seek job opportunities. These Dalits were the most able to take advantage of reservations. The bulk of the Untouchables were not, however, able to benefit in this way (Galanter 1984, 541–546). Only those who were able to avail themselves of such opportunities could ride the tide and get ahead.

The educational experiences of many Dalit girls in were not often happy. On the whole, they had to make use of the nearest school available, as their parents would not let them travel long distances on public transport to better establish-ments. The nearest schools were generally the poorest ones. Their mothers in particular feared for their safety outside the home and were often reluctant to release them from their household duties to attend school. Nor were home environments often conducive to study. Lower-class parents often did not take any detailed interest in their children's studies and lacked knowledge of educational opportunities. They believed that it was the teacher's job to teach and the child's to study. Some had imbibed the prevailing high-caste attitudes towards learning, seeing it as something to be forced upon reluctant children through strict discipline, including physical beating, to make them memorise their lessons.

Many of the informants commented on the low standard of the teaching they received in municipal schools. Many held arrogant attitudes that smothered poor and low-caste pupils. Dalit girls, in particular, were accused of being dullards who were 'not worth teaching'. Even some parents and relatives joined in this chorus, agreeing that girls were not suited to study beyond a certain level. It was a rare teacher – and there were a few – who made a point of teaching well and encouraging Dalit girls to excel. These exceptional – often idealistic – individuals guided them in their progression to the next stage of their education and advised them about scholarships and other opportunities. There was also the problem of the constant sexual harassment of girls by boys in schools, as well as by teachers. Few women were prepared to vocalise their concerns and experiences in these respects publicly – most preferred to remain silent so as to preserve their reputations. Many families also practised gender discrimination, favouring sons' education over daughters'. They *gendered* education: engineering became the domain of men and arts of women. However, many women also emphasised how their parents supported their education in non-conventional fields.

Elite Dalit parents who were committed to educating their daughters, on the other hand, also overburdened them with expectations. At this level, parents were more likely to take an active interest in their children's education, pushing and coaxing them in their studies – often using corporal punishment. They also tried to inculcate in their children 'respectable' middle-class habits and encouraged various extra-curricular activities. In this way they sought both to build their social, economic, cultural and religious capital and to counter the negative stereotypes which upper castes commonly voiced about Dalits. Living in a middle-class locale in itself suggested that the children came from good homes, and that their parents – and thus they themselves – were people of good character.

Highly educated Dalit women desired and earnestly worked on assembling such capital for their children and grandchildren, and to develop a 'taste' in them for sports, arts, music, dance, culture and science. At the higher levels of education, or in 'better' schools in the middle-class localities, the Dalit pupils were invariably outnumbered by caste Hindus, which created its own tensions. These elite children often harassed the Dalits, making cutting remarks and taking very obvious care not to be touched by them. Peer groups often formed along caste lines. Some Dalits felt that they were better off in the 'poorer' schools, where at least they could hold their own or even predominate. On the whole, Dalits preferred English-medium schools, both because English was associated with the sort of non-Hindu modernity for which Ambedkar had strived and because they were less likely to be dominated by the Brahmans who staffed so many of the Marathi-medium schools.

Post-schooling marginalisation of middle-class Dalits

This study has shown that educated Dalit women often failed to achieve the broader liberation that seemed at one time to be inherent in the modern promise of education. Education on its own, therefore, does not emancipate women from their subordinate existence in the quotidian domestic life. Middle-class, urban Dalit children were brought up in a more culturally and intellectually stimulating environment and were able to situate themselves on the ladder of middle-class privilege. Although they enjoyed some rewards of upward social and economic mobility, life in the middle class engendered problems of 'passing' and 'code-switching'. Many Dalit girls tried to imitate Brahmani culture in their everyday lives, even changing their names to hide their origins. They also tried to conceal their home addresses, moved into 'better' (middle-class, mixed-caste) areas, and adopted a cultured, nasal-toned Marathi. Without a backward glance, such Dalits accommodated themselves to caste Hindu culture and the dominant ethos, trying to erase their Untouchable identities. At the same time however, many other Dalits affirmed their Dalithood with pride.

Once employed, Dalits aspired to climb the ladder of social and economic mobility. Many scholars have argued that class and educational levels have been the chief determinants of employment chances in post-independence India. Instead, this study has found that caste and gender discrimination, as they operated through the education system, stymied the life chances of many Dalit women. Very rarely did the congruence of caste, gender, rank and class work in Dalits' favour. Many Dalit women wanted to be employed, and there were no caste restrictions on women working outside the home in public. Educated women wanted to obtain respectable jobs and to avoid the historical economic and sexual exploitation of Dalit women in 'public'. On the whole, the jobs they obtained were at the lower end of the scale. Several respondents mentioned the difficulty of obtaining satisfactory employment. Some managed to build their own businesses.

Most women married before they were in a position to look for a job, and much depended on the attitude of their husbands and their families to such employment. The main attraction of a wife working was that it brought in extra income for the family. Even then, women were often expected to carry out domestic work within the home on top of their outside employment, slogging away like bullocks tied to the oil-press. Women were valued as 'secondary' earners, but this did not affect their position within the family. In some cases they had to forgo promotion. Even staunch Ambedkarite men held such attitudes towards working women. This raised questions about practices of patriarchy among the Dalits. My research has shown that change will not occur solely through movements for Dalit assertion – as is the case in the battle with the higher castes – but through the assertion of Dalit women against the men of their own community.

Dalit women were and are caught in a web of interlocking identities – as women and as Dalits. In contrast to romanticised views of the supposedly more liberated lives of Dalit women (in comparison to upper-caste women), I have sought to show that they have been subjected to a double patriarchy: that of the high castes and men of their own community. While the Dalit male controlled the Dalit woman's sexuality in private and public, high-caste male teachers both marginalised and sexually exploited Dalit pupils within the school environment. Some educated elite Dalit males dreamt of the bourgeois Victorian-Brahmani ideal of companionate marriage, thereby confining women and buttressing the gendered division of labour.

There has been internal dissent along gender and class lines within the Dalit community. The community would, of course, like to resolve these within the confines of the *ghar*, 'family' or 'home'. As a result, they have therefore downplayed such internal conflicts in order to forge Dalit solidarity. Yet, as I have revealed, Dalit women continue to experience domestic violence. Disempowered Dalit men try to exercise some measure of power over Dalit women by using physical and symbolic violence against them. As a result, some women were afraid of talking to me within the confines of their 'private' homes. Moreover, this fear was not confined to the 'private' and the 'community'; it infiltrated the 'public', in that Dalit men attempted to control women's sexuality in public. Some Dalit men were free to pursue their sexual ambitions, which were not confined to Dalit women alone, while insisting that Dalit women rein in their sexuality. Men did not always follow Ambedkar's ideal of granting 'personal independence' and seeking 'equal partnership' with women. Once again, like women in general, Dalit women have to perform a *taarevarchi kasarat* in order to balance their private and public roles.

Moreover, Dalits refused to be confined by the prisons of sanskritisation and did not simply imitate and reproduce upper-caste gendered idioms and norms. Although the conjugal family ideal did offer women and men the chance to challenge existing patriarchal structures, the family also often became a site full of tensions and allowed for the generation of 'new' patriarchies. The power of men within families was arranged differently. Nevertheless, Dalit women appropriated and animated upper-caste, bourgeois idioms and transformed them by building a *masculine womanhood* to uplift the family, community and nation. Some second- and third-generation educated Dalit women became increasingly assertive, and their education and employment were significant contributing factors towards this independence. Some men would also help women to aim higher, continue higher studies and dream bigger.

The Dalit community is grappling with a wide range of changes, and all the Dalit women with whom I spoke emphasised that they were definitely in different and better times than those of their mothers. Some middle-class women even believed that their marriages were more 'companionate', however unequal they remained. Some of the second- and third-generation learners said that Dalit families were changing and granting more independence and freedom to women, and that their status was no less than their husbands'.

Ambedkar did not anticipate some changes. Education and employment were both enabling and disabling: many women gained greater independence and confidence, yet they also differentiated and reconstructed caste, class, sexuality and gendered norms. Working outside the home could bring a greater sense of self-assurance and independence for women. Some spoke of how it was a relief to be able to go to work, escaping the constant demands of in-laws and family quarrels. They got to know the outside world and gained confidence in dealing with it. Some middle-class women even blamed poorer women for not working hard enough and not being able to 'make it'. Even feminists could not engage with their 'sisters' who were less educated and distanced themselves from their home communities.

Reservations have also proved contentious. There has been increasing competition among both Dalit women and men to seek compensatory reservations. Dalit women did not achieve any additional provision on the basis of gender and had to compete with Dalit men for reserved places in education and employment. Many middle-class Dalits ended up with a split consciousness in this respect. They sought to inculcate upper-caste culture and ways of life; on the other hand, they knew that their Dalit identity had economic and political benefits. Although they were thus trying to reformulate their identity as middle class, they could not escape the fact that they had been born Dalits and would remain so throughout life.

The Dalit community: united and fractured

Dalit women have worked largely through an idiom of 'community uplift'. Communities believe in helping their own and will make great efforts to achieve this. Several Dalit women with whom I interacted deployed such language. Their idiom, at times, tended towards helping the immediate community – Mahar, Buddhist, Matang or Chambhar – rather than the Dalits or oppressed in general, something that Dalit radicals did not anticipate. Yet, at the same time, some women also turned whatever little education and training they had back into the larger oppressed community of women irrespective of caste, as was the case with Sheela Nikam, the leader of the Hawkers' Union in Mumbai.

Dalits were fractured along lines of language, caste practices, class and regional affiliations. Although the idea of a Dalit community was tenuous in practice, Dalits in specific historical, political and intellectual contexts not only 'imagined' a community, but also actually lived in it and shaped an agenda for social justice and emancipation.[2] Dalits have imagined and even lived in collective communities in specific historical and educational conjunctures, success has been on the whole limited and contingent. There existed continuous mutual suspicion and rivalry among Dalit *jaatis*. This served to divide the Dalit movement, to its continuing detriment. At the same time however, leaders and spokespersons belonging to different Dalit communities also made attempts to create alliances among Dalits and with non-Brahmans, Muslims and *adivasis*. It is important to pay attention to the internal challenges within Dalit community because often, in the spirit of creating Dalit unity (just as elite upper-caste leaders imagined the unity of the Indian nation), Dalits also robustly stifled questions of gender, caste and class discrimination within their own community.

To Ambedkar, the self and community were compatible: women and men were social individuals and perhaps for him, as for Marx, the 'self is not *prior to*, but is *constituted by* its relations with others' (Marx 1970, 83). Thus, 'only in the community, therefore, is personal freedom possible' (83). Hence, women and men's sociality was not subsequent to but contemporaneous with their individuality; both Dalit women and men were thus to learn to make efforts for change, to demand them, to seek delight in mobility and look forward to future transformations. We can ill afford to forget Ambedkar's earlier advice and strategies to work simultaneously on the emancipation of the self and the community, in order to constitute Dalit power and a political 'Dalit community' in early twentieth-century western India, however fuzzy or fragile it may be. He and other Dalit radicals were certainly successful in building alliances to bring diverse Dalit communities together in particular historical conjunctures; the demand for the 'right to education' in 1920 was one such occasion.

Refashioning futures

It is clear that, for many Dalits, the liberation which education promised to achieve has been only partial. Education triumphed on a number of fronts, yet the visions Dalit radicals, including Ambedkar, had of its transformative power and its role in creating gender equality cannot exist independently of the social structures in which they are embedded. As a result, new forms of hierarchies and even of gender equality have constantly been constructed as women gained an education. Thus, while education allowed Dalit women to form united communities to achieve rights and power, it also reproduced differentiations and inequalities, sometimes even at the cost of a Dalit identity, something neither Phule nor Ambedkar could have anticipated or desired.

Thus education itself never had an autonomous impact of its own; its effects were often shaped by the way it interacted with notions of caste stratification, class and gender hierarchies in the wider society, structures of regular and irregular employment, and continuing caste prejudices against Dalits, as well as institutions of kinship, family and community among them. For many Dalit women, their education has not brought any escape from a life of domestic drudgery under the domination of men. Nonetheless, significant numbers have managed to obtain a higher level of educational attainment and have benefited from the positive discrimination policies of the government. Often this merely means joining the system and forgetting about the past and the discriminations of slum life. Even then, in joining the middle classes and imitating high-caste culture, Dalit women often feel more liberated than their less fortunate, poorer 'sisters'. It is, however, a personal rather than a community liberation. Yet many elite

Dalits both inside and outside India made enormous efforts to 'uplift' their community by floating scholarships, founding educational institutions, starting libraries and study centres, donating books and bicycles, and building hostels for students.

Attempts to build a counter-hegemonic ideology and practice that validates Dalithood often became lost in the daily lives of those struggling to better themselves within a social system that continued to normalise upper-caste and middle-class mores and cultural values. Previously, inequalities had been played out in practices of touching and not touching, of access to particular spaces and resources and modes of dress and demeanour. Today, the Dalit girl first encounters a person of caste in an intimate and most impressionable way in the schoolroom, when she meets her teacher and takes instruction. They experience discriminatory upper-caste attitudes that come out through ways of speaking and interacting with supposed 'inferiors' and feel shame. Later, as a girl progresses through the education system, assuming that she has the parents' and relatives' support to do so, she finds that her peers band together in caste groups, rivalling each other in an unequal contest of caste assertion. She finds herself treated as 'public property' both by other boys and upper-caste teachers, and suffers sexual harassment by males who know too well that they can get away with such behaviour without suffering any adverse consequences because their targets are lowly Untouchable girls who, everyone agrees, 'led them on'. The shame of being a Dalit and a woman is thus implanted in the schoolroom – and a consciousness is forged. A girl, as she becomes a woman, may then use this consciousness to fight back, as some have done, or she may – as most do – keep her head down and get on with her life.

Thus these accounts of the past are constantly shifting, making a claim on the contemporary Dalit present to carve out a Dalit future. There were deep generational markers between these women as they engaged and negotiated on an everyday basis with colonial and post-colonial, nationalist, upper-caste power and with Dalit patriarchy. I have explored the ways in which some Dalit women managed to better their positions through education. Ultimately, what is important is not that Dalit activism, anxiety and authority were to an extent modelled after Indian nationalist feminism or British imperial feminism, but that Dalit women perceived the need to mobilise against caste differentiation, educational disadvantage and gender discrimination; they agitated and took organised and unorganised action towards achieving an objective. What was important was that they coveted the power of agency: reclaiming, questioning, deploying, producing, focusing on themselves and their communities. They recognised their goals and selected their means, fought and carved out their own spaces, and struggled for their rights, however limited. In the end, what mattered to most Dalit parents, children, teachers, students, spokespeople and activists was not whether schools were actually advantageous, but the historically contingent power structures in which they were located and through which emerged their capacities, skills and abilities to educate themselves in the face of discrimination, indifference, inequality, prejudice and hostility.

These tales attempt to provide a fuller account of Dalit history, one that enhances, enriches and disrupts the imagining and story of India. The stories speak to different publics – local, state, national and vernacular – in order to provide sensory detail and emotional colour as well as new methodological, theoretical and conceptual frames, themes and arguments. They suggest that the emergence, construction and sustenance of the Dalit agenda of education and the broader movement depended to an important degree on the often-unacknowledged imagination and labour of Dalit women. Women acknowledged the legacy of Phule and Ambedkar, and pointed out the inadequacies and inconsistencies in the educational rhetoric of state policy and its dreamers. When they assert their *maanuski, nischay, svaabhimaan, dhaadas* and *vyakti aani samaaj vikaas* (individuated and community improvement) – that is, their virtuous selves as entangled with their community – and narrate their lives, they construct their stability across time and space to stubbornly point out complexities, uncertainties, anxieties, inequities and injustices that have yet to be recognised or addressed.

Notes

1 I have benefited immensely from Saba Mahmood's analyses, which, although in a different context, have helped me to transgress certain universal binaries. See Mahmood (2005).
2 On such an 'imagined community' of women, see Mohanty (2003, 46). Mohanty draws on Benedict Anderson's conceptualisations of 'imagined community' and 'horizontal comradeship' to argue for potential alliances and collaborations between Third World women (Anderson 2006).

References

Anderson, Benedict. 2006. *Imagined Communities*. London: Verso.

Galanter, Marc. 1984. *Competing Equalities: Law and the Backward Classes in India*. Berkeley: University of California Press.

Mahmood, Saba. 2005. *Politics of Piety: The Islamic Revival and the Feminist Subject*. Princeton, NJ: Princeton University Press.

Marx, Karl. 1970. *The German Ideology*, trans. C.J. Arthur. London: Lawrence and Wishart.

Mohanty, C.T. 2003. *Feminism without Borders: Decolonizing Theory, Practicing Solidarity*. Durham, NC: Duke University Press.

Interviews

Some names have been changed in order to retain anonymity

Chhaya Bahule, Class 12, clerical staff member at the mental hospital, Vishrant-wadi, Pune, June 2001.

Mangala Bansode, illiterate, *Tamasgir*, September 2004 in Pune and Nagar.

Nitin Bansode, son of Mangala Bansode, Class 3/4, Nagar, September 2004.

Sudha Bhalerao, Bachelors in Commerce, officer in a bank, Ramtekdi, Pune, October 2001.

Manisha Bhalerao, daughter of Sudha Bhalerao, first-year Bachelors in Commerce, Ramtekdi, Pune, October 2001.

Nani Bhalerao, Class 7, housewife, Yerawada, Pune, and Dadar, Mumbai, May 2000.

Sarita Bhalerao, Class 7, daughter of Nani Bhalerao, housewife, Mumbai, August 2001.

Sheela Borade, Class 9, sewing class, Dapodi, Pune, July 2002.

Vaishali Chandane, Bachelors in Law, advocate, Parvati, Paytha, Pune, August 2001.

Deepa Chavan, Class 9, maidservant, Ramtekdi, Pune, May 2001.

Janhavi Chavan, Bachelors in Computer Science, works with a firm, Yerawada, Pune, May 2001.

Indu Gade, Class 5, self-employed, Aundh Road, Pune, 15–16 March 2002.

Jangam's mother Gaikwad, Class 3, staff at a preschool, Yashwant Nagar, Pune, 1 August 2004

Jyoti Gaikwad, MA, lecturer, Ramnagar, Pune, 20 May 2002.

Kamal Jadhav, BA, Assistant Commissioner of Police, Kasba Peth Karyalaya, Pune, September 2001 and June 2005.

Baby Jagtap, Class 12, typist, Sinhagad Road, Pune, February 2002.

Meera Jangam, Class 9, Yashwant Nagar, Yerawada, Pune, August 2004.

Meenakshi Jogdand, Bachelors in Commerce, member of staff, bank, Bhavani Peth, Pune, March 2002.

Jyoti Kadam, MBBS, doctor at a clinic, Dapodim, Pune, June 2002.

Sulochana Kadam, Bachelors in Science, retired, served in various positions as a senior administrative officer, Ambedkar Society, Yerawada, Pune. I visited the Kadams from 2000 until the death of Mr K.N. Kadam in 2006.

Alaka Kale, MA, lecturer, Karve Road, Pune, July 2002.

Bharati Kale, MA, telephone operator, University of Pune staff quarters, Pune, June 2002.

Alaka Kamble, BA, providing private coaching to students, Tadiwala Road, Pune, October 2001.

Nanda Kamble, Nursing Diploma, nurse, Parvati slum, Pune, August 2001.

Rani Kamble, BA, sister of Alaka Kamble, clerical staff member, Pune, October 2001.

Poonam Kasbe, BA, bureaucrat with the state, Pune, September 2003.

Sadhana Kharat, third-year BA, housewife, Bibwewadi, Pune, April 2002.

Smita Khedkar, BA, job-hunting, Ramnagar, Pune, February 2002.

Gangabai Kuchekar, illiterate, Yashwant Nagar slum, Yerawada, Pune, July 2004.

Sheela Kuchekar, daughter of Gangabai Kuchekar, literate, picks and sells rags, tin, glass, and so on, Yerawada, Pune, July 2004.

Hirabai Kuchekar, Class 12, clerk, Zilla Parishad, Sinhagad Road, Pune, January, 2002.

Suvarna Kuchekar, daughter of Hirabai Kuchekar, commerce graduate, job-searching, Sinhagad Road, Pune, January, 2002.

Jyoti Lanjewar, Professor of Marathi Literature, Ambazhari, Nagpur, 10 October 2005.

Meena Mahajan, Class 12, housewife, Mangalwar Peth, Pune, April 2002.

Maya Mane, Class 12, magician, Goregaon, Mumbai, September 2005.

Chetan Meshram, son of Sandhya Meshram, second-year Bachelors in Science, Laxminagar and Ramtekdi, Pune, 11 September 2004.

Sandhya Meshram, daughter of Draupadi Nagare, Masters in Social Work, social worker, Laxminagar and Ramtekdi, Pune, June 2001, and September 2004.

Kishori Mohite, undergraduate, Sant Janabai Hostel, Pune, July 2003.

Shalini Moré, MBBS, doctor, Sinhagad Road, Pune, June 2002.

Draupadi Nagare, Class 7, Ramtekdi, Pune, September 2004.

Sheela Nikam, Class 3, owns two food stalls, Hawker's Union, Borivili, Mumbai, October 2005.

Nanubai Pagare, literate, housewife, Siddhartha Nagar, Yerawada, Pune, May 2001.

Shilpa Pagare, daughter of Nanubai Pagare, Class 10, Yerawada, Pune, 20 May 2001.

Malavika Pawar, daughter of Urmila Pawar, Bachelors in Education and Masters in Sociology, Sangeet Visharad. She teaches and is looking for further opportunities.

Manini Pawar, daughter of Urmila Pawar, Bachelors in Science and works at a laboratory. She is an accomplished Kathak dancer. Borivili, Mumbai, 6 September 2004.

Prakshoti Pawar, Bachelor in Engineering and Masters in Business Administration, executive, Maharashtra Board Housing Society, Pune, April 2002.

Ratnaprabha Pawar, Class 12, diploma in education, municipal schoolteacher, Bibwewadi, Pune, April 2002.

Urmila Pawar, MA, Borivili, Mumbai, 5–7 September 2004.

Kumud Pawde, MA, retired, Dhantoli, Nagpur, October 2005.

Apurva Pawde, MBBS, MD, son of Kumud Pawde, Dhantoli, Nagpur, October 2005.

Amita Pillewar, Masters in Social Work, researcher, Karvenagar, Pune, July 2005.

Surekha Punekar, literate, *Tamasgir*, Kasba Peth, Pune, September 2004.

Lalita Naik, daughter of Nanubai Pagare, Masters in Commerce, bank officer, Ramtekdi, Pune, May 2001.

Meena Ranpise, MA, lecturer, Pune, May 2001.

Gita Rithe, Masters in Commerce, Ambedkar Society, Pune, June 2001.

Jyotsna Rokade, daughter of Sulochana Kadam, Masters in Commerce, bureaucrat, Yerawada and Vishrantwadi, Pune, August 2004.

Poonam Rokade, daughter-in-law of Jyotsna Rokade, Bachelors in Engineering, works in Mumbai, Mundhawa, Pune, August 2004.

Yashoda Salve, Class 7, hospital attendant, Pune, February 2002.

Konica Sathe, Masters in Social Work, Karve Nagar, Pune, July 2005.

Lakshmi Shinde, Class 12, self-employed, Parvati slum, Pune, October 2000.

Parvati Shinde, Lakshmi's mother, illiterate, self-employed, owns a spice mill, Parvati slum, Pune, October 2000.

Bharati Sonawane, second-year BA, daughter of Sneha Sonawane, September 2002.

Sakubai Sonawane, Class 10, teaches at a preschool, Yerawada, Pune, September 2002.

Rajni Tribhuwan, SSC, Mayor's Office, Pune Corporation, Pune, November 2005.

Swati Waghmare, MBBS, doctor, Vishtrantwadi, Pune, November 2004.

Index

Page numbers in *italics* denote tables, those in **bold** denote figures.